NATO ASI Series

Advanced Science Institutes Series

A series presenting the results of activities sponsored by the NATO Science Committee, which aims at the dissemination of advanced scientific and technological knowledge, with a view to strengthening links between scientific communities.

The Series is published by an international board of publishers in conjunction with the NATO Scientific Affairs Division

A Life Sciences B Physics	Plenum Publishing Corporation London and New York
C Mathematical and Physical Sciences D Behavioural and Social Sciences E Applied Sciences	Kluwer Academic Publishers Dordrecht, Boston and London
F Computer and Systems Sciences G Ecological Sciences H Cell Biology I Global Environmental Change	Springer-Verlag Berlin Heidelberg New York London Paris Tokyo Hong Kong Barcelona Budapest

NATO-PCO DATABASE

The electronic index to the NATO ASI Series provides full bibliographical references (with keywords and/or abstracts) to more than 30000 contributions from international scientists published in all sections of the NATO ASI Series. Access to the NATO-PCO DATABASE compiled by the NATO Publication Coordination Office is possible in two ways:

- via online FILE 128 (NATO-PCO DATABASE) hosted by ESRIN, Via Galileo Galilei, I-00044 Frascati, Italy.
- via CD-ROM "NATO Science & Technology Disk" with user-friendly retrieval software in English, French and German (© WTV GmbH and DATAWARE Technologies Inc. 1989).

The CD-ROM can be ordered through any member of the Board of Publishers or through NATO-PCO, Overijse, Belgium.

Series F: Computer and Systems Sciences Vol. 111

The ASI Series Books Published as a Result of Activities of the Special Programme on ADVANCED EDUCATIONAL TECHNOLOGY

This book contains the proceedings of a NATO Advanced Research Workshop held within the activities of the NATO Special Programme on Advanced Educational Technology, running from 1988 to 1993 under the auspices of the NATO Science Committee.

The books published so far as a result of the activities of the Special Programme are as follows (further details are given at the end of this volume):

Vol. F 67: Designing Hypermedia for Learning. 1990.
Vol. F 76: Multimedia Interface Design in Education. 1992.
Vol. F 78: Integrating Advanced Technology into Technology Education. 1991.
Vol. F 80: Intelligent Tutoring Systems for Foreign Language Learning. 1992.
Vol. F 81: Cognitive Tools for Learning. 1992.
Vol. F 84: Computer-Based Learning Environments and Problem Solving. 1992.
Vol. F 85: Adaptive Learning Environments: Foundations and Frontiers. 1992.
Vol. F 86: Intelligent Learning Environments and Knowledge Acquisition in Physics. 1992.
Vol. F 87: Cognitive Modelling and Interactive Environments in Language Learning. 1992.
Vol. F 89: Mathematical Problem Solving and New Information Technologies. 1992.
Vol. F 90: Collaborative Learning Through Computer Conferencing. 1992.
Vol. F 91: New Directions for Intelligent Tutoring Systems. 1992.
Vol. F 92: Hypermedia Courseware: Structures of Communication and Intelligent Help. 1992.
Vol. F 93: Interactive Multimedia Learning Environments. 1992.
Vol. F 95: Comprehensive System Design: A New Educational Technology. 1993.
Vol. F 96: New Directions in Educational Technology. 1992.
Vol. F 97: Advanced Models of Cognition for Medical Training and Practice. 1992.
Vol. F104: Instructional Models in Computer-Based Learning Environments. 1992.
Vol. F105: Designing Environments for Constructive Learning. 1993.
Vol. F107: Advanced Educational Technology for Mathematics and Science. 1993.
Vol. F109: Advanced Educational Technology in Technology Education. 1993.
Vol. F111: Cognitive Models and Intelligent Environments for Learning Programming. 1993.

Cognitive Models and Intelligent Environments for Learning Programming

Edited by

Enrica Lemut

Istituto Matematica Applicata, C.N.R.
Via De Marini, 6, Torre di Francia, I-16149 Genova, Italy

Benedict du Boulay

School of Cognitive and Computing Sciences
University of Sussex, Falmer, Brighton BN1 9QH, UK

Giuliana Dettori

Istituto Matematica Applicata, C.N.R.
Via De Marini, 6, Torre di Francia, I-16149 Genova, Italy

Springer-Verlag
Berlin Heidelberg New York London Paris Tokyo
Hong Kong Barcelona Budapest
Published in cooperation with NATO Scientific Affairs Division

Proceedings of the NATO Advanced Research Workshop on Cognitive Models and Intelligent Environments for Learning Programming, held near Genova, Italy, March 17–21, 1992

CR Subject Classification (1991): K.3.2, D.1

ISBN 3-540-56580-9 Springer-Verlag Berlin Heidelberg New York
ISBN 0-387-56580-9 Springer-Verlag New York Berlin Heidelberg

Printed in Germany

Typesetting: Camera ready by authors
40/3140 - 5 4 3 2 1 0 - Printed on acid-free paper

Preface

The papers in this book derive from an Advanced Research Workshop on "Cognitive Models and Intelligent Environments for Learning Programming", sponsored largely by the NATO International Scientific Exchange Programme and also by the Istituto per la Matematica Applicata del CNR, Genova, Italy; the Joint ESRC/SERC/MRC Initiative in Cognitive Science and HCI in the UK; the Area della Ricerca di Genova, Italy; and Sun Micro-system Italia, Italy. The workshop was held in the agreeable surroundings of S. Margherita, near Genova, in March 1992, and gathered 47 participants from several countries and different backgrounds (mathematics, psychology, computer science, system engineering). The best papers were refereed and reworked for the present volume.

The workshop employed a number of rapporteurs who provided feedback and overview commentaries both at the event and to the organizers. We have drawn on their material extensively in the following introduction and acknowledge help from (in alphabetical order): Rosa Maria Bottino, Peter Brusilovsky, Albert Corbett, Walter Daelemans, Simon Davies, Margherita Fasano, Chronis Kynigos, Laura Leventhal, Nicolina Malara, Maria Teresa Molfino, João da Ponte, Maria Reggiani, Warren Sack, Zahava Schertz, Jean Sholtz, Francisco Simplicio-Filho, Gyulane Szendrei, Barbee M. Teasley, Haruki Ueno.

To all of them, as well as to the referees: Nicholas Balacheff, Rosa Maria Bottino, Giampaolo Chiappini, Albert Corbett, Simon Davies, Françoise Détienne, Marc Eisenstadt, Paola Forcheri, Dominique Guin, Chronis Kynigos, Laura M. Leventhal, Gordon McCalla, Maria Teresa Molfino, Janine Rogalsky, Warren Sack, Renan Samurçay, Zahava Scherz, Jean Scholtz, Inge Schwank, Francisco Simplicio-Filho, Mark K. Singley, John Sumiga, Rosamund Sutherland, Barbee M. Teasley, Haruki Ueno, Gerrit C. van der Veer, Boris Velichkovsky, M. Felisa Verdejo, Willemien Visser, Gerhard Weber, and to all those who in some way contributed to make this book possible, we wish to express our sincere gratitude.

February 1993 Enrica Lemut, Benedict du Boulay, Giuliana Dettori

Table of Contents

Introduction

Preparing a book from a number of papers from different authors requires classifying them in some way, grouping them by interest area. In the case of learning programming, several classifications are possible, such as:

- what kind of programming language is learned;
- who is the learner, novice or expert;
- where the learning occurs, in an educational or in a professional environment;
- which kind of teaching/learning environment is considered, human or automatic;
- what aspects of programming are considered, the whole process of programming or some particular parts of it.

None of the above classifications give a clear and exhaustive description of the problems of the field, hence we thought that none of them could be adopted, alone, for organizing the book. Therefore, we chose a mixed classification, based on more than one point of view, taking also into consideration the fact that the title suggests two topics of different nature. This difference, however, is only apparent since the aim of the book is to stress the importance of cognitive models in any learning/teaching process or environment.

Hence, the papers in this collection are subdivided into three partially overlapping fields. First, there are theoretical and empirical studies on *understanding programming*, including analyses of expert/novice differences and of the nature of programming expertise. Second, we include papers on the design and evaluation of *environments for learning programming*, including environments with a strong tutorial component. Finally, there are studies concerning the introduction to *programming in school environments*, based mostly on problem solving or on learning elementary concepts of mathematics.

Understanding Programming

Papers on understanding the programming process and how novices are transformed into experts here can be subdivided into two classes. Some papers are concerned with a broad-based theory of the underlying psychological processes while others are more narrowly focused on particular aspects of programming.

General Theory of Programming Knowledge

Rogalsky and Samurçay provide a detailed account of the kinds of subtasks involved in programming and of the kinds of knowledge and skill that need to be brought to bear by skilled programmers. They offer a way of thinking about learning programming that allows them to classify a wide range of different approaches to the task of teaching programming. *Van der Veer* provides an intriguing discussion of the rich variety of mental models his team has found in over 1000 protocols. His results make life awkward for programming environment and ITS designers who might rather wish to address their designs to a more homogeneous audience. *Pirolli* outlines a unified model of learning to program, intended to address program writing and comprehension, and the processing of instruction in standard didactical forms, as well as more complex interactive forms.

Design was one aspect of programming that the workshop brought into sharp focus. We have included in this section papers on "design" because it runs right through almost all aspects of programming. *Détienne*'s paper looks at the kind of design strategies that professional programmers use for an object-oriented language (OOP). The issue here is to evaluate how the characteristics of the design strategies depend on the experience of the programmers in OOP languages. Also on the theme of design, *Sumiga* offers a cognitive model of the design process, based on protocols of designers, that encompasses both opportunistic and goal-directed behaviour. Interest in "opportunism" was quite widespread and the theme turns up in other papers also (see, e.g., Davies and Simplicio-Filho below).

Theories of Particular Aspects of Programming Knowledge

Teasley argues for the adoption of an ecological paradigm in the study of program comprehension, in particular taking account of the context in which program comprehension is taking place. *Simplicio-Filho* presents an engineering model of cognitive behaviour in the task of specification understanding. The model focuses on the control mechanisms that drive opportunistic and goal-oriented behaviours, in particular on its reactive and distributed characterization. *Leventhal*'s work indicates the problem that program testers tend to see what they want to see and tend to work toward confirming hunches rather than systematically testing. Her results are in line with other fields (e.g., medical diagnosis) where "confirmation bias" has also been found. *Dagdilelis* relates the processes of constructing a program to that of validating it; he analyses student's behaviour to validate an algorithm on the basis of a proposed hierarchy of seven categories. In his view, students work simultaneously at different levels, but tend to revert to the most primitive ones when dealing with an evaluation of correctness.

Environments for Learning to Program

Work on environments for teaching programming can be divided into those that describe systems which are essentially "pure" environments and those that undertake tutorial interventions.

Intelligent Tutoring Systems

Brusilovsky describes an ITS for a mini-language that embodies a course in elementary programming, together with various tools to assist the learner who may either work in an exploratory manner, or under the guidance of the tutor. A similar combination of exploratory environment and tutor is offered by *Ramadhan and du Boulay*. They sketch results of an empirical study which supports the belief in the importance of exploratory learning as an introduction to tutored problem solving. *Corbett and Anderson*'s work on the Lisp Tutor is well known. Their paper in this volume describes an experiment to evaluate the accuracy of the underlying rule-based model of programming skill. One of the features of learning Lisp with the Lisp tutor is that there is quite a lot of control over the degree of complexity experienced by the novices. The paper by *Singley, Carroll and Alpert* describes a system, Goalposter, which tries to infer automatically what the programmer is doing and then displays the information for the programmer as an "aide-memoire". *Verdejo, Fernández and Urretavizcaya* describe the methodology and design issues in Capra, a system aimed to teach novice students the design of elementary programs. Its tutorial methodology relies on the use of schemas or plans for reasoning about program construction and takes into account the current student's intention, either explicitly expressed or inferred from the communication process. The final paper in this section, by *Davies and Castell*, neatly encapsulates some of the objectives of the workshop, in that it offers a critique from a psychological point of view of a number of well known tutoring systems for learning programming. In particular, they are concerned about the role that programming plans have played in the development of such systems and about the psychological validity of the notion of top-down planning.

Pure Programming Environments

The work by *McCalla and Greer* involves development of both ITS and learning environments. Their SCENT system is able to match a student's answer to a Lisp program against a set of solutions coded as hierarchic structures. The system can undertake the matching of student and teacher answers at various levels of granularity. They also describe the PETAL environment which provides novices with different ways to understand recursion. The MEMO system, by *Forcheri and Molfino*, is a computer based laboratory on abstract algebraic specifications, intended as a tool to enable software engineering students to reason about programming problems abstractly. In this lab, parts of specifications used inside a program are automatically implemented. *Weber* describes ELM-PE, an intelligent programming environment for learning Lisp, supporting example-based learning, able to classify and retrieve earlier programming examples for use as analogies for the current problem. *Eisenstadt, Price and Domingue* go as far as arguing that the traditional Intelligent Tutoring System approach cannot succeed in general and is based on a number of "fallacies". They argue that systems for novices (and for experts) need rather to provide a software visualization facility which will enable debugging, for example, without explicit teaching.

Learning Programming in School Environments

The paper by *Cohors-Fresenborg* offers an unusual combination of both a system, the Registermachine, for introducing a range of fundamental computing concepts and also insights from cognitive science to justify the design. His work acknowledges the importance of individual differences and the possibility that there may be systematic cognitive preferences which affect the way that computing concepts can come to be known by different students. Systematic individual difference in the way that students construct and analyse algorithms are widely discussed in *Schwank*'s paper. This result has important repercussions for the way that different classes of individuals should be taught to program: a notion that has not yet been taken up by designers of ITSs. *Kynigos*' paper describes a case study, focusing on the cognitive process by which pupils concurrently learned programming in LOGO and geometry, developing understanding of structured programming while they were learning geometric ideas. Also in *Sutherland*'s work, learning basic programming can be achieved as a side-effect of learning a mathematical topic by using LOGO or a spreadsheet environment. Her emphasis is on thinking and interacting with symbolic language as opposed to first developing a method and then translating this method into the appropriate symbolism. In *Arzarello* et al.'s paper, learning to program is described as a cognitive apprenticeship, where the interaction between pupil and teacher is aimed at overcoming certain cognitive conflicts, such as performing versus designing, syntax versus semantics, machine notion, etc. They outline some methodological tools to overcome these conflicts.

* * *

While there is, at present, a general consensus on the nature of the problem of learning programming, there are different opinions on what forms an effective environment for learning programming. It is generally recognized that the development of a mental model is a formidable task for the student and that learning programming is a complex activity that depends heavily on metacognitive skills. This activity is not simply reducible to building a model of the machine operation (the notional machine); it also requires the achievement of a more general understanding of the relational structures that underlies program functions (in several senses of the word) at higher levels of abstraction.

Problem comprehension, as well as the design, construction, testing, debugging and verification of programs, are recognized as ideally being interdependent skills, each requiring complex analysis, as each can be decomposed into a number of subskills. In practice, these skills may develop in a relatively independent manner in particular novices. The application of these skills in program construction is not strongly constrained to a particular temporal order, and the learning of these individual skills may proceed at different rates for different students (and indeed may be tackled in different orders by different students). A consequence of this view is the belief that there is unlikely to be a single path from novice to expert. Another consequence is that the structure of the final product (the program) may be less constraining on the process by which it comes into being than some would advocate. For example, top-down problem decomposition may not be (and in the case of novices sometimes cannot be) the only route to well-structured programs.

Task Analysis and Cognitive Model as a Framework to Analyse Environments for Learning Programming

Janine Rogalski and Renan Samurçay

CNRS–Université de Paris 8 – URA 1297, Equipe de Psychologie Cognitive Ergonomique,
2 Rue de la Liberté, F-93526 Saint-Denis Cedex 2, France

Abstract: Elements of a theoretical framework are presented for analysing programming tasks and identifying potential cognitive difficulties depending on training stages. Programming is considered in its professional meaning, as the whole task starting from a "problem in the world" and developing up to the status of an "implemented program". By "operative tools" we mean all "external support systems", whether they are computer-based or not, which aim to support learning activity in the domain of programming. The theoretical framework is used to define criteria to analyse operative tools for learning programming. Potential functionalities of training aids are analysed in relationship with the target programming knowledge and tasks.

Keywords: programming, didactics of informatics, cognitive tools, problem-solving, planning, operational knowledge

Introduction

Programming is known to be complex design activity. Since the 1960s, improving work efficiency and training have been permanent aims of the informatics[1] community. Solutions for reaching the first goal were first oriented, on the one hand, towards the design of programming methods to constrain and aid programmers in various stages of their activity [23], and on the other hand towards systems for program debugging: syntax error identification and data flow analysis for specific languages were two dominant orientations in these first efforts (a brief survey is presented in [13]). Systems were then designed, at the end of the 1970s, for helping students to debug their programs [1, 27]. These systems remained mainly prototypes and there are few or no evaluations of their efficiency on student's training. However, they led to the implementation of – at least – syntactical control in current programming environments.

Elsewhere, all through the 1980s, research in cognitive psychology looked at programming as a specific and interesting case of problem-solving. The "novice/expert" paradigm was

1 We use the term "informatics" instead of computer science in order to stress the community with other disciplinary fields as mathematics or physics. In the same way we will use "informatical device" as the system including computer, input and output devices, the operating system, the software in use.

widely used for research on programming knowledge acquisition. Emphasis was mainly put on algorithmics and planning (point of view of subject's activity), and on the programming control structures involved as "primitives" in program design (conditional statements and iteration) [21]. The same period saw the rapid development of issues, system design and research concerning Intelligent Tutoring Systems. In this last perspective, several goals appeared to be aimed at: either tutoring is oriented towards improvement of programming knowledge acquisition (initial training) [20] and/or knowledge management (in students or professionals) [5, 3], or the key point may be cognitive modelling for itself, programming being one possible content area among many [4]; finally, ITS may be designed with the main aim to implement theories on teaching and training [7, 16].

All studies and products on programming learning environments, are based on implicit or explicit theories of what programming is, what the knowledge acquisition processes or mechanisms might be, and could be efficient teaching methods. The theoretical framework we use for analysing adequacy between cognitive activities (and operative tools designed for supporting them) is based on an epistemological and constructivist approach, relating programming tasks and subjects' cognitive activities). It expresses models of subjects' knowledge in strong relationship with knowledge content and defends the hypothesis that knowledge is constructed and assessed through problem-solving [21]. Hence, we will first present an analysis of programming tasks and activities, then infer required knowledge and needs for training and operative tools for supporting programming learning.

Analysis of Programming Task

Like Janus, informatics presents two faces: it can be considered as a scientific field, with its own concepts, notations, typical problems and methods; it is also a set of professional fields (depending on the domains of tasks). We will adopt the latter point of view of informatics as a "science for action", starting from a schematic analysis of programming as "problem in the world" identification and continuing through programming as a "maintenance" task. Analysis will be refined by presenting two contrasting ways to decompose the global task as representation and processing tasks. These "poles" in programming are related to computational and functional programming paradigms, reflecting respectively a dynamic and a static point of view on programming problem-solving. From this analysis will be inferred the cognitive competencies required at various stages, depending on problems. Starting from a task oriented approach in didactics of informatics allows the target knowledge (knowledge to be learned through the teaching process) to be adapted to the various learning purposes depending on the subjects themselves. Analysis of training requirements are the object of the following part.

The Global Programming Task

Schema 1 below presents the complete loop of programming activity for a professional software designer. This schematic decomposition is present for any problem domain and level of complexity. The four phases or sub-tasks can be more or less extended depending on the programming task context ("school cases" and "programming in the large" do not lead to the same expansions).

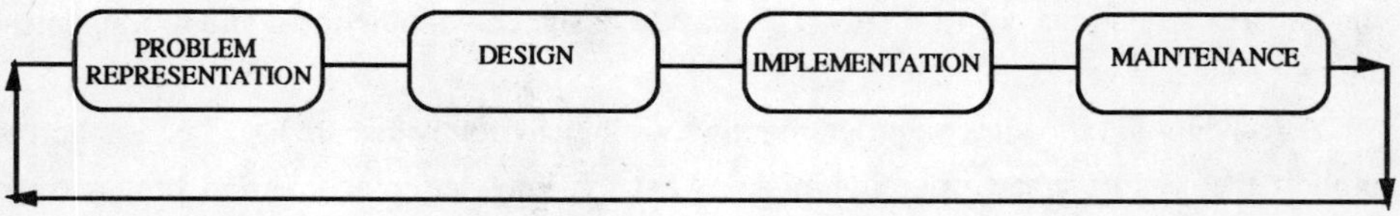

Schema 1. Loop of the programming task for a professional software designer

In training situations, problem representation may be a quite limited task if the problem is clearly defined, in a well known domain (e.g., enter a sequence of numbers until a sentinel value is reached and compute the average for high school students). Design is the phase whose function is to produce the required results (a target state of data) from the initial data (initial and final data being identified in the previous task). Its complexity (and later decomposition) depends on the required algorithms (well know or to be constructed) and on the problem domain complexity (computing fact(n) or designing an information system in a factory do not lead to the same design task complexity). Implementation concerns expression in a chosen language, on a chosen device, taking into account resources (programming environments for instance) and constraints (like execution time). Maintenance can be restricted to its lowest level sense of program testing and debugging or can concern the whole life of an evolving product. This last case can introduce a dynamic dimension to the generally static design task; object oriented design can be a way to deal with these flexibility requirements, but methods in the field present their own obstacles [3].

These programming sub-tasks have multiple interconnections and each requires various types of knowledge such as domain knowledge, design strategies, programming algorithms and methods, debugging, testing [19]. It is clear that cognitive requirements are not uniform for all these tasks, and that training cannot be seen as a linear knowledge accumulation. This necessitates a wide range of operative tools for supporting the various tasks. For instance, problem representation requires modelling activity. Methods exist for supporting such modelling in complex information system design [17, 26]; however, they concern professionals and require specific training on which there is no published research. Even for simpler problems, as is well known in mathematics, problem representation and modelling is one of the most difficult activities to teach : at best, coherence of the produced model can be directly controlled by a computer-based support.

Cognitive Activities Involved in Program Design Tasks

Cognitive activities involved in design tasks can be analysed along two dimensions : representation and processing. In fact, there are two ways for individuals to move from a real world problem (defined in the previous phase) to a program text implementable on a given device : the real-world problem can first be solved in the domain and then "translated" into a program text, or, alternatively, it can be approached by a direct representation in a programming language or any "pseudo-language" that could later be translated in (almost) any classical one, and directly solved in this programming context. Studies as well as existing supporting tools for training are mainly centered on the first alternative.

In fact, real programming activities are not guided strictly by "representing first" or "processing first" strategies. Rather anticipation about operations that would be processed on data may orient representation choices, while anticipation about the informatical constraints may intervene when a programmer is choosing a way to solve the "problem in the world". Pure novices, with little mathematical and logical background have little other choice than starting form a known solution, and translating it step by step in a computational, processing oriented approach. A lot of previous knowledge allows professionals to use more flexible strategies, moving between levels [12]. At a first glance, supporting novices strategies appears easier than helping experts because of a more homogeneous behavior : but it's a long way from "Doing it " to "Having it done by" as shown by C. Duchateau (preproceedings of the workshop for this volume).

Two programming paradigms may be used for relating the given initial data and the target data in the specification of a programming problem. In the "computational paradigm" a program can be seen as a sequence of computation on data, starting from the given data. In the "functional" paradigm a program is considered as a function; this analysis is developed in [18] and Schwank (in this volume). The first paradigm reflects the novices' approach, supported by a mental execution; the second one is more "static", corresponding to more expert strategies [12]. Poles and paradigms are not independent : the functional paradigm is mainly used with an initial representation of the world entities, while the computational one is more often present when an algorithmic solution of the "problem in the world" is processed first.

Moreover, even in case of simple iterative problems, it can be necessary to introduce a "static", functional, point of view, in order to design a correct iterative solution, without a lot of trial and error on initialization, loop body and exit condition. Expressing a method to help students -or more advanced programmers- in managing the creative part of this design activity appears to be a complex goal [5]; implementing such an operative tool in some tutoring system seems to be more than a challenge.

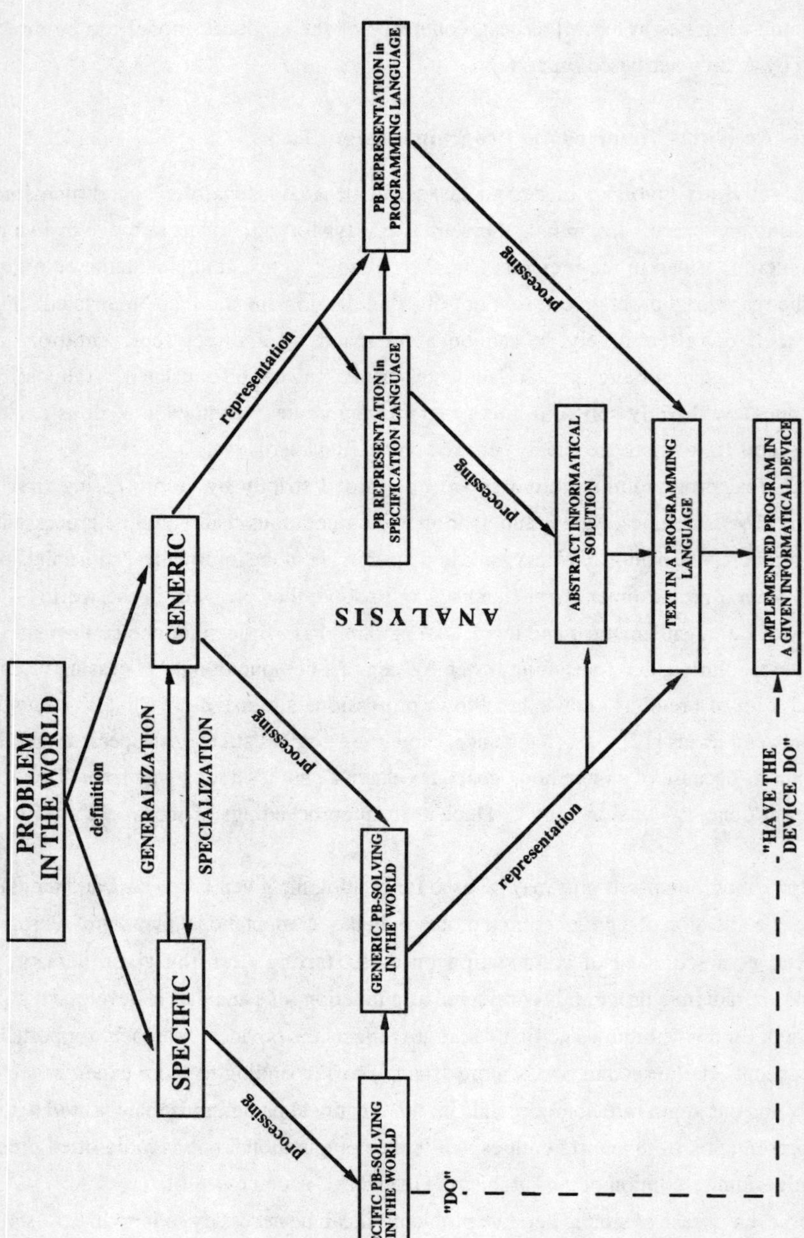

Schema 2. The schema presents a fine grained decomposition of the program design task. Two dimensions are represented: generalisation and programming paradigms. One paradigm consists in first representing the world objects and situations then processing informatical entities. The second one consists in first processing the world entities and then representing the solution in informatical terms.

Schema 2 mainly develops the design part of programming tasks. Program specification, as well as program reading, understanding, debugging, testing and maintaining have also to be analyzed for designing support systems for training (or even for a professional use). The schema 2 represents different paths which can be followed in program design when going to the problem defined in the world to the program implemented in a given informatical device. Two dimensions can be distinguished: generalisation (of problems, procedures and representations) and programming paradigms (computational versus functional) used in design. A given problem can be considered either as a specific problem or a specific case of the problem category. For instance, the well known rainfall problem can be considered as a particular problem or a specific case of iterative problem with guard value. On the other hand, attention may be focused either on the processing first or on the problem representation. For instance, the very beginner programmers usually follow the first path (going from the specific problem solving in the world to its implementation in a device), in which the problem is solved first by using the existing procedures in the world and by trying to translate theses procedures in the programming language.

This schema presents possible paths in programming tasks analysis, depending on programming pradigms and/or cognitive styles. In this respect, it can be used to analyse what are the main tasks that are supported by learning environments. It can also be used to classify the existing operative tools supporting the design activity. For instance tools such as programming methods (LCP, SADT, JACKSON, MAYDAY) aim to support the design activity through follow the paths going from the representation first to the processing after. Although these tools are efficiently used by experienced programmers their use by beginners necessitates specific training.

Constructing Competencies Involved in Programming

This very brief analysis of the programming task shows that learning and teaching programming cannot be a simple task. Competences depend on the problem domain complexity itself, particularly on its requirements in terms of data organization and depth of planning. Another point has to be stressed: implementing a solution in an effective way requires the "logic" of the solution (as an algorithm or a function) be linked to the "logic" of the physical informatical device. The device processes finite, limited entities: so that for instance numbers are not mathematical numbers, even for natural ones, and consumes time: so that a quite logical solution may lead to a "combinatorial explosion", and processes in a quite constrained sequential way, with neither parallelism nor anticipation).

Knowledge Requirements in Programming Activities

Programming activities require integration of knowledge defined at various levels and issued from various domains. Even though there are few studies analysing the nature of knowledge used by efficient professional programmers in their activities, some invariants can be identified. Modelling activity – representation of world problem objects in terms of the informatical objects to be processed by a given machine – constitutes a main dimension of programming competence. This activity requires an integrated knowledge both about the problem domain and the informatical device (notional machine, operating system, etc.). Representations of the informatical device involve also different points of view on the system: functional, topographical, physical and temporal (flows of information through the system); each level provides criteria for solution choices and evaluation.

Another dimension concerns problem analysis: various studies have shown that, by experience, expert programmers have constructed criteria to categorize problems and operative ways to solve them. This type of knowledge constructed by problem solving becomes an orientation basis for expert programmers when dealing with new problem domains. This can be expressed in terms of schemas construction [13], or in terms of "compiled strategies" [21]. It differs slightly from the automatic learning mechanisms of Anderson's ACT * theory implemented in LISP-Tutor [4], in that these structured knowledge may be produced not only by automatisation of frequent procedures but also by explicit activities such as generalization and discrimination. This last conception is implemented in the Interactive Learning Environment (ILE) prototype presented by Verdejo (this volume).

Experience with problem-solving also structures knowledge about data structures (char, list, record, array, tree structure,...), programming concepts (control structures, data types, variables, functions,…), and general algorithms (sorting, listing, computing). This structuring process produces encapsulated notions which lead to use more powerful units than primitives to solve problems. When expert programmers' knowledge for well known problems is elicited, it is not surprising to observe that the knowledge about primitives is organised in terms of schema such as loop plans or conditional plans [13]. But it should not be forgotten that these structures, which are attractive for training purposes result from long-term processes, and cannot be easily transposed for beginners' training – except for syntactical or specific notions.

More, it is important to mention that professionals are working with highly integrated operative tools supporting planning, computation and control such as programming environments and programming methods, which "take care" of a part of their cognitive tasks. Using these tools necessitates specific knowledge acquisition: which programming paradigm is implemented in the support? What are the strategies that are compatible with the constraints and resources of these tools? What is the semantic of the system of notations used by the system? Even experienced programmers may encounter difficulties with these issues [12].

Schema 3 below presents a model for operational knowledge, coordinating the four components defining competence: organisation of knowledge (concepts organisation), experience acquired in the field, available operative tools, classes of problems that can be tackled. This model, KEOPS, is concerned with fields like programming or other fields that involve specific and structured scientific/technical knowledge or operational professional knowledge. It extends the model of "conceptual fields" developed by G. Vergnaud [27] to analyse students' acquisition and training situations in mathematics (for instance, early counting activites involve a numerical conceptual field; managing cartesian products or computing bidimensional relationships in physics refer to the conceptual field of multiplicative structures; and measuring length, area or volume refer to a spatial conceptual field).

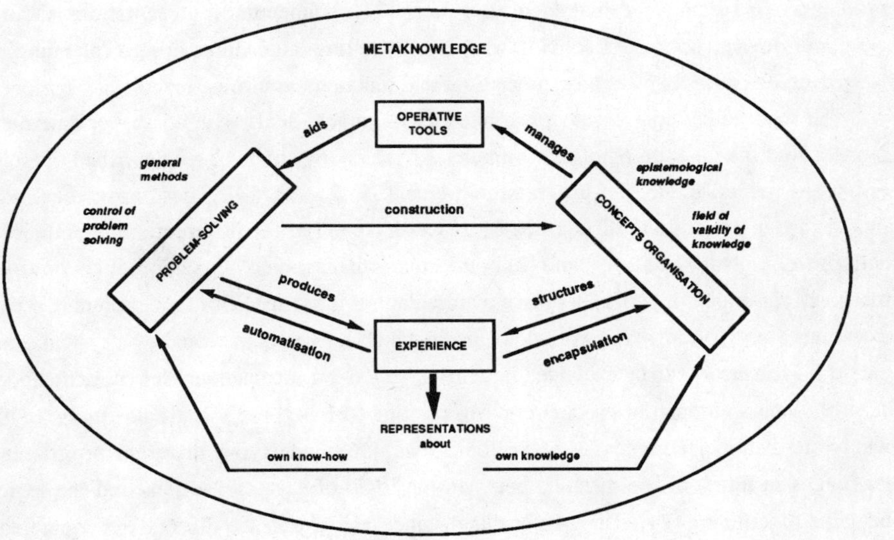

Schema 3. KEOPS model of operational knowledge in a disciplinary or professional field as programming. K(nowledge) is an organisation of concepts: programming notions as variables, functions, control structures, data structures, algorithms,..; E(xperience) includes previously encountered programming situations and tasks; O(perative tools) may be programming environments, programming methods; P(roblem)-S(olving) links classes of programming problems to classes of programs (sort algorithms aso).

Developing individual competences in programming is the result of multiple interactions between the components. Helping students to solve problems with programming environments (operative tools) contributes to the construction of new concepts or new relationships between yet acquired concepts, controlling concept understanding is a way to tackle new problems and to develop transfer abilities, and allowing students to acquire a lot of experience produces procedural automatisation in problem-solving, as well as construction of chunks of knowledge.

Finally, "programming in the large" is no longer an individual activity, but involves programmer teams. As a collective activity, it requires development by programmers of knowledge about mental models and strategies used by other actors, and metaknowledge about their own strategies and their functional place in teamwork. From this point of view, programming environments and methods may play a constructive role in a "common referential" between members of programmers teams. This collective perspective is absent in systems devoted to training beginners.

Cognitive Difficulties Along the Acquisition Process

In the past ten years a lot of data have been collected about novices' misconceptions and strategies [25]. The difficulties novice programmers encounter when solving programming problems can be analyzed mainly in four parts [21]: conceptual representations about the computer device (notional machine), problem modelling, algorithms design (planning) and programming concepts (variables, procedures and functions, control structures).

The main knowledge to be constructed by beginners deals with an appropriate mental model about the functioning of the computer device. Many studies have described the role of erroneous mental models in programming errors [9, 21, 22, 24]. These erroneous mental models are mainly due to difficulties beginners have (1) in the differentiation of their own actions from the device's ones; and (2) in the conceptualisation of execution of actions by the machine. This problem of mental device representations is not specific to programming activity: in various highly automatized work domains, in which activity is mediated by a system, a large part of human errors can be explained in terms of lack of an adequate device representation and control (such as industrial process control, piloting, driving, etc.). We have analyzed elsewhere the relative complexity of notional machines underlying different programming languages in terms of the distance between the logic of subject's actions and the logic of machine functioning [21]. The greater this distance, the greater the difficulty encountered by subjects in constructing a mental model. Several tools have been developed to help beginners to construct an appropriate mental model of device execution [8]. They are all based on the principle of the "visualisation" of machine execution, under the implicit or explicit hypothesis that visualisation produces understanding.

When they program, novices most often work within a problem domain they know (usually simple numerical or logical problems for which modelling activity is not solicited) and construct plans which are compatible with their existing RPS (representation and processing system) [12]. These plans reproduce how the novice executes his/her own actions, they are then translated into a program text by mental execution or by using another program text as example (syntactic adaptation). Some types of errors concerning the lack of control conditions can be explained by this model. A learning environment such as Bridge tries to support the learner's activity by allowing him/her to implement an action plan which is incompatible with the functioning of the device and by helping him/her to "translation" this plan into an executable one. The question remains open if this kind of support helps really learners to construct a new RPS.

In terms of strategies, novices' programs are often constructed in a bottom-up and forward way and reflect the difficulties they have in constructing plans compatible with the functioning of the machine. In order to guide the beginners' strategies in an optimal way, some learning situations are based on learning programming methods first. The difficulties in teaching methods, whatever the domain of activity, are now well known. However there is also evidence that at an appropriate knowledge level, teaching programming methods may not only help strategy acquisition, but also the acquisition of programming concepts.

Research has also shown that there exists a strong interaction between logic, programming knowledge and the mental model of the informatical device in the novices' errors . Studies have shown this interaction by analysing pupils' programs involving treatments of strings which have no homologue in the subjects' own action repertoire [15]. In the same direction, other studies cite evidence that the subject's pragmatic model of conditional statements may not be compatible with the device's logical model of conditional [22].

It is evident that beginners have to progress simultaneously in different domains. The acquisition process has to be represented in a spiral form rather than a linear and cumulative one. This explain why it is difficult to construct efficient didactic situations going from simple elementary problems to compositions of these units. The difficulties we have described above concern not only the initial acquisition of computer skills (what we call "computer literacy"). Some of these difficulties are encountered as well in in-service training of professional programmers when problem complexity or concept complexity increases [14]. Some examples of recurrent misconceptions we call "epistemological obstacles" concern the concept of variable and recursive structures. For instance, Detienne's study (in this volume) shows that in learning a new programming language (here it is an object oriented language), professionals with procedural language experience, have troubles with the concept of class and hyperclass which correspond to the variables in the new language. Likewise, they transfer their previous procedural strategies to the target language, therby creating obstacles in many situations.

We can add to these specific problems some more general elements concerning human biases in formal reasoning which play an important role in programming activities. For instance, to construct some iterative and recursive structures, it may be necessary to use the conditional reasoning: "if I had done this ... I could do that" without knowing anything about the plausibility of the "if" or the way to do "this". Construction may also require reasoning "by sufficient conditions" which is more difficult than reasoning by "necessary conditions". It is easier to conduce a retrospective plan when the data to be constructed in a backward way may be derived from the final data by some necessity regarding the problem content itself [5].

Needs and Criteria for "Operative Tools" in Programming

From training experiences it is pretty clear that subjects should or could be helped to perform programming tasks. Decomposing cognitive requirements for programming reveal that aids may concern a variety of purposes. As for other complex tasks, the needs for "operative tools" are aimed at decreasing cognitive load on programmers and at structuring and controlling sub-tasks and activities in problem-solving. At the same time, tools for supporting learning appear as a possible solution to the difficulties encountered in teaching and training. Two main kinds of tools may be designed for these purposes: (1) (computer-based) environments, that is, artifactual tools, and (2) methods for programming (programming being a specific case of problem-solving) [23], that is, cognitive tools. These tools can be analysed along three main dimensions: (1) Are they devoted to knowledge acquisition (new concepts, new languages,...) or to knowledge management (using newly acquired knowledge in problem-solving)? (2) What are the potential user's characteristics in terms of previous programming knowledge and general cognitive background? (3) What is/are their function(s) with respect to programming task analysis?

Knowledge Acquisition or Knowledge Management? Novices or Experienced Programmers?

According to the first dimension, operative tools can be schematically classified into three categories: "tutors", oriented towards knowledge acquisition, "bugs finders and debuggers" intermediate tools that keep beginners from being overwhelmed by interactions between misconceptions on a new notion and unrelated errors in a program text and that allow programmers to disregard low-level programming tasks, and "programming methods and environments", mainly dealing with knowledge management in problem solving [23]. These tools can concern beginners (novices, with no previous programming knowledge), intermediate programmers (who have at least some "computer literacy" or may have programming knowledge – like students learning recursion), experienced programmers (who know a lot in a given domain or in a given class of programming languages), or high-level expert programmers.

User's characteristics and tools classes are not completely independent. Programming methods or environments generally assume important user programming knowledge and their aim is to help professional programmers [3, 12, 17, 26]. Actually, some environments require that programmers acquire new specific knowledge, for instance, when they are based on complex logical and mathematical concepts. So recursion is a typical obstacle, but not the only one, that face programmers with real difficulties [14] (See also F. Detienne, this volume). Tutors are developed for beginners from the point of view of programming knowledge. It must be stressed that "beginners" is a fuzzy user's categorization. Some tutors for learning a programming language (using student modelling) concern real novices but still require general cognitive abilities, for instance answering questions about expected program behavior (DIALOGUE for Prolog) [9] or DIPLOMAT [6], or to interpret proposed choices and representations (such as LISP-Tutor for LISP) [4]. Others can be used only with some previous programming knowledge : PROUST implicitly requires minimal knowledge about conditionals, variables and program structure (for understanding explanations about errors, for instance) [13].

Programming environments aimed at training can be considered as user independent, as programming languages themselves are user independent. Configuration and problems can be chosen in a way adapted to the student's level: BOXER could be used with LOGO beginners for turtle geometry, or might train advanced students in building an adequate representation of local and global variables (no evaluation of BOXER is available at the moment) [9]. ALADIN – a language constraining structured programming – has been used with beginners in a wide range of previous knowledge (logic, mathematics, programming) – nevertheless they all were adults with high school level [20]. The Registermachine (E. Cohors-Fresenborf and I. Schwank, this volume) was used with 7th grade students from the very first concepts about variable until recursive programs and debates on program analysis (program tree) and evaluation.

The existing programming tools can be analyzed into six main categories: tools which aim to make the construction of the notional machine easier (Boxer, Registermachine, Prolog tracer,...); tools that handle syntax, notation errors and control structures expressed in the language code (Lisp-tutor,...); tools supporting plan construction (PROUST, BRIDGE, DIALOGUE); tools supporting problem representation and data structuring (LCP, HOOD, ALADIN, MAYDAY); and tools supporting algorithmic activity [16] and design activity (MERISE [26] Jackson , MAYDAY [12]).

As far as evaluation is available (training programming tools often exist only as prototypes), a common point seems to appear: effective training techniques depend on the initial learner's competence or even cognitive style, and depend on the didactical use of these tools. It may be expected that mere "face-to-face" between student and system may less effective than reflection between teacher and students – or between students – on the activity they developed with the tool, as it is confirmed by the importance of metaknowledge in the use of LISP-Tutor as underlined by Pirolli in this volume.

Integration of training tools in the whole long-term didactical process may also be a condition of students' acquisition. For instance, ALADIN is a programming environment that imposes heavy constraints on the form of the students' programming activity. Several "paper and pencil" sessions are introduced in the training process using ALADIN. Some of them make meaningful these constraints. Others reinforce acquisition of structured programming by requiring students to transfer the procdures they have used in the ALADIN context in the a situation without this interactive environment.

Even for experienced programmers, familiarity with the programming environment itself is a factor of efficiency [12]. Time management is not the easiest issue when trainers want to integrate training tools, because they can feel that they are wasting time when focusing on familiarisation with a new way of approaching a problem.

Conclusion

In this paper we have tried to present a set of cognitive criteria which can be used in the characterisation of the tools and environments that have been developed to help trainees to learn programming. There is no good or bad tool independent of the task and the user for which it is devoted.

In fact, several goals are integrated in teaching programming, and programming training tools are more or less adapted to these goals at each point in the training process. Constructing a common referential for the trainees and the support system itself is a primary goal: it is a precondition to any productive human–machine dialog. Interaction between programming concepts, precursors in other knowledge fields and the problem domain also has to be managed: "open" environments" seem to be more adequate to this purpose. Defining, executing and controlling strategies is a key point in programming: methods and support systems are quite able to impose constraints on students' strategy, but are less efficient for flexible aid.

New trends are appearing in computer-based training toward Interactive Learning Environments (ILE), that try to offer intelligently selected/chosen situations to student activity and to organize interaction between students and situations. Operations on and reflection about problems can be a core of these situations. In this orientation student modelling, direct explanation of system problem-solving could be replaced by an interaction where the locus of control is devolved to the system for low-level activities (such as expression of plans in a given programming language) and to the student for the highest levels (proposing strategy, classifying problems, form recognizing) [7]. They could enlarge possibilities for the design of systems integrated in current training.

References

1. Adam A., Laurent J.-P.: LAURA: a system to debug student programs. Artificial intelligence 15, 75-122 (1980)
2. Barnard D.T.: A survey of syntax error handling techniques. Tech. Rep. University of Toronto 1976
3. AFCET: Objectifs Objets. Interfaces 103/104 (1991)
4. Anderson J.R., Boyle C.F., Corbett A.T. & Lewis M.W.: Cognitive modelling and intelligent tutoring. Artificial Intelligence 42, 7-49 (1990)
5. Arsac J.: Préceptes de programmation. Paris: Dunod 1991
6. Barril P.: DIPLOMAT , un logiciel intelligent pour l'apprentissage de la programmation logique. Thèse. Université Paris VI 1989

7. Delozanne E.: Explication en EIAO. L'exemple d'ELISE. Thèse. Le Mans: Université du Maine 1992
8. DiSessa A.A., Abelson H.: Boxer: a reconstructible computational medium. In: Studying the novice programmer, (E.Soloway & J.C.Spohrer, eds.), pp. 467-481. Hillsdale: Lawrence Erlbaum1989
9. Du Boulay B.: Intelligent systems for teaching programming. IFIP TC3, Frascati 1987
10. Frasson G., Gauthier G. (eds.): Intelligent tutoring systems. At the crossroads of artificial intelligence and education. Norwood: Ablex 1990
11. Green T.R.G.: The nature of programming. In : Psychology of Programming, (J.-M.Hoc, T.R.G.Green, R.Samurçay, D.Gilmore, eds.), pp. 21-44. London: Academic Press 1990
12. Hoc J.-M.: Towards effective computer aids to planning in computer programming: theoretical concern and empirical evidence drawn from assessment of a prototype. In: Working with computers: theory versus outcome. pp. 215-247. London: Academic Press 1988
13. Johnson W.L.: Understanding and debugging novice programs. Artificial Intelligence 42, 51-97 (1990)
14. Kitchenham, Charn: Research and practice: software design methods and tools. In: Psychology of programming. (J.-M.Hoc, T.R.G.Green, R.Samurçay, D.Gilmore, eds.). pp. 271-284. London: Academic Press 1990
15. Lagrange J.-B.: Des situations connues aux traitements sur des données codifiées: représentations mentales et processus d'acquisition dans les premiers apprentissages en informatique. Thèse. Université Paris VII 1991
16. Lelouche R., Malouin J.: Fondements pédagogiques et éléments de design d'un système d'EIAO de l'algorithmique. In: Deuxième Colloque francophone sur la didactique de l'informatique. pp. 267-285. Presses Universitaires de Namur 1990
17. Lim K.Y., Long J.B., Silcock N.: Integrating human factors with structured analysis and design methods: from conception to an extended Jackson System Development method. Ergonomics 33, 12 (1989)
18. Pair C.: Programming, programming languages and programming methods. In: Psychology of programming. (J.-M.Hoc, T.R.G.Green, R.Samurçay, D.Gilmore, eds.), pp. 9-19. London: Academic Press 1990
19. Pennington N., Grabowski B.: The task of programming. In: Psychology of programming (J.-M.Hoc, T.R.G.Green, R.Samurçay, D.Gilmore, eds.) pp. 45-62. London: Academic Press 1990
20. Richard P.: ALADIN Une contribution méthodologique et logicielle à l'enseignement de l'algorithmique. Thèse. Université Paris VI 1991
21. Rogalski J., Samurçay R.: Acquisition of programming knowledge and skills. In: Psychology of Programming. (J.-M.Hoc, T.R.G.Green, R.Samurçay, D.Gilmore, eds.). pp. 157-174. London: Academic Press 1990
22. Rogalski J., Hé Y.: Logic abilities and mental representation of the informatical device in acquisition of conditional structures by 15-16 year old students. European Journal of Psychology of Education. 4(1), 71-82 (1989)
23. Rogalski J., Samurçay R., Hoc J.-M.: L'apprentissage des méthodes de programmation comme méthodes de résolution de problème. Le Travail Humain. 51(4), 310-320 (1988)
24. Samurçay R.: The concept of variable in programming: its meaning and use in problem solving by novice programmers. In: Studying the novice programmer. (E. Soloway, J.C. Spohrer, eds.). pp. 161-178. Hillsdale: Lawrence Erlbaum 1989
25. Soloway E., Spohrer J.C. (eds.): Studying the novice programmer. Hillsdale: Lawrence Erlbaum 1989
26. Tabourier Y.: De l'autre côté de MERISE. Systèmes d'information et modèles d'entreprises, Paris: Les Editions d'Organisation 1986
27. Vergnaud G.: Théorie des champs conceptuels. Recherches en Didactique des Mathématiques 10, 3-28 (1990)

Mental Representations of Computer Languages - a Lesson from Practice

Gerrit C. van der Veer

Department of Computer Science, Free University, Amsterdam, The Netherlands
Department of Ergonomics, University Twente, Enschede, The Netherlands

Abstract: An important aspect of human variation in working with computers is related to the concept "mental model", which indicates the mode and structure of knowledge representation employed by different programmers and computer users when interacting with a system. The assessment of the qualitative aspects of mental models of computer languages and of programmable machines asks for a special methodology. The user of a computer system has to be provoked to explicate his mental representation of the language aspects of human-computer interaction.

In our contribution we will present a method to achieve this: let the computer user "teach-back" his personal representation to a virtual partner, who has to be defined in such a way as to focus on the interaction language aspects of individual knowledge. The teach-back method will be explained and illustrated for a variety of different computer applications. Standard methods of scoring teach-back protocols will be shown to improve the reliability of the relevant indexes.

Several dimensions of systematic individual differences have been detected in the quality of individual representations of interaction languages. Important destinctions are the levels of representation (related to the functionality of the system and to the syntax and lexicon of interaction), and the mode of representation (verbal or spatial/visual, the use of graphical elements in the lexicon, procedural vs declarative representations).

These different ways of individual representation turn out to be related to both the type of interaction language prescribed by the computer system, and to representations provided in the teaching process.

Keywords: mental model, computer languages, individual differences, representations

Introduction: Why Bother about Mental Models

In modern society, the computer seems to be a general tool for a growing variety of jobs. Computers tend to be common pieces of furniture in schools, and even at home the machine is increasing popular. Using the computer, however, is far from trivial. Especially when the user of a system has to plan, or even has to organise his plan, elements of programming will be part of the skill of managing the machine. Programming a computer is not a "natural" human behaviour.

Learning to program is much more than just learning a formal language. A special way of analysis (of a problem) and of synthesis (of a solution) have to be developed. The first course in programming is in this respect a crucial phase in the life of prospective computer users. De Hoog [7] mentions an average of 20 per cent drop out during the course, and a further 60 per cent who never practise any programming past the last exercise in the introductory course. He estimates a 20 percent "success" rate in introductory courses for university students. Coombs, Gibson, and Alty [3] mention 50 per cent drop out during programming courses.

This type of observation stresses the importance of taking into account the prospective user when developing computer languages, programming environments, and programmable machines. Users will differ in several aspects, and both the training for computer use, and the design of the user interface and the language have to take this into account. Teachers and designers need to be aware of the relevant variety of computer users. As user interfaces and programming environments tend to behave in an increasingly "intelligent" way, the machine itself might be designed to adapt to this variety, by incorporating a model of the user (or the programmer) in the interface.

Both for teaching, design, and for adaptation, knowledge of potential users is needed. Modelling the user not only requires knowledge of human information processing, but also knowledge of human variation. An important aspect of human variation in this respect is the mode and structure of knowledge representation employed by different programmers and computer users [15].

The notion of "mental model" is a core concept in this respect. The term generally refers to some kind of internal representation that is individually developed by human beings in order to cope with complexity in the environment. The computer, especially when used as a programmable machine, is such a complex device, only to be mastered if adequate mental representations of its internal structure are available.

In section 2 we will elaborate the notions of mental models and mental representations, based on cognitive psychological theory. Section 3 will briefly review method for investigating human knowledge, and elaborate a method to conceptualise mental representations in its relevant aspects. The richness and variety of individual representations is illustrated in 4, leading to the derivation of some viewpoints on representational issues for teaching and design.

Mental Models or Mental Representations

Studies on mental models often approach this type of phenomena either from a nomothetical point of view (presenting a general model of human knowledge representation) or from the point of view of individual experience from a small collection of atypical experts. When applied to teaching and design of computers as programmable devices, both viewpoints have a certain validity:

a. A model of an adequate mental representation (i.e., complete, correct, consistent with perceivable aspects of the machine), might function as a standard or prototype in teaching.

b. Mental models of experts provide a clear insight of what actual adequate mental models might look like. They point to the typical knowledge structures, skills, and strategies that characterise expert behaviour.

However, experts are not born as such. Mental models develop as a result of training and experience, influenced by prior knowledge and references to metaphors and analogies. In as far as teaching and design focus on the development of the mental model, the issue of representation is relevant. In order to choose helpful representations there is a need for a clear insight in the quality and variations of mental representations, as developed by novice computer users.

A Need for Theory

The intuitive ideas that until recently underlay most notions of "how users think", or "how programmers imagine their machine" were based on the individual experience of the designer himself. A systematic study of mental models of programmable machines has to start with a review of theory. Only if we are aware of the relevant aspects and characteristics of the phenomena, will we be able to develop systematic methods for the investigation of mental representations.

A main problem is the fact that mental models are mental. They cannot be observed directly. Theory needs to show us the relation between observable behaviour and hypothetical internal phenomena. We will focus on theories that provide a basis for empirical studies.

Not all types of mental model that are hypothesised as basic for human behaviour, however, are considered to be consciously available to the user of a complex system. Moray [11] and Stassen, Johanssen, and Moray [14] point out aspects of skill in computer use, that have to be explained by internal models that are "not ... accessible to consciousness". Although we do not consider this type of model less important for programming or the use of computers, this study is restricted to mental representations of which the computer user is aware, i.e., to which he is able to refer.

A Short Review of Theoretical Issues

In this section we provide an overview of some relevant theoretical approaches. We do not pretend to be in any way complete. Many authors apply the term "mental model" or related concepts, but there is a large variety in viewpoints.

a. Mental models as explanation of behaviour.
   Gentner and Stevens [4] edited a volume on this topic, that opens with an introduction by Norman [12]. Norman refers to mental models as models that, in principle, should be runnable. However, mental models are characterised by the following phenomena: they are incomplete, they have vague boundaries (different systems with certain similarities are being mixed up), they are unstable over time (details may be forgotten), they contain aspects of superstition (as a trade off for mental effort). According to Young [17] in the same volume, mental models may be of different types: strong resemblance to the system to be represented, surrogate (a physical of notational analogue), mapping between user's behaviour towards the system and system as such, knowledge in the form of a collection of terms, problem space, or a psychological grammar. The general idea of this volume is that mental models are any type of internal representation or knowledge that is used in predicting, planning, and interpretation of the behaviour of complex situations or systems.

b. Mental models vs. mental logic.
   Johnson-Laird [8] refers to mental models as an alternative for the theory of "mental logic". He makes a distinction between different kinds of mental representation: mental models (structurally and syntactically analogous to the represented world), propositional representations, and images (perceptual correlated). Anderson [1] and Anderson, Farell, and Saunders [2] also mention different representations: temporal strings, spatial images, and abstract propositions, which they relate to problem solving behaviour. Problem solving requires the derivation of procedures from knowledge that is represented in production rules. Declarative knowledge has to be transformed to "interpretive productions", in order to be applied in complex situations.

c. The imaginative character of cognitive models
Lakoff [9] stresses the imaginative character of thought. He lists four types of cognitive models: proposition models, image-schematic models, metaphoric models, and symbolic models. The first two types characterise structure, the two other characterise mappings that make use of structural models.

d. Induction and the flexibility of mental models.
Holland, Holyoak, Nisbitt, and Thagard [6] describe the development of mental models as a trade off between accuracy and efficiency. Analogy, rules, and defaults plays an important role in their account of the this process. They stress the flexible way in which human beings cope with failures of mental models.

Different authors stress different functions of mental representations. In most sources, a variety of different mental representations are indicated, although the term "mental model" is sometimes restricted to a single type. The characteristics of mental models are considered relatively general in relation to the types of phenomena that are represented.

Mental Models of World Aspects

Several publications in this volume refer to the phenomena of mental representations. An important distinction between these references seems to be related to what aspects of the world are represented.

One group of authors applies the concept mainly to the representation of task-related concepts. Mental models of the task domain, and of learning, are addressed in the contribution of Pirolli. The internal (and external) representation of mathematical concepts is is the focus of Schwank's analysis of cognitive structures. Velichkovsky, in his discourse on social interaction, refers to mental models of interpersonal attitudes and of communication.

Another group of references regards mental representations of the computer as a device or as a programmable machine, or on mental representations of programming concepts. Duchateau focuses on the mental representation of the constraints induced by the computer ("as a performer"). Rogalski and Samurcay deal with internal representations and knowledge of both the computer device, and algorithmic and programming concepts. Detienne refers to "meta-schemas" (grouping actions) used by programmers in planning their activities.

Our focus will be mainly related to the last group. We will investigate mental models of the computer as a device for delegating tasks with the help of "computer languages" and as a programmable tool for solving problems.

A Pragmatic Definition

In order to apply the concept of mental representations to situations of programming and computer languages, we are concerned first of all with the aims of the representations. All internal representations that human computer users apply in planning and executing task delegation, evaluating results, and interpreting system's behaviour [12] are relevant candidates for our investigation. In order to attain the goals set in the introduction (modelling for teaching, design, and adaptation), we should consider any type of mental representation humans tend to develop for this situations. As such, we will not restrict ourselves to a single type. On the other hand, we will only study representations that can be reproduced by the human computer user via conscious processes. We are aware there are forms of "tacit knowledge" [13] which, however, we will not discuss in our contribution.

Conceptualising Human Knowledge

Collecting knowledge of mental models and mental representations is a problem. Norman [12] mentions "the scientist's conceptualisation of the mental model", indicating the need for a systematic methodology for eliciting this type of knowledge. According to the above mentioned theories, mental models are one source of variation in human behaviour towards the represented phenomena, and, as such, behaviour should enable the study of underlying mental models. On the other hand several authors (e.g.,[4]) apply techniques of verbal protocols, in order to study mental representations.

If one tries to collect systematic data on user knowledge and the representation users apply in working with computers, several methods are commonly used. An indication of user knowledge may be derived from behaviour in interaction with a system or in programming activities (error data, statistics on user actions and action sequences). User knowledge may be deduced from performance on questionnaires and knowledge tests (error diagnostics). Both types of indication of knowledge, however, are rather indirect. The knowledge is derived from behaviour or from test data. The validity of these indices may be quite acceptable as far as "quantitative" aspects of knowledge are concerned, but the information derived on representational aspects of knowledge will be rather poor.

Let Computer Users Teach Us

The assessment of the qualitative aspects of human knowledge representation asks for a different methodology. The user of a computer system has to be provoked to explicate his mental representation of the language aspects of human-computer interaction. We will present a method to achieve this: let the computer user "teach-back" his personal representation to a virtual partner, who has to be defined in such a way as to focus on the interaction language aspects of individual knowledge.

A Methodology

A set of considerations guided our methodology:

a. understanding the goal of the method.
The general idea behind our method is to let computer users represent externally how they model the system internally. First of all, one has to clearly explain the goal of this method. The idea of being evaluated on knowledge should be avoided. The subjects should understand that any representation they provide is valid and "correct", in as far as it reflects their internal representation.

b. A reason to explicate.
In order to motivate external representation, the subject should be enabled to focus on a virtual (or real) partner to explain his representations to. In general, it is needed to make sure the subject assumes this partner knows about the tasks to be delegated to the computer system (in order to avoid bothering the subject by explaining characteristics of the task domain). It is also essential that the subject assumes the partner does not know how to communicate with the system, i.e., does not know the computer language.

c. Focus on the language.
Providing the subject with a circumscribed task that belongs to the general task domain for which the system is designed, enables him to focus on the way he represents the

interaction with the machine. The task, to this end, should not be bizarre or exceptional, and consist of sufficient subtasks to enable the subject to show a variety of parts of his knowledge and representation.

d. Freedom of representation.
It is essential to allow any way of representation. Actually, in our research we restricted subjects to representations where paper and pencil were the only media provided. This artificially prohibited the representation of movements and skills that might have been perceived if subjects could have demonstrated their representations by interacting with the machine. On the one hand, we lost traces of tacit knowledge (which is only to be indicated from actual skillful behaviour), on the other hand, we forced any mental representation that would precede behaviour, to actually be revealed.

The Teach-back Method

The teach-back method, as we designed it, always has to start with a brief explanation of what we intend to collect, e.g. "We are interested in the way you imagine the system XXX internally. To that end we ask you the following question".

Using diagrams and/or words show how you would explain to someone who has never user an electronic mail system how to perform the following task:

Examine your mail, deleting any message from Tom or Dick, saving any message from Fred in the file "fredmail" without their titles, forwarding any message from Harry to John.

Figure 1. Example of a teach-back task

The question is printed on a sheet of paper that is completely blank, apart from the question, and has a continuation sheet. Figure 1 shows an example. In this case, both the element of freedom of representation, as well as the reason for representation (first paragraph in the figure), and of the indication of the task in order to focus on the language (second paragraph) are explicitly present.

The protocols can be interpreted and scored according to a "hermeneutic" method and scoring rules [16] that focus on 4 different aspects.

a. The levels of description users apply in representing the interaction with the system. We found the top four levels Moran [10] distinguishes to be regularly found in these protocols, either single or in combinations: task level descriptions (referring to the external task domain - i.e., a system independent knowledge representation), semantics of the interaction language (representing the functionality of the system), syntax of the language, and key-stroke representations of the interaction.

b. The style of representation shows different elements. Representations may have elements of
- verbal descriptions (indicating a relation between at least two verbally expressed concepts),
- visual-spatial images (graphically indicating a relation between at least two concepts),

- use of icons (graphical elements in the representation lexicon, indicating a single concept),
- sets of production rules (a declarative representation),
- program structures (procedural representation, indicating temporal order and flow of control)

c "Correctness" indicates the relation between the represented knowledge and the actual system or interaction language.

d. The completeness score reflects the amount of detail and the coverage of the representation in relation to the teach-back task description.

Reliability

Interpretation and scoring of these protocols needs a considerable amount of training. Guided scoring of 100 protocols enabled different raters to reach acceptable interrater reliability. Standard methods of scoring teach-back protocols [16] for a sample of 188 protocols from a homogeneous group of novice personal computer users showed reliability coefficients of .73 - .89 for the style indices, .66-.82 for the level indexes, .70 for correctness and .83 for completeness.

Individual Differences

This analysis is based on a collection of about 1000 protocols that refer to mental representations of different types of computer systems and applications, collected from users of varying age and levels of experience. The four aspects at which teach-back protocols may be rated indicate relevant dimensions of systematic individual differences [16] regarding the quality of individual representations of interaction languages.

In the current study we focus on the levels of representation (related to the functionality of the system and to the syntax and physical elements of interaction), and the mode of representation (verbal or spatial/visual, the use of graphical elements in the lexicon, procedural vs declarative representations).

In table 1 an example is presented of a study of mental representations of the interaction with operating systems, for a group of 607 secondary school students who participated in an investigation after their first 10 lessons in working with a personal computer.

aspects of representation	% of protocols
style:	
verbal	91
image	25
icons	28
production rules	6
program	34
level:	
task	8
semantics	30
syntax	49
key-stroke	78

Table 1. style and levels of mental representation for 607 secondary education students [16]

These data are illustrative of the kind of variability in mental representations as found with the teach-back method. Although these data are collected in a population of novices of ages 12-18, the same kind of differences are to be found in adult samples. In the example data, it show that most students represent at least part of their knowledge in a verbal way, although 25 per cent of the representations have image elements (some are completely image representations). Icons are a common representation for concepts for which a verbal reference seems to be either not present, or too cumbersome to produce. Program format models are quite common in this group, though declarative representations are an exception (this is different for most of the adult groups we investigated).

Scoring the levels of representation reveals that often more than one level will be found in a single representation. In that case the occurrence of adjacent levels is a common phenomenon. Characteristic for the secondary education sample is the focus on the lowest levels of representation. Key-stroke representation is most common, task representations are very rare. This is different for the adult samples we investigated.

Variability of Representations

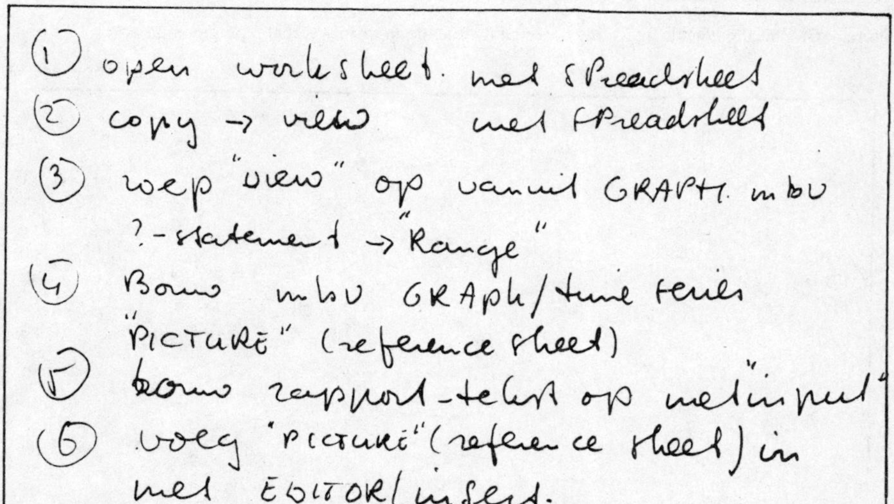
(1) open worksheet. met spreadsheet
(2) copy -> view met spreadsheet
(3) roep "view" op vanuit GRAPH. mbv ?-statement -> "Range"
(4) Bouw mbv GRAPH/time series "PICTURE" (reference sheet)
(5) bouw rapport-tekst op met "input"
(6) voeg "PICTURE" (reference sheet) in met EDITOR/insert.

Figure 2. Verbal protocol, showing procedural structure by lay-out (numbering)

**find: dir you will get a directory,*
a table with names of files (content)

**a hard copy: print:"   "*

**make a copy: first insert disk a, next key in: diskcopy a: b:*
remove disk a and insert disk b

Figure 3. Example of declarative representation

Many different combinations of styles and levels are found in the protocols of novice computer users. "Pure" verbal protocols still will show (in the lay-out) visual structure that indicates either a procedural (see figure 2) or a declarative (figure 3) representation.

```
TYPE MAIL ↵            This shows last letter to have
                              arrived
   If letter is from Tom of Dick
Type d ↵
   If letter is from FRED type w FREDMAIL
   If letter is from Harry type m John
Continue in this way typing + ↵ to arrive at
the previous letter.
   If in doubt type ? ↵ This gives
   help information.
   If you have "goofed" type MAIL    this allows
a restart
   at end type q ↵

   After last + ↵ type d ↵ this deletes last
   letter
```

Figure 4. Graphical elements indicating procedural structure in mainly verbal representation

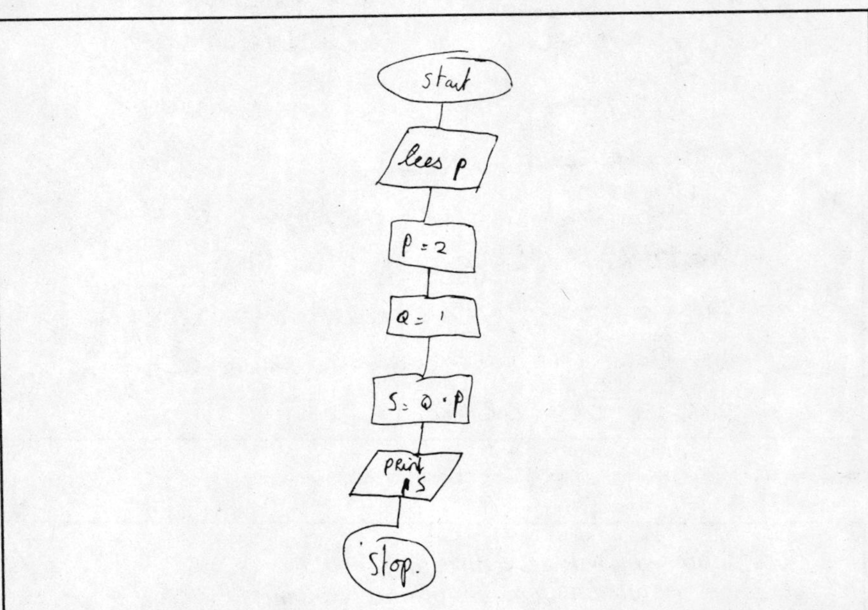

Figure 5. Procedural representation in pure image format

Image elements in representations are, however, much more common to represent procedural representations (figure 4 shows a mixed verbal / image representation, figure 5 illustrates a completely image representation of a procedural model).

Figure 6. Icons representing conceptual objects

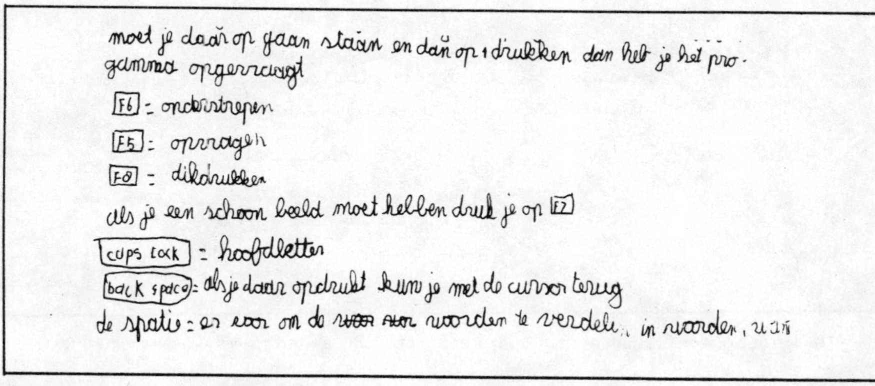

Figure 7. Iconic representation of key-strokes

Icons may represent both conceptual objects (figure 6) and represent non-verbal aspects of the physical interface or keystrokes (figure 7).

Image representations can either reflect the physical appearance of the system (figure 8) or indicate conceptual relations (figure 9). "Pure" image representations are relatively rare.

Figure 10 shows an example of a completely non-verbal spatial representation at semantic level. This protocol from a novice computer user shows the task-decomposition of searching for a text in memory (the text string "ZOEKTEKST" indicates the Dutch command name), copying the text (labelled "COPIE" in the figure) and printing, where the system's "memory" is represented by a maze, and the search and storing activities are represented by paths through the maze. The labels "tekst" and "copie" are added to the image to identify the objects "text" and "copy of the text" respectively.

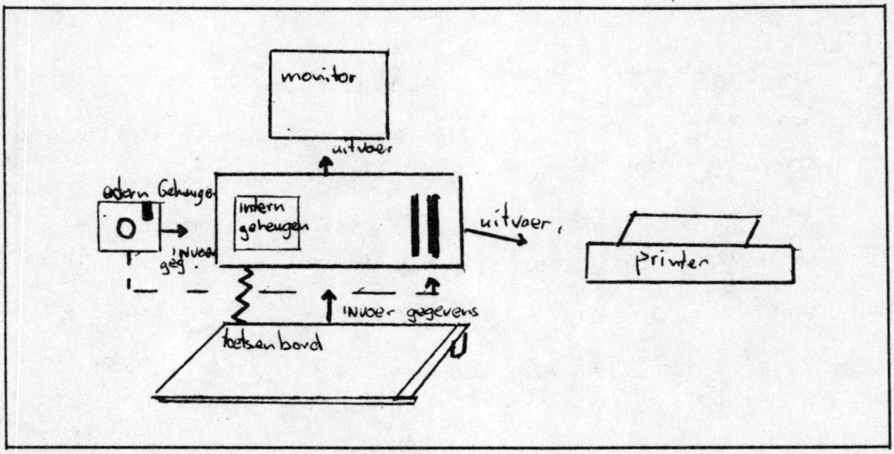

Figure 8. Image representation of physical aspects

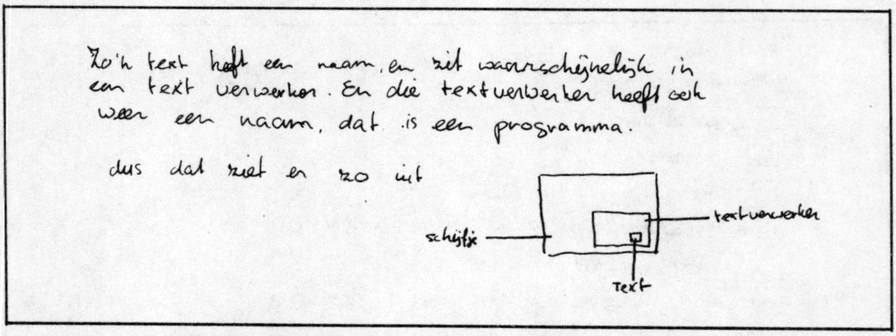

Figure 9. Image of conceptual relations (indicating a disk, containing a word processor, containing a text)

Variability in Relation to Type of Computer Language

In a study that compared mental representations of command interfaces (MS-DOS) and direct manipulation interfaces [16], MS-DOS users showed significantly more key-stroke representations. In the same study, direct manipulation users showed significantly less iconic representations. We may interpret this phenomenon as an illustration of the characteristic of mental models that Norman [12] refers to as "parsimonious", indicating that computer users tend to represent only the bare minimum of necessary information. As direct manipulation interfaces most of the time show iconic representations of the interaction language elements, and readily present visible indications of the possible physical actions, there is less need to mentally represent this than in the case of command systems.

In the same study we found MS-DOS users to mentally represent significantly more procedural knowledge (and there was no indication of differences in declarative knowledge). In itself this observation is difficult to interpret, but it points in the same direction as the study by Halio [5] who found direct manipulation interaction to be related to less well structured user performance (for tasks in the domain of creative writing). The lack of perceptible structure in command interfaces may force users to be more structured in their mental representations of the objects and systems they are working with.

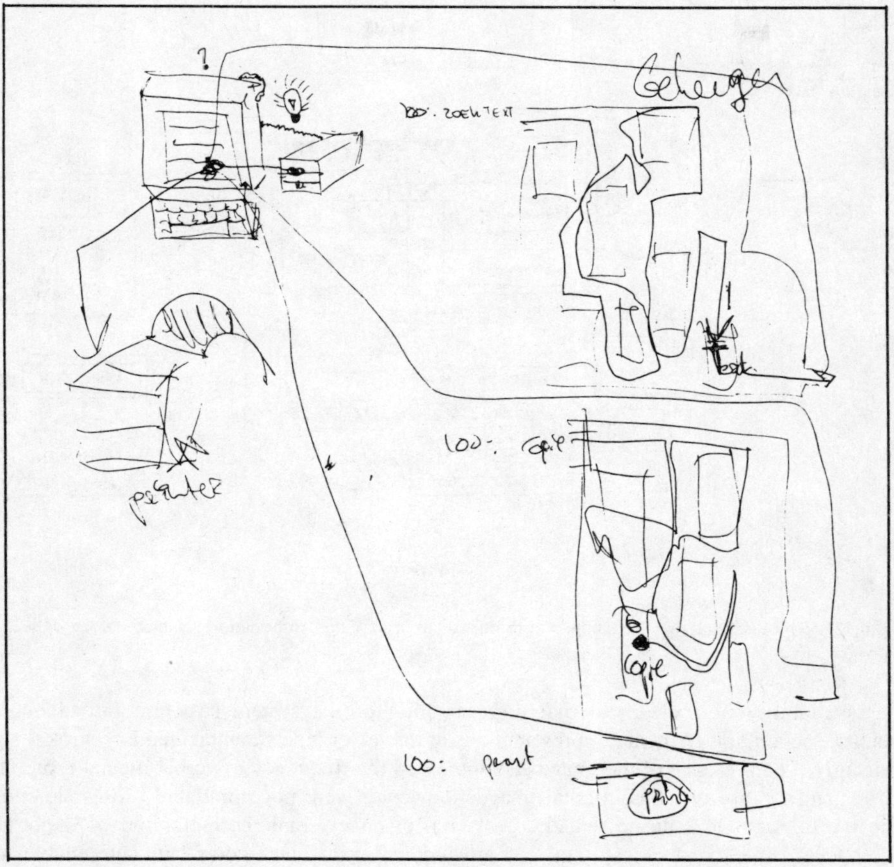

Figure 10. Completely non-verbal image of interaction at semantic level

Providing Additional Representations for Computer Users

Providing additional representations might be expected to influence the development of mental models. We performed a field study of MS-DOS users in in secondary education [16] in which we provided teachers with a single visual-spatial representation of the general system semantics and of structural aspects of information and information flow (figure 11). The teacher was merely required to show the picture (printed on an overhead sheet) to the class for a couple of minutes during his second lesson and indicate which aspects of the image would be relevant for the course. Moreover, a paper copy of the same figure was handed out to the students.

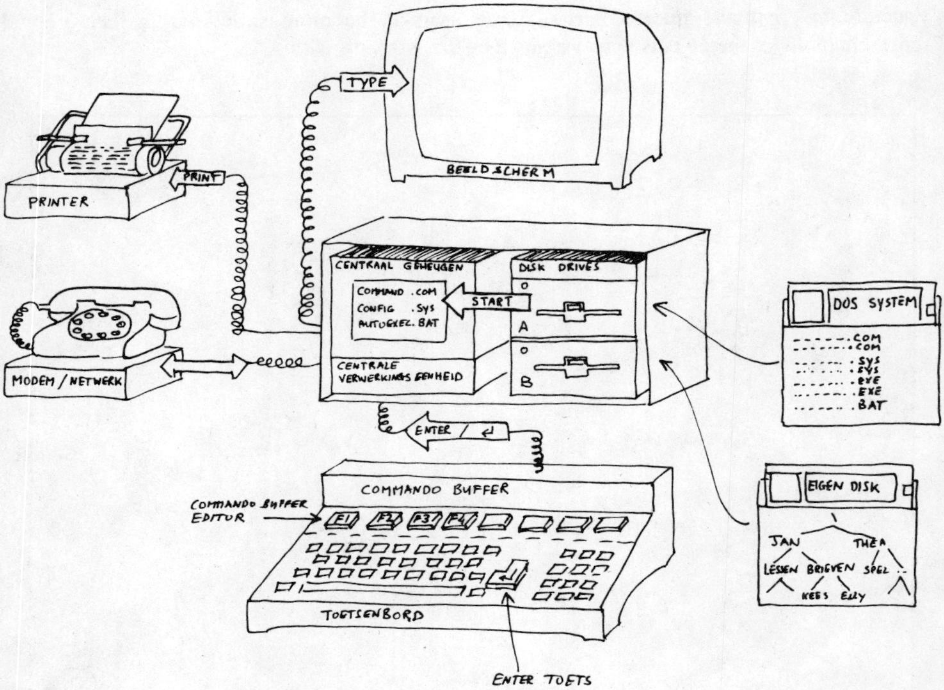

Figure 11. Visual-spatial representation of information transport and information structure of an MS-DOS machine

The availability of a clear external representation of the system structure turned out to increase the amount of mental representations at the lower levels (syntax and key-stroke) significantly. The presence of the image also increased the frequency of verbal mental representations and the use of icons. Mental images, however, were not stimulated in this situation. The results seem to indicate that the provision of an external representation of important (high level) aspects of the system that are hidden in the interaction language enable the development of mental representations (of different modes of knowledge and of lower level aspects) that are still not externally available during computer use.

Conclusions: Lessons from Teach-back

The teach-back method turns out to be applicable as a relatively simple way of collecting information on mental representations of computer users. Scoring teach-back protocols requires considerable training, but the resulting indices may be derived in a reasonably reliable way.

The investigations referred to in the previous sections show the possibility to collect information on mental representations of computer systems and interaction with programmable machines. The richness in variability validates the notion of mental models as broad concept, including the representation of both structural and observable aspects of systems. Mental representations may show characteristics of declarative or procedural knowledge.

Visual-spatial structures do occur, as do purely verbal representations.

individual representation turn out to be related to both the type of interaction prescribed by the computer system, and to elements in the teaching process. Our investigations show interesting systematic effects of differences in interaction languages. If interaction is designed in a way that provides relevant representations (at the interface) to the user, the need for internal representations of certain types decreases. On the other hand, providing (off-line) representations of structural aspects or interaction improves the novice computer user's ability to develop relevant mental representations, even of aspects not externally represented.

References

1. Anderson, J.R.: The architecture of cognition. London: Harvard University Press 1983
2. Anderson, J.R., Farrell, R. and Sauers, R.: Learning to Program in Lisp. *Cognitive Science*, 8, (2), 87-129 (1984)
3. Coombs, M.J., Gibson, R. and Alty, J.L.: Acquiring a first computer language: a study of individual differences. *In* "Computing skills and the user interface" (Eds. M.J. Coombs and J.L. Alty). London: Academic Press 1981
4. Gentner, D. and Stevens, A.L. (Eds.): Mental Models. Hillsdale, N.J.: Lawrence Erlbaum 1983
5. Halio, M.P.: Student writing: can the machine maim the message? Academic Computing, jan. 1990, 16-45 (1990)
6. Holland, J.H., Holyoak, K.J., Nisbett, R.E. and Thagard, P.R.: Induction: Processes of inference, learning, and discovery. Cambridge, Mass.: The MIT Press 1989
7. Hoog, R. de: Sociaal-wetenschappelijk onderzoek en het ontwerp van gebruikersinterfaces. *In* "Programmatuur naar menselijke maat - cognitieve ergonomie van mens-computer systemen" (Eds. G.C. van der Veer and E. Lammers). Amsterdam: Stichting Informatica congressen 1985
8. Johnson-Laird, P.N.: Semantics and cognition. Cambridge, Mass.: MIT Press 1983
9. Lakoff, G.: Women, fire, and dangerous things. Chicago, Ill.: The University of Chicago Press 1987
10. Moran, T.P.: The Command Language Grammar: a representation for the user interface of interactive computer systems. *International Journal of Man-Machine Studies, 15*, 3-50 (1981)
11. Moray N.: A lattice theory of mental models of complex systems. Report EPRL-88-08, Engineering Psychology research laboratory. Urbana Il.: Univ. of Illinois at Urbana-Champaign 1988
12. Norman, D.A.: Some observations on mental models. *In* "Mental Models" (Eds. A.L. Stevens and D. Gentner). Hillsdale, New Jersey: Lawrence Erlbaum 1983
13. Rasmussen, J.: Information processing and human-machine interaction: an approach to cognitive engineering. Amsterdam: North-Holland 1986
14. Stassen, H.G., Johannsen, G., and Moray, N.P.: Internal representation, internal model, human performance and mental workload. Report EPRL-88-01, Engineering Psychology research laboratory. Urbana Il.: Univ. of Illinois at Urbana-Champaign 1988
15. Van der Veer, G.C.: Individual differences and the user interface. *Ergonomics*, vol. 32, 1431-1449 (1989)
16. Van der Veer, G.C.: Human-computer interaction: learning, individual differences, and design recommendations. Alblasserdam.: Haveka 1990
17. Young, R.M.: Surrogates and mappings: two kinds of conceptual models for interactive devices. *In* "Mental Models" (Eds. D. Gentner and A.L. Stevens). Hillsdale, New Jersey: Lawrence Erlbaum 1983

Towards a Unified Model of Learning to Program

Peter Pirolli

School of Education, University of California at Berkeley, Berkeley, CA 94720, USA

Abstract: This paper outlines a Soar model of learning to program. The model is intended to address program writing, program comprehension, and the processing of instruction in standard didactic forms as well as more complex interactive forms. The model reveals fine-grained regularities underlying the acquisition and development of programming skill. Recent work on the model suggests that it can be extended to address individual differences in learning strategies and the comprehension of instruction.

Keywords: student models, Soar, programming

Introduction

In this paper, I outline a unified cognitive model of learning aimed at addressing the sorts of situations and phenomena that occur in introductory programming courses. The development of the model has been motivated primarily by studies of people using the CMU Lisp Tutor [4, 11, 14], and by our attempts to come to an integrated understanding of our observations within the Soar theory [10]. Only pieces of the model have been implemented so far, and many details require substantial refinement. However, the broad outline of this model suggests that this complex learning domain can indeed be understood in an integrated way. To a large extent, such integration is motivated by the notion that it insures a better understanding of learner psychology [10]. Moreover, such models can serve as a foundation for more complex measurement and diagnosis techniques to be used in learning environments, or more specifically as student models in interactive learning environments [15].

Table 1. Range of issues to be addressed by the model

Tasks	Learning	Influences on Learning
Programming writing	Skill acquisition and practice	External environment
		Examples & texts
Program comprehension	Transfer of cognitive skill	Hypermedia
Instruction comprehension	Declarative knowledge	Individual differences
	Program models	
	Task models	Aptitude-treatment interactions
	Models of learning	

Table 1 presents the main aspects of learning to program that we are trying to encompass in the model. Roughly, the model is intended to address performance on certain categories of programming tasks, learning to perform those tasks, and factors that appear to influence learning. Much of the focus of our empirical work has been on program writing in Lisp, in which students face problems involving some mix of familiar and novel programming goals. More recently, we have been interested in how people comprehend already written programs (e.g., examples used in instruction).

By observing people as they solve sequences of programming problems, one can track the acquisition and practice of individual elements of cognitive skill associated with programming [4, 13]. Related to such analyses, one can determine how cognitive skills transfer from earlier programming experience to new programming problems [14]. Recently, we have been interested in how people acquire mental models important to programming. Such models include models of the function and structure of programs, and their operation, models of how programming tasks are performed, and models of how to effectively learn about programming.

Across several studies, we have examined factors that influence learning in pedagogical experiments. It seems clear that examples play an important role in learning to program and their influence on future performance can be analyzed quite precisely using our model [13]. Furthermore, the particular explanations of those examples can have a great impact on learning efficiency [13]. Recent work in our lab has examined how people acquire knowledge from interactive hypermedia environments that differ in how they structure information. Finally, we are beginning to extend our model to address findings of individual differences in learning strategies [5] and how the relative effectiveness of these strategies seem to vary across different learning environments (or what are traditionally called aptitude-treatment interactions).

Overview of Soar

In the rest of this paper, I outline the model we are developing to address the features listed in Table 1. Although the model has been developed piecemeal, we are attempting to integrate the pieces in the Soar architecture. Soar performs tasks by problem space search and universal subgoaling, and uses a base learning mechanism called chunking. Problem spaces comprise sets of states, with operators that move from state to state. The achievement of desired states within a problem space constitutes task accomplishment. Knowledge is used to define and select problem spaces, to guide progress towards desired states, and select and apply operators All long-term knowledge is stored in a content-addressable memory, represented as a production system.

The processes generated in performing a task are focused by *goal contexts* that are stored on a *goal stack.* A goal context is basically a four-slot frame with slots for a goal, a problem space, a state, and an operator. The conditions of the productions test for patterns in the goal stack, which is stored in a working memory, and the production actions can add new information to working memory. Some complex operators may involve significant search for their implementation, and thus may be implemented as tasks themselves in appropriate problem spaces. In addition, the process of operator selection itself may be implemented as a complex task in problem spaces . Thus, the full power of problem space search can be applied to any subcomponent of a task.

Soar operates by iterating through *decision cycles*. Each decision cycle includes an *elaboration phase* and a *decision phase*. In the elaboration phase, knowledge relevant to the current task context is retrieved by the parallel firing of productions. The actions of some productions will deposit *preferences* about possible actions to take. Preferences are basically assertions stated in a domain-independent format concerning the selection, rejection, or comparison of problem spaces, states and operators for goal contexts on the goal stack. That is, preferences are statements about how the slots in goal contexts should be changed, and thus determine changes in problem spaces, states, and operators. For example, given a particular goal context containing a specific problem space, state, and operator, a production may assert that a new state is "best" for that goal context. Such a preference would achieve the application of the operator by moving from the current state to the new state.

The end of the elaboration phase occurs when all relevant productions have been fired (i.e., *quiescence* is achieved). At this point, the decision phase is invoked and the set of preferences is examined to determine a unique action to take using a task-invariant comparison scheme. Frequently, the available knowledge is insufficient or conflicting in determining an action. Such a situation gives rise to *impasses*, which automatically generate a subgoal. Thus, new goal contexts are added to the goal stack solely through the generation of impasses. In these subgoals, knowledge can be brought to bear in selecting new problem spaces and in guiding search in order to overcome the impasse. When an impasse is overcome, the subgoal disappears from the goal stack.

The resolution of impasses triggers the chunking mechanisms, and in this manner Soar learns from experience. New productions (chunks) are created with conditions that test for information that was available in the pre-impasse task context, and that was used to generate the results that lead to the resolution of the impasse. The actions of these chunks contain the results that resolve the impasse. This chunk will be fired in future situations similar to the impasse-generating situation, and an action will be taken without progressing through an impasse subgoal.

The Soar Analysis of Programming Tasks

Several models of program writing in Lisp have been developed in research surrounding the CMU Lisp Tutor [1, 2, 3, 11, 12]. These have mostly been developed in the GRAPES production system language. Generally, each GRAPES production rule either (a) decomposes a programming goal into subgoals, or (b) directly carries out a basic programming action (e.g., writing some code). The translation of such models, and especially the student model contained in the Lisp Tutor, is very straightforward. Each GRAPES production rule just corresponds to an operator in Soar.

The operation of a Soar model for writing programs is illustrated in Figure 1. Imagine that the model is faced for the first time with the task of writing a Lisp program to compute factorials and the resulting solution is:

```
(defun fact (n)
    (cond   ((zerop n) 1)
            (t (* n (fact (1- n))))))
```

Also assume that the system has all the relevant knowledge for proposing, selecting, and applying the relevant problem-solving operators. This would be roughly equivalent to a programming student who has solved several similar programming problems. Each triangle in Figure 1 represents a problem space. The circles represent states within a problem space, and the labelled arrows indicate operators that change problem solving states. Given the goal to write the factorial function, Soar selects a *code* problem space to achieve that goal (top of Figure 1). The initial state in that problem space contains specifications relevant to the program, but no program structure. The desired (goal) state is to have a written program that satisfies the specifications. Given this initial and desired state, production rules select a *code* operator to specify the factorial function. The system does not immediately have the knowledge to write the program, so an impasse results.

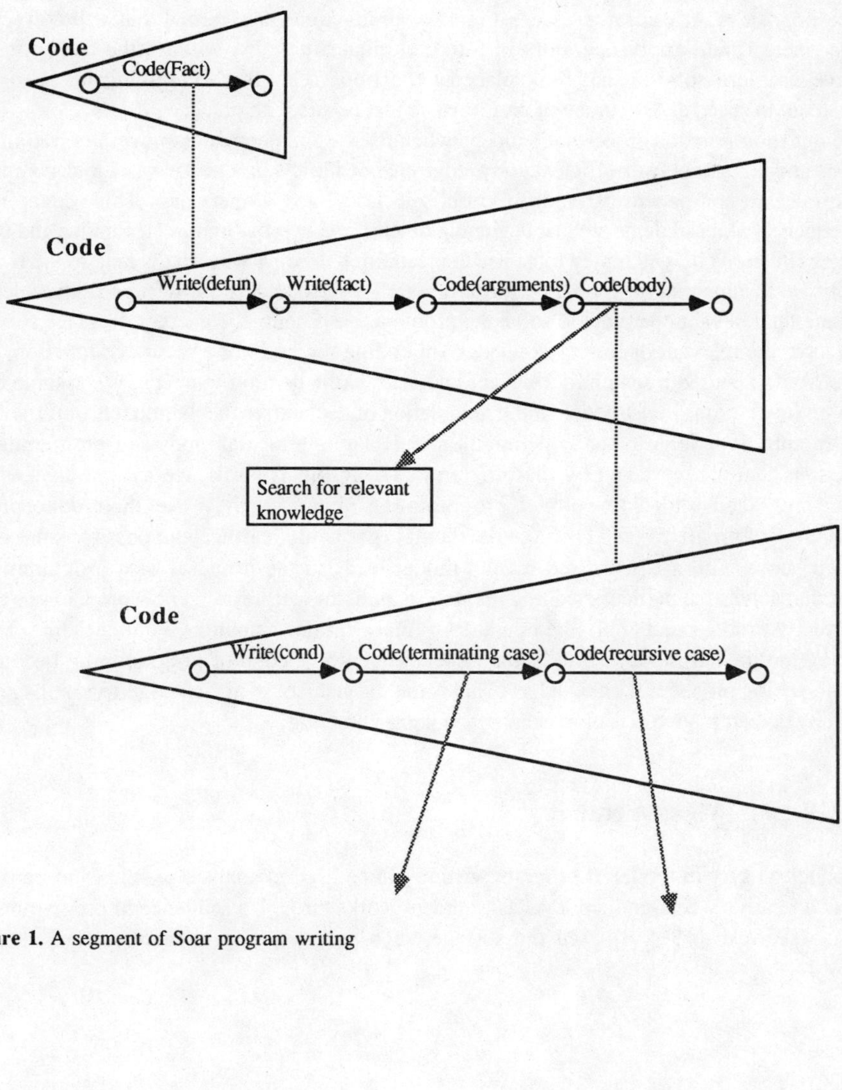

Figure 1. A segment of Soar program writing

The dotted line leading down from the code(fact) operator to the lower code problem space indicates that the impasse leads to the proposal of another code problem space that will resolve the impasse (the middle problem space in Figure 1). In this lower problem space, the specification of factorial is decomposed. Operators apply to write "defun", the name of the function, "fact", the argument to the function, "n", and an operator is selected to code the body of the function. Again, the system does not immediately have the knowledge to implement the body of the function, so another impasse results.

The impasse results in the selection of another code problem space (at the bottom of Figure 1), in which operators apply to write "cond," and to code the two conditional cases of the the function. The coding of each of these cases in turn results in impasses. This subgoaling on impasses continues many layers deep until all of the function has been written. In total, about 30 operator applications are required to correctly write the factorial program.

Soar chunking mechanisms create productions that summarize the problem solving that resolves impasses. At each impasse, in Figure 1, productions are learned that will correctly, propose, select, and apply operators in future similar situations, without the need for the extensive problem solving that took place in the impasses. Such chunking leads to the improvement in speed and accuracy of performance that occurs with practice [10].

The question remains as to what happens when the system encounters novel programming situations at which there is insufficient knowledge encoded in the production rules to decompose the solution into component parts, or propose, select, and apply operators. This occurs with great frequency when students are just beginning to learn a new programming technique and they encounter situations in which they must use the technique in some way that is new to them. At this point we assume that the model performs a search for declarative knowledge from which it can induce the relevant operators to solve the problem. In Figure 1, for example, if the system did not have the relevant operator knowledge for coding the body of a recursive function, the impasse would result in a search for relevant knowledge (the box in Figure 1). We assume that this search involves the construction and manipulation of declarative mental models of programs (their structure, functionality, and operation), and declarative mental models of programming (i.e., actions that can be taken by the programmer). In other words, we assume that when students are faced with some novel programming situation, they use their conceptual understanding of programs (and how to write them) to explicitly reason about possible solutions.

When successful, a constructed mental model leads to the proposal of a programming operator that solves the particular coding impasse. Chunking will result in new productions that will correctly propose and apply the operator in future similar situations without the need for consulting the mental model. In this way, declarative knowledge of programming becomes situation-specific procedural knowledge. This is the mechanism by which cognitive skills arise from highly contemplative acts of reasoning about programming.

Model-Based Measurement

The production system model of program writing can be used to analyze practice and transfer effects at a relatively fine-grained level as a student works through a sequence of programming problems (see also [17, 19]). On the surface, such programming behavior seems almost intractable to analyze. In some places the students' performance is seemingly effortless, and in others unbearably difficult. How can one predict such variation?

The production system model can provide a detailed task analysis of each programming problem that a student encounters. This task analysis can be used to segment the stream of problem solving into more fine-grained situations in which some specific operator (or operators) could apply to yield an observable programming action. Our models segment the stream down to the level at which individual atoms (e.g., "defun") are coded, which typically take less than 20 seconds. Figure 2 illustrates such an analysis. Over the course of several problems, one can use the production system model to identify the sequences of operators, q_i, that might apply. These operators can be used to segment the observed problem solving into a sequence of situations, S_i, and we can observe what actions, A_i, were exhibited by a student and compare them to the actions predicted by the model.

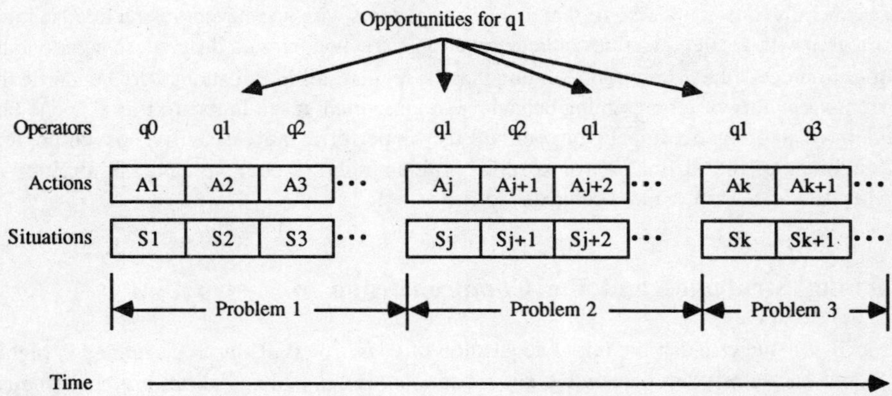

Figure 2. The model-driven analysis of problem solving behavior

Once problem-solving behavior has been segmented this way, one observes systematic practice effects on the selection and application of individual operators. That is one can pick a particular operator, such as q_1 in Figure 2, and observe its application both within and across problems. The observed probability of error in applying a particular operator q_i, after t opportunities for practice is $Q_i(t)$, and it typically follows a power law

$$Q_i(t) = a_i\, t^{-c} \qquad (1)$$

with c as a learning rate parameter, $0 < c < 1$, and a_i is the probability of error on the very first opportunity to use q_i [13]. The time to apply such operators also decreases as a power function [4]. Under certain conditions [13], one may observe that error rates decrease exponentially with practice,

$$Q_i(t) = b_i\, e^{-ct} \qquad (2)$$

So, the difficulty of any particular situation that occurs while solving a programming problem can be largely determined by identifying the operator q_i that applies to that situation, and determining the degree of practice that has occurred on that operator. The overall difficulty of the programming problem (e.g., the total number of errors that will occur; the amount of time that will be required) is simply the sum of the performance on the operators required for the problem.

This analysis can be extended by including the effects of pedagogical manipulations that influence the initial acquisition of programming operators [13]. For instance, it is possible to determine which programming operators in a learning situation can be induced by analogy to example programs presented in instruction. The relevant example materials improve the initial application of the operator by some amount, d_i, but do not change the rate of improvement due to subsequent practice, i.e.,

$$Q_i(t) = (a_i - d_i)t^{-c} \qquad (3)$$

More generally, one could assume that $d_i = 0$ for operators with no relevant instruction, and that d_i increases with greater quantities or better quality instruction, or with differences in individual abilities to process the instruction. Finding that the regularities in Equations 1 to 3 underlie the apparent variability of programming behavior is an important result in itself. It is also one that could have a dramatic impact on our ability to perform more sensitive psychological measurement of the difficulties of specific problem solving contexts and the abilities of individuals with respect to those contexts [15].

Learning Strategies and the Comprehension of Instruction

This analysis suggests that the initial acquisition of cognitive skills in programming is highly dependent on the relevant declarative knowledge that is available. Indeed, protocol studies, production system simulations, and pedagogical experiments [13, 16] show that declarative conceptual models of instructional texts and example programs have a significant impact on the acquisition of programming skill. Lately, we have been particularly interested in the strategies learners use in interpreting instruction and reflecting upon their own problem solving. These strategies, and the conceptual understanding they produce, varies across learners and appears to have an impact on the development of their cognitive skill.

Pirolli and Recker [14] studied subjects using the CMU Lisp Tutor who were videotaped while thinking aloud. Part of our protocol analyses focused on understanding *self-explanation strategies* involved in interpreting or explaining instructional texts and examples. Based on their performance with the Lisp Tutor, we divided subjects into "good" and "poor" performers. In summary, we found:

- Good subjects exhibit higher quantities of indicators of (a) awareness of their own states of knowledge, (b) awareness of the structure of instructional materials and activities, and (c) explicit plans or strategies for structuring their learning.
- Good subjects produced richer explanations of the examples and were more likely to connect these explanations to novel concepts that were introduced in the instructional texts.
- Good subjects were more likely to begin a self-explanation in reaction to a self-imposed learning goal.

We hypothesized that learners vary in their knowledge (or beliefs) about how to focus their own learning. Guided by this exploratory research, Bielaczyc, Pirolli, and Brown [5] developed a set of instructional interventions aimed at teaching effective learning strategies. Subjects working with the CMU Lisp Tutor were divided into a control group and a group receiving instruction on self-explanation strategies using modelling, scaffolding, and fading techniques. These strategies were presented to subjects as sets of questions they were to ask themselves, and these included self-questions about:

- form and meaning of example code,
- main (new) ideas introduced in text,
- connecting the text material and the examples,
- self-monitoring of understanding.

Analyses of verbal protocols and of the Lisp Tutor data revealed a significant gain in performance on the Lisp Tutor for the instructional group in comparison to the control group. This gain in performance was correlated with qualitative and quantitative improvements in self-explanation and metacognition.

Our model of these self-explanation processes (see also [20]) builds upon theories of mental models [7], discourse processing [8], and explanation-based learning [6, 9]. The model assumes that a goal of self-explanation is to produce integrated coherent mental models of the programming situations and tasks described by instructional texts and examples. Following Johnson-Laird [7] and Kintsch [8], we assume that instructional text is processed into a set of interrelated verbal propositions. The comprehension of these propositions (i.e., understanding the meaning of the propositions) involves their interpretation with respect to mental models. These interpretation processes take the verbal propositions as input and construct, extend, evaluate, or revise mental models [7].

Table 2. A sentence of instructional text and its underlying propositional base

Text	Propositions	
When a function calls itself as a helping function we say it is making a *recursive call.*	P1.	(FUNCTION X)
	P2.	(CALL X X)
	P3.	(HELPING-FUNCTION Z)
	P4.	(MANNER:AS P2 (CALL X Z))
	P5.	(RECURSIVE-CALL P2)
	P6.	(DEFINE P5 (P1 P2 P3 P4))

Table 2 presents the propositional analysis for a piece of instructional text used in several of our experiments. The text defines the notion of a *recursive call* based on ideas that have been introduced earlier in the text. Figure 3 is a schematic illustration of a mental model that is consistent with these propositions. Each box in Figure 3 is a token in the mental model and the solid lines indicate relations among the tokens. The ovals in Figure 3 stand for the propositions in Table 2, and the grey arrows indicate the links between propositions and mental model elements.

The critical proposition in Table 2 is P6, which defines a recursive call in terms of other propositions. P6 is used to construct a *meta-model* element of knowledge that indicates that whenever certain conditions are satisfied in a mental model, then the model can be elaborated in certain ways. In Figure 3, this meta-model element is indicated by the two grey boxes connected by the double arrow. This element is basically a new piece of domain theory that can be used in the construction of future mental models. It indicates that whenever an ensemble of mental model elements conforms to those indicated on one side of the double arrow, one can infer the elements on the other side.

This construction of the mental models from discourse is made difficult by two factors. First, the texts typically describe programs and programming in a very abstract manner, and consequently the construction of concrete referents in the mental model is difficult or uncertain at best. Second, because it is instructional discourse, a number of new concepts and propositions are introduced for which the learner cannot possibly already have the machinery for directly constructing the corresponding interpretation in a mental model.

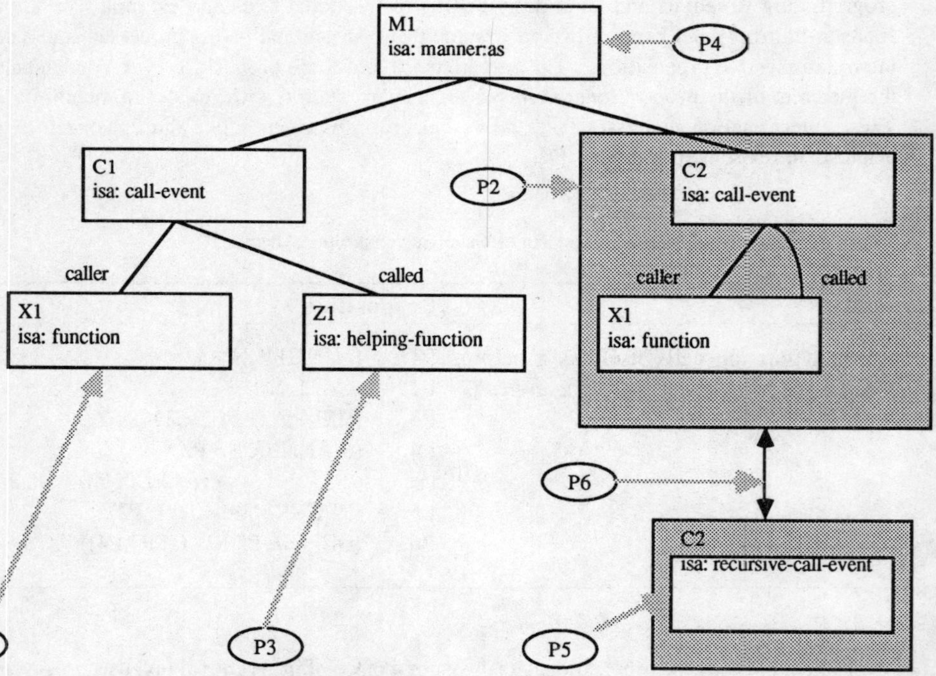

Figure 3. A model constructed from propositions

Examples can be used to solve both difficulties by providing concrete referents for abstract discourse and newly introduced concepts and propositions. In general, it appears that students prefer to construct mental models of example programs and then elaborate these models using propositions from the text rather than vice versa. We have been exploring ways of implementing a variation of explanation-based learning in Soar (for another variation, see [18]). Here, the learning involves constructing explanation structures in the mental model by using available and newly constructed domain knowledge. Chunking mechanisms lift new pieces of domain knowledge from the explanation process.

In the case of programming examples, one might imagine two sorts of explanation structures being generated. One kind of explanation might be directed at explaining how the example program satisfies the specifications for the program. A second sort of explanation process might be directed at explaining how novel concepts introduced in the instructional discourse are instantiated in the example program. Our protocol analyses indicate that subjects (to varying degrees) engage in both sorts of explanations.

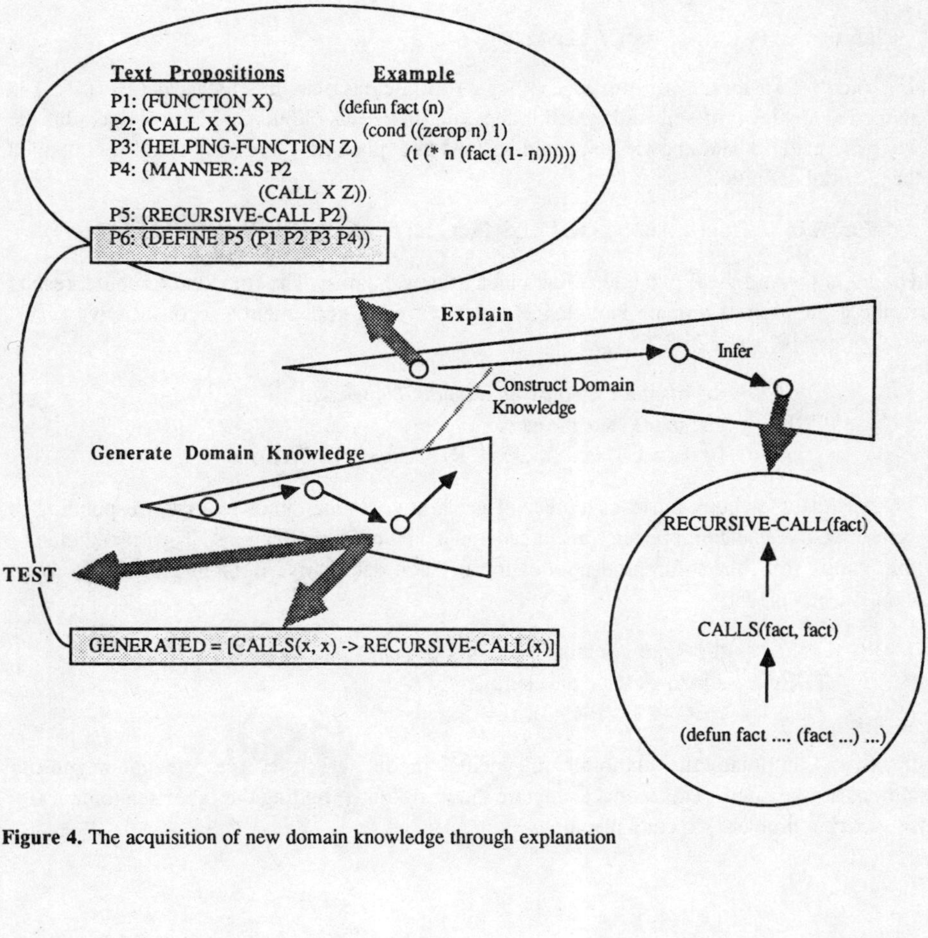

Figure 4. The acquisition of new domain knowledge through explanation

The general scheme is illustrated in Figure 4. To illustrate how a new piece of domain knowledge gets learned consider the novel concept introduced by the text in Table 2. In the top problem space (labelled *explain*) in Figure 4, the system is attempting to construct a mental model that encompasses the factorial example and interprets the text propositions within that mental model. The large oval at the top left of Figure 4 illustrates the contents of the problem state. The elaboration of the mental model of factorial in the *explain* problem space involves frequent impasses into the *generate domain knowledge* subspace. In this subspace, pieces of declarative domain knowledge are generated and tested against the text discourse and then used to elaborate the mental model. In the *generate domain knowledge* subspace the meta-model element (Figure 3)

CALLS(*x*, *x*) <-> RECURSIVE-CALL(*x*)

is generated and successfully tested against the text proposition P6. This constructed domain knowledge is then used in an attempt to infer some additional information about the factorial example.

Assume that some domain knowledge about the the concept of "function calls" has already been acquired,

(defun *x* ... (*y* ...)**...)** -> CALLS(*x*, *y*),

where the list structure **(defun** *x* ... (*y* ...)**...)** indicates that the list structure (y ...) is contained at any level of embedding within the outer list. This old domain knowledge, plus the newly generated domain knowledge, could be used to explain how a recursive call is contained in the factorial definition,

(defun fact ... (fact ...) ...) -> CALLS(**fact**, **fact**) -> RECURSIVE-CALL(**fact**),

and chunking would yield two interesting kinds of new chunks. The first kind of chunk results from the generation of domain knowledge and it serves to implement a reconstructive *recall operator* (see [10], pp. 326-345):

IF the operator is *construct-domain-knowledge*
THEN add to the state the element:
(defun *x* ... (*x* ...) ...) -> RECURSIVE-CALL(*x*).

In other words, the chunk retrieves a piece of declarative domain knowledge corresponding to the text discourse that could be interpreted and applied by other productions. The second kind of chunk results from the inferential application of such declarative domain knowledge to an evolving mental model:

IF the state contains **(defun** *x* ... (*x* ...) ...)
THEN add to the state the element:
RECURSIVE-CALL(*x*).

Such chunks automatically elaborate the mental model whenever the relevant triggering conditions are satisfied. This seems to capture the well-known finding the experts automatically perceive richer problem structure than novices.

Learning from Hypermedia

Our earlier studies of self-explanation examined students as they read through relatively standard-looking texts and then solved problems with the CMU Lisp Tutor. Although the textbook material was carefully crafted (for experimental purposes), it was like the sort of didactic instruction usually encountered in schools. Partly motivated by a desire to explore some of the claims for interactive hypermedia instruction, Margaret Recker developed a hypertext *Explanation Environment* that was intended to promote the construction of productive self-explanations. In part, we were also interested in examining the interaction of learning strategies with such environments. The Explanation Environment was designed to enable students to make links between example and text material, to allow a hierarchical structure of presentation, and to provide the learner with greater control over the progress through the material. The design incorporated the following five features:

- a hierarchical structure in the presentation of instructional texts,
- the presence of explanatory elaborations embedded with the example programs,
- the presentation of programming abstractions,
- metacognitive support through the highlighting of new terms for which the learner could provide and store explanations
- navigation support through a global navigation maps and buttons in addition to the local navigation buttons

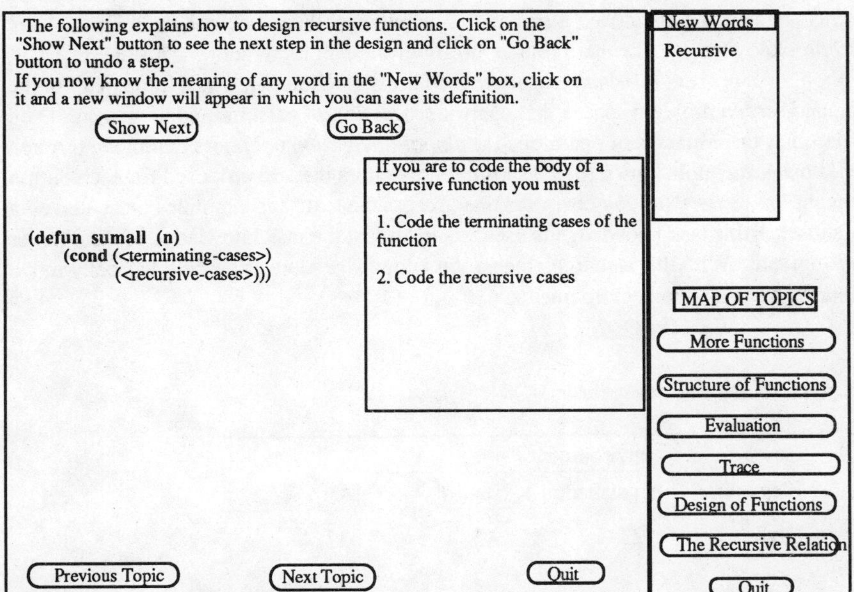

Figure 5. A screen from the Explanation Environment

Figure 5 shows a screen from the Explanation Environment in which the design of recursive functions is presented. The *Show Next* and *Go Back* buttons can be used to see how the example function is decomposed, and the box next to the example presents the underlying program design plan. The buttons along the bottom are for local navigation and the map at the lower right is for global navigation.

We compared the performance of subjects learning from the Explanation Environment with subjects who learned in a control condition. In this control condition, subjects used a learning environment that contained the same texts and examples as the Explanation Environment, but the information was presented in a linear fashion (i.e., just like turning the pages in a book). Contrary to our expectations, the Explanation Environment did not produce better learning. Rather we found an aptitude-treatment interaction: The Explanation Environment appeared to be beneficial for subjects who were already performing well, and seemed to hurt subjects who were already performing poorly.

Table 3 illustrates this significant interaction. All subjects had gone through the same four Lisp Tutor lessons prior to working with the learning environments. We tested subjects on these four lessons and divided them into high vs low performers. Table 3 shows the mean error rates in programming with the Lisp Tutor for these high and low performers, after they had gone through the Explanation Environment or the control environment. The errors are averages over all opportunities for applying a novel programming operators.

To help us understand this interaction, Margaret Recker has developed a set of Soar models that simulate individual subject strategies on the two learning environments. The screens and buttons of the hypermedia environments are simulated by a set of Lisp functions that can be "read" into Soar working memory. For each environment, there is a set of common *task implementation* knowledge. For the Explanation Environment, there are four problem spaces, including a top-level *process-instruction* space that controls the global traversal through all of the instruction, and *screen* problem spaces that control processing of each individual screen. Each problem space has three classes of operators: (a) *global-navigation* operators that move through the hypertext using the global map, (b) *select-button* operators that are proposed for each button on a screen, and (c) *comprehension* operators that process the texts and examples presented on a screen. A subset of this task knowledge is used to implement the task knowledge of the simpler control environment. With this task implementation knowledge alone, Soar will basically move at random through the learning environments.

Table 3. Mean error in applying new operators

Prior	Environment		
Lisp Score	Explanation	Control	Mean
High	.23	.45	.37
Low	.75	.24	.49
Mean	.53	.35	.43

Note: N = 16

The task implementation knowledge yields some interesting measures. The Explanation Environment requires 102 productions for navigation whereas the control environment requires only 64 productions. The Explanation Environment requires that up to four problem spaces be on the goal stack, whereas the control environment never exceeds a two-level goal stack. Together, these imply that that navigating the Explanation Environment is both a more complex task, and produces a higher working memory load.

To simulate individual subjects, additional *search control* knowledge is provided. This knowledge selects among the various operators available, and simulates the tendencies or strategies of individual subjects. For instance, the best subject (lowest number of programming errors) is simulated by adding search control knowledge that prefers the *comprehension* operator and the *select-button(example)* operator that selects the viewing of examples. This simulation learns 68 chunks of lisp knowledge from the material. In contrast, the worst subject (highest number of programming errors) is simulated by search control knowledge that selects the *select-button(example)* operator, and the *select-button(next)* operator which moves to the next screen. This simulation only learns three chunks of Lisp knowledge.

Although more subject simulations need to be developed, the work so far (and the protocol data) suggests that (a) low performance subjects were more prone to simply move through the instruction (i.e., selecting the next button) than high performance subjects, who tended to be more driven by their self-explanation (comprehension) strategies, and (b) the low performance subjects may have been more susceptible to the greater complexity and cognitive load of the Explanation Environment.

Summary

One of the practical motivations for developing an integrated model of learning to program is the idea that it could lead to better instruction. The parts of the model we have developed suggest that it is possible to track students in highly interactive learning environments, identify the declarative domain knowledge they are acquiring, and how they are transferring that knowledge into practice. Moreover, it appears that it is possible to detect differences in learning strategies, and it is possible to teach better ones.

Acknowledgements

This research is supported by a National Science Foundation grant, no. IRI-9001233. I would like to thank Kate Bielaczyc and Margaret Recker for their significant contributions to this work.

References

1. Anderson, J. R.: Learning to program in LISP. Cognitive Science. 8, 87-129 (1984)
2. Anderson, J. R., C. F. Boyle, A. Corbett and M. W. Lewis: Cognitive modelling and intelligent tutoring. Artificial Intelligence. 42, 7-49 (1990)
3. Anderson, J. R., C. F. Boyle and B. J. Reiser: Intelligent Tutoring Systems. Science. 228, 456-462 (1985)

4. Anderson, J. R., F. G. Conrad and A. T. Corbett: Skill acquisition and the LISP tutor. Cognitive Science. 13, 467-505 (1989)
5. Bielaczyc, K., P. Pirolli and A. Brown: The effects of training in explanation strategies on the acquisition of programming. University of California, Berkeley, CA Tech. Rep. CSM-3, 1991
6. DeJong, G. and R. Mooney: Explanation-based learning: An alternative view. Machine Learning. 1, 145-176 (1986)
7. Johnson-Laird, P. N.: Mental models. Cambridge, MA: Harvard University Press 1983.
8. Kintsch, W.: The role of knowledge in discourse comprehension: A construction-integration model. Psychological Review. 95, 163-182 (1988)
9. Mitchell, T. M., Kellar, R. M., and S. T. Kedar-Cabelli: Explanation-based generalization: A unifying view. Machine Learning. 1, 47-80 (1986)
10. Newell, A.: Unified theories of cognition. Cambridge, MA: Harvard University Press 1990.
11. Pirolli, P.: A cognitive model and computer tutor for programming recursion. Human-Computer Interaction. 2, 319-355 (1986)
12. Pirolli, P.: A model of purpose-driven analogy and skill acquisition in programming. In Proceedings of the Tenth Annual Conference of the Cognitive Science Society. Hillsdale, NJ: Lawrence Erlbaum 1987.
13. Pirolli, P.: Effects of examples and their explanations in a lesson on recursion: A production system analysis. Cognition and Instruction. 8, 207-259 (1991)
14. Pirolli, P. and M. Recker: Knowledge construction and transfer using an intelligent tutoring system: The role of examples, self-explanation, practice, and reflection. University of California, Berkeley, CA Tech. Rep. CSM-1, 1991
15. Pirolli, P. and M. Wilson: Measuring learning strategies and understanding: A research framework. University of California, Berkeley, CA Tech. Rep. CD-1, 1991
16. Pirolli, P. L. and J. R. Anderson: The role of learning from examples in the acquisition of recursive programming skills. Canadian Journal of Psychology. 39, 240-272 (1985)
17. Polson, P. G., S. Bovair and D. Kieras: Transfer between text editors. In Proceedings of CHI '87 Human Factors in Computing Systems and Graphics Interface Conference. New York: Association for Computing Machinery 1987
18. Rosenbloom, P. S.: Mapping explanation-based generalization onto Soar. In Proceedings of the Fifth National Conference on Artificial Intelligence (AAAI-86). Los Altos, CA: Morgan-Kaufman 1986
19. Singley, M. K. and J. R. Anderson: Transfer of cognitive skill. Cambridge, MA: Harvard University Press 1989.
20. VanLehn, K., R. M. Jones and M. T. H. Chi: Modeling the self-explanation effect with Cascade 3. In Proceedings of Annual Conference of the Cognitive Science Society. Lawrence Erlbaum 1991

Acquiring Experience in Object-Oriented Programming: Effects on Design Strategies

Françoise Détienne

Project of Ergonomics Psychology, Institut National de Recherche en Informatique et Automatique, Domaine de Voluceau, Rocquencourt, BP 105, 78153, Le Chesnay Cedex, France

Abstract: The goal of the present study is to analyse the design activities of professional programmers using an object-oriented programming (OOP) language. An issue is to discover which characteristics of the design strategies are common or different according to the experience the programmers have in the OOP language in question. This is evaluated for different types of problems.

Keywords: design strategies, schemas, object-oriented programming, expertise

Design Strategies in Programming

Most often, empirical studies of program design have been conducted either with experts or with novices in programming. Insofar as new programming languages are becoming increasingly available to experienced programmers, the design activity of experts using new languages seems an important psychological issue to address. The original contribution of the present study is to draw comparisons between design activities of experienced programmers with varying degrees of experience in a new language.

Empirical studies of programmers have highlighted various characteristics of design strategies [1, 7, 9, 10, 11, 12]. Distinctions are made between top-down or bottom-up strategies, breadth-first or depth-first strategies, prospective or retrospective strategies, procedural or declarative strategies, use of simulation, use of software design knowledge and problem domain knowledge.

Design strategies tend to vary according to the programmer's expertise and to characteristics of problems. Experienced programmers tend to use top-down and breadth-first strategies whenever they solve familiar problems. Whereas the design strategies of experts tend to be prospective, the design strategies of novices tend to be retrospective: novices construct new solutions in a backward manner. Problem characteristics also seem to influence the nature of design strategies. For declarative problems [8], the data structure guides program development whereas, for procedural problems, the structure of the procedure guides the program development.

Evolving from novice to expert involves constructing knowledge structures such as schemas of programming[1] [3, 4] and also using different strategies. Experts have at their disposal a greater number of strategies enabling them to use their knowledge efficiently [6].

The goal of the present study is to analyse the design activities of professional programmers using an object-oriented programming (OOP) language. An issue is to discover which characteristics of the design strategies are common or different according to the experience the programmers have in the OOP language in question. This will be evaluated for different types of problems.

The O2 Experiment

An experiment was conducted to study the activity of program design developed by programmers experienced in classical procedural languages as they use an OOP language[2]. Eight professional programmers participated in this experiment. All had several years of programming experience with classical procedural languages such as C, Cobol or Basic. Four of them were "beginners in OOP". The four others, "experienced in OOP", had practice with the object-oriented language under study. Each subject had two management problems to program with an object-oriented system, the O2 system, using the CO2 language:

- a financial management problem which was a slightly modified version of a problem classified in a previous experiment [8] as a declarative problem
- a library management problem which was a slightly modified version of a problem classified as a procedural problem.

The task domain was familiar to the subjects. The order of problems presentation was counter-balanced. The beginners in OOP had one day for programming each problem whereas the programmers experienced in OOP had half a day[3]. Prior to the phase of program design, the four beginners in OOP received a day of theoretical training.

All subjects had at their disposal a manual for the system, a theoretical paper on OOP and an example-program, i.e., a program written with the CO2 language solving a problem different from the experimental ones. We collected the subjects' verbalizations, successive versions of programs under development, notes, and the order in which the different traces of

---

[1]These knowledge structures are also called "programming plans" by Soloway's group. However, to be more precise, the term "plan" will refer to a representation constructed during design which guides the activity whereas a schema is a knowledge structure, stored in memory, which may be evoked during design for elaborating a plan.
[2]Previous analyses of this experiment were focused on knowledge transfer [2] and software code reuse [5].
[3]It proved to be sufficient to develop the program at least as much as the beginners. As an indication, the maximum size of programs written by subjects was 300 lines.

the activity were made. The final versions of the programs were given for evaluation to experts in OOP.

The O2 System

The O2 system is an object-oriented data base system. A "classical" language is used mainly to write the methods. In the version of the system used for our experiment, this is the CO2 language, which is a slightly modified version of C. An object-oriented layer, the O2 language, is added to the "classical" language.

There is an important difference between the object-oriented paradigm and the procedural paradigm. With a procedural paradigm, data and functions are separated, whereas with an object-oriented paradigm, they are integrated. Objects are the program entities which exhibit this integration. Objects are instances of classes. A class is defined as a structure (a type) and methods. A method is a function attached to a class that describes one part of the behavior of the objects which are instances of this class.

A program is composed of two parts:

- a *declarative part* in which computational entities and the relations between them are defined. This part is called the "model of classes" and is written in O2. It consists of the type specification, i.e., the names of classes, the types and names of attributes, the relations between classes and the method specification, i.e., the signatures of methods which are names and parameters of methods
- a *procedural part* which consists of the bodies of methods. This is written in CO2.

Design Strategies: Common Characteristics

Whatever their experience in OOP, a plan subjects try to follow when designing their program is to define the model of classes before defining in detail the processes which are expressed by methods. Thus they try to define declarative aspects of the program composed of classes, relations between classes and associations between classes and methods before defining the procedural part. This ordering is driven by specific characteristics of the O2 system under study. A constraint of order is as follows: in a method body, it is not possible to use a class or an object which has not been completely specified before. The plan programmers try to follow is hierarchical. They first try to develop the most abstract aspects of the solution before writing the code of methods which refines the functionalities defined in the declarative part.

Design Strategies: Different Characteristics

The data have been analysed to determine how design strategies vary with the experience of the programmers in OOP.

Number of modifications to the abstract solution

While refining their solutions, all subjects tend to modify the abstract solution developed beforehand. Developing the procedural part in more detail makes them modify the model of classes. When they refine the functions by writing the code of methods, programmers are able to refine some characteristics of the structure of objects already defined at higher levels of abstraction, e.g., they add attributes in a class or add parameters in a method signature. However they also make more drastic changes to the declarative model: they add new classes and new methods, and move methods from one class to another.

This result exhibits the difficulties subjects have in articulating declarative characteristics of a solution with more procedural characteristics of a solution. In doing the mapping between problem entities and computational entities in order to define the model of classes, they need knowledge of the procedure they will develop in the procedural part so as to develop the static aspects of the solution, i.e., the structures and the functionalities of classes.

Figures 1a and 1b present the numbers of modifications made in the models of classes while the subjects developed the procedural parts of their programs.

	Beg1	Beg2	Beg3	Beg4	Exp1	Exp2	Exp3	Exp4
procedural problem	16	22	21	32	22	29	10	9
declarative problem	7	46	29	15	9	6	23	13

Figure 1a. Total number of modifications made in the model of classes

	Beg1	Beg2	Beg3	Beg4	Exp1	Exp2	Exp3	Exp4
procedural problem	13	13	18	20	7	12	10	9
declarative problem	4	38	22	12	4	4	14	3

Figure 1b. Number of method modifications made in the model of classes

Not surprisingly, more modifications are made by beginners in OOP than by programmers experienced in OOP. Whereas this difference is not significant when we consider the total numbers of modification ($F(1/6)=3.015$, $P<0.13$), it is significant when we consider only the methods modifications ($F(1/6)=6.187$, $p<0.04$), e.g., adding/modifying/removing a method and moving a method from one class to another. There is neither a significant effect of the problem type nor a significant interaction effect.

Depth-first versus breadth-first elaboration of the solution

When a solution is elaborated in a breadth-first manner, the complete solution is elaborated at a given level of abstraction before being developed at the next level of abstraction. In terms of methods defined in the model of classes, the solution would be elaborated in a breadth-first manner if most methods were simply named and listed before any code was written. A strictly depth-first strategy would consist of defining a method and writing the code before defining another method. Figure 2 presents the numbers[4] of methods defined in the model of classes before the elaboration of the procedural part: these numbers are given for both kinds of subjects and both kinds of problems.

	Beg1	Beg2	Beg3	Beg4	Exp1	Exp2	Exp3	Exp4
procedural problem	9	8	8	2	9	11	19	4
declarative problem	18	5	3	4	12	13	13	9

Figure 2. Number of methods defined in the model of classes before developing the procedural part

The numbers shown in Figure 2 do not reveal purely depth-first strategies (none of the numbers is one). However, low numbers indicate a more depth-first strategy and high numbers indicate a more breadth-first strategy. Numbers less than seven represent half of the observations for beginners in OOP but only one of eight observations for programmers experienced in OOP. This suggests that beginners in OOP tend to adopt either a depth-first strategy or a breadth-first strategy whereas programmers experienced in OOP tend to adopt a breadth-first strategy. The type of problem does not seem to have an effect on the type of strategy used.

Procedurally-driven versus declaratively-driven strategy

When first elaborating the model of classes, the entities evoked and used by programmers are objects, actions and different types of links between them. When describing the model of classes in terms of the programming language, objects should be mapped to computational entities such as classes static description, i.e., the class name, its type and attributes, actions

[4]Absolute numbers are presented. A working hypothesis is that the total number of methods which should be defined in a complete solution would be the same for all subjects.

should be mapped to computational entities such as methods definition or parts of methods and links should be mapped to computational entities such as inheritance links and composition links between classes and associations between classes and methods.

An analysis of this early phase of design has been conducted in order to describe how objects, actions and links between them are elaborated and how they are mapped with computational entities allowed in the model of classes. Strategies differ in the following ways:

- *integration versus no integration between actions' description and objects' description:* For some subjects, an intermediary representation consists of a separate description of objects and actions. In this case, the analysis of notes taken by subjects shows that objects are listed and actions are listed without explicit links between objects and actions.
- *declaratively-driven versus procedurally-driven strategies:* Using a declaratively-driven strategy, the subject first lists the objects as classes. Then, for each object, the subject lists actions associated with it. With this strategy, the representation of objects is most important and the subjects elaborate actions in reference to the objects. Using a procedurally-driven strategy, the subject first lists actions as methods. Then, for each action, the subject infers one or several objects the action should be associated with. With this strategy, the representation of actions is most important and the subjects infer the association between actions and objects in reference to the actions.

Beginners in OOP (four of eight observations) tend to describe objects and actions separately more often than programmers experienced in OOP (one of eight observations). Furthermore, beginners in OOP (three of eight observations) tend to follow the procedurally-driven strategy more often than programmers experienced in OOP (one of eight observations).

When the strategy is declaratively-driven, the subjects generate a list of actions for each object in turn. When elaborating actions they may infer an action which may be associated to several objects. In this case, some subjects associate this action to the various objects whereas other subjects associate it to the object under current consideration only, then associate it to the other objects when they are under consideration.

We would expect, at least for beginners in OOP, the strategy to be procedurally-driven for procedural problems and the strategy to be declaratively-driven for declarative problems. Our data show that the choice of strategies does not seem to be related to the problem type. However, beginners in OOP tend to integrate objects'descriptions and actions'descriptions more often for procedural problems (three of four observations) than for declarative problems (one of four observations).

Objects, actions and associations between them are defined in an iterative manner. For one subject, a shift of strategies was observed. Whatever the strategy followed by beginners in OOP, we observed that many questions were raised about the associations between actions and objects. The choice of the association between objects and actions is sometimes postponed until the elaboration of the procedural phase.

With the inheritance property, methods associated to the superclass are inherited by subclasses. Whereas programmers experienced in OOP tend to associate these methods to the most general class first, beginners in OOP tend to associate them to subclasses first before associating them to the superclass. This result suggests that experienced programmers tend to develop a more general solution first whereas beginners tend to start from particular solutions before abstracting the more general solution.

Use of exemplars

Exemplars of solutions may be provided by the example-program or by programs developed by the programmers beforehand (this is the case for programmers experienced in OOP). The way exemplars of solution are used varies greatly depending on the subjects' experience in OOP.

Beginners in OOP often use the example-program. They use it in various ways. First, given a problem, the programmers may use the example-program to search for a solution. This analogical problem solving process may produce errors. The nature of the analogy may be semantic or syntactic. Second, beginners in OOP may have elaborated a solution and tried to infer the rules of validity of this solution from information extracted from example-program understanding. Third, beginners in OOP may have obtained an error message after compilation and may have a hypothesis about the cause of the error. They use the example-program to search for information confirming or contradicting their hypothesis. These last two ways of using exemplars of solution will be developed in the next section.

Programmers experienced in OOP rarely use the example-program. Whenever they do, they read a part of it to verify the form of a syntactic component in their programs. One subject used parts of programs he had developed before. An analysis of his verbal protocols [5] showed that reused solutions represent instantiations of schemas possessed by the programmer. It appears that the evocation of a schema and the extraction of information from understanding the detailed source-solution code allow the elaboration of an abstract representation of the source-solution which can be described as a set of subgoals to achieve. This representation provides the programmer with an abstract plan to follow in order to construct a detailed target-solution for solving his current problem.

Inferring/using validity conditions of solution/schema versus generate/test/debug

Experienced programmers are able to use decision rules and inferred constraints for anticipating the correctness of a solution without having to develop it at a detailed level. The use of specialized design schemas frees them, at least partially, from reliance on weak problem-solving methods.

A previous analysis of our data [2] highlighted the effect of knowledge transfer mechanisms. It was shown that beginners in OOP, but also programmers experienced in OOP, transfer schematic knowledge of classical procedural languages, of the task domain and of a design methodology. It was shown that transfer mechanisms sometimes produced errors and inelegances in programs, particularly for the beginners in OOP programs.

Although both kinds of subjects evoke and use schemas of programming, an important difference is the way they determine when and how to use these schemas. Beginners use schemas but they lack decision rules or they use erroneous decision rules associated with schemas. This may lead them to produce errors. However they use strategies which avoid making errors.

One strategy is to analyse exemplars of a solution to infer the rules of validity of a given solution. This was observed many times for some subjects using the example-program. Looking at some part of the example-program may give them information about the conditions in which a solution, chosen for their current problem and instantiated in the example-program, is valid.

Another strategy is to use weak problem-solving methods such as generate-test-and-debug for evaluating a solution. As the analysis below reveals, beginners in OOP use this strategy much more extensively than programmers experienced in OOP.

In order to determine whether or not the programmers used a weak problem-solving strategy such as generate-test-and-debug, we analysed when compilations were run during program elaboration. Compiling the program is a way to test solutions whenever they are developed at the code level. Figure 3 presents, for each subject and for each type of problem, whether or not compilation is postponed until the whole declarative part and procedural part have been coded[5].

	Beg1	Beg2	Beg3	Beg4	Exp1	Exp2	Exp3	Exp4
procedural problem	(?)	no	yes	no	yes	yes	yes	yes
declarative problem	no	no	no	no	yes	no	yes	yes

Figure 3. Postponements of compilations per problem type and per subject

Data show that compilation is postponed mostly by programmers experienced in OOP. These subjects tend to write the code of the whole programs then compile it. Beginners in OOP tend to write pieces of code corresponding to one or several methods then compile it or them.

[5]For the subjects "Exp2" and "Exp3" no compilations were run for the procedural problem. However, the subjects wrote the code of their program and, when the experimentator told them the experiment was over, they remarked that they would not have time to compile their programs. So it appeared that compilation had been postponed. On the other hand, for the subject "Beg1", the subject wrote pieces of code only with paper and pencil so we cannot tell whether or not, when using the O2 system, this subject would have intended to postpone compilation.

So, they use a generate/test and debug strategy, the evaluated units being one method or several methods. When they receive an error message they make hypotheses about the error. Then either they modify and compile their solution again or they use other exemplars of solution to test whether or not their hypothesis is correct. They use the example-program to search for information confirming or contradicting their hypothesis. In this case, subjects find that verifying hypotheses in this way is more economical and cautious than modifying their current programs and compiling them again. This behavior of hypothesis testing using information extracted from the example-program was not observed for programmers experienced in OOP.

Conclusion

The use of strategies has not been shown to be related to the type of problem used in our experiment. However, the use of strategies has been shown to be related to the experience programmers have in OOP. The beginners in OOP tend to use either a depth-first strategy or a breadth-first strategy. The programmers experienced in OOP tend to follow a breadth-first strategy exclusively.

For the beginners in OOP, the strategy is either declaratively-driven or procedurally-driven and they first tend to separate objects'descriptions and actions'descriptions. Programmers experienced in OOP tend to follow a declaratively-driven strategy. This suggests that different meta-schemas are used for planning their activity: either schemas grouping actions according to objects or schemas grouping actions by procedure. The former type of schemas may be developed through practice with OOP languages and are more adapted to the constraints which must be taken into account in designing with this kind of languages, e.g., making explicit the links between objects and actions.

Evaluation mechanisms are related to the experience programmers have in OOP. Whereas both kinds of programmers possess and use schemas of programming, beginners in OOP either do not know the conditions in which to use schemas or they use wrong conditions. Although this leads them to make errors, they also use strategies to avoid making errors. One strategy is to analyse exemplars of solution so as to infer rules of validity of a given solution. Another strategy is to use weak problem-solving methods such as generate-test-and-debug for evaluating their solution. Whereas the latter strategy has been shown to be used also by complete novices in programming, the former strategy is a way to use exemplars of solution which may be specific to experienced programmers.

These results emphasize the diversity of strategies used by experts in using a new programming language. Aiding systems should support the use of these various strategies. Furthermore transfer mechanisms of schemas have been shown to produce errors whereas strategies are used in order to avoid making errors. Aiding systems would support these transfer mechanisms, in particular, by providing feedback about the validity of the transferred schemas at levels of abstraction higher than the implementation level.

Acknowledgements

The study was conducted under a research contract with the GIP Altaïr (Altaïr is a consortium funded by IN2, INRIA and LRI University Paris XI). Thanks to Pascal Claudel for collecting the protocols and to Philippe Delsol for participating in one part of the protocol analysis. Thanks to Willemien Visser for help in the preparation of this paper.

References

1. Adelson, B. & Soloway, E.: The role of domain experience in software design. IEEE Transactions on Software Engineering. 11 (11), 1351-1360 (1985)
2. Détienne, F.: Difficulties in designing with an object-oriented language: an empirical study. In: Human-computer interaction, proceedings of INTERACT'90 (D. Diaper, D. Gilmore, G. Cockton & B. Shackel, eds.). pp. 971-976. North-Holland 1990
3. Détienne, F.: Program Understanding and knowledge organization: the influence of acquired schemas. In: Cognitive ergonomics: understanding, learning and designing human-computer interaction (P. Falzon, ed.). pp. 245-256. London: Academic Press 1990
4. Détienne, F.: Expert programming knowledge: a schema-based approach. In: Psychology of programming (J-M. Hoc, T.R.G. Green, R. Samurçay, D. Gilmore, eds.). pp. 205-222. People and Computer Series, Academic Press 1990
5. Détienne, F.: Reasoning from a schema and from an analog in software code reuse. In: Empirical studies of programmers, Fourth Workshop (J. Koenemann-Belliveau, T. Moher & S. P. Robertson, eds.). pp. 5-22. Norwood, NJ: Ablex 1991
6. Gilmore, D.: Expert programming knowledge: a strategic approach. In: Psychology of programming (J-M. Hoc, T.R.G. Green, R. Samurçay, D. Gilmore, eds.). pp. 223-234. People and Computer Series, Academic Press 1990
7. Guindon, R.: Knowledge exploited by experts during software system design. International Journal of Man-Machine Studies. 33(3), 241-360 (1990)
8. Hoc, J-M.,: Towards effective computer aids to planning in computer programming: theoretical concern and empirical evidence drawn from assessment of a prototype. In: Working with computers, theory versus outcome. pp. 215-247. London, Academic press 1988
9. Rist, R.: Knowledge creation and retrieval in program design: a comparison of novice and intermediate student programmers. Human-Computer Interaction. 6, 1-46 (1991)
10. Soloway, E., Ehrlich, K. & Bonar, J.: Tapping into tacit programming knowledge. Human Factors in Computer System, 15-17, 52-57 (1982)
11. Soloway, E. & Ehrlich, K.: Empirical studies of programming knowledge. IEEE Transactions on Software Engineering. SE-10 (5), 595-609 (1984)
12. Visser, W. & Hoc, J-M.: Expert software design strategies. In: Psychology of programming (J-M. Hoc, T.R.G. Green, R. Samurçay, D. Gilmore, eds.). pp. 235-249. People and Computer Series, Academic Press 1990

Programming and Design

John Sumiga

School of Computing and Information Technology, Wolverhampton Polytechnic, Wolverhampton, UK. and Centre for Systems Methodologies, Department of Computer Science, Swinburne Institute of Technology, Hawthorne, Victoria 3122, Australia.

Abstract: An important component of programming is the process of design and this should be taken account of when developing cognitive models of the programming activity. Most empirical studies of programming neglect this dimension because of the absence of a theory, the difficulties associated with collecting and analysing empirical data and a commitment to the top-down philosophy of design. This paper reports work that has been carried out in modelling the conceptual design activity in both the software engineering and mechanical engineering domains. A novel method for analysing verbal protocols, based on functional discourse analysis is outlined and a blackboard based model of conceptual design is presented.

Keywords: Cognitive Modelling; Design; Blackboard Model; Psychology of Programming

Introduction:

This paper takes a broad view of what is meant by programming and takes it to mean more than the construction of algorithms in a particular executable notation. Programming is viewed as the process of developing software, i.e. Software Engineering, and should be thought of as encompassing all of the stages characterised by the lifecycle model and not just those following the design phase. Until comparatively recently, however, most studies of programming in both the Computer Science and Psychology domains have concentrated on the lower level activities associated with software construction and comprehension, e.g. algorithm construction, use and effect of syntax, debugging etc. What has been neglected has been the higher level activity of design, i.e the process of creating a solution specification from a problem specification (the design brief). The lower level activities mostly involve the transformation of the solution (i.e. program or system) specification into a functioning artefact. Whilst there are many questions associated with this transformation, it is also crucial to investigate how a solution specification is derived by a designer. In general, methodologies and other techniques such as formal specification methods do not aid in this process as they do not provide any criteria for the decomposition of a problem into appropriate components. Neglecting this aspect of programming would be a serious omission in that many of the difficulties currently being experienced by the software engineering community, i.e. the 'software crisis', can be interpreted as resulting from high level design problems.

The main efforts associated with resolving the software crisis have involved the development of methodologies, with their associated notations and CASE tools. Methodologies attempt to provide a structured way of carrying out the software development process, such that it can be successfully managed. In so doing, they provide guidelines for how to carry out the process. The focus of methodologies is, however, the development of software and not its design, i.e. they are concerned with constraining the product once it has been designed. Many methodologies are based on the waterfall model, a model which has been criticised as being unrealistic and idealised [13, 24], because of its reliance on hierarchical top-down ideas. Blind adherence to this approach can lead to enormous difficulties because of the cognitive requirements made of the user. The success of a methodology will be determined by the amount of dissonance between the method and its user. This becomes even more relevant when considering CASE tools, where the major issues become those of usability and effectiveness [20].

One foundation stone of this work is that appropriate support is most easily developed on the basis of reducing the dissonance between the cognitive processes of the user (of a tool, method etc.) and the cognitive requirements for the effective use of the entity concerned. It is, therefore, concerned with developing an understanding of the cognitive processes associated with the software development activity, with an emphasis on the design process, in order to aid the development of appropriate support tools and environments for both the novice and experienced programmer.

Psychology and Programming

This section is not intended to be a full review of the literature, studies or models in the area. More detailed reviews have recently appeared [19, 22]. It is, however, worth noting that there are several imbalances in the attention received from empiricists. Two main issues have to be raised concerning the general aspects of studies of the software development process. Firstly, many of the studies reported in the literature have utilised small numbers of individual non-expert subjects solving artificial problems under laboratory conditions.

This is rightly criticised as being potentially flawed [9]. Recent studies have attempted to overcome these difficulties [17] although earlier studies have investigated the behaviour of 'expert' programmers [2]. The vast majority of studies have also concentrated on individual programmers and their activities, i.e. "programming in the small". What has been neglected is the study of "programming in the large" [23]. Again, attempts are being made to redress the balance [10] and deal with the factors associated with software development teams and their organisational context.

The second general point is that there is not an even distribution of studies over the main stages of the development life cycle. The number of empirical studies and attempts to develop models increases with the tangibility of the deliverables of the stage. Thus, very little work has been carried out in the specific area of analysis, whilst the majority of the work has involved coding and program comprehension. There is a simplistic explanation for this in that the less tangible the output of the activity, the more difficult it is to establish satisfactory controlled experimental conditions. Most of the work carried out on the analysis and design phases has used protocol analysis as the experimental methodology [12], whilst investigations of, for instance, coding behaviour submit more readily to manipulation [6, 16]. There have been a number of methodology based criticisms of empirical studies [6, 28, 29, 37]. There is, however, a small, but growing body of work which attempts to use controlled experiments to investigate analysis and/or design [25] and to test hypotheses generated from models and theories [11, 14]. This work is, however, still in its infancy in that most of the proposed models are not sufficiently refined to allow the generation of testable hypotheses, and investigations of analysis and design using techniques other than protocol studies are few and far between.

However, from what is known of programming, the common cognitive tasks which need to be dealt with in models of the software development process are: mappings between structures (problem descriptions, specifications, designs, algorithms etc.); dealing with uncertainty, ambiguity and conflict; object recognition; analogical reasoning; inferring structure and process, i.e. creating, refining and expressing a working mental model; searching, browsing and foraging; evaluation; prediction and testing; composition, decomposition and refinement of both structure and process.

Whilst no existing model is capable of dealing with all of these issues, there are several which either attempt to address a sub-set of them or which could be extended in scope to deal with them. An early model [5] attempted to create an information processing theory sufficient to describe the coding process in the construction of FORTRAN programs. Its focus of attention, however, is coding and not design. A further model [31, 32] is concerned with knowledge and memory structures and is insufficiently refined. The well-known GOMS model [7] assumes perfect expert behaviour and that programming involves a notional machine plus the creation of instructions for this, using an editor. Again, the emphasis is on programming, not design. The ACT* model [3], which is a general model of cognition, has been successfully used to model the generation of LISP code. Interestingly, this assumes that LISP programming is largely a top-down planning activity. This approach to software design was suggested by earlier work [21] and has been much utilised by the work on programming plans [1, 26, 32]. The psychological reality of programming plans is questionable [14] and the top-down assumption does not appear to capture the opportunistic aspects of programmers' behaviour. Various similar models have been suggested to overcome this failing [17, 31, 34-36]. The earlier stages of software development are being increasingly recognised as important [13, 33], but they have not been the focus of attention. The remainder of this paper attempts to characterise the design process and outlines a model of conceptual design.

The conclusion that must be drawn from this brief survey is that there is yet much work to be carried out in that many of the cognitive tasks involved in the software development process have yet to be incorporated into a unified model of sufficient refinement to generate testable hypotheses for future empirical studies and to form the basis of appropriate support for programmers and programming.

Design can be considered from two different perspectives; as a form of problem solving or as a form of planning. These are not dissimilar[34]. The most complete characterisation of design as a form of problem solving [15] argues that design is a generic activity, independent (other than for various forms of knowledge base) of the domain in which an artefact is being designed. It is a form of problem solving which takes place in a task environment with particular properties. The key observations, amongst others, are that designers: carry out extensive problem structuring, involving information gathering, the application of personal knowledge, particularly kernel ideas, and the application of constraints; make extensive use of performance modelling and simulation; make use of personalised heuristics; utilise limited commitment control strategies with nested evaluation; make and propagate commitments; create 'leaky' solution decompositions; mediate through the use of abstraction and abstraction hierarchies; use artificial symbol systems. Whilst this study provides a rich set of observations about the design process, it does not provide a detailed coordinated model which can be used to simulate the process and aid further understanding and development.

As mentioned earlier, several recent studies of design [17, 31, 34-36] have observed that it is inherently opportunistic in nature and has much in common with Opportunistic Planning [18]. A model of the design process, based on the OPM blackboard architecture, is proposed. This has been developed from observational studies utilising verbal and video protocols of both software and professional mechanical designers and has been used to account for the protocols in both domains [27, 34]. Before giving details of the model, it is pertinent to say a little about how protocols are analysed.

Protocols are analysed in two stages. Firstly, principles from functional discourse analysis are used to break down the protocols into utterances, yielding an analysis at the function and task levels. Secondly, the analysed protocols are traced on to a blackboard model, based on OPM [18].

Discourse analysis has been used to study verbal interaction in a large number of disciplines [8]. It has not, to our knowledge, been used to analyse think-aloud protocols prior to this study. The closest usage to that reported here involved the design of an intelligent interface, based on a blackboard architecture, following a study of the interactions between a user, an on-line information system and an intermediary [4].

Discourse analysis attempts to account for meaning and coherence in discourse. Functional discourse analysis is one model proposed by discourse analysts and is based on the idea that the unit of analysis in discourse is the utterance, which need not be coextensive with a grammatical sentence. Utterances perform "functions" which give structure to discourse. The function of an utterance, for our purposes, is that which the utterance achieves. This approach is extremely useful in protocol analysis, where the objective is to trace a search in a problem space or to identify the processes by which a task is accomplished. Identifying the function of a subject's utterances yields important information about the problem solving activity. Also, linguistic features can be used to parse a protocol, if these features can be found to be reliable indicators. In protocol analysis, there are many types of statements or utterances. Some express evaluative judgements, some express intentions and strategies, others express commitment to a particular course of action, others are inferences from perceived facts or queries. In the analysis at the functional level, of both software and mechanical designer protocols, the following functions can be identified from utterances: Defining the problem (express current understanding of the problem); Prioritising (declare intention to conduct design activity according to certain principles); Searching (seek to establish relevant facts); Setting down a requirement (elaborate the perceived performance features of the artefact); Modifying a requirement (modify understanding of a requirement); Self assessment (assess own performance or knowledge of the domain); Task assessment (assess state of the problem, what is needed to make progress or how much has been done so far); Moving on (decide what to do next); Generating a proposal (suggest a design concept for the artefact) Elaborating a proposal (work out a function structure for the artefact); Evaluating (make comparisons or set evaluation criteria); Modifying a proposal (suggest a modification to a proposal); Coming up against a constraint (discover a limiting condition); "Skirting along" (talk around the problem without a clear objective); Making a commitment (articulate intention to carry out or reject a proposal); Deferring commitment (postpone making decisions at a detailed level). These were extremely useful in providing a first level analysis of verbal protocol data.

A Blackboard Framework for Modelling Design

The framework used to model the conceptual stage of design is the Opportunistic Planning Model (OPM), (Hayes-Roth and Hayes-Roth, 1979). The use of OPM can be viewed at three different levels: as an implementation formalism; as a formalism on to which data can be matched; as a theory of how knowledge is used to solve a category of problems (in this case design problems). As an implementation formalism, OPM can be used to specify a simulation of planning (and related) tasks. This is the end goal of this work. Secondly, its use as a set of categories for mapping data provides an intermediate stage between raw data and a computational implementation. Thirdly, OPM is, at least implicitly, a partial theory of planning. The analysis presented here will argue the validity of generalising from this to allow the use of OPM as a model for other ill-structured problems such as design.

The blackboard framework was used because it allows attention to be focussed on the sub-processes involved in conceptual design and the control and coordination of those processes. The sub-processes of interest are: problem understanding and interpretation; conceptual and mental modelling; evaluation and mental execution; analogising; problem feature identification; feature comparison; assessment. Control issues include: hierarchical top-down or bottom-up coordination; heterarchical (opportunistic) coordination, with island formulation and island driving [34].

Designers have models or mental representations of artefacts upon which they build solutions to new problems. They tend to have ill-defined representations of the problem scenario for unfamiliar problems, so they have to build a cognitive model before they started designing. It is not possible for them to break down the problem into subproblems as they have no well-defined representation to work with. Conceptual design is characterised as the process of constructing a hypothetical representation of an artefact. Constraints are very important in these early stages of design, as they are the criteria against which the designer evaluates the suitability and feasibility of a proposed artefact.

In OPM, a planner makes different kinds of tentative decisions at different levels of abstraction. Current decisions can lead to further decisions at arbitrary points in the planning space. There is no overall abstract plan to guide the whole process. Planning actions depend on current decisions and weak strategies. The current work suggests differences and similarities between design and planning. In both activities, the solution is constructed incrementally and decisions are made at different levels of abstraction. There are, however, three differences which must be accounted for.

Firstly, constraints must be made explicit in a design model, because many decisions made by designers concern the identification and satisfaction of constraints. Designers make decisions either to satisfy constraints or to minimise the effects of these on the solution. OPM does not explicitly deal with constraints and, particularly, does not emphasise them as playing a part in shaping the final plan. In the design task, constraints are too important to be dealt with in such a manner and are, therefore, objects in the blackboard which can be created, modified and accessed for the purpose of evaluating design options. Secondly, designers are constantly reviewing and assessing the state of the problem. This has implications for the control part of the model, as many decisions depend on the designer's own assessment of the progress made in carrying out the task at a particular point in time. Planner behaviour in OPM is event driven to a greater extent than is designer behaviour. Designers have well defined ideas of how design should be carried out and tend to adhere to their overall strategies with opportunistic episodes [11]. Thirdly, designers' reasoning is best characterised as model driven. Design solutions are built from basic design concepts and designers' efforts are focussed on testing the proposed solutions in terms of suitability and feasibility. Moreover, designers may generate a number of different options. Thus, there is a different control regime necessary when building a design model, as compared to OPM. Not only are there different categories of decisions (constraints and options) that must be made explicit but there are other factors affecting the control of the model (model driven reasoning, a larger number of options to be managed and situation assessment). These differences are a reflection of the greater complexity of the design problems when compared to the planning problem used in OPM. The following global architecture (see Fig. 1) has been used in the model:

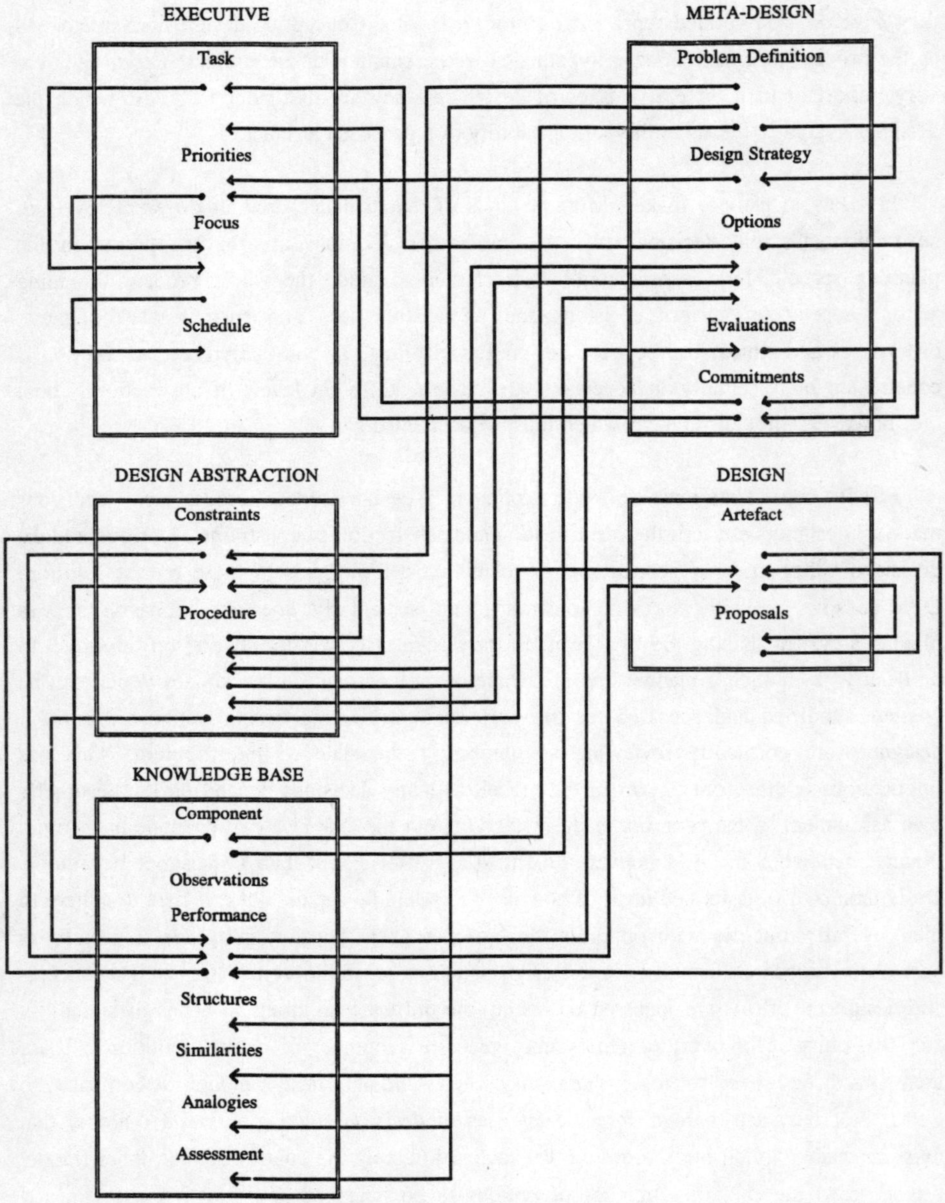

Fig. 1: A Blackboard Model of Conceptual Design

The Executive Plane represents the organisation and control aspects of design activity. It consists of four levels. The Task level represents the designer's current assessment of the task. The Priorities level reflects the designer's current priority. The Schedule level records which, from among a number of appropriate actions, is selected to be carried out. The selection process requires conflict resolution, taking into account the following factors: the actions listed at the schedule level; the current strategy operating on the blackboard, recorded on the Strategies and Priorities levels; the existing options at the Options level; the situation assessment as recorded at the Task level. The Focus level indicates the section of the blackboard where action is due, given the most recent event triggered on the blackboard and any strategies operating on it. The most recent events triggered at the Options and Task levels are also taken into consideration.

The Meta-design Plane represents the designer's understanding of the problem and their evaluation of the evolving solution at different stages of the design process. It consists of five levels. The Problem Definition level contains the problem description as in the design brief. As the designer works through a problem, new information may be recorded at other levels of the blackboard, as the designer may selectively read the problem statement. Some problem details may be disregarded, others may be expanded with new information. The problem may also be set in particular domains or high level interpretations of the problem may be articulated. These are all recorded on this level. The Design Strategy level records decisions about how to carry out the design process. Generally, this takes the form of a statement of intention. The Options level records the existence of different design options or alternative solutions. Generally, an option is expressed as a design concept, a method or simply some technology upon which the artefact can be built. The more alternatives considered by the designer, the more necessary it is for the model to "manage" the options. The Evaluations level records the judgments made about: the artefact being designed; the constraints acting on the solutions; the designer's knowledge; the design process itself. These judgments form the basis for modifications, queries, further evaluation and new ideas. As a result of these types of evaluations, the designer makes decisions to pursue a particular design option or to abandon it. The Commitments level records recommendations concerning particular design options. These often take the form of modifying, accepting, rejecting, reinstating or postponing a design option.

The Design Abstractions Plane contains a representation the designer has of an abstract artefact. With unfamiliar problems, designers have poor or incomplete representations of the artefact being designed. Most of their activities are directed at constructing and refining a design model. These initial representations are referred to as models, but they can be viewed as hypotheses that are generated and elaborated by the designer, in order to build a blueprint for the artefact. Requirements and constraints form the backbone of the evolving design. This plane consists of the two levels. The Constraints level, records constraints expressed as either performance requirements the artefact must satisfy, or as some limiting condition that must be taken account of in the design. These are usually expressed as "do's" and "dont's". The Procedure level contains descriptions of how the artefact will perform the various procedures which will functionally satisfy the requirements. This level can be further elaborated in order to model the later stages of design [34].

The Design Plane which records the evolving specification of the artefact. Designers find it difficult to verbalise about this aspect of the design process and, consequently, most of their activity is recorded as sketches and notes. It consists of two levels. The Artefact level, where decisions are recorded about the general layout of the evolving artefact. Again, this can be further elaborated to capture the later stages of design. The Proposals level records deferred commitments. Typically, designers focus on the major features of the artefact and defer commitment on details or even on important aspects that do not demand an immediate resolution.

The Knowledge Base Plane contains domain knowledge needed to support the reasoning processes associated with the Design abstraction and Design planes. It consists of seven levels. The Component level, which records relevant features of the components involved in the problem. This information is obtained by examination, questioning, measurement or the formulation of assumptions based on past experience and stored knowledge. The designers also make inferences based on this knowledge. The Observations level, where inferences based on domain knowledge are recorded. The Performance level records assessments of how feasible a proposed (inspection or handling) procedure might be. The Structures level records observations made about structural features of the problem. The Similarities level records perceived similarities between structures. The Analogies level records analogies made by the designer, in particular those involving problems they have previously solved. Finally, the Assessment level records the designer's perception of the difficulty of a particular task.

The specialists associated with this model are considered to be condition-action rules. The condition part has two components: a knowledge component and a trigger. The former is matched against an existing entry on the blackboard. The latter is a test of the specialist's relevance and is used at the Schedule level to determine whether the specialist can be executed. The conflict resolution factors determine whether the specialist is relevant to the context of the problem. Specialists are processes which can create other objects and place them on the blackboard or they can modify existing objects. These objects can be considered to be frame-like in nature, the modifications being carried out consist of alterations to or entries in slots.

Finally, the model is, like OPM, event driven. It runs in "cycles" or sequences of events. On each cycle, the current focus causes a number of specialists to be invoked. These are placed on the agenda, which carries out the various conflict resolution strategies.

Conclusion:

The work reported here is part of a larger project aimed at developing support for the early stages of software development. In order to do this, it is considered important to develop a full understanding of the psychological processes involved in those early stages in order that the dissonance between users and support tools and methods is minimised. As such, this work is also relevant to the process of teaching or training. Even expert designers exhibit some opportunistic behaviour when dealing with unfamiliar problems, resulting in satisficing rather than optimising behaviour. The approach taken to training in any domain that involves design as an activity should take this into account. This is particularly relevant to Software Engineering, where design plays such a key role.

References:

1. Adelson, B. and Soloway, E.: A Cognitive Model of Software Design. In: Nature of Expertise. (M. Chi, R. Glaser, M. Farr, eds.). 1984
2. Adelson, B. and Soloway, E.: The Role of Domain Experience in Software Design. IEEE Trans. Software Engineering. Vol. SE-11 (1985)
3. Anderson, J.R.: The Architecture of Cognition. Cambridge, Mass. Harvard U. P. 1983
4. Belkin, N.J., Brooks, H.M. and Daniels, P.J.: Knowledge elicitation using discourse analysis. Knowledge-Based Systems. Vol. 1, 107-24 (1988)
5. Brooks, R.: Towards a theory of the cognitive processes in computer programming. Int. J. Man-Machine Studies, 9, 737-751 (1977)
6. Brooks, R.: Studying Programmer Behaviour Experimentally: The Problems of Proper Methodology. Comm. ACM, 23, 207-213 (1980)
7. Card, S.K, Moran, T.P. and Newell, A.: The Psychology of Human-Computer Interaction. Hillside, NJ: Lawrence Erlbaum Ass. 1983
8. Cook, G.: Discourse. Oxford: OUP 1989
9. Curtis, B.: By the way, did anyone study any real programmers? In: Empirical Studies of Programmers. (E. Soloway and S. Iyengar, eds.), Ablex 1989

10. Curtis, B.: Modelling the Software Development Process. Sixth Symposium on Empirical Foundations of Information and Software Science. Atlanta GA. 1988
11. Davies, S.P.: Characterizing the program design activity: neither strictly top-down nor globally opportunistic. Behaviour and Information Technology. 10, 173-90 (1991)
12. Ericcson, K.A. and Simon, H.A.: Protocol Analysis: Verbal Reports as Data. Cambridge, MA.: MIT Press 1980
13. Ghezzi, C., Mehdi, J and Mandrioli, D.: Fundamentals of Software Engineering. Englewood Cliffs. N.J.: Prentice-Hall 1991.
14. Gilmore, D.J. and Green, T.R.G.: Are 'Programming Plans' Psychologically Real - Outside Pascal? Proc. INTERACT 87, (H.J. Bullinger and B. Shackle, eds), Stuttgart 1987
15. Goel, V. and Pirolli, P.: Design within Information Processing Theory: The Design Problem Space. AI Magazine. Spring 1989
16. Green, T.R.G., Sime, M.E. and Fitter, M.: Thoughts on Behavioural Studies of Programming. AISB Quarterly, May 1978.
17. Guindon, R., Krasner, H. and Curtis, B.: Breakdown and processes during the early activities of software design by professionals. MCC Technical Report STP-283-87 1987
18. Hayes-Roth, B, and Hayes-Roth, F.: A Cognitive Model of Planning. Cognitive Science. 3, 275-310 (1979)
19. Hoc, J.-M., Green, T.R.G., Samurcay, R. and Gilmore, D.J.: Psychology of Programming. London: Academic Press 1990
20. Howard, S. and Sumiga, J.H.: Computer Aided Software Engineering: Methods and Styles. 25th. Annual Conference of the Ergonomics Society of Australia (ESA89), Canberra. 1989
21. Jeffries, R., Turner, A., Polson, P. and Atwood, A.: The processes involved in designing software. In: Cognitive Skills and their Acquisition. (J.R.Anderson ed). Hillside, NJ.: Lawrence Erlbaum 1981
22. Koubek, R.J., Salvendy, G., Dunsmore, H.E. and LeBold, W.K.: Cognitive Issues in the Process of Software Development: Review and Re-appraisal. Int. J. Man-Machine Studies, 30 (1989)
23. Parnas, D.: Software Aspects of Strategic Defense Systems. Comm. ACM, 28(12). 1326-35 (1985)
24. Parnas, D.L. and Clements, P.C.: A rational design process: how and why to fake it, IEEE Trans. SoftwareEngineering, 12(2), 251-7 (1986)
25. Ratcliff, B. and Siddiqi, J.I.A.: An empirical investigation into problem decomposition strategies used in program design. Int. J. Man-Machine Studies, 22 (1985)
26. Rist, R.: Plans in Programming: Definition, Demonstration and Development. In: Empirical Studies of Programmers. (E. Soloway and S. Iyengar, eds). Ablex 1986
27. Rivera, R. and Sumiga, J.H.: Conceptual Design: A Cognitive Model. Dept. Computer Science Internal Report SIT-CS-1/92. Swinburne Institute of Technology, Australia 1992
28. Shiel, B.A.: The Psychological Study of Programming. ACM Computing Surveys, 13(1) (1981)
29. Shneiderman, B.: Empirical Studies of Programmers: The Territory, Paths and Destinations. In: Empirical Studies of Programmers. (E. Soloway and S. Iyengar, eds.), Ablex 1986
30. Shneiderman, B. and Mayer, R.: Syntactic/Semantic Interactions in Programmer Behaviour: A Model and Experimental Results. Int. J. Computer and Information Sciences. 8(3) (1979)
31. Siddiqi, J.I.A. and Sumiga, J.H: Empirical Evaluation of a Proposed Model of the Program Design Process. Proc. Fourth Symposium on Empirical Foundations of Information and Software Sciences, Atlanta Ga. 1986
32. Soloway, E. and Ehrlich, K.: Empirical Studies of Programming Knowledge. IEEE Trans. Software Engineering, 10(5), 595-609 (1984)
33. STARTS Guide: Department of Trade and Industry 1987
34. Sumiga, J.H.: Modelling Software Design. Dept. Computer Science Internal Report SIT-CS-2/92. Swinburne Institute of Technology, Australia 1992
35. Sumiga, J.H., Khazaei, B. and Siddiqi, J.I.A.: A Cognitive Model of Program Designer Behaviour. Proc. ECAI, 1988. Pitman 1988
36. Sumiga, J.H., Siddiqi, J.I.A. and Khazaei, B.: Use of a Blackboard Framework to Model Software Design. Sixth Symposium on Empirical Foundations of Information and Software Sciences, Atlanta, Ga, 1988.
37. Vessy, I. and Weber, R,: Research on Structured Programming: An Empiricist's Evaluation. IEEE Trans. Software Engineering, 10(4) (1984)

Program Comprehension Skills and Their Acquisition: A Call for an Ecological Paradigm

Barbee Mynatt Teasley

Computer Science Department, Bowling Green State University, Bowling Green, Ohio 43403, USA

Email: bteasle@opie.bgsu.edu

Abstract: Current theories of program comprehension suggest that the process is either top-down or bottom-up. However, recent research challenges these monolithic generalizations. This paper overviews these challenges and suggests that an ecological paradigm must be used in studying program comprehension and the acquisition of comprehension skills. Specifically, factors encompassing aspects of what is being comprehended, who is doing the comprehending, and for what purpose the comprehension task is undertaken must be studied. Furthermore, the interaction of these factors must be explored in order to fully understand comprehension processes and their acquisition.

Keywords: program comprehension, expertise, ecological paradigm

Introduction

To understand how programming is learned we must first ask "What do programmers know?" One way to answer this questions is in terms of the skills programmers possess. Pea and Kurland [25] broadly categorize these skills as the ability to understand a programming problem, to design a programming solution, to write the program code implementing the solution, to debug a program, and to comprehend a written program. The focus here will be on the last of these, program comprehension. What are the processes involved in program comprehension, and what do we know about how this ability is acquired? What are the limitations of current models of program comprehension and its acquisition?

Current Models of Program Comprehension and Its Acquisition

Current models of program comprehension processes can be broadly categorized as bottom-up or top-down. In bottom-up models, the programmer first understands individual lines of code and procedural information. Next, aggregates of lines are comprehended, and finally the program's function (i.e., its application or purpose) is understood [e.g., 33, 3]. Pennington [26, 27] also proposes a bottom-up model in which programmers extract lower-level types of knowledge (e.g., operations) before higher level types of knowledge (e.g., program function). Top-down models suggest that programmers start with a hypothesis about the function of the program [e.g., 4] or plans [e.g., 35, 9, 28] as a basis for comprehension. They then attempt to verify their hypothesis or fill in the details of a plan by searching the program for additional information. Wiedenbeck's work on the role of beacons in program comprehension tasks [42, 43, 44] also supports function-based, top-down comprehension.

Research contrasting experts and novices suggests that they differ in their comprehension processes, with experts apparently using a top-down approach and novices using a more bottom-up approach. Studies using the method of free recall of scrambled versus meaningful programs have found that experts are better than novices at recalling meaningful programs, but are equal to novices in recalling scrambled programs [e.g., 20, 1, 31, 30]. These results suggest that experts' knowledge of programming is more organized than novices, and that this organizational knowledge is activated during comprehension, providing a top-down framework for comprehension. Soloway and Ehrlich [34] studied the effects of violations in stereotypical program structures (rules of discourse) on comprehension and found that experts' performance was more affected by such violations than novices. This research supports the idea that experts have expectations about program structure and content which are called into play in a top-down manner during comprehension. Thus, although a specific theory of the acquisition of program comprehension skills does not exist, it appears that it involves a transition from the use of a bottom-up to a top-down strategy, and the the acquisition of organized knowledge that enables the use of a top-down approach.

Challenges for Current Models of Comprehension

Recent research offers serious challenges for both models of the comprehension process, and thus for our understanding of its acquisition, as well. One example is Adelson's [1] study. In this study, expert and novice programmers were given programs accompanied by flow charts describing either the functions of the program (e.g., "make a field of 20 rows") or the step-by-step procedural logic (e.g., "J ¨ J + 1"). The programmers were then asked questions about both the functions and logic of the programs. Experts were better overall when the content of the questions matched the content of the flow chart and they were superior in answering questions about functions after being given the logic flow chart. Surprisingly, when given the function flow charts, the novices were actually better than the experts at answering questions on logic. Adelson speculates that the subjects were given an implicit task demand (i.e., set) dependent on the type of flow chart they saw. Experts who were given function flow charts formed representations that included *only* information about function, and did not include details of procedural logic. Novices, on the other hand, tended to form representations including *both* sorts of information, no matter which flow chart they had seen. Adelson's study challenges a strict top-down or bottom-up comprehension model because it suggests that more than one type of knowledge representation can be created during the comprehension process. Furthermore, the results show that the type of representation formed is a product of two different factors: the expertise of the subjects and implicit task demands. It is this second point - that two simultaneous independent variables produce an unexpected interaction - that particularly deserves further attention. The claim is that we cannot hope to understand program comprehension and its development unless we take into account a variety of aspects simultaneously by using what I label an *ecological paradigm.* This is similar in concept to the ecological approach to perception founded by Gibson [12]. Gibson stressed that in the domain of vision, what is perceived by an organism bears little resemblance to unidimensional variations in physical stimuli such as size, brightness or wavelength. Instead, what he termed higher order affordances, such as *looming*, are extracted automatically from the physical stimuli.

More specifically, program comprehension, as in reading comprehension [45], can be seen as the result of the interaction of three ecological factors:

- what is being comprehended
- who is doing the comprehending
- for what purpose is the comprehension being done.

The following sections will discuss each of these factors. An outline is presented in Table 1.

The Role of *What* is Being Comprehended

Pennington (based on Kintsch) makes a distinction between two sorts of meaning a program can have and their associated representations. A program model represents the surface meaning of the text and its structure (program operations). A situation model represents what the program means in reference to the application it performs (the domain of the program). Most research on program comprehension makes no distinction between the two sorts of knowledge. No research has specifically looked at the effect that domain knowledge has on program comprehension, although it has been examined in software design [e.g., 41, 6, 2].

Characteristics of the particular programming language that the program is implemented in also affect comprehension. Green [15] proposes the idea of cognitive dimensions of notations to highlight the need to consider computer languages as notations, and to explore how features and characteristics of a notation relate to both the cognitive strategies of the user and the circumstances of its use (i.e., the environment). One of the dimensions he proposed was role-expressiveness. Role-expressiveness is "a property of the language that enables the automatization of the mapping between problem and programming knowledge." Gilmore and Green [14] demonstrated that role-expressive notation facilitates comprehension. Mynatt, Leventhal, Instone and Rohlman [23] did a longitudinal study of the acquisition of sensitivity to

Table 1: Examples of variables related to what is being comprehended, who is comprehending, and for what purpose, that influence program comprehension.

What Is Being Comprehended
- Domain
- Language the program is written in
- Complexity of the algorithm
  - formal
  - psychological
- Programming style
  - broad (e.g, structured vs. OOP)
  - fine-grained
  - aesthetics
- Surface features

Who Is Doing the Comprehending
- Expertise
  - breadth of knowledge
  - organization of knowledge
  - knowledge of comprehension strategies
- Cognitive style
- Intelligence and ability
- Personality
- Motivation

For What Purpose
- Naturalistic
  - learning
  - program review/assessment
  - debugging
  - enhancement or modification
- Artificial
  - memorization
  - to answer questions
  - recognition test
  - fill-in-the-blank

---

role-expressiveness. Using a variety of comprehension tasks, and looking at computer science students across a span of up to three years, they found that sensitivity to large differences in role-expressiveness increased with increasing expertise. However, sensitivity to small differences in role-expressiveness did not change. Furthermore, they found that comprehension strategies showed an interaction of role-expressiveness and expertise. With low-role-expressive materials, comprehension tends to be more procedural (bottom-up). As expertise and role-expressiveness increase, however, comprehension becomes more functional (top-down).

Surface features of program source code, such as naming style, indenting and commenting have also been postulated to effect program comprehension, and have been shown to have differential effects based on expertise. For example, Mynatt [22] and Teasley [38, 37] review earlier studies and present results from several experiments showing that naming style in programs affects program comprehension by novices, but not by more advanced students or experts. Teasley [38] also showed that while naming style affects the comprehension of program function (high-level knowledge), it did not affect the comprehension of lower-level knowledge, such as operations or program states. Gellenbeck and Cook [11], on the other hand, reported that meaningful variable and procedure names did aid discovery of Pascal program function for advanced students, although not as much as code beacons, such as the swap operation in a sorting routine.

Program complexity has also been shown to affect comprehension. Formal measures of complexity, such as lines of code, McCabe's complexity metric and Halstead's metrics have shown some correlation with number of errors, development effort and other measures related to ease of comprehension [e.g., 7]. Mynatt, et al., [23] found differences in comprehension as measured by a fill-in-the-blank test related to formal complexity. Mynatt [21] postulated that factors beyond formal complexity, i.e., semantic complexity, would also affect comprehension. She compared recall performance for three pairs of Pascal programs. The pairs were approximately equal in formal complexity as measured by Halstead's metrics and each pair performed the same task. However, one member of each pair was hypothesized to be more semantically complex. The pairings included recursion versus iteration, "nonobvious" versus "obvious" algorithm, and less-familiar versus more-familiar data structures (linked lists versus arrays). There were no differences in immediate recall among any of the pairs. However, performance on hand-execution of the more complex algorithm was worse; and in surprise delayed recall, the more complex member of each pair was less completely recalled. The poorer delayed recall and hand-execution performance suggests lower comprehension when the programs were initially presented.

The Role of *Who* is Doing the Comprehending

Clearly, expertise is an important characteristic of the comprehender which has an impact on comprehension. What does expertise involve? The general literature on expertise delineates three dimensions: breadth of knowledge, knowledge organization and problem solving strategies (see 16 for a review). Most research in program comprehension has focused on the kinds of knowledge programmers have and its organization (e.g., chunks, beacons, plans, function). More recently, attention has turned to strategies used by comprehenders [e.g., 39, 10, 13].

One aspect of breadth of knowledge is knowledge of one or more programming languages. Pennington [26, 27] found that Cobol programmers were better at answering questions concerning data flow than were Fortran programmers, while the Fortran programmers were better at answering questions concerning control flow. (It is possible, of course, that this difference is due to the languages themselves, rather than the prior experience of the subjects.) Stone, Jordan and Wright [36] likewise found differences in comprehension and debugging ability related to language knowledge. They compared novice COBOL and Pascal programmers and found that Pascal education is a better predictor of debugging performance, results in superior debugging performance and appears to lead to enhanced comprehension of program goals and plans.

An open question is how and to what extent expertise in areas other than just programming languages influences comprehension. Domain knowledge has already been mentioned as a possible influence. A study by Davies [8] suggests that knowledge of software design skills can affect comprehension. He found that Basic programmers with formal instruction in software design were better able to detect errors in Basic programs with highlighted plan structures than those with no such training.

Besides expertise, characteristics of the comprehender such as intelligence and ability, personality, motivation and cognitive style are no doubt related to skill in comprehension. Although no direct research has been done relating these factors to program comprehension, some research is suggestive. For example, Campbell and McCabe [5] found that SAT scores, grades in high school mathematics and science, and number of high school mathematics and science course are all significantly correlated with success as a first-year computer science major at a university. These factors are also correlated with ability and intelligence. Neal [24] showed that a personality factor, risk aversion, plays a role in success with structure-based program editors.

The Role of *Purpose* in Comprehending

Although it has not been studied systematically, it seems likely that the purpose or goal of the comprehender can effect the comprehension strategy used. The Adelson study mentioned above is an example of how task demands can influence comprehension. She found that the type of flow chart given to the subjects before they read the programs influenced the type of mental representation they formed. Pennington [26, 27] likewise found task-related effects. She noted that subjects asked to perform a program modification task exhibited a shift toward comprehension of the domain-related function of the program at the expense of comprehending control-flow information.

Studies of program comprehension during debugging have demonstrated that experts use a variety of comprehension strategies, including both top-down and bottom-up approaches [e.g., 18, 19], and that novices and experts use different mixtures of strategies [17, 39, 40]. Thus, these studies suggest that comprehension processes may vary when a naturalistic task is studied, compared to comprehension tasks typically used in experiments.

Conclusions

The material presented here is not intended to be an exhaustive review of the related literature. The goal is to present some highlights of what we know and do not know about program comprehension and the acquisition of comprehension skills, and to suggest goals for a comprehensive theory of program comprehension. This overview suggests several conclusions. First, evidence has repeatedly surfaced that (at least) expert comprehenders have both top-down and bottom-up strategies of comprehension available to them. Thus, theories of comprehension and its acquisition must account for this fact. A "one-strategy-fits-all" theory of comprehension will not be rich enough to explain program comprehension. Second, theories of program comprehension must start bringing into their scope a wider variety of factors related to the comprehension task and comprehension skills than they have to date. Differences related to expertise have been the primary focus thus far. However, as the present paper points out, there are many other factors that can influence comprehension. These factors encompass aspects of what is being comprehended, who is doing the comprehending, and for what purpose the comprehension task is undertaken. Finally, it will be necessary to explore the *interaction* of factors related to comprehension. Some of the studies presented here showed, for example, that expertise can interact with task demands [e.g., 1] and role-expressiveness [e.g., 23] to differentially affect comprehension processes. It is likely that additional insights into the comprehension process can be gained by systematically exploring interactions.

This paper has suggested that a theory which takes account of all these aspects of comprehension will be ecological in nature. It seems likely that such a theory may incorporate three primary components. One component is the use of plan-like structures to represent certain types of knowledge, combined with a top-down down approach to the activity of comprehending those types of knowledge. That is, comprehension may be carried out through the activation and/or recognition of plans, followed by activities designed to fill in the relevant plan knowledge. Herein the term "plans" is being used in its global sense [29], meaning goals which can be applied in several contexts, and which can be independent of a particular domain problem (e.g., a control loop to read data from a file). A second component of an ecological model may encompass the use of bottom-up activity to extract and represent other aspects of comprehension, including domain-specific and language-specific facts, details of operation, and conclusions regarding style, aesthetics and grammatical structure. The third component is the overseer of the other two components. This component conducts meta-comprehension activities. It takes into account the current ecological aspects of the task at hand- the *what, who* and *for what purpose*. It selects an appropriate strategy and directs the comprehension process by proportioning activity appropriately between the other two components. The overseer would also monitor the success of the comprehension process as it is taking place. If the chosen strategy does not appear to be resulting in successful comprehension, another strategy might be attempted. Finally, the overseer would decide when comprehension is complete, or when unsuccessful attempts to comprehend are to be concluded. Under this sort of model, learning to comprehend programs would involve not only learning to recognize and build different sorts of knowledge structures, but the acquisition of various strategies for comprehension, and learning to recognize under what circumstances to use each strategy.

Acknowledgements

The author would like to thank Diane Schertler Rohlman and Keith Instone for their aid in editing and revising the paper, and Laura Marie Leventhal for her helpful comments.

References

1. Adelson, B.: When novices surpass experts: The difficulty of a task may increase with expertise. *Journal of Experimental Psychology: Learning, Memory and Cognition*. 10, 483-495 (1984)
2. Adelson, B. and Soloway, E.: The role of domain experience in software design. *IEEE Transactions on Software Engineering*. 11, 1351-1360 (1985)
3. Basili, V. R. and Mills, H. D.: Understanding and documenting programs. *IEEE Transactions on Software Engineering*. SE-8, 270-283 (1982)
4. Brooks, R.: Towards a theory of comprehension of computer programs. *International Journal of Man-Machine Studies*. 18, 543-554 (1983)
5. Campbell, P. F. and McCabe, G. P.: Predicting the success of freshmen in a computer science major. *Communications of the ACM*. 27, 1108-1113 (1984)
6. Curtis, W., Krasner, H. and Iscoe, N.: A field study of the software design process for large systems. *Communications of the ACM*. 31(11), 1268-1287, (1988)
7. Curtis, W. , Sheppard, S. B., Milliman, P., Borst, M. A. and Love, T.: Measuring the psychological complexity of of software maintenance tasks with the Halstead and McCabe metrics. *IEEE Transactions on Software Engineering*. SE-5(3), 96-104 (1979)
8. Davies, S. P.: The nature and development of programing plans. *International Journal of Man-Machine Studies*. 32, 461-181 (1990)
9. Detienne, F.: Expert programming knowledge: A schema-based approach. In: *Psychology of Programming*. (J.-M. Hoc, T. R. G. Green, R. Samurcay and D. J. Gilmore, eds.). New York, NY: Academic Press 1990
10. Detienne, F. and Soloway, E.: An empirically defined control structure for the process of program understanding. *International Journal of Man-Machine Studies*. 33, 323-342 (1990)
11. Gellenbeck, E. M. and Cook, C. R.: An investigation of procedure and variable names as beacons during program comprehension. In: *Empirical Studies of Programmers: Fourth Workshop*. (J. Loenemann-Belliveau, T. G. Moher and S. P. Robertson, eds.). Norwood, NJ: Ablex 1991
12. Gibson, J. J.: *The Ecological Approach to Visual Perception*. Boston: Houghton Mifflin 1979
13. Gilmore, D. J.: Expert programming knowledge: A strategic approach. In: *Psychology of Programming*. (J.-M. Hoc, T.R.G. Green, R. Samurcay and D.J. Gilmore, eds.). pp.223-234. New York: Acedemic Press 1990
14. Gilmore, D. J. and Green, T. G. R.: Programming plans and programming expertise. *Quarterly Journal of Experimental Psychology*. 40A, 423-442 (1988)
15. Green, T. G. R.: Cognitive dimension of notations. In: *People and Computers. Vol. V*. (A. Sutcliffe and L. Macaulay, eds.). Cambridge: Cambridge University Press. 1989
16. Kaplan, S. Gruppen, L. D., Leventhal, L. M. and Board, F.: *The Components of Expertise: A Cross-Disciplinary Review*. Ann Arbor, MI: The University of Michigan 1986
17. Kessler, C. M. and Anderson, J. R.: A model of novice debugging in LISP. In: *Empirical Studies of Programmers*. (E. Soloway and S. Iyengar, eds.). Norwood, NJ: Ablex. 1986
18. Koenemann, J. and Robertson, S. P.: Expert problem solving strategies for program comprehension. *Human Factors in Computing Systems: CHI '91 Conference Proceedings*. Reading, MA: Addison-Wesley. 1991
19. Letovsky, S.: Cognitive processes in program comprehension. In: *Empirical Studies of Programmers*. (E. Soloway and S. Iyengar, eds.). Norwood, NJ: Ablex 1986
20. McKeithen, K. B., Reitman, J. S., Reuter, H. H. and Hirtle, S. C.: Knowledge organization and skill differences in computer programmers. *Cognitive Psychology*. 13, 307-325, (1981)

21. Mynatt, B. T.: The effect of semantic complexity on the comprehension of programs. *International Journal of Man-Machine Studies.* 21, 91-103 (1984)
22. Mynatt, B. T.: Why program comprehension is (or is not) affected by surface features. In: *Human-Computer Interaction - INTERACT '90.* (D. Diaper, D. Gilmore, G. Cockton, B. Shackel, eds.). New York, NY: Elsevier Science. 1990
23. Mynatt, B. T., Leventhal, L. M., Instone, K. and Rohlman, D. S.: Longitudinal studies of the relation of programmer expertise and role-expressiveness to program comprehension. In: *User-Centered Requirements for Software Engineering Environments: NATO Advanced Research Workshop.* New York, NY: Springer-Verlag. (in press)
24. Neal, L.: User modelling for syntax-directed editors. In: *Human-Computer Interaction - INTERACT '87.* (H.-J. Bulliger and B. Shackel, eds.). NY: Elsevier 1987
25. Pea, R. D. and Kurland, D. M.: On the cognitive effects of learning computer programming. *New Ideas in Psychology.* 2(2), 137-168 (1984)
26. Pennington, N.: Comprehension strategies in programming. In: *Empirical Studies of Programmers: Second Workshop.* (G. M. Olson and E. Soloway, eds.). Norwood, NJ: Ablex 1987a
27. Pennington, N.: Stimulus structures and mental representations in expert comprehension of computer programs. *Cognitive Psychology.* 19, 295-341 (1987b)
28. Rist, R.: Search through multiple representations. In: *User-Centered Requirements for Software Engineering Environments: NATO Advanced Research Workshop.* New York, NY: Springer-Verlag. (in press)
29. Rist, R. S.: Plans in programming: definition, demonstration and development. In E. Soloway & S. Iyengar, Eds., *Empirical Studies of Porgrammers.* Noorwood, NJ: Ablex Publishing (1986).
30. Robertson, S. P., Davies, E. F., Okabe, K. and Fitz-Randolf, D.: Program comprehension beyond the line. In: *Human -Computer Interaction - Interact '90.* (D. Diaper, D. Gilmore, G. Cockton and B. Shackel, eds.). pp. 959-963. New York:Elsevier Science Publishing Company 1990
31. Schmidt, A. L.: Effects of experience and comprehension on reading time and memory for computer programs. *International Journal of Man-Machine Studies.* 25, 399-409 (1986)
32. Shepard, R. N.: Ecological constraints on internal representation: Resonant kinematics of perceiving, imaging, thinking, and dreaming. *Psychological Review.* 91(4), 417-447 (1984)
33. Shneiderman, B. and Mayer, R.: Syntactic/semantic interactions in programmer behavior: A model and experimental results. *International Journal of Computer and Information Sciences.* 8, 219-238. (1979)
34. Soloway, E. and Ehrlich, K.: Empirical studies of programming knowledge. *IEEE Transactions on Software Engineering.* SE-10, 595-609 (1984)
35. Soloway, E., Ehrlich, K. and Bonar, J.: Tapping into tacit programming knowledge. *Proceedings of Human Factors in Computer Systesm..* pp. 52-58. Gaithersburg, MD. 1982
36. Stone, D. N., Jordan, E. W. and Wright, M. K.: The impact of Pascal education on debugging skill. *International Journal of Man-Machine Studies.* 33, 81-95 (1990)
37. Teasley, B. M.: Experimental studies of the effects of naming style on program comprehension. Computer Science Department, Bowling Green State University, Technical Report # 91-103 (1991).
38. Teasley, B. M.: The effects of naming style and expertise on program comprehension. *International Journal of Man-Machine Studies.* (in press)
39. Vessey, I.: Expertise in debugging computer programs: A process analysis. *International Journal of Man-Machine Studies.* 23, 459-494 (1985)
40. Vessey, I.: Toward a theory of computer program bugs: An empirical test. *International Journal of Man-Machine Studies.* 30, 23-46 (1989)
41. Visser, W.: More or less following a plan during design: Opportunistic deviations in specification. *International Journal of Man-Machine Studies.* 33, 247-278 (1990).
42. Weidenbeck, S.: Organization of programming knowledge of novices and experts. *Journal of the American Society of Information Science.* 37, 294-299 (1986a)
43. Weidenbeck, S.: Beacons in computer program comprehension. *International Journal of Man-Machine Studies.* 25, 697-709 (1986b)
44. Weidenbeck, S.: The initial stages of program comprehension. *International Journal of Man-Machine Studies.* (to appear)
45. Wright, P.: Feeding the information eaters: Suggestions for integrating pure and applied research on language comprehension. *Instructional Science.* 7, 249-312 (1978).

A Distributed Model of Cognitive Behaviour in Specification Understanding

Francisco C. Simplicio-Filho

Imperial College, Department of Computing

180 Queen's Gate, London SW7 2BZ, UK. E-mail: fcs@doc.ic.ac.uk

Abstract: This paper presents an engineering model of cognitive behaviour in the task of specification understanding. The model is an attempt to pesent some established hypotheses on the cognitive system functioning, in a way amenable to more precise analysis. It focuses on the control mechanisms that drive opportunistic and goal-oriented behaviours, in particular on their reactive and distributed characterization. The models proposed is based on an interpretation of the *model human processor* [2, 13] and described in terms of a set theoretical visual formalism, the state-graph, able to represent concurrent and distributed components. As a conclusion, in contrast to the view in which opportunistic behaviour is described as plan violation, the model suggests that opportunistic behaviour does not totally rule out goal-oriented behaviour. A number of understanding activities can operate in parallel and, to some extent, this enables the cognitive system to keep the course of actions according to plan while undertaking other cognitive activities. The model provides a plausible explanation for the mechanisms that underlie this concurrence.

Keywords: Specification understanding, cognitive behaviour, understanding, opportunistic behaviour, goal-oriented behaviour, reactive behaviour.

1 Introduction

Programming is nowadays considered as a stage in the software development process. The importance of the specification in this process has increasingly been recognized. The comprehension of specifications is a part of this process that plays a much more important role in software engineering than has commonly been thought. Using a given specification to achieve understanding is a common part of many activities dispersed throughout the life cycle, including learning, design, programming, inspection, maintenance and reuse. The key to the specification's role is precision and understanding [17]. Specification is a process of achieving common understanding at a suitable level of precision. In contrast with formal methods research, which focuses on precision, our work focuses on the complementary issue of understanding. Many issues regarding how people understand specifications seem intimately related to human cognitive or problem solving limitations. Suitable tools and techniques may help to overcome some of them [5]. However, the development of such tools based on a sound engineering foundation requires a detailed comprehension of the cognitive requirements in this task.

Among the many attempts to provide this comprehension, two broad groups are noticeable: 1) attempts that focus on the development of specialized representations, and 2) attempts that focus on the development of models of the understander's behaviour. In the first approach, research on the development of specialized representations addresses the knowledge held by the understander, its structure and its relationships. Representations such as "plans" [4] and "design schemas" [6,16], to name a few, offer different, but related constructs to describe different organizations of the understander's knowledge [1]. This group of approaches is based on the assumption that our ability to automate parts of the understanding process may be increased if more information can be captured in mechanically processable forms. A major problem with models of understanding based on knowledge representation is their inherent incompleteness. The background knowledge cannot be represented as a set of explicit propositions [19]. The overwhelming nature of knowledge may make it difficult, impossible perhaps, to construct a complete explicit representation.

In the second approach, knowledge organization is not everything; instead, the mechanisms that use knowledge are equally relevant. A scientific account of how knowledge is acquired, retained, and used in interpreting the world does not necessarily call for a complete specification of all knowledge [11]. In order to understand how knowledge is used, research focuses on the cognitive behaviour, in particular on the control mechanisms that produce the behaviour and guide the understander in deciding what to pursue and which parts of the problem to work on next. The emphasis is on assisting the activity of understanding rather than automating it. Models of these dynamic processes are in their infancy.

Following this second approach, the development of a model able to describe cognitive behaviour faces some representational difficulties. The characterization of complex behaviour in a way that aids understanding and at the same time is amenable to more precise analysis has been an issue in software and system engineering. One of the difficulties of this characterization relates to the description of the model's reactive character, through which the system continuously reacts to external and internal stimuli. The reactive behaviour can not be adequately described in terms of simple relationships between inputs and outputs, as commonly used to describe other less complex systems; the allowed combination of inputs and outputs may vary in time and depend on internal states of the system. Such behaviour is better described in terms of the set of allowed sequences of events, actions and conditions restricting them. Another difficulty of this characterization relates to describing concurrence and distribution. In concurrent and distributed systems several processes, which operate concurrently and without hierarchical relationship, should communicate and be controlled. This characteristic can not be adequately described in terms of relationships between states of the system because it is very difficult to get a coherent picture of the system global states. Systems with concurrent components may involve a large number of possible global states which result from the Cartesian product of all sequences of states and events of the components.

Blackboard models have been used to characterize cognitive behaviour, as an example of this second approach [18]. Actually, cognitive modelling and blackboard models share a similar basic approach: both try to locate the source of cognitive activity in the characteristics of the underlying machinery. However, in contrast to blackboard models, cognitive modelling is not directly concerned with how the model is to be implemented; neither is it limited by the computational tractability of its model. Since its origin, the potential of blackboard models for dealing with concurrence and distribution has remained an attractive possibility. In fact, most recent blackboard implementations are conceptually parallel and distributed models. However, the promise of multiprocessing and distributed blackboard models remains largely untapped. Constructing effective sequential blackboard based applications has been hard enough [3]. The system's approach to control determines its potential behaviour, its coherence and comprehensibility. Control of reasoning in blackboard models is still an active research area [10]. Nevertheless, analogies can be drawn between cognitive models and blackboard models, so sometimes it may be useful to describe the one in terms of the other from which more knowledge is available. However, we found that the implementation oriented approach of blackboard model imposes unnecessary constraints on discussing cognitive behaviour.

A set-theoretical visual formalism called hygraph has been proposed for describing complex systems [7-8]. A hygraph-based extension of the standard state-transition diagrams, the statechart, has been proposed for describing behaviour of reactive systems [9]. It provides a means of representing complex relationships between components, like concurrence and depth, to produce a concise diagram. It also allows the representation of a broadcast mechanism for communication between concurrent components. A hypothesis put forward in this paper is that this formalism may be used to describe and discuss cognitive behaviour.

In this paper we advance an engineering model of cognitive behaviour. The model makes use of the hygraph representation in order to convey some established hypotheses on the cognitive system functioning. It is based on existing models, in particular on the *model human processor* [2, 12, 13]. As such, it can be described as an attempt to provide a statechart based interpretation of a subset of that model. An advantage of this interpretation is that it provides a basis for discussing these hypotheses in more objective terms. It also enables the elaboration of more complex combinations of behaviour. Here, three layers of behaviour are discussed. Section 2 introduces the basic representation of the cognitive system components and the first and second layers of behaviour. These layers allow the discussion of the basic mechanisms of understanding. At the first and lower layer, a pattern of behaviour termed *dispersion* is counteracted by another pattern termed *focusing*. They are used to explain *spontaneous* and *rational understanding*, at the second abstract layer. Section 3 discusses the third layer in which *opportunistic* and *goal-oriented behaviours* are explained. As a conclusion we suggest that goal-oriented behaviour and opportunistic behaviour can co-occur. A number of understanding activities can operate in parallel and, to some extent, this enables the cognitive system to keep the course of actions according to plan while undertaking other cognitive activities.

2 A Distributed Model of Understanding

This model is based on the description of the underlying cognitive components and their possible interaction. This description is presented in figure 1. A detailed account of the development of this interpretation may be found in [15]. In the diagram, rounded rectangles represent states; arrows represent transitions between states or sets of states; dashed lines represent orthogonal, parallel partitions of states. Small dotted arrows represent initial states. When a state occurs, it may cause further transitions in other components. This is represented by the condition *[in (state)]* related to a transition. It reads: if *state* occurs then the related transition also takes place. The recurring rectangles in the working memory illustrate that a number of activations may be stored simultaneously.

Based on this description, sequences of states can be inferred. Sequences of states represent behaviour. Some patterns of behaviour described in the model human processor can be discussed in terms of particular sequences of states. For example:

- Many memory retrieval failures are explained in terms of a spontaneous decay over time. This spontaneous decay is explicitly represented as a transition into the working memory, leading to the state w-clear, which represents the fact that the information is no longer available in the working memory.
- The memory retrieval behaviour depends on the time elapsed between the storing and retrieval of the information. This period will determined which memory, if any,

holds the information. For retrievals done shortly after storing, information may be held in both memories. Given a start state [*w-stored*], which means that there is information in the working memory, a subsequent state [*activated*] in long term memory represents the behaviour in which the information is stored simultaneously in both memories. For retrievals done long after storing, information is retrievable only from long-term memory. This fact is illustrated by the following sequence: [*stored, activated, lt-stored, w-clear*].

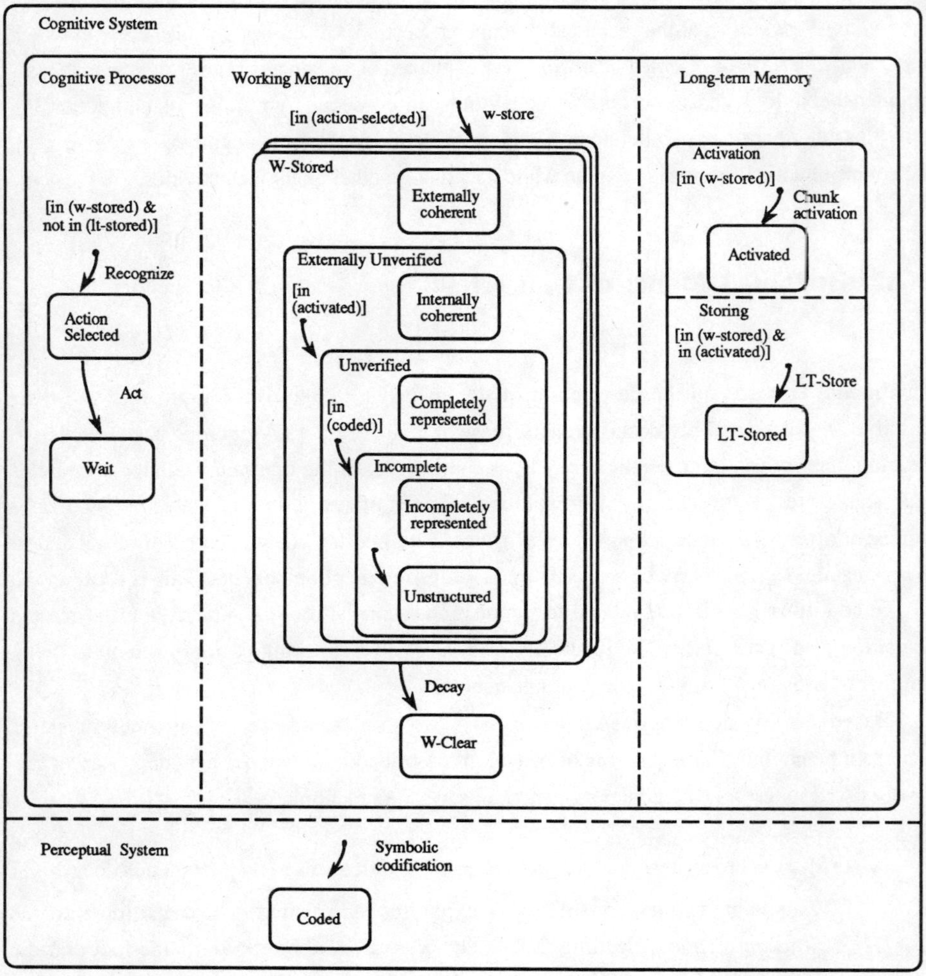

Figure 1. A statechart interpretation of the cognitive system components and their interaction. Rounded rectangles represent states; arrows represent transition between states or set of states; dashed lines represent orthogonal, parallel, partition of states. Small dotted arrows represent initial states.

- The recognize-act cycle in which the cognitive processor operates is represented by the sequence [*action-selected*, *wait*]. This sequence takes place when the state *w-stored* occurs in the working memory. This description suggests that the cognitive processor does not hold the control of the system activity. Its operating cycle is a consequence of information available in the working memory and the term "cycle" is not really a proper term.

2.1 Dispersion and Focusing

More complex patterns of behaviour can be represented by combining layers of sequences of states. In the basic layer, two counteracting patterns of behaviour emerge from figure 1 as the core of cognitive behaviour: dispersion and focusing. On the one side, during memory retrieval there is no guarantee that activations in long-term memory include the desired information; activations are hypothetical. In figure 1, the relationship between memories is represented in terms of a cyclic reference: the transition activation is initiated by the condition [in (*w-stored*)]. The transition w-store, on the other hand, is initiated by the condition [in (*activated*)]. For example, the partial behaviour [*w-stored*, *activated*] points to a recursive repetition of itself, leading to cycles that stop when the information stored in the working memory decays and reaches the state w-clear. These cycles produce an effect that we term dispersion tendency. This effect provides an explanation of the phenomenon of "activation spreading" described in the model human processor. It suggests that particular information stored in the working memory tends toward dispersion: the previously activated information becomes less accessible and new related information arises continuously. Since there is no guarantee the activation involves the proper information, the cycles increase the chances of an appropriate retrieval. It is important to note that these cycles are autonomous. They will happen independently of the kind of information being activated or its source.

Focusing, on the other side, is related to the cognitive processor action. The sequence [*action-selected*, *wait*] on which the cognitive processor operates, takes place when the state *w-stored* occurs in the working memory. The cyclic reference between the working memory and the cognitive processor, represented by the condition [in (*action-selected*)] in the transition w-store, leads information selected by the cognitive processor to be re-stored in the working memory. The model human processor broadly refers to this as a "refresh". A primary effect of this is to focus the system on particular relevant information. A secondary effect is to restrict the dispersion tendency. This restriction happens because dispersion is based on storing new related information in the working memory; refreshing old information reduces the chances for dispersion.

2.2 Autonomous and Rational Understanding

Unlike dispersion, focusing is not an autonomous behaviour. Therefore its action must be driven by mechanisms in a higher abstract level. A second layer of cognitive behaviour may be built based on the specification of: 1) what the understander is trying to achieve, 2) what cognitive actions may support the attainment of this goal and, 3) what constraints the task faced by the understander imposes on these actions.

First, what the understander is trying to achieve defines what we term *understanding target.* The primary understanding target is to build a symbolic representation suitable for storing information in, and retrieving it from long-term memory [14]. Input information is said to be understood when a memory structure is found that indicates how and where to store information in long-term memory. The understanding target is achieved when the component *lt-store* in long-term memory is able to store information leading to the state *lt-stored*. For the sake of clarity, we are distinguishing the term *target*, which we relate to the result of understanding as a process, from the term *goal*, which we relate to intentions of the understander. For example, understanding targets may be achieved irrespective of understander goals. In other words, understanding may occur independently of intention.

Second, two different ways to support the attainment of the understanding target may be distinguished: autonomous understanding, which results from immediate match with memory retrievals, and rational understanding which results from the cognitive processor action. During the process of understanding, old structures from long-term memory are called into play. When this retrieval succeeds in matching the information at hand, the understanding target is achieved; the new information "makes sense". However, when a proper memory structure is not immediately found, then understanding requires: finding an applicable old structure, determining to what extent it differs from the current situation and, adapting it to fit the new situation. These actions are carried out by the cognitive processor, to which we relate the term "rational". The cognitive system's ability to achieve the understanding target without involving rational actions is in part due to the dispersion tendency. As a result of dispersion new activations will be produced continuously. If the storing component can find a match between the information at hand and an activation, then it may be stored with the old one. This is represented by the sequence [*w-stored, activated, lt-stored*]. Rational understanding is illustrated by the sequence [*w-stored, action-selected, lt-stored*]. It is relevant to observe that since these two forms of understanding are based on different and concurrent components, one approach does not exclude the other.

Third, in the context of software specification, at least two restrictions set out the conditions that ordain what processes are necessary to the attainment of the understanding target. In addition to necessarily dealing with some form of symbolic representations, understanding also involves the notion that information may exhibit different elaboration levels in terms of completeness and consistency.

2.3 Elaboration Levels and Promotions

Information being manipulated by the cognitive system may exhibit different levels of completeness and consistency. In ideal terms, at the highest level all relevant information is collected and expressed in a selected representation scheme that is coherent with all other structures available. At the lowest level, information symbolically represented provides simple associations between external stimulus and knowledge eventually activated in memory. In the continuum between these extremes, we distinguish five discrete points that we term elaboration levels. Information may be: unstructured, incompletely-represented, completely-represented, internally-coherent and externally-coherent. High elaboration levels are desirable properties of the information used by the cognitive system. Nevertheless, this is not always required or attainable. In order to provide a proper response to the environment, it may be necessary to elaborate the available information to higher levels. This elaboration we term promotion. Four promotions are conceived. Promotion 1 seeks to lead information from the state *unstructured* to the state *incomplete*. Promotion 2 aims to lead information from *incompletely-represented* state towards *completely-represented*. Upgrading from *completely-represented* state towards *internally-coherent* state is carried out by promotion 3. Finally, from the *internally-coherent* state promotion 4 seeks to lead to the *externally-coherent* state. A detailed description of the promotions is not necessary here. It is relevant to observe that understanding may be achieved at any elaboration level and that promotions may involve different patterns of behaviour.

2.4 The Control Mechanism of Understanding

The cognitive system components are not equally able to deal with all elaboration levels; some are restricted to handle only lower levels. This is represented in figure 1 by the conditions [in (*state*)] associated with transitions in working memory. The perceptual system activity is restricted to *incomplete* states. This is represented by the condition [in (*coded*)]. The long-term memory retrieval is restricted to *unverified* states by the condition [in (*activated*)]. The cognitive processor activity is related to all states by the condition [in (*action-selected)*]. This indicates that only the cognitive processor is able to deal with all elaboration levels. All components may deal with promotion 1, so several patterns of behaviour may lead to this promotion.

Since some promotions may be accomplished by different means, the cognitive system faces a possible choice between them. For example, the promotion 1, from *unstructured* to *incompletely-represented* states, may be carried out by both, long-term memory activity and cognitive processor. This is represented by the sequences [*coded, unstructured, activated, incompletely-represented, lt-stored*] and [*coded, unstructured, action-selected, incompletely-represented, lt-stored*]. These sequences are possible because both long-term memory and the cognitive processor can deal with those levels of elaboration. However, because the first sequence results from the autonomous behaviour characterized by autonomous understanding it will take place first.

Autonomous understanding comes before rational understanding. However, because they share the same target, there will be no need to pursue the second unless the first fails to accomplish the understanding target. A detailed mechanism to explain how long-term memory informs the cognitive processor that it has failed is not necessary here. The cognitive processor will be aroused to action if long-term memory fails to match information and an activation. This is represented by the condition [not in (lt-stored)] in the cognitive processor in figure 1. Once aroused to action it should recognize what actions are appropriate to deal with the present elaboration level. Understanding may be accomplished by promoting information to higher levels of elaboration. If the new elaboration level can be still handled by memory activity, then again, autonomous understanding will be attempted first. If autonomous understanding finds its limit of action, in the *unverified* elaboration level, then promotions can be carried out only by rational understanding.

3 Cognitive Behaviour in Understanding

In summary, we have examined patterns of behaviour in terms of sequences of states built into a description of the cognitive components. Two layers of behaviour have been discussed. At the basic layer, two counteracting patterns have emerged as relevant: dispersion and focusing. At the second layer, two other patterns, autonomous and rational understanding support the attainment of the understanding target of building a representation able to be stored in and retrieved from long-term memory. The control mechanism of understanding was described by combining these ways of achieving understanding and differences in the nature of the information at hand which may exhibit different elaboration levels for completeness and consistency. This mechanism underlies a third layer in which the cognitive behaviour is discussed.

3.1 Goal Processing as Understanding Based Activity

Reasoning about goals and ways to achieve them calls for the construction of plans. This notion highlights a functional distinction between control knowledge, characterized in terms of plans, and other uses of knowledge, which can be called problem knowledge. In the context of software specification understanding, the distinction between plans and problem knowledge corresponds to distinguishing between 1) reasoning about what to understand, and 2) the actual understanding. At first glance, the importance of consistent plans as a way to succeed in dealing with the world may suggest that the cognitive capability of building and revising plans should be carried out by a special component of the cognitive system, or at least, by a specially adapted mechanism. However, there is no evidence of a component or processor specifically allocated to this function. Goal processing shares the same cognitive resources used for processing other forms and use of knowledge. The distinction between them is simply functional. Therefore, goal processing is based on the same cognitive mechanisms used for understanding. Plans will have to be understood in the same way that problem knowledge is understood. This view of goal processing amounts to saying that goal-oriented behaviour is based on plan understanding.

Since goal processing and other information processing share the same cognitive resources, they may eventually be in competition. If goal-oriented behaviour is based on plan understanding then it is supported by autonomous understanding, or when that fails, rational understanding is called into play, so two different situations may be envisaged. On the one hand, plans that are frequently used acquire stable representation and effective memory links, so proper activations can increase the chances of autonomous understanding. In addition, usually there is no need to have plans represented in high elaboration levels, so autonomous understanding is enough. Because the process of activation is concurrent with the process of storing in long-term memory, and the working memory may hold a number of activations simultaneously, it follows that goal-oriented behaviour based on autonomous understanding may operate in parallel with other processing. On the other hand, when autonomous understanding fails then goal processing will be based on rational understanding. In this case, the need for goal processing may compete for the use of the cognitive processor with other needs of information processing. This competition is possible because the working memory is able to store several activations simultaneously, but the cognitive processor is able to focus on only one at a time.

3.2 A Competing Situation

We devise the following example to illustrate this competing situation. This example was inspired by the empirical study conducted by Visser [18]. Let us suppose an understander verifying the external coherence of an arbitrary specification segment. To be in this state implies that this specification segment was not autonomously understood; a representation scheme was activated from memory to accommodate it; this representation was promoted to the internally coherent elaboration level, and now, it is being promoted to the externally coherent elaboration level. This promotion may involve testing consequences of the description against scenarios of the problem domain. During the promotion the cognitive processor is focusing on a particular activation, so, autonomous dispersion is restricted to very closely related activations. For example, dispersion may help to activate information about scenarios of the domain. Nevertheless, the understander may also activate the representation of another specification segment which is analogous to that segment at hand, which is also not fully understood, but whose domain the understander is more familiar with. This activation could provide the basis for autonomous understanding of that first segment. However, because the new specification segment is not yet understood and because memory is not able to deal with information at this high elaboration level, the promotion will probably continue. But, which segment will be focused on? The understander may continue with the first segment or deviate to the second segment with which he is more familiar. The decision of focusing on one activation leads to abandoning the other. The abandoned segment will fade away and will be lost from the working memory. There is no guarantee that the lost activation can be retrieved later on.

To prevent losing one of these activations, a plan has to be built to include the goal of dealing with the abandoned activation in the future. Two issues arise in this case: 1) when should the postponed activation be dealt with properly and, 2) where to store the plan in memory in order to retrieve it in due time. This plan may be simple enough to be processed in terms of autonomous understanding. In this case, the plan is restricted to low levels of elaboration and there is a relative high risk that it will not be activated in due time. For example, if at the right time the situation is handled in terms of autonomous understanding then the system will probably provide no focusing to activate this plan. Also, the future situation may not happen in the way it was conceived; the plan representation may not be suitable for representing the future event. So, an effective plan to deal with this conflict will require rational understanding. The problem in this situation is that by focusing on the plan, the two segments of the specification are at risk of being lost from memory, even for very simple plans. This configures a competing situation. For example, the understander may decide to follow dealing with the first segment with an interruption just long enough to take notes and guarantee that the second segment may be dealt with later. But, because taking notes very probably requires translating the information into a different representation scheme, carrying out this plan will call for rational understanding. As a consequence the first segment is bound to fade in memory.

3.3 Opportunism as a Promising Behaviour

The competing situation illustrated above may be summarized as: 1) the understander is focusing on a specification segment ***a;*** 2) a related segment ***b*** is activated in memory as opportune; 3) there is a goal of dealing with both segments; 4) building a plan able to support the achievement of this goal may result in losing one or even both specification segments from memory. The underlying issue is which segment has better chances of being recovered later. An answer to this issue lies in the plan that was actually being followed before the activation of the segment ***b***, that is, the plan that was driving the behaviour to focus the segment ***a***. If this plan can be recovered, then segment ***a*** may also be recovered. Three situations may hold: 1) If the plan is general, such as following the text of the specification, it probably can be recovered easily because the text will provide the auxiliary memory to help the plan resumption. 2) If the plan is specific and at a high elaboration level then it probably can also be recovered by reasoning about the plan itself; 3) If there was no plan, then focusing ***a*** or ***b*** will make little difference, so other distinctions, such as the relevance of each segment may be considered. However, in the same way that to build a plan to deal with segments ***a*** or ***b*** may lead to the lost of one or both segments, considering which one is more relevant may also put them at risk of fading in memory. As a conclusion, segment ***a*** offers, in its worst case, the same chance of being retrieved as segment ***b***.

If instead of building a plan to deal properly with segment ***a*** or ***b***, the understander just deviates to segment ***b***, then there will be less risk of losing relevant information in the future. In addition there will be less effort spent on rational processing. In general, segment ***a*** is more likely to be retrieved later than segment ***b***; building a plan to deal with the situation may not improve the chances of success; and segment ***b*** will be lost if it is not dealt with at once. Thus, opportunistic behaviour constitutes the more promising way to succeed in dealing with unpredictable events. Since many world events are of this sort, opportunistic behaviour is the typical way of reacting. It is a way of taking advantage of the knowledge available at the time. To behave opportunistically corresponds to following the general rule: if something has to be done, it is better to do it at once.

One might suggest that, in the long run, to follow opportunistic behaviour in the way described above will lead the cognitive system to chaos. However, it should be observed that this does not exclude goal-oriented behaviour totally. Since goal-oriented behaviour may also be carried out by autonomous understanding it may function effectively in parallel. This means that the cognitive system is able to keep track of general and simple plans while undertaking opportunistic behaviour. A restriction to this sort of plan is that it is limited to low elaboration levels. This is a characteristic of autonomous understanding. For example, this plan is not capable of registering multiple layers of deviations; it is local. Yet, there is no need for plans to be at high elaboration levels to succeed in many frequent activities.

However, autonomous understanding may not be enough to provide understanding. This may occur in both cases: in understanding the plan or in understanding the problem. In the example above, autonomous understanding may fail while understanding the specification segment and also while keeping the course of actions according to a plan. Exceptions are bound to happen, which requires rational understanding. When the process of understanding the problem is what fails, then this does not necessarily require changing the general plan. A local plan may be activated in order to deal with this situation in an opportunistic way. As we have pointed out, opportunistic behaviour will provide better chances for achieving understanding and the retrieval of the abandoned activations later on. The general plan may be resumed afterward. However, if in addition to the failure in understanding the problem, the process of understanding the plan also fails, then we have a breakdown: what one was trying to do has failed, and there is no new plan to indicate what to do next. In this case goal processing will require rational understanding, and this may be found competing for the use of the cognitive resources with the need for understanding the problem.

4 Conclusions

In conclusion, this paper focuses on modelling the cognitive control mechanisms that guide an understander in deciding what to pursue and which parts of the specification to work on next during the activity of software specification understanding. Current research stresses the distinction between goal-oriented behaviour, in which a plan is followed, and opportunistic behaviour, in which no plan is observable. One view of opportunistic behaviour describes it as plan deviations [18]. This view assumes that the cognitive system follows a comprehensive and well defined plan that is interrupted when new information or new events are perceived as opportune. In contrast, this paper suggests a rather different view in which opportunistic and goal-oriented behaviours to a certain extent can proceed concurrently. A number of autonomous understanding activities can operate in parallel and this allow the cognitive system to keep the course of actions according to a plan while undertaking other cognitive activities.

The model introduced here analyses these mechanisms and provides the basis for further work to discuss how software specification understanding may be supported by providing an appropriate interaction between the understander and a set of software tools.

Acknowledgements

I wish to thank Thomas Maibaum and Anthony Finkelstein for invaluable comments in earlier versions of this paper.

References

1. Brooks, R.: Categories of programming knowledge and their application. *Internat. Journal of Man-Machine Studies*. 33 (3), 241-246 1990
2. Card, S., Moran, T. and Newell, A.: *The psychology of human-computer interaction*. Lawrence Erlbaum Associate 1983
3. Corkill, D.: Design alternatives for parallel and distributed blackboard systems. In V. Jagannathan, R. Dodhiawala and L. Baum (eds.) *Blackboard architectures and applications*. Academic Press (1989)
4. Détienne, F. and Soloway, E.: An empirically-derived control structure for the process of program understanding. *Internat. Journal of Man-Machine Studies*. 33 (3), 323-342 (1990)

5. Guindon, R. and Curtis, B.: Control of cognitive processes during software design: what tools are needed?. In E.Soloway and S. Iyengar (eds.) *Empirical studies of programmers*. First Workshop, pp. 263-269. Ablex 1988
6. Guindon, R.: Designing the design process: exploiting opportunistic thoughts. *Human Computer Interaction*. 5, 305-344 (1990)
7. Harel, D.: On visual formalisms. *Comm. of the ACM*. 31 (5), 514-530 (1988)
8. Harel, D.: Statecharts: a visual formalism for complex systems. *Science of Computer Programming*. 8 (3), 231-274 (1987)
9. Harel, D. and Pnueli, A.: On the development of reactive systems. In K.R.Apt (ed.) *Logics and models of concurrent systems*. NATO ASI Series F, vol.13, pp. 477-498, Springer-Verlag 1985
10. Hayes-Roth, B.: Control issues in blackboard architectures. In V. Jagannathan, R. Dodhiawala and L. Baum (eds.), *Blackboard architectures and applications*. Academic Press 1989
11. Johnson-Laird, P.: Mental models. In M. Posner (ed.) *Foundations of Cognitive Science*. MIT 1989
12. Lewis, C.: A research agenda for the 90s in human-computer interaction. *Human Computer Interaction*. 5, 125-143 (1990)
13. Newell, A. and Card, S.: The prospects for psychological science in human-computer interaction. *Human-Computer Interaction*. 1, 209-242 (1985)
14. Schank, R.: Explanation patterns: understanding mechanically and creatively. Lawrence Erlbaum Associates 1986
15. Simplicio, F.: A model of cognitive behaviour in software specification understanding. Research Report 92/3, Imperial College of Science, Technology and Medicine, Department of Computing (1992)
16. Soloway, E. and Ehrlich, K.: Empirical studies of programming knowledge. *IEEE Trans. on Software Engineering*. 10 (5), 595-609 (1984)
17. Turski, W. and Maibaum, T.: *The specification of computer programs*. Addison-Wesley 1987
18. Visser, W.: More or less following a plan during design: opportunistic deviations in specification. *Internat. Journal of Man-Machine Studies*. 33 (3), 247-278 (1990)
19. Winograd, T. and Flores, F.: *Understanding computers and cognition. A new foundation for design*. Ablex 1986

How Confirmation Bias Affects Novice Programmers in Testing and Debugging: Research Strategies and Implications for Tools

Laura Marie Leventhal

Computer Science Department, Bowling Green State University, Bowling Green, Ohio 43403, USA

Abstract: Learning to be a skilled programmer involves the acquisition of skills in many areas, such as program design, comprehension, generation, program debugging and program testing. Among novice programmers, testing and debugging appear to be particularly problematic. We believe that software testing and debugging involve processes of hypothesis generation and verification. As such, we feel that confirmation bias is likely to be manifest in both testing and debugging.

We have focused our current research on whether and to what extent testers seek disconfirmation in software testing. In our current research,we have found strong evidence of confirmation bias in testing; the bias is mitigated to some extent by increasing tester expertise, increasingly detailed specifications, and the presence of software errors. In future research, we intend to broaden the scope of our program testing work, as well as to explore issues of confirmation bias in debugging.

Keywords: Confirmation bias, software testing, experimental research.

Introduction

Learning to be a skilled programmer involves the acquisition of skills in many areas, such as program design, comprehension, generation, program debugging and program testing. Among novice programmers, testing and debugging appear to be particularly problematic. For example, behavioral studies of debugging and testing have found that the performances of novices is often quite poor [30, 31, 35], particularly compared to more expert subjects [8, 17, 21, 27, 28, 29]. In addition, Sheppard, Curtis, Milliman & Love [22] reported much more variance in debugging performance among programmers of lower expertise levels than among programmers of higher expertise levels and Gould & Drongowski [5] and Gould [6] reported that debugging performance improved with practice.

One explanation for poor novice performance in debugging and testing is that typically in learning to program, novices receive no formalized training in testing and debugging. Consequently, their skills are quite weak, or their comprehension of programs is limited [8,

27]. However, training and knowledge alone do not insure optimal performance in testing and debugging. Even among practitioners, failures of testing and inadequate debugging can lead to substantial and costly problems. For example, software failures have been estimated to cost $900 million a year in Great Britain alone [18].

In my current work, I suggest that this lack of effectiveness in program testing and debugging may be partially the result of psychological limitations. Specifically, I argue that the phenomenon of *confirmation bias* may impede effective software testing and debugging. At Bowling Green State University, I, along with my colleagues Barbee T. Mynatt, Diane S. Rohlman, and C.R. Mynatt, have developed a program of research to investigate the role(s) of confirmation bias in program testing and debugging, especially for novice programmers. We are also interested in the implications of our results for tool design. In this paper, I will briefly overview existing research on confirmation bias, our research, and our recommendations for tool design.

Confirmation Bias

Behavioral research on hypothesis testing has shown that people often test hypotheses and rules in ways that tend to confirm, rather than disconfirm them. This tendency has been labeled *confirmation bias* and is an example of a larger class of biased behaviors, called cognitive biases [cf. 23, 25] have identified the following behaviors as manifestations of confirmation bias:

1. Failure to seek disconfirmatory evidence in testing a hypothesis
2. Failure to use disconfirmatory evidence in evaluating a hypothesis, even when it is available
3. Failure to test alternative hypotheses
4. Failure to evaluate evidence in light of alternative hypotheses.

As an example of Category 1, Wason [34] asked college students to discover an experimenter-defined rule for generating number triples. Subjects were given an example of a triple which fit the rule ("2-4-6") and told that they could test their own hypothesized rule by generating more triples. After each triple the experimenter would tell the subjects whether the triple fit the true rule or not. The subjects were also asked to state what hypothesized rule they were testing and were told to announce the correct rule when they thought they had discovered it.

Based on the experimenter-supplied triple, most subjects generated an initial hypothesized rule something like "even integers increasing by two". This response was actually a subset of the true rule, which was simply "increasing numbers". Eighty percent of the subjects erroneously convinced themselves that they had discovered the correct rule. In testing their rules, subjects generated *four times* as many test triples which were consistent with their rules as triples which were inconsistent. In other words, subjects who were testing the "even integers increasing by two" rule generated four test triples such as "8-10-12" for every one such as "1-2-3" or "3-2-1". This failure to seek disconfirmation has also been shown in a variety of other laboratory settings, such as Wason [33].

The effect of confirmation bias has been shown to be quite general and robust, across both laboratory studies and among practitioners. For example, Mitroff [16] has shown that NASA geoscientists, working with the Apollo moon program, tended to investigate moon rocks in ways that supported their hypotheses about the rocks. [See also 15, 24, 33, 34]. In some studies, confirmation bias appears to be lessened somewhat by increasing subject expertise levels [e.g. 10]. Across the confirmation bias literature, ratios of confirmatory tests to disconfirmatory tests of 4:1 are typically reported, and ratios as high as 10:1 often are described.

Does Confirmation Bias Have a Role in Software Testing and Debugging?

We believe that software testing and debugging involve processes of hypothesis generation and verification. Other authors have articulated this position as well [cf. 1, 9, 20, 27, 28]. As such, we feel that confirmation bias is likely to be manifest in both testing and debugging.

Indeed, there is some preliminary evidence that this is so in software testing. For example, Zweben, Stringfellow & Barton [35] had introductory programming students test their own and someone else's program. The test data typically included only valid, but not invalid, data.

Several previous behavioral studies of debugging also have found indications that debugging behavior is affected by confirmation bias. For example, in a protocol study of expert and novice debuggers, Vessey [27] found that novice debuggers considered far fewer alternative hypotheses when looking for the source of a program error than did experts. In another study of expert and novice programmers, Guggerty & Olson [8] found that expert programmers tested fewer hypotheses than novice subjects. However, they noted that the experts often started with the correct hypothesis, so that the testing of many hypotheses would have been inappropriate. We interpret these results within the Tweney, Doherty & Mynatt definition of confirmation bias as suggesting that performance of debuggers is sometimes poor because the subjects fail to test alternative hypotheses of the causes of errors during debugging.

Brooke & Duncan [2] found that subjects in a debugging task had only limited advantages when they used a flowchart description of a program instead of a program listing. We speculate that subjects' performances were virtually identical, whether they had flowcharts or listings, because both notations were low-level and unhelpful in the formation of alternative hypotheses.

Our Research

Because prior research, such as Zweben, et al. [35] has suggested that confirmation bias is manifest in software testing as a failure to seek disconfirmation, we have focused our current research on whether and to what extent testers seek disconfirmation in testing. To date, our research has focused specifically on functional software testing. In our research, we have taken a two-faceted approach. On the one hand, we have conducted studies of subjects actually engaging in testing and debugging tasks, and interpreted their behaviors within the framework of confirmation bias. Our goal here is to identify, in applied settings, how these biased behaviors manifest themselves. Our other approach has been to reformulate the basic tasks of testing and debugging into the classic laboratory tasks that have been used to study these phenomena, and then study subject behaviors on the tasks. Our goal from this type of research is to identify which features of testing and debugging are transferable to standard laboratory tasks.

Applied Studies

In our model, we have operationally defined a "confirmatory test" to be any test case which tests a defined program function from the program specification. In this definition, we identify equivalence classes of inputs which would test these defined functions, and label representative tests as "confirmatory." Tests which test inputs from equivalence classes outside of the specifications are defined as "disconfirmatory." Then, under this definition, a tendency to use more confirmatory tests than disconfirmatory tests would be considered a manifestation of confirmation bias.

Our procedure across several studies has been to present subjects with a written program specification. Then subjects are presented with a Pascal program in a simulated MacPascal environment. Subjects are instructed to test program to see if the program meets the specification. They are told to execute the program as many times as they want to. Subjects are not allowed to change the program code. In our experiments, we have varied the level of subject expertise, the completeness of the specifications, and the presence or absence of errors in the program. For generalizability, we have used different types of programs in our experiments. The typical data that we collect are the number of confirmatory and disconfirmatory tests that subjects run. We also collect data that we call "coverage data," which describes what percentage of possible confirmatory and disconfirmatory tests have been executed, for the various equivalence classes. Finally, we sometimes ask subjects, at the completion of their tests, to rate how confident that they are that the program is correct and that they have tested it thoroughly.

Across several studies, where subjects were asked to test programs, we have found overwhelming evidence of the use of a confirmatory testing strategy. For example, in a study reported in Mynatt, Leventhal, Mynatt and Rohlman [17], subjects tested a numerical program. Subjects generated approximately four times as many total confirmatory tests as total disconfirmatory tests and covered about twice as many of the possible confirmatory tests as disconfirmatory. These ratios are consistent with studies reported in Mynatt, Leventhal, Mynatt and Rohlman [17], Leventhal, Mynatt, Rohlman and Mynatt [11] and Leventhal [12].

Previous studies of biased behaviors in testing have found some evidence that clarifying the problem statement to make disconfirmatory tests more salient may moderate the bias [e.g. 7, 26]. In Mynatt, Leventhal, Mynatt and Schertler Rohlman [17] and, Leventhal, Mynatt, Rohlman and Mynatt [12], we described studies in which we varied the completeness of the software specification; the goal was to vary the salience of the disconfirmatory tests to the testers. In one variation, the specification was stated in the positive ("this program will do...") and the negative ("this program will not do ..."). Using the same operational definition of confirmatory and disconfirmatory tests, we found that making the disconfirmatory tests more salient did improve subjects testing of disconfirmatory tests. However, even in these situations, subjects tended to test more confirmatory tests that disconfirmatory tests.

Some previous studies of bias have found that increasing subject expertise tends to reduce biased behavior [e.g., 10]. However, observational studies of practicing scientists show a strong tendency among scientists toward biased behaviors [e.g. 15, 16, 24]. Consistent with the [10] finding, in Mynatt, Leventhal, Mynatt and Rohlman [17], we found that we found that increasing levels of expertise led to increasing use of disconfirmatory tests, across two different testing tasks.

Several previous studies of biased behaviors have found that error feedback may tend to diminish biased behaviors [e.g. 32]. In studies reported in Leventhal, Mynatt, Rohlman and Mynatt [12] , we found that subjects who found errors during testing tended to perform more tests overall. In some cases, subjects generated noticeably more disconfirmatory tests that they did in the error-free condition.

Tweney, Doherty & Mynatt [25] have identified the failure to consider disconfirmatory evidence as a manifestation of confirmation bias. In addition, Lichtenstein and Fischhoff [13] and Lichtenstein, Fischhoff and Phillips [14] have suggested that people are often overconfident of their own performance, as evidenced by poor calibration. In Leventhal [11] and Leventhal, Mynatt, Rohlman and Mynatt [12], we asked subjects to test programs and then to subjectively rate their confidence that the programs were correct. We found that even when programs failed, subjects appeared to be poorly calibrated. These subjects had lowered confidence in the correctness of the programs; however, even these subjects rated the programs as "somewhat correct."

We are currently collecting verbal protocols of subjects testing programs, to better understand the hypotheses that subjects hold while they are testing. In these verbal protocol studies, we are varying the types of specifications and the presence of errors. To better understand the effects of expertise on testing, we have also varied the amount of specific training in functional testing among these verbal protocol subjects.

Modifications to Traditional Laboratory Tasks

In our research, we have also attempted to extract some critical features of software testing and map those activities onto the traditional laboratory tasks that have been used to study confirmation bias.

The Wason 4-Card Selection Task is a task in which subjects are ask choose test data to falsify a rule (cf. Wason, 1960). Some previous experiments have considered the impact of expertise in science or mathematics in performance on the selection task [e.g.10]. In our version of the 4-Card Selection Task, we Used subjects of various expertise levels, and a combination of program testing scenarios and other scenarios, we found advanced computer science students did better on the program testing instantiation of the 4-card task, than did two other control groups.

The Wason 2-4-6 Task was described in the literature review section of this paper. It is a task in which subjects are asked to discover a rule [34]. To solve the problem, subjects generate a hypothesized rule and then execute tests of their hypothesis. In an unpublished modification of the 2-4-6 task, Rohlman provided a specification of the rule and asked subjects to determine if the provided rule was correct. She varied the completeness of the specifications, similar to Mynatt, Leventhal, Mynatt & Rohlman [17] and Leventhal, Mynatt, Rohlman, and Leventhal [12], and found similar patterns of results. The data from this study reveal that giving subjects expanded rule specifications influences the proportion of rule triples tested by the subjects.

Future Work

Currently we are performing verbal protocol program testing tasks to determine more precisely the nature of program testers' hypotheses as they test. Our initial results suggest that testers' hypotheses are, in fact, closely related to the program specification, similar to our operational definition that we used in prior studies. In future studies, we plan to study testing behaviors, using professional programmers. We will also study testing behaviors in a variety of testing environments, varying the programming languages and CASE tools available.

Our testing results are encouraging that confirmation bias is manifest in software engineering tasks. In future studies, we intend to extend our work to debugging studies, as well. Since previous studies of debugging have suggested that debuggers often fail to consider alternative hypotheses in debugging, our focus will be to identify the hypotheses that debuggers generate and test.

Implications for Tools

We feel that enhanced tools for debugging and testing might mitigate some of the effects of confirmation bias. One approach for an enhanced testing tool would be to present the task of program testing as a task that one complete using a strictly confirmatory strategy. In a previous study by Mynatt, et al. [17], we provided program testers, at various expertise levels, with complete software specifications (typical positively-worded specification, plus the specifications stated negatively). These complete specifications transformed software testing into a task that was strictly confirmatory. Testers of all levels improved their testing performance with the complete specification. We speculate that a testing tool that generated a complete software specifications (positively- and negatively-worded) would be useful in improving testing behaviors.

Typical contemporary debugging tools are often low-level [cf. 1].. These tools are not necessarily designed to help a person form hypotheses about the cause of errors in a debugging task. An alternative approach to an enhanced debugging tool would be to develop a tool that presented alternative hypotheses to the person who was debugging. Such a debugging tool would operate at a higher level of abstraction than most contemporary tools. [cf. 19].

Our third tool strategy would be to develop enhanced training systems. As was noted above, more highly expert programmers are better than novices at both debugging and testing. We believe that differences in confirmation bias are involved in these expert-novice differences. Recent research concerning other cognitive biases, outside of confirmation bias, has suggested that relatively short, intense training periods are sufficient to overcome much of the bias effect [cf. 3, 4]. We are hopeful that a training tool that teaches subjects to seek and use disconfirmation and multiple hypotheses might be useful as well.

Conclusions

Program testing and debugging are difficult skills to learn and to execute. In our research, we have found compelling evidence that confirmation bias explains many limitations in testing and debugging. Across several experiments, we have found that program testers tend to test programs with confirmatory test cases, although this tendency may be mitigated to some extent by tester expertise, by the quality of the program specification, or by the presence of errors. These findings have implications for future empirical study of testing and debugging behaviors, as well as for tool development.

Acknowledgements

I would like to thank Barbee Teasley, Diane Schertler Rohlman, and Keith Instone for their help in preparing this paper.

References

1. Araki, K, Furukawa, Z. and Cheng, J.: A general framework for debugging. IEEE Software. 14-20 (1991)
2. Brooke, J.B. and Duncan, K.D.: Experimental studies of flowchart use at different stages of program debugging. Ergonomics. 23(11), 1057-1091 (1980)
3. Cheng, P.W., Holyoak, K.J., Nisbett, R.E. and Oliver, L.M.: Pragmatic versus syntactic approaches to training and deductive reasoning. Cognitive Psychology. 18, 293-328 (1986)
4. Fong, G.T., Krantz, D.H. and Nisbett, R.E.: The effects of statistical training on thinking about everyday problems. Cognitive Psychology. 18, 253-292 (1986)
5. Gould, J.D.: Some psychological evidence on how people debug computer programs International Journal of Man-Machine Studies. 7, 151-182 (1975)
6. Gould, J.D. and Drongowski, P.: An exploratory study of computer program debugging. Human Factors. 16(3), 258-277 (1974)
7. Griggs, R.A. and Newstead, S.E.: The role of problem structure in a deductive reasoning task. Journal of Experimental Psychology, Memory & Cognition. 8, 297-307 (1982)
8. Guggerty, L and Olson, G.M.: Comprehension differences in debugging by skilled and novice programmers. In: Empirical Studies of Programmers (Soloway, E. and Iyengar, S., ed.s). pp. 13-27 Norwood, NJ: Ablex Publishing Corporation 1986
9. Katz, I.R. and Anderson, J.R.: Debugging: an analysis of bug-location strategies. Human-Computer Interaction. 3, 351-399 (1988)
10. Kern, L. H., Mirels, H. L. and Hinshaw, V. G.: . Scientists' understanding of propositional logic: An experimental investigation. Social Studies of Science. 13, 131-146 (1983)
11. Leventhal, L.: Program testing and confirmation bias among experts and novices: An exploratory study. Bowling Green State University Computer Science Department Technical Report. 91-JAN-02, 1991
12. Leventhal, L.M., Teasley,B.M., Schertler Rohlman, D.M. and Mynatt, C.R.: Evidence of Confirmation and Positive Test Bias in Software Testing. Bowling Green State University Computer Science Department Technical Report. 92-JUN-01, 1992
13. Lichtenstein, S. and Fischhoff, B: Do those who know more also know more about how much they know? Organizational Behavior and Human Performance. 20, 159-183 (1977)
14. Lichtenstein, S., Fischhoff, B. and Phillips, L.D.: Calibration of probabilities: The state of the art to 1980. In: Judgement Under Uncertainty: Heuristics and Biases (Kahneman, D., Slovic, P. and Tversky, A., ed.s). pp. 306-334 . New York: Cambridge University Press 1982
15. Mahoney, M. J. and DeMonbreun, B. G.: Psychology of the scientist: An analysis of problem-solving bias. Cognitive Therapy and Research,. 1, 229 - 238 (1978)
16. Mitroff, I.: Norms and counter-norms in a select group of Apollo moon scientists: A case study of the ambivalence of scientists. American Sociological Review. 39, 579 - 595 (1974)
17. Mynatt, B.T., Leventhal, L.M., Mynatt, C.R. and Rohlman, D.S.: (1991) "Why Software Testing is Often Ineffective: Evidence of Positive Test Bias in Software Testing. Bowling Green State University Computer Science Department Technical Report. 92-MAY-01, 1992
18. Neuman, P.: Risks to the public in computers and related systems. Software Engineering Notes. 13 (1988)
19. Olsson, R.A., Crawford, R.H., Ho, W.W. and Wee, C.E.: Sequential debugging at a high level of abstraction. IEEE Software. 27-36 (1991)
20. Pennington, N and Grabowski, B.: The tasks of programming. In: Psychology of Programming (Hoc, J.-M., Green, T.R.G., Samurcay, R. and Gilmore, D.J., ed.s). pp. 45-62. San Diego, CA: Academic Press LTD 1990
21. Rohlman, D.S., Mynatt, C.R., Mynatt, B.T. and Leventhal, L.M.: The Influence of Expertise on the Four-Card Selection Task in the Domain of Software Testing. Midwestern Psychological Association Annual Meeting. Chicago, Illinois, 1992
22. Sheppard, S.B., Curtis,B., Milliman, P. and Love, T.: Modern coding practices and programmer performance. Computer. 41-49 (1979)
23. Tversky, A. and Kahneman, D.: Judgement under uncertainty: Heuristics and biases. Science. 185. 1124-1131 (1974)
24. Tweney, R. D.: Faraday's discovery of induction: A cognitive approach. In: Faraday Rediscovered. (D. Gooding, and James, R., ed.s), pp. 159-206. London: MacMillan 1985
25. Tweney, R.D., Doherty, M.E. and Mynatt, C.R.: Hypothesis testing: the role of confirmation. In: On Scientific Thinking (Tweney, R.D., Doherty, M.E. and Mynatt, C.R., ed.s). pp. 113-128. New York: Columbia University Press 1981
26. Tweney, R. D., Doherty, M. E., Worner, W., Pliske, D., Mynatt, C.R., Gross, K., and Arkelin, D.: Strategies of rule discovery in an inference task. Quarterly Journal of Experimental Psychology. 32, 109-123 (1980)

27. Vessey, I.: Expertise in debugging computer programs: a process analysis. International Journal of Man-Machine Studies. 23, 459-494 (1985)
28. Vessey, I.: Expertise in debugging computer programs: an analysis of the content of verbal protocols. IEEE Transactions on Systems, Man, and Cybernetics. 16, 621-637 (1986)
29. Vessey, I.: Toward a theory of computer program bugs: an empirical test. International Journal of Mn-Machine Studies. 30, 23-46 (1989)
30. Waddington, R. and Henry, R.: The effect of program authorship on novice debugging performance. In: Designing and Using Human-Computer Interfaces and Knowledge Based Systems (Salvendy, G. and Smith, M.J., ed.s). pp. 113-120. Amsterdam: Elsevier Science Publishers B.V. 1989
31. Waddington, R. and Henry, R.: Selective information hiding: A debugging technique to address some of the problems of novice programmers. In: Human Aspects in Computing: Design and Use of Interactive Systems and Work with Terminals (H.-J. Bullinger, ed.). pp. 592-596.Amsterdam: Elsevier Science Publishers B.V. 1991
32. Walker, B. J. and Harper, D. R.: Decision-making under system failure conditions. Final report to Air Force Office of Scientific Research, (1990 - Unpublished manuscript).
33. Wason, P. C.: On the failure to eliminate hypotheses in a conceptual task. Quarterly Journal of Experimental Psychology. 12, 129-140 (1960).
34. Wason, P. C.: Reasoning about a rule. Quarterly Journal of Experimental Psychology. 23, 273-281 (1968)
35. Zweben, S. H., Stringfellow, C. and Barton, R.: Exploratory studies of the software testing methods used by novice programmers. Third Software Engineering Institute Conference on Software Engineering Education. (1989)

The "Private" Relation of the Student with Systematic Programming and Validation

Vassilios Dagdilelis

Laboratoire de Structures Discrètes et Didactique, IMAG, Université Joseph Fourier, Grenoble, France

Abstract: The focus of this research is on what students (at university level) do when they have to validate an algorithm. Validating an algorithm is strongly related with building it. We propose a hierarchy of several categories of methods to construct a valid – or to validate an – algorithm. A general student's conception is also presented – the mechanistic conception – which could give a general frame to better describe a student's behavior.

Keywords: Didactics of informatics, programming learning modeling, student models, novice programmers

1. Introduction

Programming is in general recognized as a very complex intellectual activity. Teaching programming seems to be in the center of interest of an increasing number of researches which have been carried on all over the world, and many theoretical models and frames have been proposed for analyzing the student's behavior in "programming situations". For example, the question of which methods and strategies students use for solving a programming problem, or more generally the question of modeling – in some way – student's behavior, was a central theme in several researches [1,2,3,4].

A question which seems to be less studied in a direct way, although indirectly it is treated in many researches, is the correctness of algorithms. The main focus of our research is on what students (at university level) really do when they have *to construct a correct algorithm.* We need to make some remarks to define our target in a more precise way.

- It is evident that the study of student's behavior is important to derive an optimal organization of teaching and, from this point of view, teaching programming is difficult because often, as professor J. Arsac says [5], students sometimes do - or we think they do - nonsense. This can mean that students behavior sometimes seems absurd. We shall try to present a frame for the description of the process of writing and validating algorithms - a kind of classification of those behaviors. Furthermore, we shall try to present a major student's misconception and to give a framework within which student's behavior may become less absurd, more coherent.

- The notion of valid algorithm is ambiguous and not all computer scientist would agree with the same definition. For example, a valid algorithm can be a correct one, when its function corresponds with its specification, or a robust algorithm which reacts "logically" even to a question without an answer (for example in the case of division by zero), or something else close to both of these. We are mainly interested in the correctness of algorithms, more precisely in the methods that students use to assure themselves that an algorithm is correct - we consider that the correctness is the crucial point of the validity of an algorithm.

- It is certain that there is a close relation between both methods used to build an algorithm and methods used to study or establish its validity. Computer scientists have already underlined this close relation rather early [6] . For example, it is difficult to prove, with a formal method, the correctness of an algorithm built with the help of hand-paper simulations only. However, this is not just a technical relation. The methods which have been used for constructing or validating an algorithm can be also considered as witnesses of a certain rationality, that is, they implicitly determine which are the "legitimate" ways to perform a task. Let us give an example, from another science: there are entirely different ways to prove that two triangles are equal. For a 12 years old pupil, this can mean that he has to superimpose one sheet of paper over the other one, but for a mathematician this means to produce a proof. It is clear that the pupil and the mathematician do not have the same point of view on triangles; their triangles are of different nature. Euclid's axioms, definitions, inference rules and all kind of notions that are necessary to treat triangles mathematically, define a " universe" in which superimposing sheets of papers is quite meaningless - while it is meaningful for the pupil. The employed tools can be witnesses of the nature of treated objects. In our case, we consider that the means that students use can be a pertinent indicator of the nature of the algorithm - what students think that an algorithm is. Hence, if we want to study students' behavior, we need to study in parallel he process of building and of validating algorithms.

- Validating and building an algorithm are not independent of the constraints due to the situation in which the algorithm is built. If, for example, the legitimate means for solving a problem can be defined in a general way, the choice between multiple possibilities depends on the characteristics of the situation itself: it is possible that the methods used for an algorithm which is built just for pleasure will be different to those used as part of a huge program for managing a nuclear centre.

For this purpose, we have organized some experiments with students. In our experiments, students work in pairs to solve a problem (typically to produce an algorithm to count words, paragraphs or characters). Working in pairs constitutes a specific environment of work, because students are obligated to explain their choices in conflict situations, and this is a source of information for the observer. Their products, i.e. the resulting algorithms, would be examined (by other students in some experiments or by a fictitious employer in another one) - so that students had an interest in producing a correct algorithm and in providing explanations of their choices.

We have organized our experiments with students from the the second year of the University, scientific disciplines: this could be significant because other courses taken by the students were mathematics and physics, where proofs are the standard or very common way for validating. The students could be considered as relative novices, because they had an experience of only 1 1/2 year of programming.

These students had also been taught systematic programming, that is, teaching programming was based on the systematic application of typical schemes of (mostly sequential) processing. Complex problems were decomposed into simpler ones and so on until the decomposition was simple enough to be directly programmed. Typically, the solutions were accompanied by (at least) two kinds of comments: the Dictionary, i.e. a detailed description of types and variables used in each procedure, and a description of the initial and final states of each procedure.

In order to teach programming, several researchers have proposed a " natural" and interesting solution: what must be taught is a methodical and explicit way to apply some general schemes - classes of algorithms - which can be used in a whole class of situations or problems (see for example [1, pg.857]).

The objectives of a first introductory course are to acquire a " plan/schema library" (i.e. a set of abstracts schemes) and be able to recognize problems that belongs to these solution classes. Learning is organized as a three steps cycle of progressive deepening.... classifying a problem by means of the association of a generic schema...[7, pg.73]

Actually, the real aim seems to be not only the acquisition of a library of plans and corresponding rules to apply to them, but ,something deeper, some acquisition of a general methodology as well.

2. A Hierarchy

We have tried to distinguish different categories of ways to construct and to validate the algorithms - a schema borrowed from works in mathematics teaching [8]. These categories are characterised by a progressive renunciation of pragmatic and the concrete for the benefit of intellectual and abstract - we mean objects and their relations. In what follows we will present this hierarchy and explain the differences between the proposed categories. To make our examples more understandable we have chosen them from the same experiment: students work in pairs, and the proposed problem is to write an algorithm to count words and sentences and to eliminate the redundant spaces in a stream of telegrams terminated by a special word ZZZZZZ [9]. The categories that we propose are as follows:

1- Sometimes the construction of a part of an algorithm seems to be almost immediate and there is no production of any kind of explanation. In this case the organization of the treatment can be the result of evidence: probably the way to proceed is so clear to the student that there is no need to produce any explanation, any justification. A characteristic example is the student's way of structuring the whole program: very often the " tailoring" of the whole program into procedures is made by following a kind of mental execution with no any justification at all.

2- The ostentation is a way to convince - or to be convinced - when the functioning of the algorithm is exposed to be seen. In this case there is care to produce an explanation but it looks as this explanation is in the constructed object itself. Even more, since an algorithm can be viewed as a mechanism, very often this mechanism must be set in motion to see it functioning:

An algorithm must be seen to be believed and the best way to learn what an algorithm is all about is to try it. The reader should always take pencil and paper and work through an example of each algorithm immediately upon encountering it in the text [10, pg.4].

Hence it is possible that the author refers to this particular mechanism which permits him to "see" and to be convinced about the correct functioning of the algorithm without formulating any kind of arguments. Sometimes the exposition for observation allows one to deviate from the formulation of the problem. In the following example Pierre, a student, " shows " to Christophe that his plan is simple:

Figure 1

Pierre : don't you think that this is simpler?

Christophe : I can't quite catch what you've said.....

Pierre : I'm telling you ....I'm getting a telegram ABCDEF ... from here you're getting here...I put an A in my chain...

Christophe : go on..go on.. it works ..it looks good... now I can see what you want to explain...

(at the same time, Pierre draws under each letter).

Christophe seems to have been convinced that Pierre's method *works* and *is good* probably because he can comprehend and can see with the simulation's help what Pierre has proposed.

3 - The crucial experience is a kind of " experiment" organized to confront two opposite propositions, or one proposition and his negation; this has been observed in conflict situations or when it was necessary to adopt one of two possible solutions. We give the example of Bertrand who, after constructing a procedure AVANCEMOT, is not sure that "it works" and comments:

will it work? there are no chances... I don't know if it works...we must test it with an example... we must test it in a general case and then...

We consider that this general case has its value precisely because this generality involves the validity of the algorithm in all cases. Hence, for Bertrand, the problem of the field of validity of the algorithm exists only implicitly.

4 - The generic example is a real, concrete example of data used as a support to develop or verify an algorithm - but this example is supposed to represent a class of equivalent data, and its value resides precisely in the fact that it represents a whole class. Even if this equivalence is not explicit, the problem of the field of validity of the algorithm is present. Paper simulations of the execution of an algorithm are often applied to data supposed to represent a class of "similar" data - even if it is not explicit what this "similarity" is.

Invariance and relations that are characteristic for the chosen examples are characteristic for the whole class of equivalence. But this invariance are not explicit. They can remain hidden because the situation claims only that the two students must agree with the point that the example is really representative; there is no obligation to make the properties of the data explicit.

We report the example of Françoise and Bertrand who are working on an example of a flow which is constantly used as reference during the writing of the algorithm:

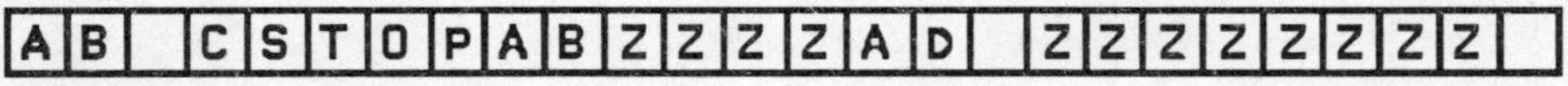

Figure 2

This flow has in some way all the characteristics that all flows must have. This example - and all similar examples - differs from limit cases (such as empty texts etc.) which are treated separately, with special data invented ad hoc. Hence, this string is general, because it represents a class of telegrams with the same characteristics. Moreover, we note that what is important is not its content but its structure: that is, the words are ABC or even C. The description of a treatment of this string is valid for all other strings with the same characteristics.

From our point of view, what characterizes the chosen example as generic is its permanent use as a support for the construction of the algorithm. Based on this flow, the two students explore the properties of all flows; they try to find the invariance and to plan their actions. We observe anyhow that all these invariances and properties remain implicit: the chosen flow has some properties but they are never formulated explicitly.

5 - The assimilation of the characteristics of the data, i.e. the invariance of their structure, is a condition for the realization of <u>mental experiments</u>. We think that the following cases belong to this general category:

It is possible to work with some kind of symbolic representation where concrete objects and concrete data have disappeared and are not present any more. What remains are the properties of the data, their structure. The work of the construction or the validation of an algorithm continues, but on a different basis. In the case of generic data, the chosen data also have a structure - as in the above cases. But now the work is made <u>directly</u> on the structure and not on concrete data that represent the structure. Hence, it seems that an important step has been done in the direction of abstraction .

An important question is the following: how are expressed these properties of the data? Sometimes it is necessary to work in a specific system of representation - mostly a graphic one, where are represented the structure of the data, their invariance; the work of building an algorithm, or explaining it, is realized with this representation. For instance, Christophe designs a first example saying: *there is nothing...you shall have words in that way with spaces...*

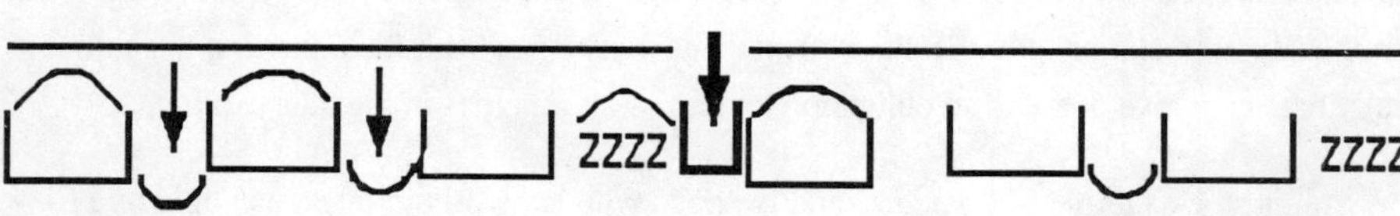

Figure 3

Words here are "physically" absent - with the one exception of the word ZZZZ, which marks the end. What is clearly represented is the structure of the string expressed with this graphical support.
In another example, Philippe makes the following drawing:

Figure 4

and says:
STOP... STOP... they are STOP everywhere .. and ZZZZ... an empty at the end.. and this is repeated I don't know how many times...

Once again, what is represented is mainly the structure of the flow.

The use of this kind of "scale" model, however, can be insufficient in the case of conflict; in this case, it is possible to observe a regression to more concrete representations. For example, Christophe looks for support to illustrate the fact that (for him) telegrams are not necessarily separated with spaces. For this reason, he uses a kind of "materialization" of his abstract model, a detailed representation of a part of the flow - precisely the part at the end of a telegram:

Figure 5

Christophe : so you have ABC ABC good...ZZZZ
Pierre : ZZZZ wait...
Christophe : put the number of blanks that you want... it's in the telegram.. each word of each telegram...

The use of a graphical representation is not necessary; the assimilation of the structure of the data is a condition for the realization of <u>mental executions</u>: students can work mentally without any example of data. The absence of concrete examples makes the correspondence with particular cases impossible. Only properties can be invoked and accepted by students. However, the properties of the data can remain completely implicit and strongly related with the effective execution of the algorithm.For instance, Oliver, a student, says, showing his algorithm - without any example:

O.K. let's try again.. you have a word.. you arrive there and then nia nia nia..yes and.. imagine that you are in an ZZZZ...

The mental execution permits Oliver not only to construct or verify his algorithm but also to show Philippe why there is an error in a specific place; Oliver invites Philippe to imagine a specific place in a string:

Oliver : well you get there ... you are... lets imagine that we get direct to the ZZZZ...
Philippe : yes...
Oliver : well you'll find.. there is no STOP in the other side.. and nia nia nia .. it will be ZZZZ..

We remark that the mental execution remains strongly related to a certain action - after all, we speak in terms of mental execution. However, what is important is the fact that the work is made directly on the structure - not with concrete examples.

6 - We consider that the direct application of <u>typical schemes of treatment</u> (for example the sequential treatment) is a step of detachment of the execution (simulated or mental). Scheme application not only requires the recognition of a certain structure of the data, but also means that the student can apply an algorithmic scheme without examining the particularities of the data - in this case there is a strong similarity with the application of methods, theorems or formulas in mathematics. What is important is the recognition of the fact that only the structure of the data and the kind of treatment that we want to apply are significant - the nature of objects is irrelevant because the scheme can be applied to any kind of data such as words, numbers, paragraphs etc.

A typical example is the student who describes this scheme:
it is necessary a sequential treatment.. start... next element... while not... process... next element

Two remarks are imposed:
- first, it seems that the recognition of a serial disposition of the data does not necessarily imply the recognition of a sequential structure; we mean that recognizing the fact that the elements are placed "one after the other" does not always imply students recognizing the typical structure of sequential problems. In a sense, there are at least two different levels of recognition: at a first level, there is recognition of a sequential disposition of objects - recognition of a pattern. This is

not the same as a level of recognition of a particular structure, characterized by some invariance, for example, one which implies the application of a while or a repeat scheme.

We can give the example of a square: a square can be considered in different ways and the recognition of a "square" geometric form does not mean that automatically there will be recognition of a particular structure (for example a fundamental structure which is repeated 4 times).

- A second remark is that we have observed that this way of proceeding was fairly marginal. Even students that had started applying this scheme have often abandoned it. We observed that there is a tendency to apply more pragmatic methods - maybe because they are believed to be more reliable. For example, students can recognize the possibility of applying such a scheme quite early:
Pierre says *there is a loop for the entire text and one for each telegram* - but this comment will remain without following. It is not easy for us to interpret this fact. But this way of proceeding sometimes seems to be too complicated and students avoid it. *I can't follow you... I can't do it like this...you deal with the entire problem at once...* says Salima when her friend wants to apply a scheme.

7- We can also expect the application of formal methods and explanations based not on the execution of an algorithm but on relations between its parts: for example, the description of the state of the system before and after the execution of a procedure (initial and final state of the system) is a typical example of this kind of explanation which is well known by students. But in general very few arguments of this kind were observed.

3. Remarks on specifications

Even if specifications are not our main subject, it is important to remark on them: in some way data specifications, specifications of results and specifications of procedures constitute a kind of "operational" definition of objects - the treatment of underlying objects depends on these definitions. Once more we give the geometry example where proofs have a meaning because the objects on which they are applied are defined in a specific way. In the same way we can consider that specifying is strongly related to the treatment.

Student's specifications are characterized by a kind of opportunism - in the following sense: objects are left unspecified or, more precisely, they were implicitly defined as objects of everyday life - words, sentences, paragraphs are very common objects. But this way of specifying can be insufficient when we must operate on them - for example to measure the length of a word we must consider it - even implicitly - as a finite series of characters delimited by two other special characters. So when we deal with an object with the computer it is necessary to change one's point of view; it is necessary to study the structure of objects much more than the objects themselves. But students' behavior is mainly characterized by the absence of a systematic study of specifications - specifications were examined only when and where there was a difficulty to negotiate - a blockage - or a conflict situation. Specifications become explicit only occasionally, when the need to define them "otherwise" becomes really flagrant - it is this kind of opportunism that we talk about. We must add that even in this case the specifications were locally defined, referred only to "problematic" points and not beyond them (for example to specify all objects).

4. The mechanistic conception

To give a more general framework for the description of students behavior, we advance the hypothesis of a mechanistic conception. This means that for students an algorithm is just a mechanism . As Soloway [1] points out, a mechanism, whether it is instantiated as a transistor, a bolt, a gear, or a verbal instruction, specifies a chain of actions that, when set in motion, produces some desired effect. An algorithm could be considered as a mechanism - and for students is very often <u>only</u> a mechanism. We can find other mechanisms in everyday life - but in this case it is at least unusual to treat the problems of constructing or explaining the functioning of such a mechanism with tools detached from effective action. In most cases there is no <u>need</u> to specify, construct or test a mechanism with such abstract methods as are necessary in programming. Usually one can try, for example, to imagine the functioning of the whole mechanism when finished, and try to construct it with trial-and-error methods.

Abstract tools are well adapted to deal with abstract problems but may be inadequate or at least unnecessarily expensive - in intellectual costs - to deal with everyday-life objects. But dealing, for example, with texts in a computer environment means that the programmer recognizes a text not as an objects which he can find for example in a book, but more like a structure of elements with some characteristics which permit the application of a specific treatment.

5. A final remark

In a general way, the different categories that we propose are characterized by their relation with a kind of empirism. More precisely, the proposed categories of processes of specification, construction and validation - processes strongly interrelated - are characterized by a progressive abandonment of the pragmatic and the concrete for the benefit of the abstract, and also a by change to more systematic methods of construction.

Each student can use several types of construction when he works with the same problem. However, we observe that the more abstract methods - even when they are known - are less often used than the pragmatic ones. They seem also very fragile: even if they are used by students, they still are often abandoned in the case of a conflict situation for the benefit of the more pragmatic methods. Specifications are characterized by a certain opportunism and they stay at a pragmatic level very often - objects of everyday life remain just objects of everyday life.

From our point of view, this behavior corresponds to a global conception that we call the mechanistic conception. Hence, if we want to change the student's behavior, we probably have to change the student's whole conception and we have to try to show that there exist several intermediate levels between this point and the taught methods, so it seems that there is an important gap between them:
many works on the psychology of programming insist on the gap between the world of the task (where nearly unconscious acting is sufficient) and the artificial constraints of the world of the performer (formal treatment, language,..) [11].

Hence, the fact that these students had been taught a kind of systematic programming shows perhaps that the difficulties of adopting a radically different point of view are bigger than is often believed.

References

1. Soloway E: Learning to program = Learning to construct Mechanisms and Explanations. Communications of the ACM, Vol 29, n°9,pp. 850-859 (1986).
2. Hoc J.M.: L'étude psychologique de l'activité de programmation: une revue de la question, T.S.I. 1,5, pp. 383 - 392 (1982).
3. Rogalski J. , Samurcay R. : Acquisition of programming knowledge and skills. In: Psychology of Programming (J.M. Hoc, T.R. G. Green, R. Samurcay & D. Gilmore Eds), London Academic Press, pp.157 -174, 1990.
4. Sheil B.A. : The Psychological Study of Programming, Computing Surveys, 13, 1, pp. 106-120 (1981).
5. Arsac J.: Penser les machines. Seuil, Paris, 1988.
6. Hoare C.A.R. : An axiomatic basis of computer programming, Communications of the ACM, Vol 12, n° 10, pp. 576-580 and 583 (1969).
7. Verdejo M.F., Fernandez I., Urretavizcaya M.T.: Methodology and design in Capra, an environment for learning program construction, Preproc. NATO ARW, Cognitive Models and intelligent Environments for Learning Programming, S. Margherita, Genova, pp. 73-84, 1992.
8. Balacheff N. : Processus de preuve et situations de validation, Educational Studies in Mathematics, 18, pp. 147-176 (1987).
9. Henderson P., Snowdon R.: An experiment in structured programming, B.I.T. 12, pp. 38-53 (1972).
10. Knuth D.E.: The Art af Computer Programming, Vol 1: Fundamental Algorithms. 2nd ed., Reading, Mass.: Addison-Wesley 1973.
11. Duchateau C.: From "Doing It..." to " Having It Done by...": the Heart of Programming. Some Didactical Thoughts, Preproc. NATO ARW, Cognitive Models and Intelligent Environments for Learning Programming, S. Margherita, Genova, pp. 187-200, 1992.

Towards an Intelligent Environment for Learning Introductory Programming

Peter L. Brusilovsky

International Centre for Scientific and Technical Information, Kuusinen Str. 21b, Moscow 125252, Russia

Abstract: The paper discusses some problems of building intelligent learning environments for novice programmers. An intelligent learning environment ITEM/IP is described. The environment supports a course on introductory programming based on the mini-language Turingal. The mini-language serves as a means of mastering the main concepts of programming, the structures of programming languages and skills in program design and debugging. ITEM/IP integrates a set of tools which support students as they learn to program.

Keywords: Intelligent learning environment, novice programmer, introductory programming, mini-language.

Introduction

Intelligent tutoring systems (ITS) and programming environments can be viewed as two opposite approaches to using advanced computer technologies for learning programming. Intelligent programming environments (intelligent learning environments for programming) attempt to bridge the gap between ITS and programming environments.

Intelligent programming environments are able to offer the flexibility of microworld-like environments accompanied by an artificial intelligent coach or tutor. This paper discusses some problems of building intelligent programming environments, lists some useful components of them and suggests an approach to integrates the components. To illustrate the discussion we describe briefly ITEM/IP environment which supports a course on introductory programming based on the mini-language Turingal. ITEM/IP attempts to integrate the capabilities of a tutoring system, programming environment and on-line reference manual for programming.

1. Intelligent Programming Environments

A variety of computer systems and tools have been designed to help teachers and students at all stages of learning programming. These systems and tools can be divided roughly into two classes: tutoring systems and programming environments.

A tutoring system supports the work of human programming tutor in a traditional learning process. It presents teaching material to the student, guides or coaches the student problem solving activity and checks the student programs. Intelligent tutoring systems (ITS) employ artificial intelligence (AI) techniques to work at the level of a skilled human teacher. However, most of these systems are not aimed to replace the human teacher in the classroom, but rather to decrease the amount of non-creative classroom work of a teacher in the course of programming. The systems allow a teacher to have more time for creative work with the weakest and the strongest students.

A programming environment supports the work of a student and the process of exploratory learning. A student is provided with a set of tools which supports the design and debugging of student programs and lets the student experiment with the programs and the programming language. Advanced programming environments employ human-computer interaction (HCI) and Cognitive Science techniques to increase students' learning abilities.

The following teacher activities can be supported by ITS tools with the use of AI techniques:

- instructional planning and knowledge sequencing (SCENT-3 [16]),
- task sequencing (BIP [2]),
- mastery learning (ACT Programming Tutor [11]),
- selection of program example (ELM-PE [22], Discover [10]),
- scaffolding the student in the process of program design at all levels from plan to code (Lisp-Tutor [1], Bridge [5], GIL [17], Discover [10], SODA [14]),
- student program checking (BIP [2]),
- student program analysis or intelligent debugging (PROUST [21], SCENT-3 [15,16], ELM-PE [22] and other systems [4]),
- strategic (meta-level) instruction (Molehill [20]).

As we can see, the spectrum of supported teacher activities is quite wide, but real systems support from one to three of listed features.

The following student activities should be supported by programming environment tools:

- program design and coding,
- using pre-stored examples and previous solutions to build a new program,
- program debugging and investigation,
- querying about description of language features (on-line help).

Modern commercial programming environments, such as Turbo-Pascal 6.0, support all these activities at some level. Advanced environments use HCI technologies such as structural editors, multi-window interface, program visualization, and hypertext to support the listed activities.

From some point of view, there is no crucial difference between ITS and programming environments. Both kinds of systems can be viewed as sets of tools which support different teacher and student activities in the process of learning programming. At this level we can see good prospects for a marriage between the two kinds of systems, that is between ITS and HCI techniques [10, 15]. Good progress has been made recently in building intelligent programming environments which can be viewed as a result of this marriage. An intelligent programming environment combines the features of ITS and programming environments and emploies both AI and HCI techniques.

First, an intelligent programming environment supports both the activities of a teacher and a student, and includes tools from both the above lists. The following systems provide good examples of this: BIP [2] (task sequencing and program visualization), Lisp-Tutor [1] and ACT Programming Tutor [11] (structural editor and guided program design), Bridge [5] and Discover [10] (guided program design and program visualization), ELM-PE [22] (selection of examples, intelligent debugging, and program visualization), GIL [17] (visual editor, guided program design and visualization), and Molehill [20] (program explanation and on-line adaptive help).

Secondly, an intelligent programming environment attempts to employ both AI and HCI techniques to support all kinds of activities listed above. In particular, it means using AI techniques within the "student" list and using HCI techniques within the "tutor" list. Good examples of this are intelligent program visualization [12] and guided visual programming [17].

There are two groups of problems in the design of an intelligent programming environment: how to use the AI and HCI techniques to design a tool which supports the given student or tutor activity, and how to integrate the given set of tools into a complex environment. The above mentioned systems provide us with good examples of solving problems of the first group. Note that applying AI techniques appears to be more difficult and less cost effective than applying HCI techniques. As a result, most of the existing intelligent programming environments use both AI and non AI tools to support the required set of activities.

The problems of building an integrated intelligent programming environment seem to be less investigated. We referred above to a number of environments which are made up of several specialised tools. However, some of these environments are more boxes of independent tools than really integrated Systems. For example, the task sequencing component and visualizer in BIP [2] are absolutely independent tools. An integrated system ought to be more than just the total sum of a number of specialised components. Components of an integrated system should be interrelated. First, one component should be able to use the capabilities of another component as well as exchange or share data with it. Secondly, the results of students' work with any of the components during the session should be taken into account by all the components and used in adapting to the knowledge level and style of work of the particular student. Careful design and both AI and HCI techniques should be used to achieve these features.

To investigate the ways of building an integrated intelligent programming environment we have designed the Intelligent Tutor, Environment and Manual for Introductory Programming (ITEM/IP) [7]. ITEM/IP is an intelligent programming environment for the mini-language Turingal which is used in an introductory programming course (see the next section). Taking this simple language, let us design a complete environment with a good set of tools as well as concentrate our efforts on problems of integration. ITEM/IP supports the following student and tutor activities: knowledge sequencing, task sequencing, selection of program examples, student program checking, counterexamples selection, program editing, access to pre-stored examples and previous solutions, program debugging and investigation, and on-line help. To integrate all the listed tools we used ITS (student models [19]) and HCI (adaptive interfaces [3]) techniques. Briefly speaking, the results of students' work with the pedagogic component are reflected in the overlay student model and used by system components as a basis for adapting to the knowledge level of the particular student. A brief overview of ITEM/IP and a short description of system components are presented in the following sections. We do not discuss here the details of ITEM/IP development which can be found in the paper [7].

2. Learning Introductory Programming with Turingal

The successful application of Logo "turtle graphics" has stimulated the development of a new approach towards learning introductory programming. Beginners learn what programming is, while studying how to control an executive (the robot, the turtle, etc.) which acts in a microworld environment and can change its position and the environment according to a set of commands. The executive can be controlled by means of a simple mini-language which, in addition to these commands, includes more or less complicated structural statements (loop, condition, etc.). The environment, as well as the position of the executive in it, are permanently displayed on the screen and thus, the student is able to see the result of the command execution immediately. The Karel language [18] serves as a good example of an educational mini-language.

While learning a mini-language, the student, from the first steps, begins to write and debug the informative programs that control the executive. During this process many of the fundamental notions of programming are learned easily and quickly, and the skills of program development and debugging are acquired. For many students, the experience they get while using this language, as well as the general feeling of programming, is quite enough for achieving the desired level of "computer literacy".

The method of learning introductory programming with the aid of mini-languages is quite well developed in Russia now. A number of mini-languages are used to support introductory programming courses in Russian schools and universities. The mini-language Turingal (Turingal = Turing machine + Pascal) was specially designed to support an introductory programming course for the first-year students of the Department of Applied Mathematics and Cybernetics of the Moscow State University. This language is an alternative way to control the well-known system of algorithmic theory - Turing Machine works with a tape of symbols. The elementary operations of the mini-language are simple and visual: the movements of the machine head left and right along the tape and typing the symbols on the tape. To control the machine head, Turingal offers a wide range of control structures (conditional statement, loops, case, subroutines) with syntax and semantics similar to the structures of Pascal. The mini-language approach and the language Turingal are described in more detail in [9].

3. Learning with ITEM/IP

The following styles of learning programming are supported by ITEM/IP:

1) Exploratory learning. The student can make use of a complete set of tools for program design and debugging known as the programming laboratory. One of the functions of the laboratory is to support visual program execution. With the help of the laboratory the student can observe the "behaviour" of programs, experiment with them and gradually learn from his/her observations and mistakes. The ITEM/IP programming laboratory, like BIP [2], and the ReGIS [13] laboratories, support the exploratory style of learning: design the program - experiment (run the program) - observe - change the program - experiment again, etc. This style of work enables the student to learn the programming concepts and construction from the experience, to "discover" features, and to get an idea of programming technology.

2) Guided learning and free learning. To the inquiry of the student, ITEM/IP selects the currently optimal teaching operation and presents it to the student: it explains new programming concepts, demonstrates semantics of programming language construction, or tests the understanding of it, presents an example solution for a relevant programming problem or suggests a problem for the student to write a program solution. The optimal operation is selected using a built-in strategy that takes into consideration the knowledge that ITEM/IP has about its domain and the student. If the student is not satisfied with the embedded strategy, s/he can also choose a teaching operation from a list of relevant ones suggested by the system. The student uses the programming laboratory to experiment with presented examples and to solve problems.

3) Learning by repeating and on-line help. At any time a student can demand a re-explanation of past material, including presentation of related examples and analysis of related problems. The extent to which material is explained by ITEM/IP is inversely proportional to the current student knowledge about the material. Therefore a repeated explanation is usually more concise than the original one. This mode offers an on-line reference access to the learned material of the course.

Students spend most of the time in ITEM/IP working with the programming laboratory. With the help of the main menu, the student can at any moment call the pedagogic component for a new teaching operation, information, help, or checking the solution of the solved problem. ITEM/IP ensures the continuity of the student's work: the results of the student's work with each of the ITEM/IP components are stored by the Student Model and used by other components to adapt behaviour to the knowledge level of the student.

4. An Architecture of ITEM/IP

The main components of ITEM/IP are the pedagogic module, the programming laboratory, and the conceptual kernel, which includes the domain model, the student model and the base of teaching operations.

4.1 Conceptual Kernel

The domain model in ITEM/IP is the network which contains interconnected elements of conceptual and procedural knowledge. We use three kinds of nodes in the network: high level programming concepts (for example: loop), constructs of the studied programming language (for example: *while* statement) and skills for using the constructs in a context (for example: using negative condition in *while*). The nodes are linked with the following relations: general/specific (IsA), part-of and usage. The latter relationship links a construct-usage with the construct itself (for example: the mentioned skill is linked to *while* by an IsA link and is linked to a "negative condition" constructed by a usage link.

The Student Model, a kind of overlay model, is based on the Domain Model. For every Domain Model concept, The Student Model contains several integer counters for the purpose of indicating the extent to which the student has mastered a concept. Besides a set of counters, the Student Model includes optimal difficulties for all kinds of teaching operations. The Student Model is always kept up-to-date and supports adaptive work of all the environment modules.

The Base of teaching operations is a set of frames of three kinds: the concept frames mentioned earlier, example frames and problem frames. The pedagogic module uses these frames to build teaching operations of five kinds. Independence of frames makes it possible to expand the base with ease.

Example frames and problem frames are the two main kinds of frames. An *example frame* includes the text of the example (the language construct) and a set of input data "tests" by which this construct can comprehensively be demonstrated. Using this data, the pedagogic module organises a visual demonstration of the construct's semantics and "mental execution" tests checking the acquisition of semantics.

A *problem frame* includes a title, a problem text, a set of test data, a variant of the plan, a model solution and the problem complexity. A problem can be analysed as an example or given to the student to be solved. A special slot is used to link the Base frames with the Domain Model. This slot lists all Domain Model concepts related to the given frame. This list is called the spectrum of the frame.

4.2 Programming Laboratory

The programming laboratory is a set of special "software tools". The tools support the design, debugging and investigation of Turingal programs by the student. The laboratory includes a structured editor which makes it easier to enter and correct a program, and a visual interpreter which enables the student to run programs step by step and observe its work. The interpreter visually displays all machine head moves and symbol typing on the tape and also marks the current operator.

The student uses the programming laboratory in the *independent* mode for experiments and solving problems presented by the pedagogic module. The pedagogic module uses the laboratory in the *controlled* mode to perform teaching operations (see next section). In both these modes, the programming laboratory components adapt their work to a specific student using the student model. It is on the basis of the student model in particular, that the extent to which various language constructs must be visualized is determined: the less studied the construct is, the more detailed the visualization.

For example, when the construct of compound conditions is introduced, it will be visualized in detail as sequence of "steps" of interpretation. Each of the elements of the compound conditions will be visually checked in a separate step and the result (true or false) will be also visually presented in a separate step. On the next level of visualisation granularity stepwise condition checking is substituted with single-step checking, then the visual effect of checking switched off, and follow on. If the compound condition is already studied completely (last level) it will not be visualized at all and just will be passed by the flow of control pointer.

Error handling by the interpreter and error message generation also depends on the student model. More details about adaptive error handling and visualization in ITEM/IP can be found in [8].

4.3 Pedagogic Module

The pedagogic module controls the process of learning at the "macro" and "micro" levels. On the "macro" level the pedagogic module compiles a list of teaching operations relevant at a given moment and chooses the optimal teaching operation. The optimal operation is chosen using the student model and the built-in teaching strategy, which takes into account the tasks' spectra and complexities [6].

On the "micro" level the pedagogic module manages a dialogue with the student during the performance of the teaching operation, chosen at the "macro" level or by the student her/himself. When the teaching operation is complete, the pedagogic module evaluates the results of the students' work with the teaching operation and updates the student model. Performing a teaching operation, the pedagogic module widely uses the programming laboratory tools. The student model is used to adapt the performance to the knowledge level of the given student.

The pedagogic module deals with the five main kinds of teaching operations: presentation, demonstration, test, problem analysis and problem to solve.

Presentation introduces (or reminds the student of) a piece of conceptual knowledge: programming concept or construct. While introducing a concept (construct), its description as well as information about its relations with other concepts is presented. The description of each concept is stored in the concept's frame. The text of the description can be broken up into fragments. Each fragment is connected with the threshold value of one of the student model counters. The fragment is not presented if the counter for the concept exceeds this threshold. According to the method given above, during a re-presentation (presentation as repetition) of concept, descriptions are usually more laconic. Information about the relations of a given concept is not stored but is generated by the system. While presenting a concept, information is generated only about relations with previously studied concepts. During the re-presentation, more complete information about relations is usually given, since by this time, a greater number of concepts have been studied.

Demonstration of language construct semantics and *Tests* that check the student's understanding of the given construct are performed with the help of the interpreter using example frames stored in the Base of teaching operations. In a demonstration, the behaviour of the chosen construct is first demonstrated on a set of tests and then the student has a chance of experimenting with the example. In a test, the student is given the initial state of the tape (test), and then, having mentally executed the construct tested, s/he can enter the result. The answer is then compared to the result obtained by the interpreter.

Programming problem is the most important kind of teaching operation. The text of the given problem is displayed and then explained in the form of the "test-result" pairs. Additional explanations, a plan for solving the problem and hints as to how the program should work (visualization of model program actions without presenting the text of the actual program), can be requested as help. Solutions are checked out by the interpreter which consecutively compares the student's program's results on the given set of tests with that of the model program. If the results of any of the tests do not coincide, the mistake is fixed and "explained" by a visual demonstration of the student's program wrong behaviour on this counterexample test. Our experience has shown that this is a very effective way of remediation.

Programming problem analysis gives the student a practical idea as to how to use the skills s/he has learned. During the analysis the student is consecutively given the text of the problem, offered a plan of action and in the end given a model solution, whose work is demonstrated on tests. Next, the model program is presented to the student for experimentation. Any previously analysed or solved problem can be re-analysed on demand.

The sequence of language study in ITEM/IP is not fixed. The system can generate an optimal sequence of teaching operations for the given student. The human teacher can tune the teaching strategy to match her/his way of tutoring by setting an individual teaching order for any student [8]. The individual teaching order is a sequence of subsets of domain model nodes. At the beginning of teaching the nodes of the first subset are activated. Then the activated subset of nodes is taught with the use of the teaching operation selected by the tutoring component until the moment when the values of all counters related to the activated nodes exceed the mastery threshold or until the moment when all the relevant teaching operations are exhausted. Then the next subset of nodes are activated in the same way.

5. Progress and Status

The version of ITEM/IP described in this paper was designed and implemented for the Soviet mainframe computer BESM-6. We have tested ITEM/IP for a year in the learning process among first year students of the Moscow State University and 14 years old students of Moscow schools. A more detailed description of ITEM/IP and some experience with the system can be found in [7]. In particular, we have found that the ITEM/IP visual interpreter could strongly help the teacher to solve the problem of debugging student programs. In about four fifths of all cases to identify the bug it was quite enough for a student to run the wrong program visually with a test data suggested by the system. Only in one fifth of cases did the student (usually a weaker student) need the teacher to help to understand the bug.

The second extended version of ITEM/IP is being developed for personal computers. It is important that ITEM/IP-II will be able to update the student model while observing free student activity in designing and debugging programs.

Summary

An intelligent programming environment can be viewed as a set of tools that supports different teacher and student activities in the process of learning programming. An interesting problem is how to integrate the given set of tools into a complete environment that ought to be more than just the total sum of a number of components.

We have designed an intelligent programming environment ITEM/IP, which supports both teacher and student work in the course of introductory programming.

ITEM/IP components are tightly integrated. One component widely uses the capabilities of other components and the results of students' work with pedagogic components are stored in the student model and used by all components in adapting to the knowledge level of the particular student. The student model of the ITEM/IP performs the traditional elaborative [19] functions of a student model, as well as some adaptive interface support [3] functions of a user model.

The approach described above is not limited to learning Turingal only. It can be used to design an intelligent programming environment for Pascal, C, or another language.

References

1. Anderson, J.R. and Reiser, B.: The LISP tutor. Byte. 10 (4), 159-175 (1985)
2. Barr, A., Beard, M. and Atkinson, R.C.: The computer as tutorial laboratory: The Stanford BIP project. International Journal on Man-Machine Studies. 8 (5), 567-596 (1976)
3. Benyon, D., Murray, D.: Experience with adaptive interfaces. The Computer Journal. 31 (5), 465-473 (1988)
4. Bertels, K., Vanneste, P. and De Backer, C.: An evaluation of different approaches in novice programming analysis. In P.Brusilovsky and V. Stefanuk (eds.) Proc. East-West Conference on Emerging Computer Technologies in Education, 1992, Moscow, pp. 36-40. Moscow: ICSTI 1992
5. Bonar, J. and Cunningham, R.: Bridge: an intelligent tutor for thinking about programming. In J. Self (ed.), *Artificial Intelligence and human learning. Intelligent computer aided instruction*, pp. 391-409. London: Chapman and Hall 1988
6. Brusilovsky, P.L.: A framework for intelligent knowledge sequencing and task sequencing. In C. Frasson, G. Gauthier and G. I. McCalla (eds.), Intelligent tutoring systems. Proc. of II Internat. Conference ITS'92, Montreal. Lecture Notes in Computer Science, vol. 608, pp.499-506. Berlin: Springer 1992.
7. Brusilovsky, P.L.: Intelligent tutor, environment and manual for introductory programming. *Educational Technology and Training International*. 29 (1), 26-34 (1992)

8. Brusilovsky, P.L.: Student models and flexible programming course sequencing. In I. Tomek (ed.), Supplementary Proc. 4-th Internat. Conference on Computers and Learning, Wolfville, Canada, pp. 8-10. Wolfville 1992
9. Brusilovsky, P.L.: Turingal - the language for teaching the principles of programming. Proc. 3-rd European Logo Conference 1991, Parma, pp. 423-432. Parma: A.S.I. 1991
10. Ramadhan, H. and du Boulay, B.: Programming environments for novices. This volume
11. Corbett, A.T. and Anderson, J.R.: Student modeling in an intelligent programming tutor. This volume
12. Eisenstadt, M., Price, B.A and Domingue, J.: Redressing ITS fallacies via software visualization. This volume
13. Heines, J. and O'Shea, T.: The design of rule-based CAI tutorial. *International Journal of Man-Machine Studies*. 23 (1), 1-25 (1985)
14. Hohmann, L., Guzdial, M. and Soloway, E.: SODA: a computer-aided design environment for the doing and learning of software design. In I. Tomek (ed.), Computer Assisted Learning. Proc. of 4-th Internat. Conference ICCAL '92, Wolfville, Canada. Lecture Notes in Computer Science, vol. 602, pp. 307-319. Berlin: Springer 1992
15. McCalla, G.I. and Greer, J.E.: Two and one-half approaches to helping novices learn recursion. This volume
16. McCalla, G.I., Greer, J.E. and Scent Research Team: SCENT-3:An architecture for intelligent advising in problem-solving domains. In C.Frasson, G. Gauthier (eds.), Intelligent Tutoring Systems: At the crossroads of artificial intelligence and education, pp. 140-161. Norwood: Ablex Publishing 1990
17. Merril, D.C., Reiser, B.J., Beekelaar, R. and Hamid, A.: Making process visible: scaffolding learning with reasoning-congruent representations. In C. Frasson, G. Gauthier and G. I. McCalla (eds.), Intelligent tutoring systems. Proc. of II Internat. Conference ITS'92, Montreal. Lecture Notes in Computer Science, vol. 608, pp.103-110. Berlin: Springer 1992
18. Pattis, R.E.: Karel - the robot, a gentle introduction to the art of programming. London: Wiley 1981
19. Self, J.: Student Models: What use are they?. In P.Ercoli and R. Lewis (eds.), Artificial intelligence tools in education. Proc. of the IEP TC3 working conference on AI tools in education, 1988, pp. 73-85. Amsterdam: North-Holland 1988
20. Singley, M.K., Carrol, J.M. and Alpert, S.R.: Incidental reification of goals in an intelligent tutor for Smalltalk. This volume
21. Soloway, E.: PROUST. Byte, 10 (4), 179-190 (1985)
22. Weber, G.: Analogies in an intelligent programming environment for learning Lisp. This volume

Programming Environments for Novices

Haider Ramadhan* and Benedict du Boulay

School of Cognitive and Computing Sciences, University of Sussex, Brighton, BN1 9QH, UK.
*permanent address: Math. and Computing Dept., Sultan Qaboos University, Sultanate of Oman.

Abstract: We describe DISCOVER, a tutor for elementary programming that combines a free phase, in which students may experiment in building and executing programs of their own, with a guided phase where problems are set and their solutions monitored. The system embodies a visible, executable, concrete model of the notional machine. When setting a problem, the system offers example solutions of similar problems. A pilot experiment is described to investigate the effects on problem-solving, during the guided phase, of providing the concrete model and the similar examples.

Keywords: Intelligent Tutoring System / Programming / Visualisation / Examples

Introduction

Opponents of intelligent programming tutoring systems (ITS) argue that these systems have not fulfilled their early promise in assisting novice programmers to overcome the abstraction and difficulty found in programming, and that some hard effort is needed to come up with alternative approaches to the design of systems for novice programming. Programming systems, they claim, that are based on visualisation [7], microworlds [15] or learning by example [14] techniques may prove to be more effective than current systems (e.g. [2,9]).

The way forward, therefore, should be a joint endeavour between visualisation, microworlds and ITS. A practical example along this path is represented by the intelligent discovery programming system DISCOVER [16,17,18]. DISCOVER does not view the issue of visualisation as simply a question of animating program execution (program visualisation [13]) nor of displaying different values of variables during execution, but of supporting a high-level, integrated, conceptual and concrete environment that allows novices to relate problem-solving with the dynamic behaviour of both language and machine. To achieve this, DISCOVER integrates visibility, program visualisation, and a concrete, dynamic model of the underlying computer system, the notional machine [6], with which the novice user is interacting [10].

An Overview of DISCOVER

DISCOVER is an intelligent programming environment that synthesizes domain visualisation and microworlds with automatic, active program diagnosis and tutoring. DISCOVER works in two phases. In the *free* phase, users may construct whatever programs they like

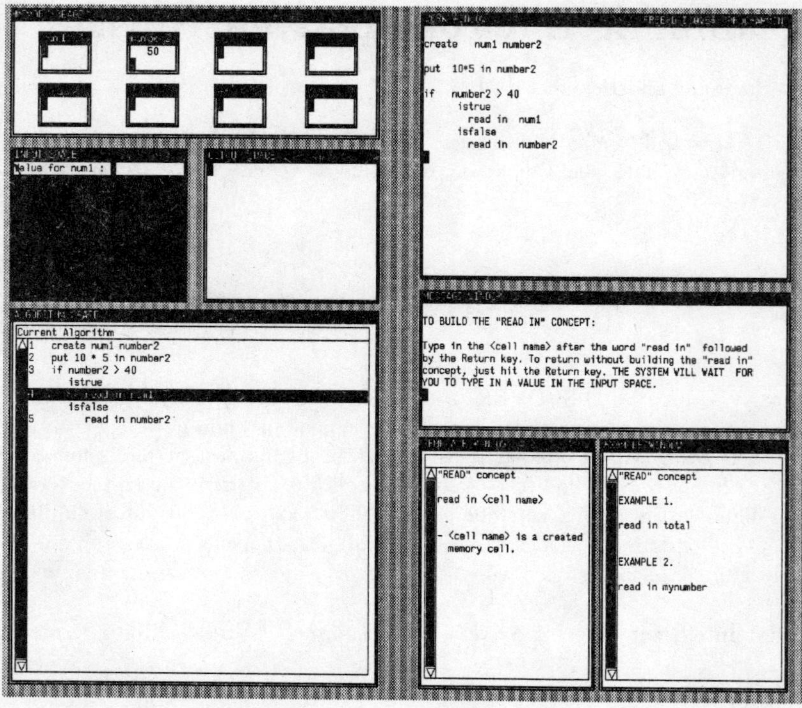

Figure 1: A snapshot of DISCOVER's free phase interface

and there is no comment on these programs from the system. In the *guided* phase, DISCOVER sets problems and monitors the users' solutions. Figure 1 gives a snapshot of DISCOVER's environment during free phase.

Free Phase

The aim of the free phase is to enable novice users to build a robust and clear mental model of the dynamic behaviour of both individual programming concepts, whole programs as well as of the underlying notional machine. The system (1) through *visibility*, helps novices visualise otherwise hidden and internal changes in some conceptual parts of the underlying computer system such as the memory space. This includes, for example, visualising how variables are named, how they get their values, and how the corresponding memory cells in the memory space are affected; (2) through *program visualisation* (highlighting the line currently being executed) it helps novices understand how their programs statements are executed and how control flows from one line to another and how their programs dynamically behave; and (3) through a *concrete model* of the underlying computer system (dynamic notional machine), helps novices conceptualise the properties of the machine they are interacting with and thus build an accurate model of its behaviour (see Ramadhan [19] for a detailed discussion on DISCOVER's main design decisions and features).

The programming language of DISCOVER is a pseudo-code based, algorithm-like language. The language is simple in order to reduce the number of abstract programming ideas and concepts and omits procedures and recursion, avoids having too many programming tricks to be learned, and avoids requiring the learning of low-level syntax details. Programming concepts supported currently include CREATE, PUT, READ IN, WRITE OUT, WHILE-ENDWHILE and IF-ISTRUE-ISFALSE. The interface (shown in figure 1) appears to the user as a collection of eight windows. The four windows on the left side of the interface, namely the *Memory Space*, the *Input Space*, the *Output Space* and the *Algorithm Space*, represent the notional machine.

The selections in the *Programming Concepts Menu* contain the beginning of phrases. Each phrase corresponds to one programming concept. When the user selects a concept, its corresponding name is inserted into the work window and all the user has to do is complete it by typing in its parameter part (e.g. the names of the memory cells to be created). Any syntactically incorrect parameter parts provided by the novice are trapped by the syntax-directed editor and reported in the *Message Window*.

Once a concept is completed it appears in the Algorithm Space Window, where the code so far entered is stored. Immediately after the statement moves across to the Algorithm Space Window, DISCOVER visually executes it and instantly shows the changes that take place in the memory space, input space or output space windows. For example, executing a CREATE concept causes a cell from the array of cells in the Memory Space Window to be named. Any assignment, either via the PUT or READ IN concept, to a memory cell shows up immediately in that cell. Input and output, via READ IN and WRITE OUT concepts, occur in the Input Space Window and Output Space Window. At any time during the free phase, the novice can load pre-stored programs and visualise their dynamic behaviour and can add, delete or modify program statements on-line in real time.

Figure 1 shows a small program being built in the Algorithm Space window which makes use of two variables (see the Memory Space window) together with some data input (see the Input Space window).

Guided Phase

The aim of the guided phase is to teach the the novice to compose and coordinate programming concepts and statements to solve given programming problems under the guidance of the intelligent programming expert, and thus build effective problem-solving skills.

The user has two main sources of help in learning how to solve programming problems. The first is the guidance he gets from the system about the adequacy of each statement he chooses to include in his solution. The second is set of pre-stored *similar* problem statements and example solutions which are displayed along with each problem to be solved.

During the guided phase, DISCOVER selects the next problem from the problems library and presents its specification in the Problem Description Window. At present, the next problem to be solved is selected by DISCOVER's domain expert in a predetermined order which does not vary across students. For each problem, the system selects a similar example problem that is relevant to the current problem and displays this example problem along with its example solution in the Example Solution Window. Again, at present, the examples are pre-determined for each problem.

The user has to build his solution to the current problem by properly putting together programming concepts shown in the Programming Concepts Menu. Once a concept is completed and accepted by the Syntax Directed Editor, it is passed to the intelligent

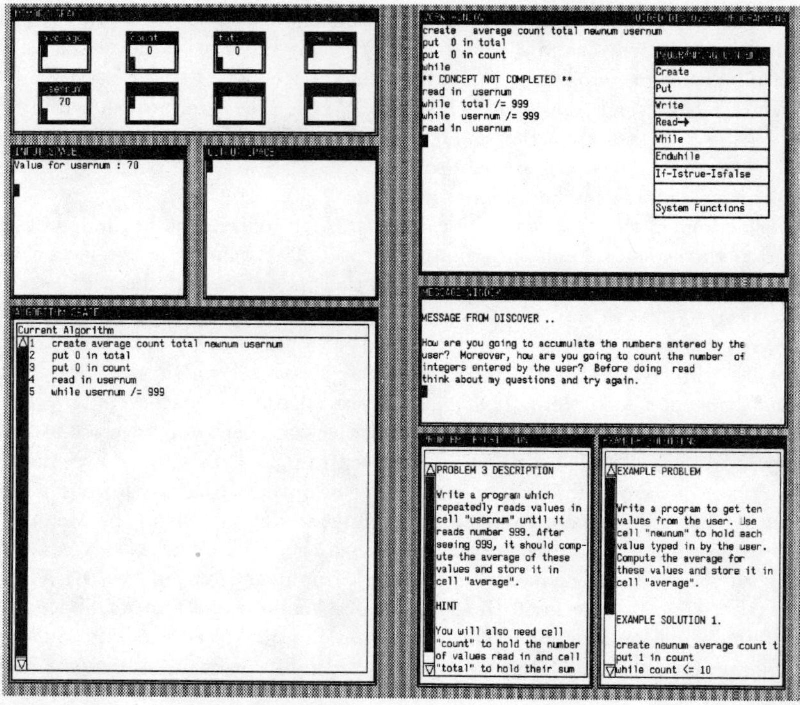

Figure 2: Dealing with a misconception in the guided phase

component of DISCOVER (the domain expert) for automatic debugging and analysis. In doing so, DISCOVER attempts to model the steps taken by the user by evaluating his actions and responses. DISCOVER analyzes the surface code of the completed statement (partial solution code) without much specific knowledge about the problem to be solved or about how to design and construct an algorithm (i.e. DISCOVER cannot solve the problem itself).

Much like Laura [1], Talus [12], Aurac [8] and Bridge [5], DISCOVER relies on a prestored reference solution (the ideal student model) for a given problem and applies various heuristics and pattern matching techniques to match the solution code provided by the novice with the reference solution in order to spot errors and misconceptions. Unlike these systems, however, DISCOVER is capable of interactively analyzing partial solution code and providing immediate feedback on both success and failure. By doing that, DISCOVER explicitly guides the novice in the process of putting together programming concepts to solve the given problem. A complementary paper [20] describes how DISCOVER represents its knowledge of the reference solution; how it conducts the automatic matching of the novice's solution to the reference solution; and how it handles the problem of nondeterminism in novices' solutions.

DISCOVER monitors the novice's actions, not on a symbol-by-symbol basis, but on a complete concept-by-concept basis. As long as each concept represents a correct goal on a solution path, DISCOVER continues guiding the novice towards the final goal, reasoning about the goals already satisfied and hinting at the goals that still remain to be satisfied. Figure 2 gives an example of error feedback and shows a problem description, a partial answer (in the *algorithm space*) together with a similar problem and part of its solution (in the *example solutions* window).

Automatic Program Diagnosis

Many automatic program debugging systems, including Proust [9], Talus [12], Aurac [8], BIP [4], and Laura [1], cannot debug partial code segments and wait until the entire program code is completed before attempting any debugging analysis. As a result, these systems lack any rich interaction with the users *during* program construction. DISCOVER is a model-tracing system capable of debugging a partial solution as is provided by the novice user. To be able to monitor users' progress in putting programming concepts together and decide when to interrupt and what to say, DISCOVER emphasizes not only the final solution but also intermediate states on the solution path that the novice has to go through during problem-solving.

Several programming systems and tutors do support the debugging of partial solutions, among which are GREATERP [2], Bridge [5], and GIL [21]. Unlike Bridge, which requires the novice to specifically request the automatic analysis of his program (passive-like mode), DISCOVER, like GREATERP and Gil, supports active, automatic debugging, and thus is capable of monitoring each step that the user may take.

Unlike GREATERP and GIL, however, DISCOVER (1) utilises goals and plans (not a production system) to represent the knowledge of its domain expertise, (2) does not keep an account, at least currently, of common error patterns (the buggy model), (3) supports an explicit planning mechanism during all stages of the problem-solving process to trace the user's intentions (e.g. by selecting the concepts from the menu during problem-solving, the user non-intrusively tells the system his intentions and goals), (4) supports an ability to give delayed feedback by increasing the grain size of automatic diagnosis to a complete programming statement (not just a single symbol or token) and an ability to do limited backtracking by giving the user some chance to delete previously entered code and restart, and (5) provides feedback not only on failure but also on success.

Empirical Investigations

To evaluate the effectiveness of DISCOVER's programming environment, we have conducted three experiments, of which one is reported in detail here. The first experiment aimed at determining the effects of domain visualisation on the way novices comprehend the dynamic behaviour of programming concepts, of whole programs and of the underlying notional machine during the free phase only. The results of this experiment suggest that novices who work through a sequence of problems and solutions using the free phase are better able to predict the behaviour of programs than novices who work through the same sequence of problems using a special version of the free phase that masks out the visualisation features.

The second experiment analysed the experience of novices who went directly to the guided phase without passing through a preliminary free phase experience. Results suggest that novices who went directly to the guided phase made more logical errors, more syntactic errors and took longer to solve problems than those who spent some time with in the free phase, even though the total time on task for the two groups was roughly comparable.

The third experiment (described below) attempted to determine the effects of domain visualisation and example-based learning on the way novices solve programming problems during the guided phase.

Eight novice programmers (with no or very little programming experience) took part in this study. Four novices used a full domain visualisation system DISCOVER while four others used a modified version of DISCOVER, which masked out all the visualisation features (e.g. memory cells, visual execution and the model of the machine) as well as relevant example cases and solutions. Both groups took a pen and pencil programming quiz prior to the experiment. The performance on the quiz showed that both groups had a reasonably compatible programming knowledge. The experiment started by showing all the subjects how to use their assigned system. Each subject explored the system in a free, open-ended mode for fifteen minutes and then moved on to solve a total of three programming problems under the guidance of an intelligent tutor.

Evaluation Measures

Only two key performance measures were considered for evaluating and analyzing the results: (1) the total number of logical errors across all three problems and (2) total time spent on these problems (speed of solution). The first measure was based on observing and computing the frequency of deviation from a correct solution path for both groups. Only logical errors were considered in this measure. Logical errors included either failure to select a correct programming concept that corresponds to the next goal on the solution path (design or goal-level error) or selecting a correct concept but failing to complete it correctly by providing relevant parameters that correspond to plans needed to satisfy the next goal (implementation or plan-level error), for example selecting "read newnum" when "read usernum" is required (and newnum has been declared).

The second measure (speed of solution) was based on how long it took the DISCOVER subjects to solve all three programming problems. This total time in minutes was compared with the time it took the control subjects to complete solving the same set of problems using the modified system.

All the syntax errors that resulted from improperly completing the selected concepts in DISCOVER's programming language, and the time associated with correcting them were excluded from the evaluation measures analyzed in this study. An example of a syntactic error would be "put usernum in 10" rather than "put 10 in usernum". In the experiment, the criterion for distinguishing between logical and syntactic errors was based on which part of the system reacted to the error.

The two key measures (number of logical errors and speed of solution) were compared to determine whether DISCOVER, through its domain visualisation and example-based learning features, had any effect on the way novices put together programming concepts to come up with higher-level plans (programs) for the given exercises. It could be argued that simply taking the total number of logical errors during problem-solving is only a weak basis for a comparison and that a more informative measure would be a comparison of the particular kinds of errors made by the two groups. We accept this criticism but argue that the comparative total numbers of errors are at least indicative of the relative difficulties faced by each group.

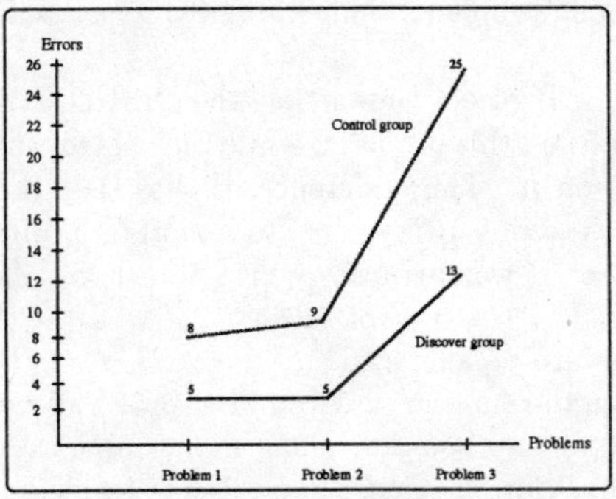

Figure 3: Error totals

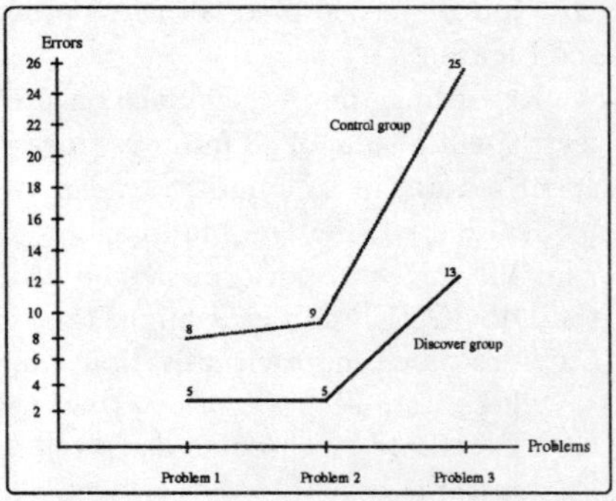

Figure 4: Solution speeds

There is also the issue of training effects on the total time spent. Both groups were learning how to master the system, the language and the problem-solving so one needs to be careful when taking absolute values of time taken. However the comparative total times do provide suggestive evidence of relative difficulty, given that the two groups were going through similar training. An experiment we have not conducted (one of many) would be to compare relative problem-solving speeds of two groups each with similar equivalent mastery of the system (modulo their understanding of the notional machine).

Number of Errors

The mean for the number of errors for the DISCOVER group across three problems during the guided phase is 5.75 and for the Control group is 10.50. This implies that the subjects in the DISCOVER group made an average of 1.92 errors on each problem, while the subjects in the control group made an average of 3.5 errors on each problem. The difference in means suggests the superior performance of the DISCOVER group. Overall, the control group made about 83% more errors to complete all three programming problems than the DISCOVER group, see Figure 3.

Problem 3 was the hardest and most difficult one. The problem was the 'Ending Value Averaging Problem', which required the inclusion of several programming concepts that would satisfy the following programming plans: a counter value plan, a running total plan, a controlled loop plan, an input plan and an averaging plan. Figure 3 shows that the DISCOVER group made a total of 13 errors on this problem, and that the control group made a total of 25 errors on the same problem. This difference implies that the control group using the modified version of the system made about 92% more errors on problem 3.

Speed of Solution

The mean for the number of minutes for the DISCOVER group across three problems during the guided programming phase is 22.75 and for the control group is 28.75. This means that the subjects in the DISCOVER group spent an average of 7.58 minutes on each problem, while the subjects in the control group spent an average of 9.58 minutes on each problem. This difference in means suggests superior performance for the DISCOVER group. Overall, the control subjects using the modified version of DISCOVER took about

26% longer to complete all three programming problems than the DISCOVER subjects, see Figure 4.

Regarding the performance on problem 3, Figure 4 shows that the DISCOVER subjects spent a total of 58 minutes (mean = 14.5) on this problem, while the control subjects spent a total of 67 minutes (mean = 16.8) on it. This difference implies that the control subjects using the modified system took about 16% longer to complete problem 3. This difference in performance on solution speed was little surprising to us. We thought the DISCOVER subjects might take longer than the control subjects, since DISCOVER provides much more visualisation information to be analyzed.

There were several reasons to expect that the superior environment provided by DISCOVER would be associated with *greater* total time spent on the programming exercises. First, after submitting the completed statement for automatic analysis and immediate execution, DISCOVER subjects consistently spent some time on analyzing the effect of that statement on the underlying computer system by scanning through the cells in the memory space. In fact, our observational data are strongly consistent with this view. Second, whenever a programming solution included a loop, DISCOVER executed the solution in a stepped-execution mode, requiring the subjects to click on the mouse to continue with the execution of the next statement in the loop. Whereas in the modified system, neither visualisation nor stepped-execution were supported. Finally, our observational data show that DISCOVER subjects spent a total of 17 minutes (18% of the total time) on analyzing relevant example solutions. This behaviour is obviously expected to increase the total time spent by the group.

Despite these reasons, the DISCOVER subjects took less time to complete their programming exercises. We do not have a good explanation for this finding other than (1) the control subjects made more errors than the DISCOVER subjects (10.50 errors/subject vs. 5.75 errors/subject). Making more errors simply implies that the control subjects had to make a new selection from the concepts menu and then re-enter the entire statement. This process obviously increases the total time spent during the problem-solving and (2) since visualisation and relevant example solutions are not supported by the modified system, the control subjects had to mentally simulate the execution of the program solution which they were completing and imagine its dynamic behaviour and side-effects: a task novice programmers normally find very difficult. Unfortunately, our observational data does not include any indication about how much time subjects in both groups spent between statements, i.e. how long it took these subjects to complete the next statement (step) after submitting the current one for automatic analysis and execution.

Conclusions

In conclusion, the analysis of this experimental study seems to suggest that DISCOVER through its domain visualisation and example-based learning features appears to help novices in solving programming problems more accurately and more quickly. It could be interpreted that (1) being able to visualise different computational states of the problem-solving process seems to help novices in conceptualising the overall solution path and direction and in satisfying individual requirements of the problem description, (2) being able to visualise the dynamic behaviour of programs and machine provides novices with a clear mental model of programming that enables them to solve problems more accurately and quickly, (3) providing novices with feedback on a successful step along the solution path which tells them how close they are to the final goal state seems to help them in getting motivated and focus them more on satisfying the remaining requirements of the problem. This feedback was not supported by the modified system. Finally and more importantly (4) providing novices with relevant example solutions seems to help novices in tackling exercises they are presented with. Among visualisation and relevant examples, we do not know for sure which contributed more to this superior performance of the DISCOVER subjects. It could be that an accurate mental model of program execution and machine behaviour that these subjects developed through visualisation resulted in this performance. Another plausible explanation for this finding may be due to the fact that the relevant example solutions, either on their own or in relation to visualisation features, made it possible for the DISCOVER subjects to conceptualise the high-level solution direction and path. Obviously, more experimental studies are needed to clarify this point. Overall, the DISCOVER programming environment facilitated the problem-solving process; greatly reducing the number of logical errors and total time spent. These results are similar to those for GIL [11] where an explicit model of execution of Lisp expressions has been found to speed learning and reduce errors, and for another visual model of Lisp, DRLP, where students were found to be better able to self-correct their programs given a visual model of data flow [3].

There are several limitations associated with the results reported here. Firstly, because of the very small number of subjects in each group, it is very difficult to generalise the findings and results of these experiments. It is quite possible that larger group sizes may generate different results. Secondly, programming exercises that were presented to the subjects were very few (three exercises only) and involved small programs, instead of many, medium-level or large programs. Finally, programming in DISCOVER covered only basic programming concepts, and the language had no provision for more abstract concepts and data types such as procedures, functions, recursion, records, arrays and lists.

Acknowledgement

DISCOVER is fully implemented in POP-11 using the POPLOG programming environment developed at the University of Sussex. Haider Ramadhan thanks the Math. and Computing Dept., Sultan Qaboos University, PO Box 32490 Al-Khod, Sultanate of Oman for their support.

References

1. Adam, A. and Laurent, J. LAURA, A System to Debug Student Programs. *Artificial Intelligence* 15 (15): 75-122, 1980.
2. Anderson, J. R., Boyle, C. F. and Reiser, B. J. Intelligent Tutoring Systems. *Science* 228, 456-462, 1985.
3. Anjaneyulu, K.S.R. and Anderson, J.R. The Advantages of Data Flow Diagrams for Beginning Programming, in C. Frasson, G. Gauthier and G.I. McCalla (Eds.) *Intelligent Tutoring Systems*, second international conference ITS'92, Lecture Notes in Computer Science, Vol. 608, Berlin: Springer-Verlag, 1992.
4. Barr, A., Beard, M., and Atkinson, R. The Computer as a Tutorial Laboratory. *International Journal of Man-Machine Studies* 8, 567-596, 1976.
5. Bonar, J. G. Intelligent Tutoring with Intermediate Representations. *Proceedings of the First Conference on Intelligent Tutoring Systems, ITS-88*, Montreal, Canada, 1988.

6. du Boulay, J.B.H., O'Shea, T. and Monk, J. The Black Box Inside the Glass Box: Presenting Computing Concepts to Novices. *International Journal of Man-Machine Studies*, 14, 237-249, 1981.
7. Eisenstadt, M. Software Visualization: Redressing ITS Fallacies. *Proceedings of NATO ARW on Cognitive Models and Intelligent Environments for Learning Programming*, Italy, 1992.
8. Hasemer, T. *An Empirically-Based Debugging System for Novice Programmers.* Ph.D. thesis, The Open University, UK, 1983.
9. Johnson, W. *Intention-Based Diagnosis of Errors in Novice Programmers.* Ph.D. thesis, Yale University, USA, 1985.
10. Mayer, R. E. The Psychology of How Novices Learn Computer Programming. *Computing Surveys* 13, 121-141, 1981.
11. Merril, D.C., Reiser, B.J., Beekelaar, R. and Hamid, A. Making Processes Visible: Scaffolding Learning with Reasoning-Congruent Representations, in C. Frasson, G. Gauthier and G.I. McCalla (Eds.) *Intelligent Tutoring Systems*, second international conference ITS'92, Lecture Notes in Computer Science, Vol. 608, Berlin: Springer-Verlag, 1992.
12. Murray, W. *Automatic Program Debugging for Intelligent Tutoring Systems.* Ph.D. thesis, Texas University, Austin, USA, 1986.
13. Myers, B. A. The State of the Art in Visual Programming and Program Visualization. *Carnegie Mellon University Technical Report*, Computer Science Department, Carnegie Mellon University, USA, 1988.
14. Neal, L. A System for Example Based Programming. *Proceedings of CHI'89 Conference on Human Factors in Computing Systems*, USA, 1989.
15. O'Shea, T. Seminar at University of Sussex.
16. Ramadhan, H. A Discovery Programming System. *CSRP Technical Document No. 200*, Computer Science and AI, Sussex University, Brighton, UK, 1991.
17. Ramadhan, H. An Intelligent Discovery Programming System. *Proceedings of ACM Symposium on Applied Computing (SAC'92): Special Track on Visuality in Computing*, Kansas City, USA, 1992.
18. Ramadhan, H. Intelligent vs. Unintelligent Programming Systems for Novices. *Proceedings of the IEEE Conference on Computer Systems and Applications (COMPSAC'92)*, USA, 1992.
19. Ramadhan, H. Intelligent Systems for Programming by Discovery: A Design Methodology. In B. du Boulay & V. Sgurev (eds.) *Artificial Intelligence V*, Proceedings of the 5th International Conference on Artificial Intelligence: Methodologies, Systems, Applications (AIMSA'92), Sofia, Bulgaria. Amsterdam: North-Holland, 235-245, 1992.
20. Ramadhan, H. Improving the Engineering of Knowledge Representation for Active, Automatic Program Diagnosis. *Proceedings of the 5th International Conference on Knowledge Engineering*, Madrid, Spain, 1992.
21. Reiser, B., Kimberg, D., Lovett, M. and Ranney, M. Knowledge Representation and Explanation in GIL, an Intelligent Tutor for Programming. *Cognitive Science Laboratory Report*, Princeton University, NJ, USA, 1988.

Student Modeling in an Intelligent Programming Tutor

Albert T. Corbett and John R. Anderson

Psychology Department, Carnegie Mellon University, Pittsburgh, PA 15213, USA

Abstract: The ACT Programming Tutor helps students as they complete short programming exercises. The tutor is constructed around an ideal student model consisting of several hundred production rules. This model allows the tutor to solve exercises along with the student and serves as an overlay model of the student's knowledge. As the student completes exercises, the tutor maintains an estimate of the probability that student has learned each rule, based on a two-state learning model. These estimates are employed to guide remediation. This paper assesses the predictive validity of this modeling process, and examines the implications for the rules in the ideal student model.

Keywords: Student modeling, intelligent tutors, mastery learning

Introduction

One of the promises of intelligent tutoring systems is increased learning rates. Tailoring the learning environment to the individual student should enable the student to obtain a higher level of understanding and performance from a given investment of time. While there are other significant characteristics of learning, e.g., fostering a student's motivation to spend time on a task, it is difficult to quarrel with this goal. Learning rate can be viewed as the issue of time on task defined at the level of cognitive modeling. If we have an accurate cognitive model of the task and a model of the student's knowledge state, we can optimize learning by (1) guiding the student toward activities that lie on the frontier of the student's knowledge and (2) providing help that mimimizes the student's floundering in acquiring new knowledge. The ACT Programming Tutor (APT) is an intelligent programming environment that is intended to further each of these goals. Much of our research over the past five years has examined the issue of error feedback and floundering [5,6]. In this paper we consider the goal of tailoring activities to the individual student. In particular, we examine the tutor's knowledge tracing mechanism which is intended to optimize remedial practice, allowing the student to achieve mastery. We report a recent assessment of this mechanism and focus on the implications for the cognitive model that underlies the tutor.

The ACT Programming Tutor

The ACT Programming Tutor is a practice environment for students learning to program [3]. It presents exercises that require the student to write short programs and monitors the student's behavior on a symbol-by-symbol basis. The program has Lisp and Prolog modules, which are used to teach a self-paced introductory programming course at Carnegie Mellon University. In this report we focus on the Lisp module. Figure 1 displays the tutor interface, near the start of a Lisp exercise. The exercise description appears in the upper left window and the student's solution is displayed immediately below in the code window. The interface is similar to a structure editor. The student enters code essentially one symbol at a time, either by typing or through the menu on the lower right. In Figure 1, the student has just entered the operator *car*. The tutor has expanded a template for this function call in the code window, providing balanced parentheses and an editor node or goal symbol, <EXPR0>, that represents an argument to the function. The student will replace this node with the Lisp expression *'(c d e)*.

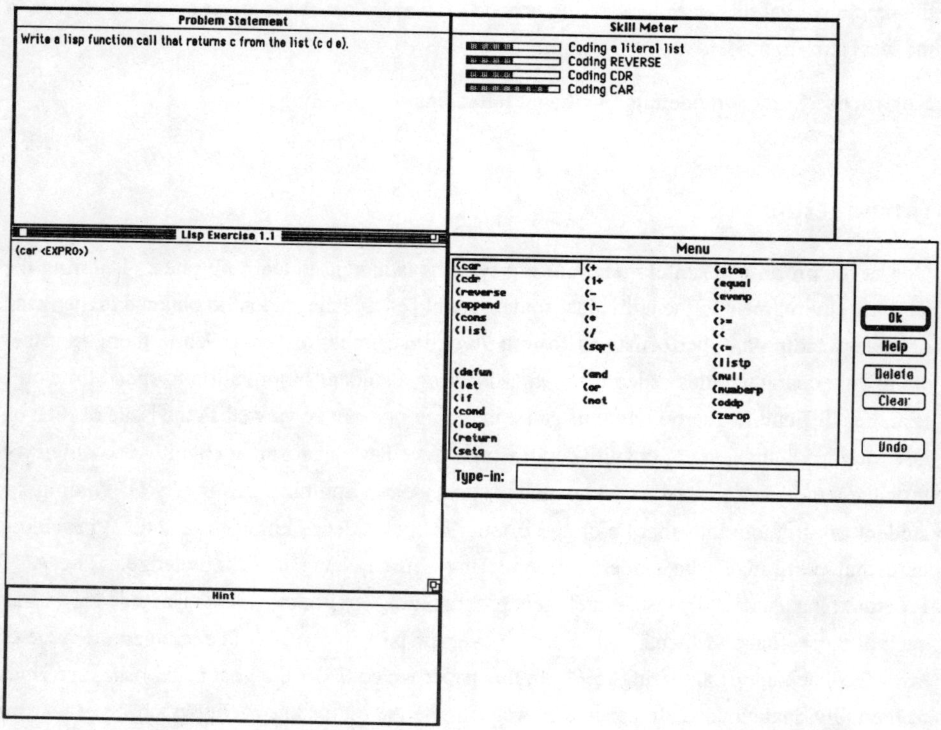

Figure 1. The APT interface near the beginning of an exercise

The tutor provides immediate feedback on each each code symbol the student enters. If the student makes a mistake, the tutor notifies the student in the help window on the lower left and does not display the symbol. The student is then free to try another symbol, ask for help, or switch to working on another node. Three levels of help are available at each goal node. In response to successive help requests at a node the tutor presents: (1) a description of the current goal, (2) an explanation of how to achieve the goal and (3) a description of the exact action to perform.

The remaining window in the upper right corner is the skill meter, which displays the tutor's model of the student. As described below, the cognitive model that underlies the tutor consists of a set of rules for writing Lisp code. As the student works, the tutor maintains an estimate of the probability that the student has learned each rule in the set, in a process we call *knowledge tracing*. The learning probability for each of these rules is displayed graphically for the student in the skill meter. In Figure 1, four rules have been introduced. The learning probability is approximately 0.80 for one rule and 0.50 for the other three rules. The present report focuses on this knowledge tracing process. A recent assessment indicates that the predictive validity of knowledge tracing is quite good [7]. In this paper we discuss how this knowledge tracing assessment can be used to evaluate the cognitive model (rule set). In the following sections we describe the curriulum under consideration, the corresponding cognitive model, the tutor's learning and performance model and finally, an evaluation of the cognitive model.

The Curriculum

This knowledge tracing evaluation focused on the first five sections of the APT Lisp curriculum. These five sections introduce two basic data types, atoms (symbols) and lists (symbols grouped in parentheses), function calls (operations) and function definitions. Students learn three extractor functions, *car*, *cdr* and *reverse*, that return information from a list, three constructor functions, *append*, *cons* and *list* that build new lists, and the operator *defun*, which is used to define new functions. An example exercise from each section is displayed in Table 1.

The Cognitive Model

The tutor was developed to test the ACT* theory of skill acquisition [1]. The theory assumes that programming knowledge can be modeled as a set of production rules. The tutor is constructed around an expert system consisting of several hundred such if-then rules for writing programs, called the *ideal student model*. Two productions would be employed in coding the first exercise displayed in Table 1. These productions are:

IF the goal is to return the first element of a list <list>,
THEN code a function call to *car* and set a goal to code <list>.

IF the goal is to code a literal list <literal-list>,
THEN code a single quote followed by <literal-list>.

This ideal model plays two roles in the tutor. First, it allows the tutor to solve the exercise step-by-step along with the student in a process we call *model tracing*. As the student enters each code symbol, the tutor attempts to match the action to an applicable rule in the model. If a match is found, the tutor accepts the symbol and updates its internal representation of the problem state. If not, the tutor requires the student to try another action. Second, in knowledge tracing, the student is represented as an overlay of the ideal model [8]. As the student works through the exercises, the tutor maintains an estimate of the probability that the student has learned each rule in the ideal model.

Table 1. Five example exercises from the APT Lisp tutor

Section	Exercise
1 Extractors	(car '(c d e))
2 Combiners	(list 'x 'y 'z)
3 Extractor Algorithms	(car (cdr '(horse dog cat)))
4 Function Definitions [a]	(defun second-to-last (lis) (car (cdr (reverse lis))))
5 More Definitions [b]	(defun replace-first (itm lis) (cons itm (cdr lis)))

[a] extractor algorithms, [b] constructor/extractor algorithms

The cognitive model for the present curriculum consists of a total of twenty-one rules. These rules are displayed in Table 2 below. Four rules introduced in the first section govern the coding of the three extractor functions, *car*, *cdr* and *reverse*, and literal lists. Two of these rules are displayed above. Four rules introduced in section 2 govern the coding of the three constructor functions, *append*, *cons* and *list* and literal atoms. Note that the same rule may apply more than once in an exercise. The rule that codes a literal atom applies three times in coding the second exercise in Table 1. Four rules introduced in section 4 concern the coding of function definitions. One codes the operator *defun*, one codes the name of the new function, a third rule applies for each variable being declared in the parameter list, and the fourth applies each time a variable is referenced in the body of the function.

In section 3 the student learns to code algorithms involving nested extractor functions. For example, in exercise 3 of Table 1, students learn to extract the second element of a list by (1) applying *cdr* to remove the first element of the list, then (2) applying *car* to return the new first element. The cognitive model assumes that the student is essentially learning to reason about nested function calls in this section and that knowledge about each of the three extractor functions will generalize from section 1. As a result, two rules in the model govern the coding of all extractor algorithms in this section. One codes the outermost function call, e.g., *car* in our example. The second rule applies in coding each nested function call, e.g., *cdr* in our example. In section 4, students learn to code function definitions involving nested extractor functions. The model assumes that the two rules learned in section 3 will generalize to the function body in section 4. In section 5, students learn to code definitions involving constructors and extractors. Three separate rules are introduced that govern the coding of the three constructors in this context, while a single rule governs the coding of an extractor or the initiation of an extractor algorithm as the argument to a constructor.

Finally, three rules model interface actions, specifically the deletion of extra editor nodes. One rule deletes an extra argument node in a constructor function call, one deletes of an extra variable declaration node in the parameter list and one deletes an extra argument node in a call to *defun*.

The Learning and Performance Model

In addition to a cognitive model, knowledge tracing requires learning and performance assumptions. For this purpose, the tutor assumes a simple two-state learning model with no forgetting. That is, each coding rule is either in the learned or unlearned state. A rule can make the transition from the unlearned to the learned state at each opportunity to apply the rule, but rules do not make the transition in the other direction. Within this framework, the task is to maintain an estimate of the probability that the student has learned each rule, conditionalized on the student's performance. The Bayesian computational procedure used is a variation of one described by Atkinson [4] and is reported elsewhere [7]. This procedure employs two learning parameters and two performance parameters:

pL_0 the probability a rule is in the learned state prior to the first opportunity to apply the rule (i.e., from reading the text)

pT the probability a rule will make the transition from the unlearned to the learned state following an opportunity to apply the rule

pG the probability a student will guess correctly if a coding rule is not in the learned state pS the probability a student will slip (make a mistake) if a coding rule is in the learned state

The values of these parameters are estimated empirically from earlier tutor data.

The goal of knowledge tracing is to implement mastery learning. In each section of the curriculum, students complete a set of required exercises that covers the set of rules introduced, then continue working on remedial exercises in the section until the learning probability of each rule has reached 0.95. The underlying model, however, also allows us to predict accuracy at each goal (step) in completing the tutor exercises. The probability of a correct response at a goal is the sum of two probabilities (a) the probability that an applicable production rule is in the learned state times the probability the student will not slip and (b) the probability the rule is not in the learned state times the probability a student will nevertheless guess correctly.

Student Modeling Assessment

The knowledge tracing mechanism satisfied a weak validity test in an early assessment [2]. Students who worked through the tutor exercises with knowledge tracing in operation performed better on posttests than students who only completed the required exercises. In the present research, however, we undertook a more detailed assessment of just the first five sections of the curriculum. We examined the results of forty-one students enrolled in our programming course in a recent semester. Knowledge tracing was in operation and the four learning and performance parameters were held constant across the twenty-one production rules as follows: $pL_0 = 0.50$, $pT = 0.40$, $pG = 0.20$ and $pS = 0.20$. Students completed an average of 14 remedial exercises, with a range of 1 to 38 exercises, in addition to twenty-five required exercises. Since knowledge tracing drives the learning probability for each production rule for each subject to a minimum of 0.95, there is insufficient variability to assess how well these learning probabilities predict posttest performance. Instead, we focused on the model's predictions for accuracy in completing the tutor exercises.

We computed actual error rates across the forty-one subjects for each of the 158 goals in the twenty-five required tutor exercises and correlated these with the predicted error rates derived from the knowledge tracing mechanism. This correlation was reliable, $r = 0.47$, $p < .05$. However, the expected values deviated systematically from the actual values. As a result, we refit the data allowing the four learning and performance parameters to vary across the twenty-one programming rules (best fitting parameter estimates were generated with a curve fitting program). This revised set of parameter estimates yielded a much better fit to the error rate data, $r = 0.85$. One consequence of refitting the data with revised parameters is that the final learning probabilities for the production rules no longer necessarily exceed 0.95. The mean learning probability for the twenty-one rules ranged from 0.89 to 1.0 across the forty-one subjects. These mean learning probabilities for the rules in the cognitive model correlated reliably with posttest performance, $r = 0.47$, $p < .05$. See [7] for more details.

Parameter Estimates: Implications for the Cognitive Model

To evaluate the cognitive model in more detail, we can examine the curve fitting results for each of the twenty-one production rules. Table 2 displays the best fitting parameters for each rule. The correlation of the empirical and theoretical learning curves for each rule is also displayed (i.e., the correlation of empirical and theoretical accuracy estimates across successive opportunities to apply a rule). The average correlation coefficient in Table 2 is 0.66, suggesting that the model is fitting the individual rules reasonably well (while the correlation of 0.85 for the overall set of 158 goals is achieved in part by fitting accuracy differences among rules). Nevertheless, inspection of the correlation coefficients and parameter estimates in the table suggest that some of the rules lack psychological validity.

Goodness of fit is the strongest indicator of the validity of a rule. By this criterion, two rules are obviously weak: Start-extractor-algorithm and Code-cons-with-extractor-argument(s). However, the parameter pT is also an important indicator of psychological validity. Recall that a low value of pT means students who don't already know a rule are unlikely to learn it at each opportunity to apply it. This suggests that the rule in the cognitive model may be too general; as students practice they are not learning a rule that generalizes across the expected contexts. By this criterion, all three extractor algorithm rules, introduced in sections 3 and 5, are suspect, as are the three constructor rules introduced in section 5.

The performance parameters pG and pS (the probability of a guess and a slip), also provide some secondary information. In curve fitting these parameters were constrained not to exceed 0.33 and 0.10 respectively. If the best fitting estimates hit these constraints, it suggests that model does not fit the data well. The pattern of r, pT, pG and pS values as a whole suggest that Code-literal-list rule in section 1 and the three combiner rules in section 2 are suspect. This result may reflect difficulties that students have in grasping the hierarchical structure of lists.

Finally, consider the three rules involving variables in section 4 (including the rule that deletes an extra node in the parameter list). The r and pT values for these rules are respectable on the whole, but the pG and pS estimates tend to be high. When we plot the learning curve for the rule that declares a variable in the parameter list, as in Figure 2, there is evidence of the difficulty some students are encountering. This figure displays error rates for successive opportunities to apply the rule. We would expect such a learning curve to be monotonically decreasing and error rates do decline fairly regularly across the first four opportunities. However they rise at the fifth and sixth goals. These two goals represent the first exercise in which students must declare two variables in a single function (exercise 5 of Table 1) and the sixth goal in particular is where that second variable is declared. The figure suggests that instead of learning the ideal rule - declare one variable for each argument to the function - some students are learning a buggy rule - always declare one variable - that happens to work for the exercises in section 4. While the curve is generally well fit by the model, the performance parameters are driven up in trying to fit the peak at goal 6 and an analogous peak at goal 11.

Table 2. Parameter estimates and correlation coefficients for the twenty-one rules in the cognitive model

	pL0	pT	pG	pS	r
Section 1					
Code Car	0.53	1.00	0.00	0.03	0.91
Code Cdr	0.93	1.00	0.32	0.00	1.00
Code Reverse	0.78	0.68	0.00	0.00	0.99
Code Literal List	0.15	0.27	0.33	0.10	0.78
Section 2					
Code Append	0.45	0.12	0.00	0.10	0.44
Code Cons	0.73	0.28	0.33	0.01	0.64
Code List	0.56	0.54	0.33	0.10	0.39
Code Literal Atom	0.17	0.43	0.00	0.00	0.92
Delete Extra Argument Node	0.13	0.96	0.03	0.04	0.97
Section 3					
Start Extractor Algorithm	0.31	0.07	0.33	0.10	0.09
Complete Extractor Algorithm	0.76	0.03	0.33	0.00	0.63
Section 4					
Code Defun	0.80	0.99	0.10	0.05	0.73
Declare Function Name	0.86	0.44	0.04	0.07	0.54
Declare Variable in Parameter List	0.43	0.76	0.33	0.09	0.65
Delete Extra Parameter List Node	0.55	0.64	0.33	0.09	0.73
Code Variable	0.53	0.09	0.33	0.08	0.67
Delete Extra Top Level Node	0.65	0.72	0.33	0.01	0.94
Section 5					
Code Append with Extractor Arg(s)	0.46	0.03	0.00	0.00	0.76
Code Cons with Extractor Arg(s)	0.56	0.04	0.00	0.10	-0.46
Code List with Extractor Arg(s)	0.12	0.39	0.06	0.10	0.87
Start Extraction Arg to Constructor	0.57	0.12	0.08	0.00	0.65

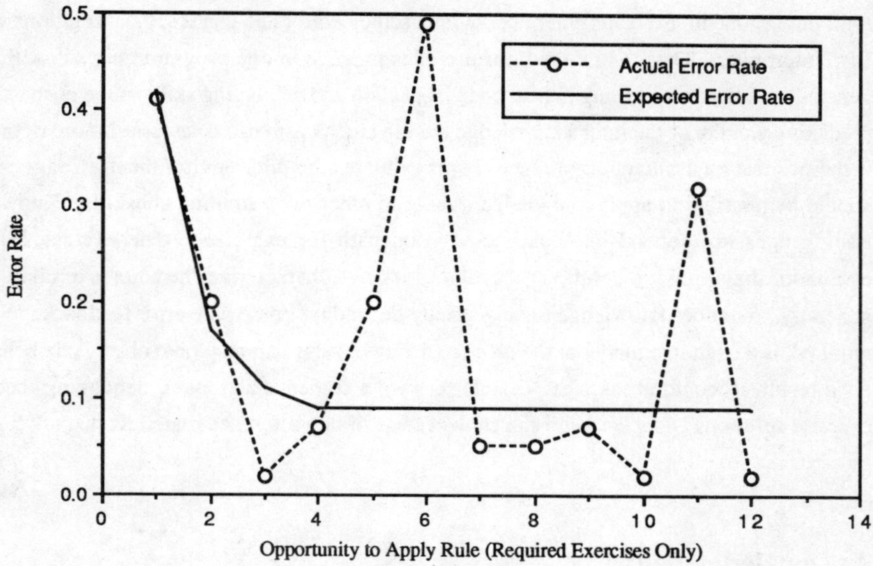

Figure 2. Actual and expected error rate across for the ideal student rule that declares a variable in a function definition across successive opportunities to apply the rule.

Discussion

The knowledge tracing procedure was quite successful at predicting tutor performance, accounting for about 70% of the variance. However, we have begun revising the cognitive model in light of the present analysis. In particular, we have restructured the literal list and the constructor rules in the early sections, the extractor algorithm rules and the rules concerning variables. The resulting cognitive model, which only covers seven Lisp operators and two data structures, has expanded to thirty-five rules. Clearly even the relatively elementary knowledge acquired in the initial phase of a programming course is complex.

The knowledge tracing procedure was reasonably successful at predicting posttest performance, accounting for 20% of the variance. There are several reasons we would not expect a stronger relationship is this assessment. Since it was conducted in the context of a course, for example, the retention interval between the tutor exercises and posttest and the amount of studying for the posttest were uncontrolled. We plan to incorporate forgetting into knowledge tracing, (i.e., allowing rules to move from the learned to the unlearned state). The current assumption that there is no forgetting may be a reasonable simplication when students are completing a short sequence of tutor exercises, but it is obviously not generally true.

There are other interesting reasons that knowledge tracing does not strongly predict posttest performance. The posttest environment in this evaluation is substantially different from the tutor environment. Students enter code with a screen editor and can test their solutions with a Lisp interpreter. Thus, while the tutor provides practice in one programming subskill, code generation, students can bring to bear code inspection and debugging skills in the posttest. The predictive validity of the tutor's knowledge tracing mechanism can be assessed more rigorously if the posttest environment more nearly approximates the tutor environment. Conversely, it should be possible to apply knowledge tracing to other programming subskills. Knowledge tracing does not depend on a unique solution path for exercises. The exercises in this evaluation have unique solutions, but that does not characterize the tutor exercises more generally. Nor does knowledge tracing strictly depend on immediate error feedback. What is required, is a cognitive model of the task consisting of rules that map onto observable behavior. As a result, it would at least be possible to trace a student's actions in debugging incorrect exercise solutions and to monitor the student's use of any reference materials that are brought on-line.

Acknowledgement

This research was supported under grant N00014-91-J-1597 from the Office of Naval Research.

References

1. Anderson, J.R.: The architecture of cognition. Cambridge, MA: Harvard University Press 1983
2. Anderson, J.R., Conrad, F. G., Corbett, A.T.: Skill acquisition and the Lisp Tutor. Cognitive Science 13, 467-505, 1989
3. Anderson, J.R., Corbett, A.T., Fincham, J.M., Hoffman, D., Pelletier, R.: General principles for an intelligent tutoring architecture. In V. Shute and W. Regian (eds.) Cognitive approaches to automated instruction. Hillsdale, NJ: Lawrence Erlbaum (in press)
4. Atkinson, R.C.: Optimizing the learning of a second-language vocabulary. Journal of Experimental Psychology 96, 124-129, 1972
5. Corbett, A.T., Anderson, J.R., Patterson, E.G.: Student modeling and tutoring flexibility in the Lisp Intelligent Tutoring System. In C. Frasson and G. Gauthier (eds.) Intelligent tutoring systems: at the crossroads of artificial intelligence and education, Norwood, NJ: Ablex 1990
6. Corbett, A.T., Anderson, J.R.: Feedback control and learning to program with the CMU Lisp Tutor. Paper presented at the Annual Meeting of the American Educational Research Association, 1991
7. Corbett, A.T., Anderson, J.R. Student modeling and mastery learning in a computer-based programming tutor. Proceedings of the Second International Conference on Intelligent Tutoring Systems, Montreal, 1992. Lecture Notes in Computer Science, Vol. 608. Berlin: Springer 1992
8. Goldstein, I.P.: The genetic graph: a representation for the evolution of procedural knowledge. In D. Sleeman and J.S. Brown (eds.) Intelligent tutoring systems. New York: Academic Press 1982

Incidental Reification of Goals in an Intelligent Tutor for Smalltalk

Mark K. Singley, John M. Carroll, and Sherman R. Alpert

IBM T.J. Watson Research Center, Yorktown Heights, NY 10598, USA

Abstract: We describe the design of an instructional system for Smalltalk that attempts to provide feedback on learners' goals and plans through a technique called *incidental reification.* We contrast our approach with other current attempts at reifying learners' goals and plans and sketch out problems and prospects for future work.

Keywords: Intelligent tutoring, object-oriented programming, cognitive modelling.

Minimizing the Smalltalk Mountain

Smalltalk, although recognized as a good platform for rapid prototyping and software reuse, is widely regarded as difficult to learn. Programming in Smalltalk involves adopting the object-oriented, message-passing model of program design and execution and becoming familiar with a large set of existing object classes, methods, and their inheritance relationships. Unlike learning a procedural language like Pascal or C, learning Smalltalk is dominated by browsing and code comprehension. Learners of Smalltalk typically experience a long, slow startup phase in which they become familiar with the hierarchy and object-oriented model but do little meaningful work (this has been dubbed climbing the Smalltalk mountain). In an industrial environment, this is particularly troublesome because of the real or perhaps perceived need to get started quickly. Many learners never make it to the top of the mountain, and abandon the language before becoming proficient in it.

Molehill is an instructional system for Smalltalk which attempts to minimize the Smalltalk mountain. Molehill combines elements of intelligent tutoring technology with more tool-like elements like hypertext and keyword search to create an instructional environment which is more structured than exploratory learning, yet less constraining than traditional tutoring. The goal of Molehill is to not only provide learners with tutoring support through a semi-structured curriculum of simple yet meaningful projects, but also provide learners with a set of tools that function both inside and outside of the tutoring context, thus minimizing the transition to real work situations. The intended audience for the system is experienced procedural programmers.

Perhaps the most important component of Molehill is an information display called the

Goalposter. The Goalposter displays the system's ongoing interpretation of the learner's actions in terms of inferred goals and plans, a kind of goal blackboard that maintains the learner's current goal tree. An important property of the Goalposter is that its contents are updated automatically and incidentally in response to the learner's conventional use of standard Smalltalk system tools. We call this property the *incidental reification of goals*, in contrast to the approach where goal structures are constructed directly by the learner. Figure 1 shows a screen image of Molehill; the Goalposter pane is in the lower-left corner.

In this paper, we outline the design of the Goalposter. We first briefly discuss several prior attempts at goal and plan-based instruction in tutoring systems, and then describe the design of our system. We motivate our design by appealing to observations we've made of the problems of novice Smalltalk programmers.

Goals and Plans in Tutoring Systems

A great deal of instructional leverage comes from an accurate and complete task analysis of the domain and the successful communication of that analysis to the student [1]. This is especially true for the more strategic aspects of a skill. Goal and plan knowledge is what drives proficient problem solving, yet its explication is typically absent from traditional pedagogy. One example of the successful communication of planning structures to students is in the Related Rates Tutor [9]. The Related Rates Tutor helps first-year calculus students solve related-rates word problems. In an initial experiment with a prototype version of the system, it was discovered through analyses of verbal protocol data that students were attempting to execute a fairly standard means-ends strategy to solve systems of equations, but were having trouble formulating and maintaining the requisite subgoals. To remedy this problem, an enhancement to the interface of the tutor was designed which allowed students to post and display the subgoals required by the means-ends strategy. As students progressed through problems, individual subgoals were boxed and shaded to indicate which were active and which had been satisfied, respectively. An experiment testing the effects of this type of planning discourse showed that student problem solving performance improved in terms of both speed and quality of moves while the goal blackboard was present.

Furthermore, many of the positive effects persisted after the goal blackboard was taken away, suggesting that the blackboard was not only a performance aid but also a learning catalyst.

This work supports the view that goal structures should be made a subject of tutorial discourse. However, the usefulness of this principle may be limited by the fact that it may be difficult to find a transparent representation for goals and plans in some domains.

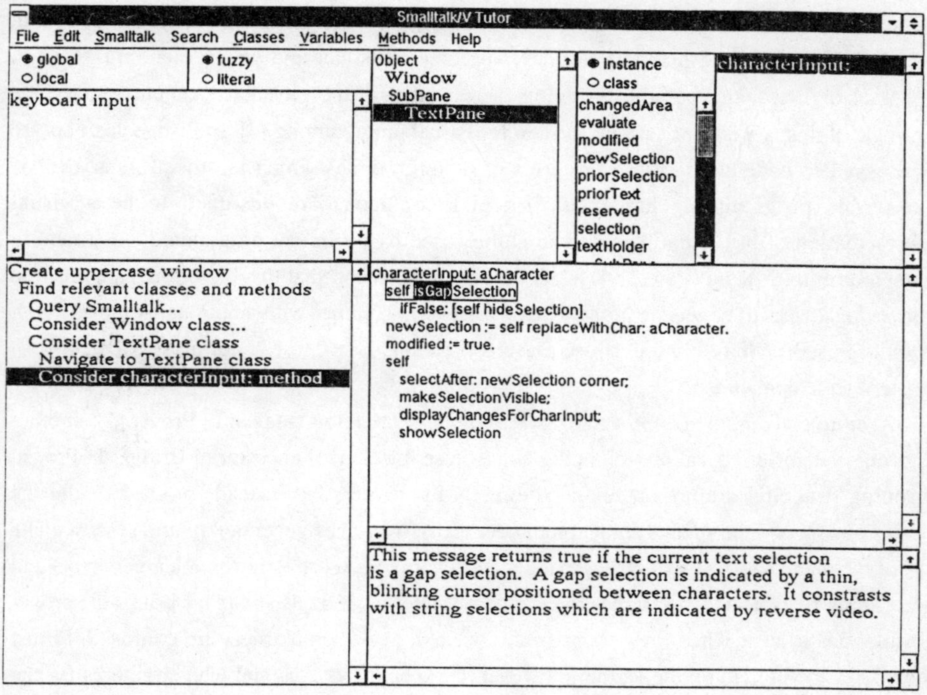

Figure 1. Screen image from Molehill. The Goalposter resides in the lower left pane. Most remaining panes belong to the class hierarchy browser. Here, the learner is looking for character input functionality and has just selected the characterInput: method defined in the TextPane class.

The problem is that the planning space is typically positioned at a level of abstraction far above what Newell & Simon [7] call the physical problem space, the space where actual operations are carried out. It may be that the goal manipulation worked in the Related Rates Tutor simply because the usual distinction between the planning space and the physicial problem space was for the most part degenerate: the goals themselves were very similar to the kinds of objects that students were manipulating in the physical problem space. This meant that students were not burdened with learning a new and abstract vocabulary for conversing about goal structures in this domain. However, in other domains, such as programming, the planning structures are more abstract and may have little meaning to the novice.

Wanting to support the planning process in their systems, some researchers have adopted the view that the planning structures they have discovered and codified can be communicated more or less directly to the student with beneficial effects. There are examples of systems in which the physical and planning problem spaces are distinct and yet learners are asked to generate plan structures prior to solving the problem in the physical problem space. One example of this is Bridge, a tutoring system for Pascal programming [3]. In Bridge, learners are first asked to code an algorithm in terms of planning icons which are themselves a fully-executable programming language. The planning icons are designed to be a visual representation of the actual planning structures used by proficient programmers as found in numerous empirical studies [12]. It is our suspicion, however, that this brute force approach to conveying abstract knowledge probably overwhelms the learner with additional complexity. It is quite possible that learning to use these formalisms is at least if not more difficult than mastering the domain itself.

A more conventional approach to goal and plan reification is taken in Proust [5], another tutoring system for Pascal programming and a close intellectual ancestor of Bridge. In Proust, planning structures are not manipulated directly by learners but instead are used "under the covers" by the system to analyze learner code. Error messages generated by the system make use of the plan analysis by referring to the underlying plans when describing learner errors and prescribing fixes. Having error messages couched in terms of goals and plans brings the proper abstractions to bear when they are critically needed, i.e. when learners are confused. Proust minimizes the burden on the learner, however, by keeping its goal and plan structures for the most part to itself. The cost, though, is that these abstractions aren't readily available and have no influence on the majority of learner problem solving. The only way a learner gets goal and plan information is by making an error, and then the information is restricted to the goals and plans pertinent to that error. The learner never receives a holistic analysis of the abstract structure of a problem.

Incidental Reification in the Goalposter

We emerged from our assessment of strategic instruction with a commitment to supporting tutorial discourse on goals and plans. We wanted to provide a holistic analysis of learner behavior, but felt it would be prohibitive to require learners to construct solutions with an abstract planning language. Our approach in the Goalposter is to have the system incidentally display an ongoing interpretation of the learner's actions in terms of hierarchical goal structures.

As learners browse the class hierarchy or write code, an object-oriented plan parser automatically updates the contents of the blackboard to reflect the system's current interpretation of the learner's actions. The interpretation may be that the student is on track and pursuing a reasonable course of action given the current project, or perhaps the student is doing something wrong. Although textual, the presentation of individual goals is telegraphic: several words at most. At any point, the student can expand any of telegraphic nodes in the goal blackboard for further explanation. The Goalposter is a facility for delivering task-oriented context-sensitive help at a level of granularity that is under the control of the student. The Goalposter is useful after a project is finished in that goal traces are saved for later inspection. It is our hope that these goal traces, if properly annotated, will support analogical problem solving outside of the context of the tutor.

Presently, only the Goalposter is permitted to post goals to the display. In order to get support from the tool, students are only required to recognize the posted goals and make the correspondence between the posted structures and their own behavior.

Empirical Observations and Design Decisions

To gain guidance for the design of our planning tool, we decided to make some observations of Smalltalk programmers working in the standard environment. Our goal was to better understand the processes of planning in Smalltalk so that we could support them without sacrificing what we felt were the strengths of the Smalltalk environment. For a more complete description of our empirical observations and how they were used to motivate the design of the system see [10-11].

To inform the design of our tool, we observed six persons of varying levels of expertise undertake an introductory yet representative project in Smalltalk: to create a window that transforms and displays all of its keyboard input in upper case. Four of these subjects performed the task on their own with no help from the experimenters; two were aided by a local Smalltalk expert acting in the role of a coach. The coach was instructed to intervene whenever it was felt to be appropriate, but to not be too directive or reveal too much of the solution in her comments. Our motivation in doing this was to observe the coach's behavior and thereby supply ourselves with a possible model for the Goalposter. This can be viewed as a fairly standard knowledge engineering situation, where the task is to extract the principles of operation from a highly-regarded yet poorly understood model (an experienced, articulate Smalltalk coach). All subjects were asked to give verbal protocols as they worked, and all were videotaped. From these observations, we tried to understand how features of the Smalltalk environment were influencing the behavior of our subjects, and further, how the problematic aspects of those features might be mitigated in our tool.

Goal Management

Many of our observations concerned problems associated with goal management. Programming in Smalltalk involves working with a large set of object classes, methods, and their inheritance relationships. Smalltalk provides a rich set of tools to help manage the complexity of the language, but these tools initially represent additional overhead for learners, making the Smalltalk mountain that much harder to climb. Anderson and Jeffries [2] documented the memory management problems plaguing beginning LISP programmers, and claimed many of their errors could be attributed to losses of information from working memory. One might expect that these problems would be even worse in Smalltalk. Indeed, our protocols contained striking examples of programmers getting confused, losing their place, and forgetting to perform stated objectives.

One of our subjects began the project by searching for those methods in Smalltalk that are responsible for processing keyboard input. After finding the characterInput: method, he deliberated over how to implement the solution, and finally announced a full-blown plan: "I'll subclass TextPane, redefine characterInput:, and change the initialization of TextWindow so that it has my new kind of pane in it." (This last goal, to modify TextWindow, is necessary because, in Smalltalk, panes do not function apart from windows.) He pursued each of these goals in turn with little difficulty. When redefining the characterInput: method, however, he simply forgot to add the message to transform the input to upper case prior to display in the pane. Thus, when he was finished, he had created a subclass of TextPane but had not overridden any of the standard TextPane functionality. Of course, when he went to test his solution, his new pane behaved like an ordinary TextPane. Rather than checking his new characterInput: method, he first reexamined the initialization of TextWindow, making sure he had in fact placed the right kind of pane in the window. Only after ruling out this possibility did he question whether he had made a mistake in his reimplementation of characterInput:. When finally discovering his error, he chided himself, "Oh, how stupid."

Based on this and other observations, it seemed clear that our subjects were having trouble managing the inherent complexity of the Smalltalk language and environment. Helping our students manage goal structures is complicated by the fact that Smalltalk's rich environment encourages incremental development and task switching. This kind of flexibility is good in terms of supporting rapid prototyping, but can only worsen task management problems for users. For example, early in the project, another subject switched freely between searching for the character input functionality, searching for the uppercase transformation functionality, and generating test code. As she switched between tasks, she spent time reestablishing the local goal context and reinstating her understanding of the state of her progress. Her protocol made us think carefully about how to update the goal display in such situations.

The Goalposter employs a variety of goal management techniques. As goals become active, they are posted to the display in green. They remain in green until they are satisfied, at which time their color changes to black. Whenever a goal is suspended in favor of some other goal, its structure collapses, i.e. only the top-level goal is shown in the display. The retention of the top-level goal in green serves as a reminder that the goal had been pursued but is now suspended.

Once the goal is resumed, the structure expands and new subgoals are added to the existing structure. Thus, the Goalposter provides a kind of fish-eye view of the current state of the project, with higher resolution shown for the currently active goal. The current goal is automatically selected in the display, which means that all Goalposter menu operations by default apply to the current goal. To the extent that goals are unordered, the tutor applies a recency principle in the delivery of help: provide the next step for the most recently posted unsatisfied goal.

Goal Evaluation

Given the complexity of programming in Smalltalk, programmers will, of course, commit errors, make poor choices, pursue incorrect paths. For example, while searching in class TextPane for the method that handles keyboard input, one subject opportunistically selected the *first* method she encountered which looked as if it might be appropriate, rather than looking more broadly for the *best fitting* method. Since methods are listed alphabetically, she happened upon appendText:, whose argument is a String object. This led to a long code modification and testing scenario, including a search for how to convert a String into upper-case, specialization of the appendText: method, and the construction of a testbed. Ultimately she determined appendText: is not the method which handles keyboard input. A similar scenario occurred for the next method she considered, appendChar:.

Extended searches can waste a programmer's time and energy and lead to goal management problems. On the other hand, investigating irrelevant methods and classes provides an opportunity for a programmer to learn about new portions of the class hierarchy. Though they may be irrelevant to the current task, they may be useful in others. Since reuse is so important in the Smalltalk environment, this sort of incidental learning is beneficial.

Informing a learner about the correctness of actions is perhaps the most basic sort of feedback a computer-based instructional system might provide. Time-consuming search episodes can be curtailed by informing leaners that certain goals should not be pursued. However, if feedback is too intrusive it can undermine planfulness [4], and, at least in this situation, can thwart opportunities for incidental learning. The Goalposter takes a compromise position: it provides feedback on the correctness of goals and actions but it remains in the background of the user's work and does not prescribe action. The Goalposter displays the text of an inferred goal colored either red or green. Green signifies an appropriate goal for the user to attempt, and red indicates a 'buggy', or incorrect or irrelevant, goal. The aim of this coloring scheme is to make salient whether the goal should be pursued. To gain a fuller understanding of the current goal state, the user may expand any red or green goal (by double-clicking on its text) to display an explanation of *why* the goal is a worthwhile one to pursue or not.

One thing we observed was that the coach reinstated learner goals when learners began to flounder. Another subject began the project by spending a protracted period in the Class Hierarchy Browser viewing numerous Window classes. He finally chanced upon the characterInput: method in the TextPane class. By this time, however, he was so completely engrossed in the vagaries of the Window subhierarchy that he had completely forgotten that the project specification had included the transformation of keyboard input to upper case, and in fact seemed to have forgotten that the project had specified any transformation whatsoever. He began to invent subgoals for himself, saying "Now what can I do with this method? Well, I could encode characters, or count them..." At this point, the coach intervened, "What do you have to do for this project?" He was surprised. "Oh, I guess I forgot." The coach reinstated the goal of the uppercase transformation, and he was on his way again.

This episode is consistent with other observations of human tutoring [6], and generally reinforced our commitment to the idea of the posting goals. Most interesting, however, was not what the coach did when learners were in trouble, pursuing inappropriate goals or forgetting goals, but what she did when learners were ostensibly on track. What we observed was that the coach delivered feedback on progress even when the learner was proceeding without difficulty. For example, the above subject often looked to his coach for confirmatory feedback for hypotheses and goals he considered pursuing. When searching for the class which handles textual keyboard input, he asked, "Will it be [a class] under ApplicationWindow?"; later, he sought confirmation when he saw and selected TextWindow as a potentially relevant class. The coach spent a significant amount of her time providing "yes, that's right" comments.

This protocol suggests that even when people are correct feedback can be useful. Such feedback encourages learners to pursue appropriate courses of action and builds feelings of confidence. In the case of the Goalposter, the system provides feedback not only on the correctness of an action but also an interpretation of why it's correct and where it fits into the overall solution. We hope this will help communicate the conceptual structure of the solution as it develops.

Goal Presentation and Representation

A major concern we have had is the comprehensibility of the Goalposter display. This concern centers on the complexity of the structure as a whole as well as the transparency of names of individual goals. We have already discussed our use of color coding and fish-eye views to try to manage the complexity of the display. A great danger is that the display will be viewed by learners as a complex addition to an already complex programming environment. In an attempt to avoid this pitfall, we have tried at every turn to simplify hierarchical relationships and use straightforward names for individual goals.

Interacting with concerns of complexity are the ambiguities inherent in plan recognition. There are many situations in which a learner is working on a programming project but the tutor does not yet have enough evidence to confidently make and display a subgoal hypothesis in the Goalposter. When we first thought about this problem, we had imagined posting fairly generic subgoals like "Find Functionality" &emdash for example this matches most ambiguous browsing episodes. But we eventually were forced to ask what was to happen when the learner takes actions that further specify the "true" subgoal, for example, selecting the characterInput: method?

Supposing that this method is part of the correct target functionality, should we post a new subgoal "Find characterInput: Functionality"? This would create rather inflated goal structures; indeed, in a sense, it creates an incoherence: "Find Functionality" is neither the parent nor the sibling of "Find characterInput: Functionality." Should we alter the original posting? This might confuse the learner, particularly if one considers other cases in which multiple subgoals might change as a consequence of a single user action. Should we reconsider having the tutor post a goal at all when it is still reasonably unsure what the current subgoal is (in this case, remaining mute until the characterInput: method is selected)?. This seriously weakens the on-line utility of Goalposter analysis as feedback to the learner. And in any case, it is not clear how long to remain mute: the learner who selected characterInput: might not have had the goal of doing so or might not have had it in the right way, to assess this (and there are still qualifications of course), we would have to wait until the learner *used* that functionality (or specialized it) later in the project. Of course, by that time it is no help at all to make this goal analysis, it is far more likely to just be confusing.

Another view of our problem is that the Goalposter combines the functions of a history of the solution process and a conceptual structure of the solution itself. The former role urges us to build the goal analysis in real time, linked closely enough to the learner's actions so that it can be an aid to making better sense of these actions. But we have to get the goal analysis reasonably right for it to be such an aid (this is the latter role), and that's difficult to do in real time. We want the learner to end up with a good conceptual representation of the problem displayed in the Goalposter. At any point in the solution process, we want the learner to have a good partial representation, one that is responsive to the learner's actions and that provides a dynamic index for help requests - but not one so good that it provides hints that undermine the learner's own problem solving.

In our current thinking on the Goalposter, we continue to struggle with this fundamental issue. Presently, the Goalposter tends to sacrifice immediacy of feedback for correctness of interpretation, i.e. the Goalposter remains mute until it is reasonbly confident it can post a subgoal that will not require updating. Another option we are considering is to create two separate tools, one to support the history list functionality of the existing Goalposter and one to support the conceptual structure functionality. The history Goalposter would provide early and continual feedback on user actions, but would be fairly non-committal in its interpretations.

The conceptual Goalposter would wait until enough behavior had been sampled to construct a reasonably strong interpretations relating user action to underlying problem structure.

Conclusion

Incidental reification as practiced in the Goalposter represents another approach toward supporting tutorial discourse on goals and plans. However, by taking this approach we are fundamentally changing the relationship between the learner and the system. Unlike a traditional tutoring system, the Goalposter provides a structured information resource which resides in the background of the learner's work and may be consulted or not at the learner's choosing. Ultimately, it is the learner who has full responsibility for managing his own help-seeking behavior. In this way, the Goalposter essentially blurs the distinction between a tutoring system and a help system. Of course, help-seeking is yet another thing for the learner to manage, and may represent an unwanted burden. However, a recent evaluation of a tutoring system for Cobol programming in an industrial setting [8] suggests that professional programmers may resent and resist the more traditional heavy-handed approach to the delivery of feedback and advice.

References

1. Anderson, J.R., Boyle, C.F., Farrell, R., & Reiser, B.J.: Cognitive principles in the design of computer tutors. In: Modelling cognition (P. Morris, ed.). New York: John Wiley & Sons 1987
2. Anderson, J.R., & Jeffries, R.: Novice LISP errors: Undetected losses of information from working memory. Human-Computer Interaction. 1, 107-131 (1988)
3. Bonar, J.: Intelligent tutoring with intermediate representations. Proceedings of ITS 1988 Intelligent Tutoring Systems Conference. New York: ACM 1988
4. Carroll, J.M., & Aaronson, A.: Learning by doing with simulated intelligent help. Communications of the ACM. 31, 1064-1079 (1988)
5. Johnson, W.L.: Intention-based diagnosis of errors in novice programs. Unpublished doctoral dissertation: Yale University 1985
6. McKendree, J., Reiser, B. and Anderson, J. R.: Tutoring goals and strategies in the instruction of programming skills. Proceedings of the Cognitive Science Society Conference. Boulder, CO: Cognitive Science Society 1984
7. Newell, A. & Simon, H.A.: Human problem solving. Englewood Cliffs, NJ: Prentice-Hall 1972

8. Radlinski, B. & McKendree, J.: Grace meets the real world: Tutoring COBOL as a second language. Proceedings of CHI '92 Conference on Human Factors in Computing Systems. New York: ACM 1992
9. Singley, M.K.: The reification of goal structures in a calculus tutor: Effects on problem solving performance. Interactive Learning Environments. 1, 102-123 (1990)
10. Singley, M.K., Carroll, J.M. & Alpert, S.R.: Synthesis by analysis: Five modes of reasoning that guide design. Manuscript submitted for publication
11. Singley, M.K., Carroll, J.M., & Alpert, S.R.: Psychological design rationale for an intelligent tutor for Smalltalk. In: Empirical studies of programmers: fourth workshop (J. Koenemann-Belliveau, T. Moher, & S. Robertson, eds.). Norwood, NJ: Ablex
12. Soloway, E. & Ehrlich, K.: Empirical studies of programming knowledge. IEEE Transcations on Software Engineering. 5, 595-609 (1984)

Methodology and Design Issues in Capra, an Environment for Learning Program Construction

M. Felisa Verdejo[1], Isabel Fernández[2], M. Teresa Urretavizcaya[2]

[1] Escuela Técnica Superior de Ingenieros Industriales, U.N.E.D. Ciudad Universitaria s/n, E-28040 Madrid, Spain

[2] Departamento de Lenguajes y Sistemas Informáticos, Universidad del País Vasco, Apdo 649, E-20080 San Sebastián, Spain

Abstract: The Capra system has been built to teach novice students the design of elementary programs. The programming methodology relies on the use of schema or plans for reasoning about program construction. The system offers interactive sessions following a Socratic style which combines explanation and verification of the different concepts of the domain. Tutoring is viewed as a process where two agents cooperate to attain some instructional/learning objectives. Under a mixed-initiative dialogue the system guides the student through its problem solving activities. The tutor dynamically plans a sequence of tutoring actions taking into account the current student's intentions expressed either explicitly or inferred through the communication process.

Keywords: Intelligent learning environments, programming environment, knowledge-base debugger

1. Introduction

Our research has focused on the teaching and learning processes involved in design activities within the domain of programming. The Capra prototype [6] is an Intelligent Learning Environment (ILE) for program construction.

The trend followed by some systems focuses on the drill and practice of a particular programming language, and as a consequence only syntactic and semantic knowledge of the selected programming language is explicitly represented. Particularly when the framework is a tutoring system, the teaching strategy is articulated on the progressive acquisition of programing language constructions. However, other works such as [1,11] propose an explicit formulation of programming as a problem solving activity. In this way, they provide means for defining classes of goals and plans, as well as tools for representing in a reified manner the whole process. Program design is then a task performed at different levels, each one involving a different degree of abstraction. Within this framework learning program construction is a multilevel acquisition of problem solving abilities, including the mastery of a programming language.

The Capra system has been built with the aim of teaching program design at an elementary level. The teaching methodology relies on the use of schema or plans for reasoning about program construction, since it has been appointed as a central issue not only in Artificial Intelligence [9] but also in programming methodology [8].

At the end of this first introductory course the student would acquire a "plan/schema library" and be able to recognize problems that belong to these solution classes. Learning is organized as a three-step cycle of progressive deepening: (1) understanding a problem (specifying data and objectives), (2) classifying a problem by means of the association of a generic schema, and (3) building an algorithm by stepwise refinement (Figure 1).

Problem
↓ COMPREHENSION
Data and Goal specification
↓ CLASSIFICATION
Basic schema association
↓ DESIGN
Abstract algorithm
↓ IMPLEMENTATION
Program

Figure 1. The learning cycle

Roughly, at least three kinds of reasoning can be distinguished: problem abstraction, association to a class of solutions, and refinement to generate a detailed solution.

Expertise is acquired by the student through problem solving activity. By solving problems, the student increases his plan library, and learn rules to perform the whole process: Abstraction rules to define goals, Association rules to select plans, as well as Refinement rules to instance and combine plans for generating a problem solution.Therefore, teaching becomes a process of conveying to the student a mixture of program schemas and the heuristic knowledge to select and apply them. Understanding the structure and functionality of a new piece of knowledge is fundamental in order to relate it with previous ones. Thus, meta-knowledge also plays an important role in the learning process.

At the moment the implemented domain knowledge base concerns exclusively the first stage of the teaching process: *Comprehension.* In this phase the student has to write the problem to be solved in a formal way, i.e. the tasks involved are:

– to establish a clear distinction of data and goals

– to write a structured description of the goals (main and secondary ones).

The teaching process provides, by a mixed-initiative dialogue, the knowledge needed about the formal specification language and how to use it. The process combines explanations and problem solving activities.

Section 2 discusses the requirements considered and the global design of Capra. Section 3 describes the operation of the system and illustrates the performance of the problem solving environment with an example. Section 4 focuses on the feedback provided by the system. A brief comment about the dialogue interface is given in Section 5 and finally a summary and main conclusions are established in Section 6.

2. Designing the System

The adaptability of an ILE is largely determined by its ability to observe and interpret the learning process of the student, especially when s/he performs problem solving activities. Current systems do not provide an adequate level of interactivity to guide and help the student along the problem solving process, due mainly to the incompleteness of the handled information either from the domain, the intention of the student, or his state of knowledge. Our approach to these difficulties is based on gathering, as much as possible explicitly, a great deal of information about the student behavior.

The main architecture of the system, as shown in Figure 2, consists of three modules: the Tutor, the Knowledge-based Debugger and the Interface. Tutor instruction [3,5] follows a Socratic style which combines explanation and verification of the different concepts of the domain.

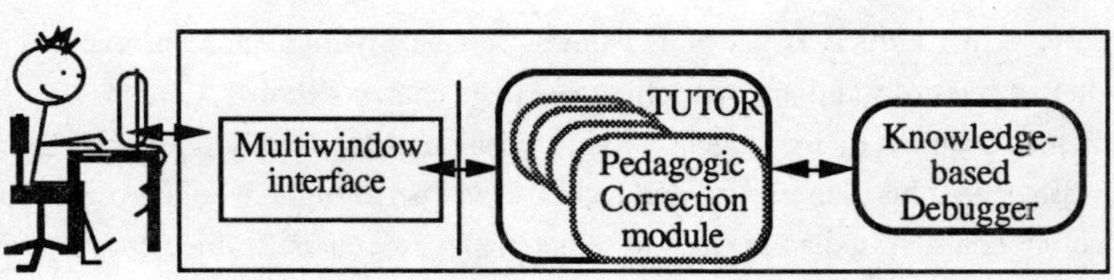

Figure 2. Capra environment

During a teaching session the Tutor puts forward exercises to check the student's comprehension of concepts. The selection of the problems is carried out based on: the student model, the concept to be checked and the current state of the session. To understand and supervise the pupil during the problem-solving activities the Tutor has an interactive Knowledge-based Debugger. The Interface acts as the communication module between the student and the system.

The Tutor Component

Three main design considerations have been taken into account:

The first concerns the role of the tutor component. Tutoring is viewed as a process where two agents cooperate to attain some instructional/learning objectives. Following a mixed-initiative dialogue, the automatic tutor dynamically plans a sequence of instructional actions taking into account the current student's intentions.

The second is related to the approach to carry out the instructional planning. This task is performed by goal-refinement at different levels of abstraction, from the most general, where the tutor decides a pedagogic strategy for the session, to the more concrete where a particular action to be carried out is executed.

The third involves knowledge representation. The knowledge needed to carry out the instructional planning is represented in a declarative way. Links with a particular domain or a student model are defined by a set of basic actions. Any class of instructional activity is described in terms of:

- a set of generic goals to be solved,
- a set of generic plans to attain a goal,
- a set of rules for deciding which plan to instance for a given goal in a particular context.

Currently the tutor architecture is made up of five modules, i.e. the instructional planning is divided on five layered levels of abstraction: pedagogic, thematic, teaching, supervising and correction. These levels where established after protocol analysis carried out on experimental teaching sessions. At the highest level of abstraction, we consider "Pedagogic Decision" where the general teaching approach is planned. Thus a teaching **session** is the result of the application of a set of strategies to reach a pedagogic goal

A typical example would consist of *a general review,* followed by *an introduction of new concepts*, then *a review of conflicting points* and finally an *introduction of new concepts*, while another one can be *a brief review of the last session* and *an introduction of new concepts.*

Two kinds of activities are carried out by the Pedagogic Decision Module:

- Choosing a combination of strategies to attain a pedagogic objective,
- Developing the strategies established in a dynamic way.

The refinement of a pedagogic objective in terms of the subject matter for each student, is carried out by goals and plans belonging to the "Thematic Decision" component. For example a thematic goal is "Determine next element to be taught". To solve these goals this component interacts with the subject-matter description and the problem library, as well as with the student model.

Once what to teach has been decided, carrying out the presentation and/or controlling the acquisition are the main tasks performed by the "Teaching component". Besides, it updates the student model and performs the communication process (managed through the Interface Dialogue Module). For instance a teaching goal that *the student know how to use concept X* can be accomplished applying the plan *explain concept X*, and *verify by means of an exercise*, which splits the goal in two subgoals, and then solving each subgoal.

The "Supervisor" focuses on the detection and resolution of conflicts arising among the tutor and student's objectives. Every time an interaction from the the student occurs a supervisor goal is created. If there are no conflicts, tutor planned activity goes on, in other cases conflict resolution plans will decide whether to consider a local change or to notify to "Pedagogic Decision" that a strategical change is needed.

Therefore each Tutor component solves a type of objectives either pedagogic, thematic, teaching, correction or conflict resolution. Every component is defined as *a knowledge base* formed by a set of objectives, plans and selection rules. An *objective* has different plans associated with it. Depending on the strategy, one of them will be selected in order to achieve the objective. A *plan* is expressed as a composition of actions and sub-objectives. The former can be described in declarative form (by rules) or procedural form. Sub-objectives will be solved invoking the current knowledge source or another one, depending on their type. A plan execution produces the raising of new objectives and the realization of elementary actions. Further details as well as the implementation are discussed in [3,4].

The Interface

The interface [2] facilitates problem solving tasks and communication activities. While solving a problem, the student communicates with Capra through a multiwindow screen as is shown in Figure 3.

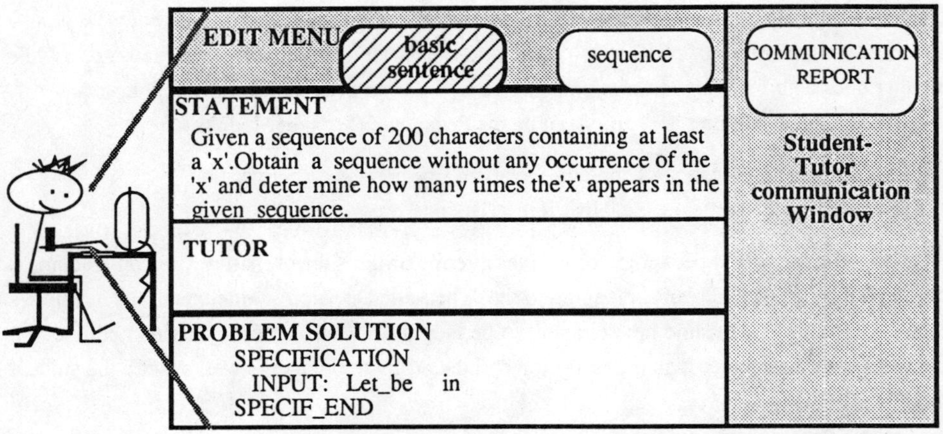

Figure 3. Student view of the multiwindow interface during the problem-solving process

There are different windows, one of them a structured space to solve the proposed problem. In this **problem-solution**-window the student writes incrementally and with the aid of a syntactic editor its solution. Partial fragments are parsed and interpreted by the debugger as soon as they are produced. The **statement** window includes the statement of the problem proposed by the Tutor (it remains fixed during the problem solving process).

The **edit** window consists of a series of menus with context-dependent options for stating the goals of the problem to be solved and the plans which may be applied to previously selected goals.

The **Tutor** window is where the Tutor makes comments, corrects or explains some concepts, and so on.

Natural language understanding is provided to enhance student-tutor communication along the teaching session. The **student-Tutor communication** window allows the student to ask questions, propose activities or comment tutor proposals using Spanish. A parser generates a message for the tutor including the student goal, Three main classes of intentions are considered: **Information**: the student gives the Tutor information about her/his understanding of concepts, examples or explanations; **Request**: the student passes on, to the Tutor, requests for teaching objects or changes of activity (an explanation with examples, a problem to solve or more information about an explanation, examples or problem statement, ...); **comment**: the student passes on to the Tutor other kind of information. The natural language component performs the parsing process using syntactic, semantic and pragmatic knowledge.

The **communication report** is a scrolling window. It can be activated to visualize the interaction carried out by the student and the Tutor through out the teaching session The tutor dynamically updates along the teaching sessions two kind of student models: a permanent model and a temporary one. The latter describes for the current session:
a) the student's intentions obtained either explicitly through the menus or inferred by the natural language understanding component,
b) the student's state of knowledge inferred from his problem solving behavior.

The Knowledge-Based Debugger

The debugger system [10] performs an Intention-based diagnosis, supported by knowledge about the domain, the specific problem to be solved and the inferred student-model. Problems are described in an abstract way, and stored in a knowledge-base. The diagnostic process is carried out interactively, and it involves matching operations between the partial version of the student solution, and the correct ones implicitly defined by the knowledge base.

The intentions of the student, explicitly stated by the options selected through the interfaces menus, are taken into account to reduce and control the design search space. Section 3 elaborates on those issues.

3. Specifying Programs with the System

The knowledge-base debugger works for the Tutor component as the student solves the problem. Figure 4 gives a general account of the debugger environment. The translation system creates the student objectives for the proposed problem. Those objectives are derived from the actions performed by the student through the edit and solution windows. The debugger designs a solution, in parallel and adapted to the student's solution. In order to carry out this task, knowledge is needed concerning the problem being worked on and the possible design plans to be applied. The former can be found in the Knowledge Base of problem descriptions and the latter in the KB of design plans.

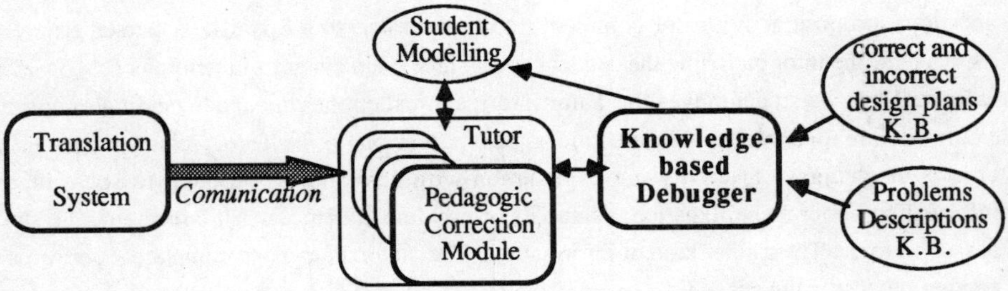

Figure 4. Knowledge-based debugger environment

The description language for problems is based on the PROUST proposal [7]. A description expresses in abstract form what must be done, i.e. the data (objects) and what results (objectives) have to be achieved in order to solve the problem. In the description there is no information on how each fragment of the objects and objectives should be solved. The plans can be found in the KB of generic design plans. Each plan expresses a way of solving a generic domain objective by further decomposing it into a sequence of subobjectives. The creation of the different instances of domain objectives (system solution tree) is carried out with information about the design decisions made by the student and the description of the corresponding problem, i.e. the choice of a plan as the debugger system operates step by step depends on the design decisions made by the student.

The student has to write a specification incrementally, following a top-down methodology using the edition menus and writing on the solution window. Thus, the student activity in the problem solving process concentrates on two aspects. On the one hand s/he should indicate by different options in the menu what goal s/he wants to solve and afterwards how s/he wants to solve it. The syntactic editor shows the generic chosen plan on the solution window.

On the other hand the student writes the solution, i.e. s/he should fill the chosen plan, by completing the sentence-pattern written on the solution window by the syntactic editor. For example, Figure 3 above shows the state of the screen after the pupil has chosen to work on the goal "input specification", and selected the option "basic sentence" to specify one of the data items. The syntactic editor has written in the problem window: "let be__ in__ ".

The knowledge-base debugger supervises the solution obtained by the student interactively to detect, diagnose, and correct the errors. This is a complex action which implies several tasks, thus the debugger system is broken down into modules that correspond to specific expertises. The **debugger** module plans the start and controls the development of the detection and diagnosis session ; the **design** module generates a solution to the problem in parallel with and adapted to the student's solution; the **verifier** module supervises the student objectives to determine the design plan he has selected (collaborating with the design module to build up the system's solution) and to detect differences between both solutions; the **diagnosis** module studies the severity of the errors detected, determining whether it is necessary to interrupt the student. On the other hand, when it has been decided to interrupt the student, the **pedagogic correction** module (included in the Tutor) selects and applies the best correction strategy to indicate the mistakes to the student.

An Example

The detection process involves matching operations between the partial version of the student, and the partial ones implicitly defined by the design plan knowledge bases. The verifier performs the process of error detection by comparing the current objective of the student to the corresponding objective of the design module. The relevant differences between them indicate possible errors. An error does not only affect the fragment where it has been detected. Errors which result from previous errors can later be detected. Thus we can say errors detected are not taken in isolation as they can combine with other errors to affect wider knowledge structures. The first kind of errors are called superficial errors and combinations of two or more errors are called global errors. A diagnosis is made of each error to determine whether it is serious enough to interrupt the student. In this process the state of the current session is taken into account as well as the information gathered from the permanent student model.

Let's comment briefly on a solution brought forward by the student, in which the strategy selected by the tutor indicates not to interrupt the student, i.e. errors are not corrected until the end of the specification process.

The Tutor's proposed problem is written in the statement window (as shown already in Figure 3):

> "*Given a sequence of 200 characters containing at least an 'x' character , obtain a sequence without any occurrence of the 'x' and determine how many occurrences of 'x' appear in the given sequence*".

The initial state of the edit and solution windows are shown in Figure 5.

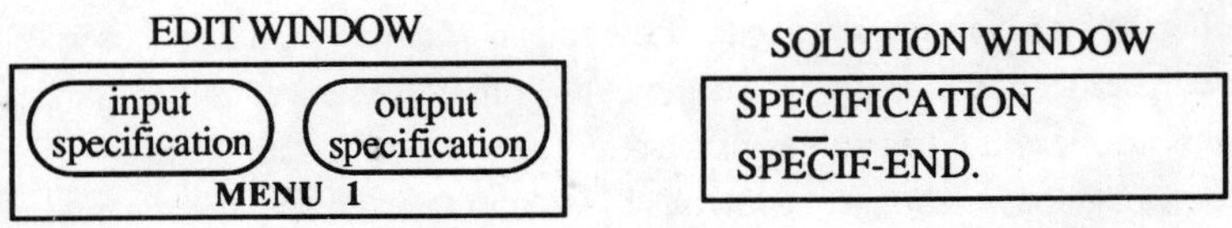

Figure 5. Edit and solution window initial state

To get, at a time, a proper perspective of (1) what the student has done, (2) what the student has not done but should be done, and (3) what s/he has done but it has been done incorrectly, its final specification follows (expressing: in normal print the point (1), in *italics* the point (2), and underlined the point (3)):

SPECIFICATION
INPUT: Let be X in CHAR such*that X= 'x'*
Let be S sequence-of CHAR such that Long(S)= 200
exist I in [1..Long(S)] S[I]= X
OUTPUT: Write T sequence-of CHAR
formed-by-the Y of S
such that Y<>X and X= 'x' and Long(S)- Long(T)
Write Long(S)- Long(T)
SPECIF-END

The student's job begins (step 1) with the selection of the "input specification"- option in the first menu. Selection of an edit option activates the Translation System and may activate the Syntactic Editor and/or modify the options of the menu. The system design process, will be realized step by step as the student's objectives are being gathered

The student first objective, **S1**, is an edit objective including the information of which part of the problem, the student wishes to develop (i.e. "input"). The design module creates in turn design expectatives which will be compared with the pupil's objective. The comparison between edit (pupil) and design (system) objectives, is directed according to the verifier rules condition. In this case a rule is fired, indicating that the pupil's design decision is correct and applying a plan to continue the process.

The second pass has the same characteristics as the first. A pupil's edit objective, **S2**, is obtained, the design module applies a design plan to the input objective and then generates an objective, **D2** (basic-sentence). Comparing both objectives their informations match and the process continues. The design module develops objective D2, applying the plan corresponding with a basic-sentence design for an Object 1 defined by a property. We have seen until now the first three passes of the process. From now on we will concentrate on those passes where errors have been detected. In steps 4, 9 and 16 errors while selecting edit objectives are detected. Whereas in pass 14, errors in filling a plan are detected.

The objective of the student in the fourth step is **S4** : "the student has finished to specify the object (data)". The design module has generated its next objective, **D4**. This one is then compared with S4. A verifier rule detects an omission error and applies the corresponding plan to solve it.

When an error is detected the design module modifies its solution tree to include the error description (**err1**, OMISSION error). And it also develops the correct design plan to have more information about the parts omitted . The error is expressed as:

{{ **err1**

TYPE-ERROR: **omission**
ASSIGNED-CONCEPT: property
CORRECT-INFORMATION: *Rep.* (X= 'x') }}

The diagnosis module will study whether the error was a superficial one or it combines with another giving way to a global error. In this case, being the first error detected it does not combine with any other. The session goes on generating the system its next objective, **D5**, and comparing it with student objective **S4**. Now the information from both objectives matches and the process continues normally (with one error pending to be corrected).

After the student has finished writing the sentence property, (Let be **S** sequence-of **CHAR** so that **Long(S)= 200**), s/he must choose what to do in the next pass.

Its election is to finish the sentence specification i.e. the student has not fully characterized the sequence and an OMISSION error has been detected. The process to deal with the new error is equivalent to the one before. An incorrect objective with error description (**err2**) is generated, and the corresponding information is created (to represent what the student should have been done).

{{ **err2**

TYPE-ERROR: **omission**
ASSIGNED-CONCEPT: quantifier
CORRECT-INFORMATION: *Rep* (exist i is-in [1..Long(S)] S[i]= X) }}

There exists still an earlier detected and not corrected error (err1) which could possibly be combined with err2. But err1 is also an OMISSION error and the combination fails.

The next error is detected in pass 14, when the student is characterizing the output sequence as a subsequence The student has indicated that the elements 'x' are not part of the sequence (i.e. Y<>X). That expression form an EXCESS error. The newly detected error is expressed in the next form:

{{ **err3**

TYPE-ERROR: **excess**
ASSIGNED-CONCEPT: expression
INCORRECT-INFORMATION: *Rep.* (X= 'x' and Long(S)- Long(T)) }}

The diagnosis module then carries out a study to determine whether err3 can be combined with any other existing OMISSION errors. Err1 and Err3 contain a property. A property is expressed by a condition which is an expression. Therefore err1 contains a property representation that can be compared to the expression representation included in err3. The diagnosis studies these representations and detects that part of the expression from err3 which combines with the property of err1 (X='x'). It then gives way to another error, **err4**, of the type BADLYPLACED and **Err3** is changed to **err3'**

{{ **err3'**
TYPE-ERROR: **excess**
ASSIGNED-CONCEPT: expression
INCORRECT-INFORMATION: *Rep.* (Long(S)- Long(T)) }}

{{ **err4**
TYPE-ERROR: **badlyplaced**
ASSIGNED-CONCEPT: property
CORRECT-INFORMATION: *Rep.Cond* (X= 'x')
INCORRECT-INFORMATION: *Rep.Exp.* (X= 'x') }}

In pass 16, the student has already finished writing the solution to the problem, indicating it by the edit option "end specification". The verifier was waiting for another output objective. A new error is detected. The error, **err5**, is of type OMISSION and the diagnoser verifies that it is a global error of type BADLYPLACED by combination with the EXCESS error, err3'. The result of this combination generates a new error description **err6**.

{{ **err5**
TYPE-ERROR: **omission**
ASSIGNED-CONCEPT: expression
INCORRECT-INFORMATION: *Rep.* (Long(S)- Long(T)) }

{{ **err6**
TYPE-ERROR: **badlyplaced**
ASSIGNED-CONCEPT: expression
CORRECT-INFORMATION: *Rep.Exp.* (Long(S)- Long(T))
INCORRECT-INFORMATION: *Rep.Exp.* (Long(S)- Long(T)) }}

When errors are detected the diagnosis module establishes their importance taking into account (1) the type of error detected, (2) the affected concept and (3) the student's model. The system will then decide whether it is necessary to interrupt the student activity.

4. Reacting to the Student

The Tutor plans and develop dynamically a teaching strategy. It means that any student intervention (either a problem solving activity or a natural language message) is taken into account, to consider the student current objectives.

The Supervisor Module detects and solves conflicts arising between the strategy followed by the TUTOR and the student's objectives. To accomplish it, Supervisor compares Tutor's objectives (current and waiting) with the student's objectives (obtained either explicitly or inferred through the interaction)

Conflicts are solved by rules which decide either to include dynamically goals in order to insert local strategies (strategic goals), or to change the general strategy. However, the solution of these strategic objectives is a task to be performed by the Pedagogic Decision Module.

The process performed by the Supervisor to respond to the student's goals splits into two phases: *to establish the student's goal to deal with*, and *to generate a plan for solving the selected student goal.*

From the list of student's objectives determined by the Interface (Translation system and Dialogue Module), the first step is to select those that are going to be treated. The process is carried out by means of rules to detect conflicts or overlapping among student's objectives. Theses rules compare the student's objectives one on one until a list of irreducible objectives is obtained; they belong to the following pattern rule:

If *conditions about Student-objective-1*
conditions about Student-objective-2
Then eliminate {student-objective-? }

In the current prototype we have assumed that it is always possible to reduce the initial list of student's goals to one single goal, and so the rules to select them give rise to a single objective. For instance, the student answer:

"I don't remember logic expressions. Give me an example."

is interpreted as the sequence of two student objectives:

(Request-Teaching-Object (Explanation, Logic-Expression)
and
Request-Teaching-Object (Example, Logic-Expression)).

In this case the following rule will select the second one to be treated.

If TYPE(ST-OBJ1) = Request-Teaching-Object and
CONCEPT(ST-OBJ1) = ?X and
REQUESTED-OBJECT(ST-OBJ1) = Explanation and
TYPE(ST-OBJ2) = Request-Teaching-Object and
CONCEPT(ST-OBJ2) = ?X and
REQUESTED-OBJECT(ST-OBJ2) = Example
Then Eliminate (ST-OBJ1)

The second phase is to generate a plan for the selected student's objective.The supervisor has several generic plans, in case of errors, the created one involves deciding what and how to say to the student.

The pedagogic correction module will carry out the feedback . In this module we distinguish two classes of plans according to two types of strategies. The first ones provide information about the error and follow afterwards with the detection and diagnosis process on the same problem (if the specification is not yet finished). These plans correspond to a *simple correction strategy*. The other ones imply total or local changes in the Tutor strategy. We refer to these plans as belonging to a *complex correction strategy*. Some examples of these two classes of strategies are given below:

COMUNICATE-FAILURE

IS-A: SIMPLE-CORRECTION-STRATEGY

USAGE: "The student failures are of little importance"

EFFECT: "The bugs are shown when the specification is finished"

EXPLAIN-WITH-WELL-SOLVED-PROBLEM

IS-A: SIMPLE-CORRECTION-STRATEGY

USAGE: "The model reflects the correct usage of the concept, related to the current error, in other problems"

EFFECT: "Explain with a correct solution previously known"

EXPLAIN-WITH-SIMILAR-ERRONEOUSLY-SOLVED-PROBLEM

IS-A: SIMPLE-CORRECTION-STRATEGY

USAGE: "The student's model has a similar error, detected in a previous problem"

EFFECT: "The Tutor reminds the student a previous problem where a similar error was detected and corrected"

EXPLAIN-WITH-EXAMPLE

IS-A: SIMPLE-CORRECTION-STRATEGY

USAGE: "It is the first time a concept is used"

EFFECT: "Explain how to solve a problem by means of an example"

RE-EXPLAIN-CONCEPT

IS-A: COMPLEX-CORRECTION-STRATEGY

USAGE: "The concept the Tutor has just verified contains several errors"

EFFECT: "The concept is explained in another way, leaving the problem pending"

DECREASE-PROBLEM-DIFFICULTY-LEVEL

IS-A: COMPLEX-CORRECTION-STRATEGY

USAGE: "There are errors affecting the explained concept and the difficulty level of the problem may also be too high"

EFFECT: "The debugger session is started again with a simpler problem. The problem remains as unsolved"

5. Dialogue Interface

In the current version of the Capra System, tutor and student can communicate in Spanish, and this has been implemented in terms of an internal message mechanism between the natural language interface and the tutor modules. This internal mechanism enables to change the kind of interface, for instance a set of pre-established menus instead of NL, provided that the same set of internal messages between the interface and the Tutor is maintained.

The dialogue component can be activated for two types of tasks:

– to send questions or pre-canned texts to the student, and

– to understand the student's interventions.

For the interface to be capable of interpreting the student's NL utterances, a model of the dialogue is needed. This model is created and updated dynamically and it represents the structure of the dialogue, the intentions of the participants, and the focus of attention [2].

The tutor provides the following information to the interface for modelling the dialogue:

– its current goal and strategy used, local and general,

– the topic focused and the main concept,

– the type of NL message to be conveyed to the student and the expectations about his/her answer.

In the second task, understanding the student NL-utterances, the interface carries out a parsing process to infer the student's objectives underlying his/her answer. These objectives are reported to the TUTOR. A categorization of student's objectives have been established [2]. Like Tutor's objectives, they include parameters whose value will be obtained in each concrete instantiation. Nine major types have been identified; some of them are:

ST-OB1:

IS-A: STUDENT-GOAL
STUDENT-GOAL-TYPE: POSITIVE-CONFIRMATION
DESCRIPTION: "The student agrees to the Tutor proposal, or the student understands last explanation, ...etc."

ST-OB4:

IS-A: STUDENT-GOAL
STUDENT-GOAL-TYPE: EVALUABLE-ANSWER
DESCRIPTION: "The student provides a (partial) solution to a proposed problem"
SPECIFICATION: *<generated answer>*

ST-OB5:

IS-A: STUDENT-GOAL
STUDENT-GOAL-TYPE: REQUEST-TEACHING-OBJECT
DESCRIPTION: "Student asks for some *teaching object*: (example problem, explanation) in order to complete his/her learning"
REQUESTED-OBJECT: *<Or EXAMPLE PROBLEM EXPLANATION>*
CONCEPT:

Communication between the NL component and the Supervisor component is carried out by means of the following MESSAGE-ANALYSIS schema:

{{ **MESSAGE-ANALYSIS**
IS-PART-OF: DIALOGUE-COMMUNICATION
MESSAGE-NUMBER: *<number of student's message sent>*
STUDENT-GOALS: *<list of student's goals>* }}

The main focus of this paper is the student–system interaction while solving a problem. Due to space limitations it is impossible to describe the natural-language interface. An account of the parser can be found in [2].

6. Summary

We have presented relevant features of Capra describing both the learning approach for a particular domain of application, program construction, and the teaching approach which shapes the system design in a more general way.

From the learning point of view, the system helps to attain the following objectives: to know the nature of an abstract class and an abstract schema, to acquire a library of schema and to learn how to solve problems by recognizing to what class they belong, selecting an applying the appropriate schema. The underlying methodology structures the learning process as a three step cycle of progressive complexity. The current test-domain is formed by a collection of one hundred problems,whose solutions use basic data types, sequences and sets.

From the teaching point of view, tutoring is seen as a process where two agents cooperate to achieve some instructional/learning objectives. This approach involves two related requirements for the system: it must be able to interpret the student behavior, and it must be able to adapt its own behavior. Capra relies on gathering as explicitly as possible a great deal of information about the student activity. Under a mixed-initiative dialogue, the automatic tutor plans and carries out a sequence of tutoring actions dynamically, taking into account the current student's intentions expressed directly through the interface options or inferred from the natural language student interventions.

The instructional knowledge is domain independent and has been represented declaratively by means of generic goals, plans and rules, organized in a modular way by types of tasks.

Capra has been implemented (details are given in [4,10]) using a two-level blackboard architecture: one level represents the instructional knowledge, as a set of knowledge sources, the other one displays control information needed to carry out the dynamic planning process.

Acknowledgments

Capra was developed from 1983 to 1990, partially supported by grants from the Spanish Research Council and Digital Equipment Corporation. The authors would like to acknowledge the contributions to the project by A. Diaz, F. Garijo, and K. Sarasola.

References

1. J. Bonar, R. Cunningham: Bridge: an intelligent tutor for thinking about programming. In Artificial Intelligence and Human Learning, pp. 391-409. Chapman Hall 1988
2. A. Diaz de Ilarraza, I. Fernández, F. Verdejo: A Natural Language Interface for Intelligent Tutoring Systems. In M. de Blasi, E. Luque, E. Scuri (eds.): Education and application of computer technology. pp. 1-12, Editioné Fratelli Laterza 1990
3. A. Diaz de Ilarraza, I. Fernández, F. Verdejo: Building a programming tutor by dynamic planning: case studies and a proposal. In Proc. Int. Conference on Intelligent Tutoring Systems, ITS-88, Montreal 1988, pp. 230- 237
4. A. Diaz de Ilarraza, I. Fernández, F. Verdejo: A Cooperative Architecture for Tutoring Tasks. In Proc. 8th Int. Workshop on Expert Systems and their Application, Avignon 1988, pp. 107 -126 (Vol. 2)
5. A. Diaz de Ilarraza, I. Fernández, F. Verdejo: Modelling an automatic tutor by dynamic planning. In Proc. IEEE-88 Int. Conference on Systems, Man, and Cybernetics, pp. 942- 948, Beijing 1988
6. F. Garijo, F. Verdejo A. Diaz de Ilarraza, I. Fernandez, K. Sarasola: Capra: an intelligent system to teach novice programmers. In Campbell, P. Cuena (eds.): Perspectives in AI, Vol. 2, pp 179 -196, Ellis Horwood 1987
7 W.E. Johnson, E. Soloway: PROUST: knowledge-based program understanding. IEEE Trans. on Software Engineering SE 10(5), 595-609 (1984)
8. M. Lucas, J.P. Peyrin, P.C.Scholl: Algorithmique et representation des données. Editorial Mason 1983
9. E. Soloway: Learning to program = learning to construct mechanisms and explanations. CACM 26(10), Sept. 1986
10. M. Urretavizcaya, M.F. Verdejo: A cooperative system for an interactive debugging of novice programming errors. In S. Dijkstra, H.P.M. Krammer, J.J.G. van Merriënboer (eds.) Instructional models in computer-based learning environments. NATO ASI Series F, Vol. 104. Springer-Verlag 1992
11. R. Waters: The programmer's apprentice: knowledge based program editing. IEEE Trans. on Software Engineering 8(1), Jan 1982

Linking Theory with ITS Implementation: Models of Programming and the Development of Programming Tutors

Simon P. Davies[1] and Adrian M. Castell[2]

[1]Department of Psychology, University of Nottingham, University Park, Nottingham, NG7 2RD, UK
[2]Information Technology Institute, University of Salford, M5 4WT, UK

Abstract: The way in which cognitive theories are implemented in intelligent tutoring systems has implications for the design and evaluation of such systems. In this paper we discuss a theory of skill development in programming centred around the acquisition of programming plans. We examine specific criticisms of the plan theory based upon recent empirical research into programming and upon an exploration of the problems relating to the way in which the original theory has been expressed in systems intended to support the learning process. Our contention is that the development of intelligent tutoring systems should not only be guided by theory but should also inform theory. In terms of the analysis outlined here, we present an example of how this might occur. In conclusion, we frame the results of this analysis in a way that might encourage a better awareness of the role of theory in the development and evolution of intelligent tutoring systems.

Keywords: Intelligent tutoring systems, programming plans, cognitive models

Introduction

Programming is clearly a complex problem solving activity which has received a significant amount of attention. This is evident in the volume of research aimed at gaining a better understanding of the cognitive process involved in programming and the consequent effort directed towards developing system to support students in the task of learning to program. Theories of skill acquisition have been instrumental in the development of such system. Moreover, in some cases, an understanding of the learning processes that such systems support has fed back explicitly into the development of cognitive theory [1]. In this paper we are concerned with an analysis of the role of theory in the development of PROUST and Bridge, intelligent tutoring systems based upon a dominant theory of programming centred around programming plans. Our primary interest is directed toward exploring the extent to which developments in our understanding of skill acquisition might inform the development of tutoring systems in this domain. Moreover, we suggest that there may be critical limitations of particular theories which only become evident when those theories are realised in systems intended to support the learning process. Our analysis is informed by an examination of specific criticisms of programming plan theory based upon more recent empirical research and upon an exploration of the problems relating to the way in which the original theory has been expressed in the Bridge system.

We begin by outlining the theory of programming plans which has been used to provide an explanation of skill acquisition in programming. This theory is based upon a description of the knowledge structures which programmers are thought to employ while developing programs and in particular those cognitive features that are known to play an important role in the development of expertise.

We then move on to discuss more recent work which has drawn into question some of the basic tenets of this theory. The next section of the paper provides an overview of the PROUST and Bridge Intelligent tutoring system. Here we consider the problems we have identified in terms of their specific implications for the students in their interaction with the system and for the way which this theory has been used to guide the development of these systems. Many of these problems stem from the lack of an explicit theory of planning, which has led to an inappropriate model of the planning process. Other problems emerge from considering plans as standard concepts/techniques and the idea that plans need to be presented explicitly to students who are interacting with the system. In the conclusion we attempt to frame the results of this analysis so as to encourage a more specific awareness of the role of theory in the development and evolution of intelligent tutoring systems.

Plan-Based Theories of Programming Skill

Soloway and Ehrlich [22] introduce the notion of the programming plan to provide a description of program fragments that are thought to represent stereotypic action sequences in programming. Plans are regarded as both language and problem independent. Hence, programs are constructed on the basis of generalised plan knowledge and specific plans are created in response to the requirements and constraints of a particular problem.

Soloway and Ehrlich report a number of empirical studies to support their contention that programmers are able to recruit tacit plan knowledge during problem solving and that the possession of such plan knowledge can be used to distinguish experts from novices. Soloway and Ehrlich reason that if advanced programmers possess and use programming plans then they should be able to recognise program fragments in plan-like versions of programs as examples of particular plans and consequently they will complete the blank line in that program with code that corresponds to the role expressed by that plan. In the case of unplan-like programs, the advanced programmer will not be able to infer the program's plan structure and they will consequently be less likely to fill in the missing line correctly. Novice programmers, who, it is claimed, have not developed a full repertoire of plans and programming conventions, will not be guided by plan structures and hence should perform with similar levels of accuracy in response to both plan-like and unplan-like programs.

Soloway and Ehrlich's results provide support for these claims. Firstly, experts were able to complete blank lines in programs more accurately than novices. In addition, subjects completed the plan-like versions correctly more often than the non-plan like versions. Finally, there was a significant interaction between program version (plan-like or unplan-like) and expertise. These results provide strong support for the idea that expert programmers use plan knowledge to guide their comprehension of programs. This knowledge provides a basis upon which expectations about program function can be constructed. Moreover, when these expectations are violated, expert performance is reduced drastically.

Recall studies reported in the same paper also provide support for the idea that the problem solving activities of expert programmers are mediated by the possession of stereotypical plan structures and that plan knowledge may be central to program comprehension. The work of Soloway and his colleagues has clearly contributed to our understanding of the use of knowledge in guiding problem solving in programming. In addition, this work has provided a useful means of describing the content of such knowledge structures and has been influential in the design of automated program analysis systems and intelligent tutoring aids including Bridge and PROUST. However, more recent work has questioned the basic adequacy of the plan theory.

Limitations of Plan-Based Theories

One of the major claims of plan-based theories is that programming plans are both language and task/problem independent. Programming plans are taken to represent generic knowledge structures that in some sense represent the deep structure of a problem. However a number of recent studies suggest the development of plan structures appears to be inextricably bound up with the way in which programming is taught, and this finding appears to pose serious implications for plan-based theories of programming expertise.

The relationship between teaching and plan acquisition is problematic because if the acquisition of plan structures is the primary characteristic of programming expertise, as suggested by Soloway and Ehrlich, then differences in teaching strategy and educational background should not affect the nature of that expertise.

Experimental work [8] suggests that the ability to extract plan structures from a program text is partially dependent upon the design experience possessed by the programmer, and that this design experience helps the programmer to construct a mapping between structures in the problem domain (plans) and structures in the language domain (programs). Additional evidence for this idea is presentend by Stone, Jordan and Wright [24], who provide experimental support for the idea that instruction in structured programming principles can improve debugging performance by increasing a programmer's comprehension of program goals and plans. Taken together these findings appear to pose significant difficulties for plan theories of programming.

Soloway and Ehrlich suggest that programming plans should be considered as schemata, however schema theory suggests that schemata acquisition is performed via an inductive process in which specific experiences are concatenated into generic schemata [22]. Schemata are not taught explicitly and we are not taught procedures which facilitate the inspection and integration of schemata. However, while the work reported above does not suggest that plans are taught explicitly, it does indicate that differences in teaching strategy may influence the kinds of representations that programmers build and the way in which programmers use these generic representations.

Another problem with the plan theory is that all the reported empirical work on program comprehension has used programs written in a single language (usually Pascal or one of its close variants). However, the plan theory gains much of its theoretical force from the claim that plan structures are language independent. For instance Soloway and Ehrlich [22] claim that their experiments support the idea that "plan knowledge play(s) a powerful role in *program* comprehension" (p. 609) (our emphasis). However, their work was concerned only with the role of plans in the comprehension of Pascal-like programs, the assumption presumably being that these effects will generalise to different languages.

Gilmore and Green [13] working with Basic programmers found that such programmers were unable to benefit from cues to plan structure (e.g., when such structures are colour highlighted) while debugging programs. On the other hand, debugging success for Pascal programmers is facilitated by plan structure cues. Basic programmers do not appear to employ an abstract plan-based representation of a particular program during program comprehension, but tend to rely more extensively upon control flow information implicit in the text structure of the program. This research calls into question one of the basic theoretical claims of plan theorists, which suggests that plan structures are language independent. Indeed, if the plan theory is not generalisable to languages other than Pascal then clearly it is of significantly less utility and therefore interest.

The above discussion also has implications for the second major claim of the plan school which states that the possession of plan structures form the basis for understanding programming expertise. One of the main problems with the plan theory is that plans are used both to explain expertise and to provide the only empirical measure of that expertise; in the studies carried out by Soloway and Ehrlich, no independent measures of expertise were established.

Davies [9] reports a study which suggests that while the existence of pans may be used to differentiate novices from experts, an analysis of plan structures does not appear to provide a means of testing out more subtle distinctions between levels of expertise. This study suggested that intermediate programmers appear to possess the same range and number of plan structures as their more experienced counterparts, but with intermediates and experts using plans rather differently.

This finding suggests that the procedures for detecting plan violations may be well developed in the case of expert programmers. The evidence concerning plan use seems to provide little support for the idea that the possession of plans can be taken as a defining characteristic of expertise. In terms of the plan theory, one would presumably expect plan structures to be gradually accumulated as a programmer becomes more experienced. However, the lack of a clear discontinuity in the number and range of plans used by intermediates and novices suggests that this view is invalid.

Oddly, the plan theory also neglects to consider planning. Davies [10,11] has attempted to outline a theory of planning in programming based upon an empirical analysis of programming strategy. One of the more important findings reported in this work is that programming strategy is opportunistic in the sense that it does not appear to follow a strict hierarchical decomposition path. Rather, fragmentary code elements may be generated at any point during development of a program and then later reevaluated and modified in respect to the particular goal currently under consideration. In addition, the development of code may be postponed at any time in order that the programmers might direct their attention to other goals or subgoals, possibly in response to the recognition of previously unforeseen interactions between code structures or goals.

Moreover, it appears that experts develop strategies which necessitate the externalization of partially generated fragments which are then later recomprehended [12,14]. In this sense, programming can be seen as an incremental process where goal structures are externalised and recomprehended when necessary. One of the major characteristics of programming expertise appears to be based upon the development of strategies for reducing working memory load by using external sources to record partial solution steps [10].

In summary, recent experimental work has suggested a number of significant problems with the plan theory of programming. Firstly, this theory has neglected to provide an account of the strategic elements of plan use: that is, a theory of planning. Secondly, the use of plans appears to depend upon the particular training experience of the programmer and upon features of the language used. This suggests that programming plans cannot be considered to be 'natural' structures that evolve independently of programming experience and exposure to particular languages. Finally, the purported relationship between expertise and plan knowledge as stated by Soloway and Ehrlich appears to be drawn into question by a number of recent studies.

Knowledge-Based Program Analysis - PROUST

The early empirical support for the idea that plan structures guide the comprehension of programs led to the development of PROUST [17-20], a system that analyses novices' programs automatically to derive a non-algorithmic, or plan-based, description of the program. PROUST employs a knowledge base of programming plans and strategies, together with a description of the bugs that are commonly associated with these plans and strategies and uses these descriptions as a basis for describing the bugs to the novice programmers. PROUST carries out an 'intention' based analysis of programs, i.e., it frames its analysis in terms of both the intended functions of the program and in terms of the programmers intention as to how a particular function should be achieved.

Clearly, programmers might implement the same goal in many different ways. In PROUST's case the system constructs a description of the intentions underlying each individual student solution. PROUST combines plans into possible implementations for each goal, and then matches the plans against the code. If PROUST is unable to match its goal decomposition of the problem with its decomposition of the students solution, it attempts to account for this mismatch between the plans and the code. To do this PROUST uses its knowledge base of plan-difference rules, which suggest bugs and misconceptions that may account for the mismatch.

Bridge and BridgeTalk - Plan-Based Programming Tutors

An evaluation [18] of the PROUST system was considered to provide support for plan-based accounts of program understanding since it demonstrated that plan-based descriptions of programs can provide a good basis for predicting and locating bugs and misconceptions. However, it has been suggested that there are a number of problems with the consultative nature of the interaction with the student. In particular, although PROUST provided powerful diagnostic facilities it was considered to lack the richness in interaction demanded of an interactive tutorial environment since it does not provide a great deal of feedback to students about their progress [5]. In a similar vein, Bonar and Conningham identify other problems with extant tutorial systems. For example they claim that the LISP tutor [2,3] is too directive and constraining in that it forces "a student to proceed in a more or less top-down manner. There is no provision for informal ideas and intermediate components in the problem-solving process" (p. 391).

Consequently, Bridge [5,6], a prototype tutorial environment for novice programmers, was designed to provide interactive feedback to students of programming. In addition, development included the explicit goal of providing a language that would allow students to discuss designs and partial goals, embodying an understanding of cognitive processes known to play a significant role in novice programming.

This system will be examined in detail here as it illustrates a number of points central to the concerns of this paper. The philosophy underlying the Bridge approach to Pascal teaching using plans raises important questions concerning both the adequacy of the theory it embodies to explain the teaching process and the nature of the educational goals to which it strives.

The fundamental assumption underlying the Bridge system is that teaching plans to students will improve their basic ability to understand and generate programs, indeed they follow Soloway and Ehrlich [22], in asserting that an understanding of these plans is crucial to the success of novice programmers.Using this approach they seek to address a number of problems commonly associated with learning from more traditional programming texts including syntactic matching [4] and plan merge errors [23].

One result of using such a plan-based approach is considered to be the ability to create an explicit and high level plan representation. This is done by moving through successively formal representations from informal natural language descriptions through plan specifications to a programming language code solution. The focus on plan specification is assumed to mitigate problems stemming from plan interactions.

The second system we wish to explore here is a further development of the original Bridge design, which seeks to capitalise on a range of additional features provided by a visual programming language. Visual programming languages are anticipated to avoid problems associated with a linear textual programming languages by virtue of enhanced flexibility and expressiveness together with a reduction of working memory load on novice programmers. BridgeTalk emphasises the nature of the interrelations between formal plan components and seeks to provide a structure for organising and understanding problem-solving.

Bonar and Liffick set out a number of design goals which they have attempted to incorporate in BridgeTalk. These include 1). the need to allow users to understand, develop and utilise their own 'informal' plans arising from everyday life; 2). the need to help novices develop a library of programming plans; 3). the aim of allowing novices to implement such plans at the level of a standard programming language; and 4). to aid programmers by concentrating on plan composition, by maintaining a continuity of representation at an 'atomic' level. The transition from the 'real-world' to standard language constructs via 'informal' plans is anticipated to be rendered much more effortless by providing a language which emphasises the connections between the semantics of objects in the real world and those existing in high level languages.

The design goals for BridgeTalk have emphasised different aims than those originally formulated for Bridge. As a consequence, BridgeTalk has addressed some of the original system but has revealed a new set of problems. The next section delimits these problems by illustrating how design decisions arising from a particular theoretical perspective have generated commitments to teaching strategies and implementation constraints which are not supported by empirical studies.

Programming Plans: A Standard Set of Concepts?

Bonar and Cunningham's assumption that programming plans represent 'standard sets of concepts' to talk about students' models of programming tasks, in the same way that expert physicists use principles of conservation of energy to understand physics tasks, does not appear to be justified. There is little evidence to suggest that the notion of the programming plan as introduced by Soloway and Ehrlich can provide a foundation for the kind of standard concepts that Bonar and Cunningham advance. Experiments looking at plan use across different tasks [21] and programming languages [13] have demonstrated that other knowledge structures play an equal or greater role in program generation and comprehension.

Nature and Utility of 'informal plans'

In addition, within the BridgeTalk system there appears to be an implicit assumption that all informal plans have the potential to be equally useful, mitigated only by task demands and the level of semantic 'connectiveness'. There appears to be no regard to variance in usefulness in respect to the cognitive effort invested in dynamically altering, updating or manipulating these plans into 'acceptable' formal plan structures. Indeed, it is possible that such informal plan structures are likely to be incomplete and/or inconsistent between and within themselves.

Comprehensiveness

Also, developing mappings between informal plans and those residing within BridgeTalk is based upon developing an understanding of the connections between their semantics. However, the range of identified plans within BridgeTalk is necessarily limited, and while facilities exist (and their use is encouraged) to create user generated plan structures, it is not clear which are the most important to teach. It seems clear that not all plans will be equally useful within a given context and that this contextualization will lead to difficulties formulating appropriate strategies for determining which plans to teach.

Rolling Awareness

Finally, one issue emerge from the BridgeTalk system relates to the question of whether the build-up of a library of plans is linearly cumulative. This gives rise to potential problems in the sense that it might be suggested that it is necessary to be well versed (that is, to have developed rich semantic connections) in the application of any single plan, before another can be understood in context and used. This reflects the difficulty of describing plan concepts at a single level of abstraction. It is clear that, in most teaching situations, students are presented with simple example which grow in complexity. However, the plan theory as it is currently articulated does not make any attempt to differentiate between levels of plan complexity. Rather, as we have seen, the emphasis is upon moving between different abstract descriptions of the same formal object. This tends to divert attention away from the seemingly important internal differentiation of plan structure which would seem to be an important requirement from an educational perspective.

Unidirectional Flow and Opportunism

It is clear from problem solving research that environments should facilitate movement between levels of abstraction in order to allow opportunistic episodes to emerge and support both top-down and bottom-up strategies [16]. As Guindon suggests, "a decision at a given level of abstraction may influence subsequent decisions at higher or lower levels of abstraction, specifying actions to be taken at different time during the process" [15; p 337]. It is not clear how Bridge enables insights gained from working at a more detailed level of abstraction to guide revision of higher level planning. For example, a student recognising familiar fragments of code at the lowest level may wish to exit that level and change a components of the requirements at a plan or natural language level. However, there is no support for managing the repercussions of such opportunistic episodes.

Bridge embodies a notion of planning which suggests that programmers should work through problems by successively decomposing the problem at more detailed levels of abstraction. However, there is no evidence from the plan literature that this model of planning is appropriate. Indeed, it has been suggested that plan theories of programming have failed to make explicit any form of planning strategy [12,7].

In addition to the inability to support opportunistic episodes the imposition of this particular form of decomposition does not well the explicit design aim of working toward a solution by successive approximation. Although this design aim may be worthwhile it does not appear to be realised in the implementation of Bridge. Bridge is anticipated to recognise a solution that is close to correct by being aware that the student is moving from a component of one representation to another representation. This presents two problems. Firstly, it is not clear how the current set of plans is able to be revised in response to detected flaws and changes in the environment because the environment would appear to constrain the student to a unidirectional mode of planning. Secondly, although Bridge is anticipated to understand student's partial solutions because of the translation from one representation into the equivalent component in another representation, the second representation is always at a lower level of abstraction.

Opportunism is also restricted by the use of the 'hints' mechanism which, as the student progresses through different levels of description, provides diagnostic and coaching information. As progression occurs through the required levels, these hints indicate the proximity to a correct solution and therefore tend to restrict opportunities for active exploration. Moreover, while Bridge attempts to understand students' partial solutions it does not appear to support their externalization, which more recent models of programming have suggested is an important aspect of skill development in programming [12].

Students are required to select a plan and then select a Pascal construct that best implements that plan or role. There is an assumption here that the student already has enough knowledge about these plans to be able to successfully choose from them the one most appropriate to the situation. However, given that one of the features of expertise in programmer appears to be the development and use of selection rules to guide plan choice [9] it seems unlikely that novice programmers would possess an adequate repertoire of rules to enable them to make successful choices.

'Priming' Plans

Novice programmers by definition, are not conversant with plans, however the Bridge developers require that the students engage in learning about plans via studying a plan workbook before exposure to the tutoring system itself. There are several problems associated with adopting such an approach. Firstly, it is open to the accusation of introducing a confounding variables in assessing the contribution of Bridge to whatever learning outcomes are to be evaluated. One of the ways in which this may be manifest is in changing the way that the students approach Bridge with respect to developing strategies and forming alternative views of the tasks. Moreover, it is likely that exposure to the plan workbook will affect the way that the students develop strategies to comprehend Pascal structures independently of strategies for using Bridge.

Secondly, the theory of programming plans implies that plans are not taught explicitly to students. Rather such plans will be acquired via the same kind of general learning mechanisms (such as induction or analogy) that are posited in schema-based accounts of cognition [22]. Schemata/plans are not taught explicitly, and providing students with a plain workbook violates what appears to be a basic premise of plan-based theories of programming.

Implementation Issues

One final issue relates to the extent to which particular hardware and software platforms have driven the implementation decision and pedagogical tradeoffs that are embodied in BridgeTalk. It seems clear that decisions about the language in which BridgeTalk is implemented "spill over" into the pedagogical process. For example, features of the object oriented implementation of BridgeTalk as inheritance and slot filling make the implementation of, for example, movement between successive levels of abstraction much easier, however this implementational feature appears to have driven the development process.

In addition, in BridgeTalk it is important to ensure that decomposing from the pseudocode level to implementable Pascal code level maintains the continuity of representation (reflected in style, movement, functions, etc.) rather than reflecting constraints imposed by the object-oriented development environment. In many ways, BridgeTalk fosters an object oriented approach to the development of Pascal code because of the flexibility of its implementation. However, it seems incongruous to highlight such an approach in the teaching of a language such as Pascal with an underlying computational model that is far from object oriented.

Another implementation issue relates to the expression of control flow and date flow in the visual language adopted in BridgeTalk. Bonar and Liffick describe the decision to make control flow explicit, (i.e., how the plans fit together), whereas the data flow is indicated by 'subtle visual cues'. The rationale for this is only explained by anecdotal reference to design decision made in a previous version. However, it seems clear that this is an important decision and it is not made clear what information was used to support it, and what implications this decision will have in the subsequent use and evaluation of the system.

Evaluation

The evaluation of PROUST was based on its ability to provide a consistent model of the intentions underlying the programs and scored highly respect to a comparison of its ability to recognise bugs against using methods such as code walkthroughs. In other words it could be evaluated against criteria independent of the theory upon which it was based. The evalution of Bridge which has been reported [5] focuses on informal reports of the problems they had interacting with Bridge and does not provide insight into its utility as an aid to Pascal programming.

It is interesting to note that while Bonar and Cunningham suggest that their students were reasonably successful at developing outline solutions using plan-based concepts, they often had some difficulty translating this into a program. They report that "Matching between the Phase 2 output and Pascal code was problematic, however. Because there is not always a simple match between a plan component and Pascal code, students will sometimes make a reasonable selection that Bridge doesn't accept". (p 409). This appears to suggest that knowing plans alone may be inadequate to explain the performance of programmers. Rather, what appears to be important is understanding how plans are used.

There is little emerging from the descriptions of Bridge to suggest which independent criteria could be used to evaluate Bridge against alternative tutoring systems in terms of its learning outcomes. Indeed it is difficult to imagine how to develop such criteria independent of the plan theory on which it stands.

Conclusion

This paper has sought to explore a number of issues which illustrate the importance of the role of theory in the development of intelligent tutoring system. In order to do this we have concentrated upon a specific theory of skill acquisition in the programming domain and its subsequent implementation in an intelligent tutoring system for teaching Pascal. Our analysis has indicated a range of problem relating to both the implementation of the theory and to the adequacy of the theory itself. It appears that a number of these problems emerge only as a consequence of considering the implementation of the theory as represented by the various incarnations of the Bridge system. The recognition of such problems imposes a requirement on the part of the developer to maintain an awareness of the behavioral and the cognitive implications of the theory upon which it is based. Development of intelligent tutoring systems informed by a more explicit and a better articulated relationship to theory may help to effect closure in the feedback loop between theory driven accounts of cognition and input derived from real-world implementations of those theories.

Hence, we would argue that the success of the instructional method reflects on the correctness of the cognitive theory and vice versa. We suggest that one way of charting and providing navigation on this difficult route is to strengthen and make explicit the way in which design choices have been informed by theory. However the symmetry of this feedback demands consideration of the relationship between the information derived from developing and evaluating the implementation and the effect that this will have on the subsequent reevaluation of the theory. Although we have focussed upon what Littman and Soloway [20] have termed internal evaluation, we feel that an increased awareness of the importance of the symbiotic relationship between theory and its expression in intelligent tutoring systems will eventually help create better teaching systems, the aim of external evaluation.

References

1. Anderson J.R.: Methodologies for studying human knowledge. Behavioral and Brain Sciences 10, 467- 505 (1987)
2. Anderson J.R., Boyle C.F., Reiser B.J.: Intelligent tutoring systems. Science 228, 456-462 (1985)
3. Anderson J.R., Farrell R., Sauers R.: Learning to program in LISP. Cognitive Science 8, 87-129 (1984)
4. Bonar J.: Understanding the bugs of novice programmers. Dissertation, University of Massachusetts, 1985.
5. Bonar J., Cunningham R.: Bridge: an intelligent tutor for thinking about programming. In Self J. (ed.) Artificial intelligence and human learning: intelligent computer-aided instruction, pp. 391-409. London: Chapman and Hall 1988
6. Bonar J., Liffick B.W.: A Visual programming system for novices. In Chang S.K. (ed.) Principles of visual programming systems. Englewood Cliffs: Prentice-Hall 1990
7. Davies S.P.: Skill levels and strategic differences in plan comprehension and implementation in programming, in Sutcliffe A., Macaulay L. (eds.), People and computers V. Proceedings of HCI'89. Cambridge: Cambridge University Press 1989
8. Davies S.P.: The nature and development of programming plans. International Journal of Man-Machine Studies 32, 461-481 (1990)
9. Davies S.P.: Plans, goals and selection rules in the comprehension of computer programs. Behaviour and Information Technology 9(3), 201-214 (1990)
10. Davies S.P.: The role of notation and knowledge representation in the determination of programming strategy: A framework for integrating models of programming behaviour, Cognitive Science 15, 547-572 (1991)
11. Davies S.P.: Expertise in computer programming: the role of working memory and display-based problem solving. (Submitted for publication)
12. Davies S.P.: Characterizing the program design activity: neither strictly top-down nor globally opportunistic. Behaviour and Information Technology 10(3), 173-190 (1991)
13. Gilmore D.J., Green T.R.G.: Programming plans and programming expertise. Quarterly Journal of Experimental Psychology 40A(3), 423-442 (1988)
14. Green T.R.G., Bellamy R.K.E., Parker J.M.: Parsing and gnisrap: A model of device use. In Olson G.M., Sheppard S., Soloway E. (eds.) Empirical studies of programmers: Second workshop, Norwood, NJ: Ablex 1987
15. Guindon R.: Designing the design process: Exploiting opportunistic thoughts. Human-Computer Interaction 5, 305-344 (1990)
16. Hayes-Roth B., Hayes-Roth F.: A cognitive model of planning, Cognitive Science, 3, 275 -310, 1979.
17. Johnson W.L., Soloway E.: PROUST: Knowledge-based program understanding. IEEE Transactions on Software Engineering 11(3), 267-275 (1985)
18. Johnson W.L.: Modelling programmers intentions. In Self J. (ed.) Artificial intelligence and human learning: intelligent computer-aided instruction. London: Chapman and Hall 1988
19. Johnson W.L.: Understanding and debugging novice programs. Artificial Intelligence 42, 51-97 (1990)
20. Littman D., Soloway E.: Evaluating ITSs: the cognitive science perspective. In Polson M.C. and Richardson J.J. (eds.) Foundations of intelligent tutoring systems. Hillsdale, NJ: Lawrence Erlbaum 1988
21. Pennington N.: Comprehension strategies in programming. In Olson G.M., Sheppard S., Soloway E (eds.) Empirical studies of programmers: Second workshop. Norwood, NJ: Ablex 1987
22. Rumelhart D.E., Norman D.A.: Analogical processes in learning. In Anderson J.R. (ed.) Cognitive skills and their acquisition. Hillsdale, NJ: Lawrence Erlbaum 1981
22. Soloway E., Ehrlich K.: Empirical studies of programming knowledge. IEEE Transactions in Software Engineering 10(5), 595-609 (1984)
23. Sopher J.C., Soloway E., Pope E.: Where the bugs are. In Borman L., Curtis B. (eds.) Human factors in computing system II, Proceedings of CHI'85, Amsterdam, North-Holland 1985
24. Stone D.N., Jordan E.W., Wright M.K.: The impact of Pascal education on debugging skill, International Journal of Man-Machine Studies 33, 81-95 (1990)

Two and One-Half Approaches to Helping Novices Learn Recursion

Gordon I. McCalla[1] and Jim E. Greer

ARIES Laboratory, Department of Computational Science, University of Saskatchewan, Saskatoon, Saskatchewan S7N 0W0, CANADA

Abstract: In this chapter we discuss two approaches to supporting students learning recursion, and then introduce a third simpler approach that may in some circumstances prove to be useful. The first approach is exemplified by the SCENT advisor which aims to provide relevant advice to novice programmers on their recursive programming strategies. In this approach knowledge of typical novice strategies is internalized in the system in order that it can understand and comment upon student code. The second approach is illustrated by the PETAL support environment in which students choose among three Programming Environment Tools (PETs) that scaffold their use of three different mental model-level problem solving methodologies as they solve recursive problems. Knowledge of the different problem solving methodologies is externalized in PETAL's design, although the system itself does not contain any internalized knowledge of student mental model-level reasoning. The third approach, reified in the G.E.N.I.U.S. PL/C advisor, does an end run around the need for deep knowledge by taking advantage of idiosyncracies in the relationship between a novice programmer and a supposed expert. Although in many ways this is a half-baked approach, it suggests the possibility of achieving robust and helpful performance with little knowledge engineering.

Keywords: recursive problem solving, knowledge-based advice, scaffolding environments, ignorance-based reasoning

Introduction

For a number of years we have been investigating issues involved in helping novices learn to program. Novices have problems at many levels. They can have difficulty in their use of language constructs, in their development of programming plans and strategies, and in their understanding of deeper mental model-level conceptions underlying the process of program creation. We have the long term objective of being able to build an integrated system that provides support to students at all these levels as they learn to program. In the shorter term we have focussed on the strategic and mental modelling levels, and have limited the domain to learning simple LISP recursion. In particular we have constructed two systems: the SCENT advisor, which provides strategy-level advice to students; and the PETAL system, which supports students at a deeper mental model-level as they create their programs. In this paper we

[1]Visiting the Learning Research and Development Center, University of Pittsburgh, 1991-1992.

will overview each system separately, and then discuss prospects for their integration into a complete programming support tool. Finally we will examine an alternative approach which hints at the possibility of an end run around the need for deep knowledge engineering at all.

The SCENT Advisor

Over the past few years under the auspices of the SCENT project [16] we have been developing a full-fledged intelligent advising system, aimed at providing intelligent strategy-level advice to novice LISP programmers. A novice LISP student presents to the SCENT advisor a program to solve a recursive LISP programming task. The advisor, in turn, provides explanations of various sorts about the student's programming strategies. The student can browse through these explanations at many levels of detail in order to help him/her to understand what he or she has done correctly or incorrectly.

The SCENT advisor is a traditional intelligent tutoring system in that it builds an internalized model of the student programmer's strategy in order to comment upon it. It is non-traditional in its use of case-based and granularity-based reasoning methodologies to help it build this model. As described below, these techniques help the SCENT advisor to overcome the usual brittleness inherent in such model-driven systems. The current implemented prototype SCENT advisor has fairly complete coverage of strategic concepts underlying single function recursive LISP programs, and will work for a number of tasks in this sub-domain. Although enhancements in coverage, recognition, and explanation have been our first priority, the prototype advisor has now undergone its initial test with students in a real world setting.

At the heart of the SCENT advisor is a recognition engine whose job it is to try determine what strategies the student has used in his/her solution to a LISP programming task. The recognition engine uses a model-based approach to recognition, comparing the student's solution to models in a fixed strategy library. There are many examples of such model-based recognition schemes, for example [10, 23]. In our approach we attempt to overcome some of the problems of model-based recognition, especially problems in robustness, flexibility, and adaptability. First, we incorporate into our models an explicit notion of granularity (a computational extension of some of the ideas of Hobbs [9] which we describe in [8]). Granularity allows the recognition engine to back off to coarser grained models if it is unable to recognize detailed student behaviour. This improves the robustness of our model-based recognition scheme. Second, we do not match the models themselves, but instead match the pattern of model instantiation of the current student behaviour to patterns of previous model instantiation. These previous patterns are effectively cases in the sense of [13]. Using cases also enhances the recognition scheme's robustness, and moreover allows the system to be better tuned to its environment since only cases that typically occur in the environment will be in the case library. Since new cases can easily be added, the recognition scheme can eventually be synchronized almost exactly to the needs of students in a domain.

The basic domain models are arrayed in a *static granularity hierarchy*. In the static hierarchy, domain concepts are represented as objects responsible for recognizing instances of themselves in the real world environment. In the LISP domain these objects represent typical

LISP programming strategies and the real world environment is a student solution to some programming task. For example a cdr recursion object would recognize a LISP cdr recursion if the student's solution contained a cdr reduction as well as a null base test. This means that objects are described in terms of their component parts, each of which is itself an object, ultimately bottoming out at observers responsible for actually accessing the environment. This *aggregation* dimension is complemented by an *abstraction* dimension that represents objects in terms of views ranging from abstract to refined. For example an abstraction of cdr recursion is recursion; a specialization is tail-end recursion. Attached to objects in the static granularity hierarchy can be descriptors containing advice that is relevant if that object is recognized in the world. Thus, in the LISP domain there could be advice of relevance to the student about the particular strategies he or she has used.

This static hierarchy is *instantiated* for particular patterns of behaviour in the environment using a *recognition scheme* that can incorporate either top-down or bottom-up control, or mixtures of the two. In bottom-up control, observers look at the environment in order to recognize primitive objects, and recognized objects simplify (aggregate or abstract) into coarser-grained objects. In top-down control, higher-level objects articulate (using aggregation or abstraction relationships) into finer grain sized objects until observers confirm that certain patterns exist in the environment. Multiple instances of objects are represented naturally, so the resulting instantiation pattern of objects is a true hierarchy. This *instance hierarchy*, complete with its recognized and partially recognized objects at various grain sizes, becomes a "fingerprint" for a particular behaviour pattern in the world. In the LISP domain the static hierarchy represents typical programming strategies, and an instance hierarchy is created for each solution (correct or misconceived) to each task. Thus, the static hierarchy is task- and solution-independent, while each instance hierarchy is task- and solution-specific. The recognition process is described in much more detail in [18].

An instance hierarchy constitutes a flexible and robust representation of the many levels of strategies contained in a LISP program. The representation is flexible in that there are various grain sizes at which analysis of the program's strategies can be examined. Even if the student's program cannot be completely recognized at the finest grain size, it can still be recognized at some level of detail. The ability to keep track of partially recognized strategies (i.e. strategies where some of the parts are missing) adds to this robustness. Thus, missing and/or highly uncertain information can be reasoned about. This robustness is further enhanced by the ability to use an instance hierarchy as the basis for a case in the Kolodner [13] sense.

A full *case* consists of a programming task description, a LISP solution, an instance granularity hierarchy corresponding to strategies in the solution, and a set of annotations on the instance hierarchy. The annotations provide a mechanism for attaching advice to specific strategy instances in the hierarchy. The annotation process is initiated by the system which copies general strategy descriptors and general explanations from the static hierarchy over to the instance hierarchy as it is formed using granularity-based recognition. Next, the knowledge engineer adds additional task- and solution-specific annotations to appropriate objects in the instance hierarchy. Cases are thus generated semi-automatically by a knowledge engineer who must supply various ideal solutions for a task the student is to work on, and then must annotate the instance hierarchies with specialized advice, but can let the system do the rest of the case creation. Cases can also represent common buggy solutions. In these cases the annotations must take into account the non-ideal nature of the solution. The knowledge engineer creates an entire library of cases, representing as many of the typical student solutions as desired for each task the student might work on.

When a student uses the SCENT advisor, he or she chooses a task to work on and provides a solution for that task. An instance hierarchy for the student's solution is automatically created by the granularity-based recognition scheme described above. This instance hierarchy is then compared to the case library to find the best match, i.e. the case whose instance hierarchy is structurally most similar to the student's instance hierarchy. Experiments with various algorithms by Coulman [5] has resulted in a very efficient matching process. Then, the explanations stored with this case, together with descriptions of the differences between the student's instance hierarchy and the case's matching instance hierarchy, can be made available to the student.

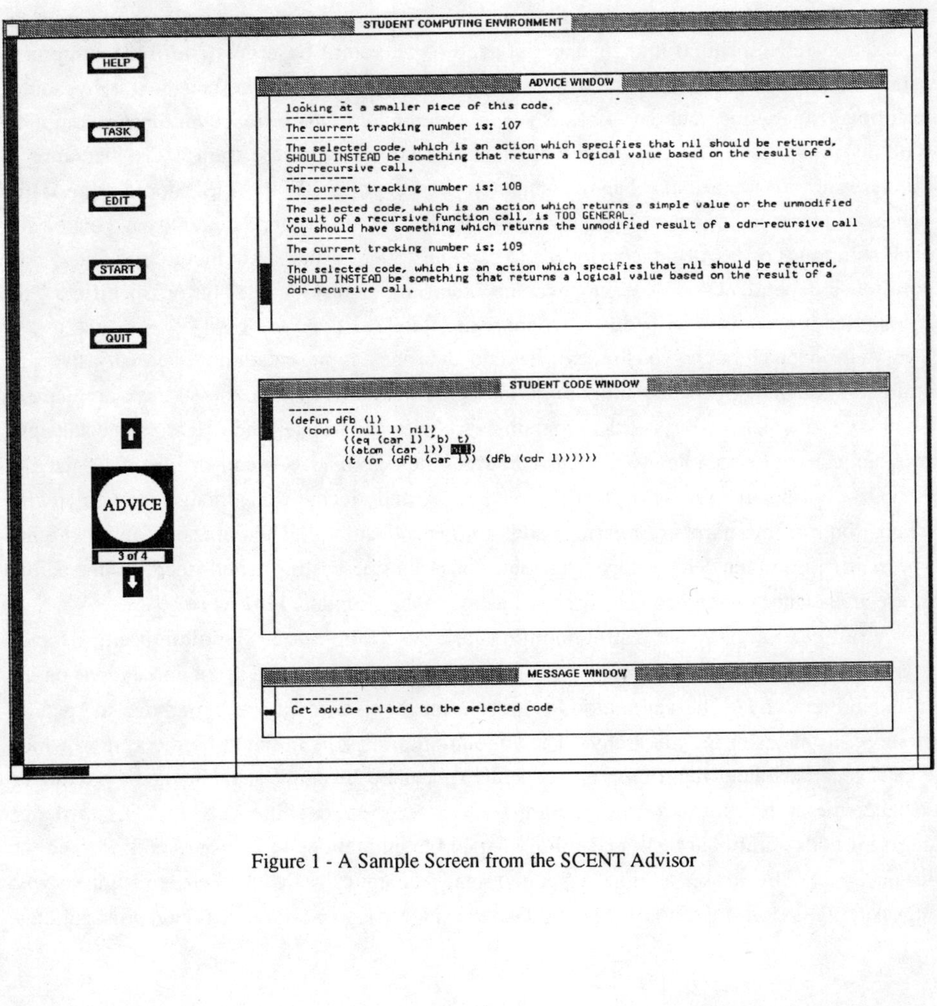

Figure 1 - A Sample Screen from the SCENT Advisor

We have designed an interface (see Figure 1) that the students can use to browse through their solution code for a task. The students enter their solution in the code window, and then the system completes its case-based analysis of the code. The student can access the advice generated in this analysis by highlighting the part of the code about which he/she wants advice (this is a decision about the desired aggregation level of the advice). Then the student selects the level of detail of this advice by clicking the up or down arrows attached to the advice button on the left of the screen (this is a decision about the desired abstraction level of the advice). The advice is scrolled in the advice window at the top of the figure, with tracking numbers separating each piece of advice. These numbers help to coordinate our experimental analysis, since they can be used in relating observer notes and students' verbal protocols with electronic protocols automatically gathered by the system.

We recently made this system available to students in an introductory artificial intelligence course. These students were novices to LISP, but were experienced in other programming languages. Preliminary analysis indicates that the system is robust, and the advice is, in the main, useful to students. However, it appears that we need more cases in the library, and we need to be able to restrict the student from going too deeply along the abstraction dimension since the advice often becomes irrelevant or even harmful at fine-grained levels. In these situations, presumably we have not accurately discerned detailed student goals, or perhaps we have, but the students themselves don't think about their strategies in such a fine-grained way.

Overall, we are pleased with the progress made on the SCENT advisor to date. Adding cases to the granularity-based recognition scheme has allowed a degree of task independence to be achieved. The knowledge engineer need only provide the basic static hierarchy of typical strategies in a given domain, find typical solutions to various tasks in the domain, and do some annotation of the static hierarchy he or she has built and the instance hierarchies generated by the system. Since recognition will happen at some grain size, instance hierarchies are certain to be created for each solution. Later, during an advising session, the case matching algorithms also are sure to retrieve a case, since the analyses of an ideal solution and the student solution are both available at various grain sizes. Any new student solutions discovered during an advising session can be easily annotated and added to the case library, allowing the system's coverage to be relatively easily enhanced. Granularity thus guarantees recognition and matching, while the case-based approach guarantees a modicum of task-independence, generality, and self-improvement in the system. Weber's ELM system [21] (this volume) gains a similar flexibility by adding a notion of cases to a model-based approach, only instead of having a knowledge engineer choose relevant cases to add, ELM incorporates an explanation-based learning scheme that automatically inserts the new cases at an appropriate level in the model hierarchies. This gains the advantage of automatic learning, but means there are lots of irrelevant cases added, and advice must be adapted from generic templates rather than tailored to individual cases.

Finally, it should be noted that there is no reason, in principle, why these methodologies should not work for any domain where users must devise strategies to solve problems, even non-programming domains that require strategic thinking. In fact, we are currently trying to expand the SCENT advisor to be a help system for programmers using complicated large scale information system development tools. This should test the generality of our approach to case-based, granularity-based recognition.

The PETAL System

The advice given by the SCENT advisor is about the strategies that students use to solve problems. Often, however, their problems lie at a deeper level: the mental model level (where the term mental model is meant in a sense similar to that in [6]). The failure to build a correct composition step in a recursion may well reflect the student's deep underlying misconceptions about recursion, for instance that a recursive call is a branch to a subprocedure, and the return is a branch back to the calling program. If the student thinks that recursion is just a loop, it is hardly surprising that the composition step is a mystery! Mental models in the programming domain such as the loop model have been investigated by a wide variety of researchers, including [1, 7, 11, 12, 14, 19].

The loop model is an example of a faulty mental model of how recursion works. There are also a variety of correct mental models of recursion. One of these is the *syntactic model*, where students abstract structural features and code templates in order to put together their solutions. A more sophisticated model is the *analytic model*, where students no longer see recursion in terms of syntactic templates, but instead analyze the problem in terms of cases, and determine input conditions and output strategies for each case. Perhaps the most sophisticated mental model of recursion is the *analysis/synthesis model*, where students are able to break a problem down into sub-problems and then combine the sub-problem solutions appropriately. Empirical studies carried out in our laboratory [3, 4] have shown that students indeed do use syntactic and analytic models, and that there is a natural progression from syntactic to analytic model as students gain experience in writing recursive programs. We hypothesize that as students become experts, they will make a final transition to the analysis/synthesis model, although the studies only ran long enough to hint at this evolution.

In the long term we have been considering the problem of incorporating a mental model level into our SCENT recognition scheme, thus enabling the system to provide advice on the deeper problems students may be having (see the conclusions, below). However, this will require us to achieve more understanding of the mental model level than we currently possess. In order to gain this understanding, we have needed a way of having students express to us in some unambiguous way what they are thinking at the mental model level. We would like this communication to be as natural as possible so that it doesn't get in the way of students' thinking as they solve programming problems.

To this end, one of our Ph.D. students, Shawkat Bhuiyan, has devised a system called PETAL [2, 4] which consists of three Programming Environment Tools (PETs) to support students in the use of the three mental models of recursion. As students use a PET, they express mental model-level decisions by actions carried out in the PET. These actions can be automatically recorded, and when correlated with external observations made by an experimenter, can yield detailed insights into the use of mental models. Better yet, students do not find this distracting, since the PETs also help them learn about recursion. The PETs provide scaffolding and support for the students as they carry out programming tasks. Thus, PETAL has two important goals: it should serve as both a learning tool and a tool for collecting empirical evidence. Because the tools support all phases of program construction from the perspective of a given mental model, we prefer to refer to them as supporting *mental methods*, rather than simply mental models. Unlike the SCENT advisor, PETAL does not build any internal model of student behaviour. On the other hand, like the SCENT advisor, it has required a good deal of sophisticated knowledge engineering based on understanding real student behaviour in order to construct it. In this sense PETAL has a sophisticated "external student model" (as the term is discussed in [15]).

PETAL consists of three PETs: PET1, supporting the syntactic method; PET2, supporting the analytic method; and PET3, supporting the analysis/synthesis method. A student using PETAL first chooses a particular programming problem to work on. A description of the problem and examples of its behaviour are then shown to the student. If the student is interested in trying to solve the problem, he or she then selects one of the three PETs. A new screen appropriate to the PET is then presented to the student.

A screen image of the analytic PET is shown in Figure 2. The PET has been initialized for the programming task the student is working on, in this case the findb problem ("return true if a list has a b at the top-level"). A student uses PET2 in three stages: (i) *intention*, where, similar to the intial stages of the Programmer's Apprentice [20], the student's basic goals are elaborated; (ii) *plan*, where these intentions are expressed at an algorithmic level similar to the plan level in PROUST [10]; and (iii) *code translation*, where actual code is produced. The PET provides menus to help students reify their choices at each stage. Figure 2 shows the support tool for stages (i) and (ii). On the left side of the screen at the top are a selection of descriptors (tuned to the findb problem, including appropriate correct descriptors as well as common distractors). With these the student is able to express at the bottom left of the screen the intended input cases and output strategies for the particular problem being solved (in this case the findb problem). Once the student is satisfied that his or her intention has been captured, he or she works on the right side of the screen selecting natural language phrases that flesh out the intention into a programming plan. This plan is built up at the bottom right of the screen, and like the intention phase description the plan is also divided into an input and output part. When done this second phase, the student presses the Coding Stage button to head on to stage (iii), where the analytic PET overlays a special PET2 editor window on top of the phase (i) and phase (ii) screens. In this window, the student generates separate LISP code chunks (again with the help of a menu containing code chunks appropriate for the findb problem) for each different piece of the stage (ii) intention-level solution. When the student wants to see the complete code, he or she clicks on the Edit Program button which overlays a LISP editor window over the PET2 screen. In this window PET2 displays the complete LISP program as devised in the coding stage, now automatically packaged by the PET into a COND, prefaced by an appropriate function header, and annotated with a commentary derived from the choices made by the student in earlier stages of the analytic PET.

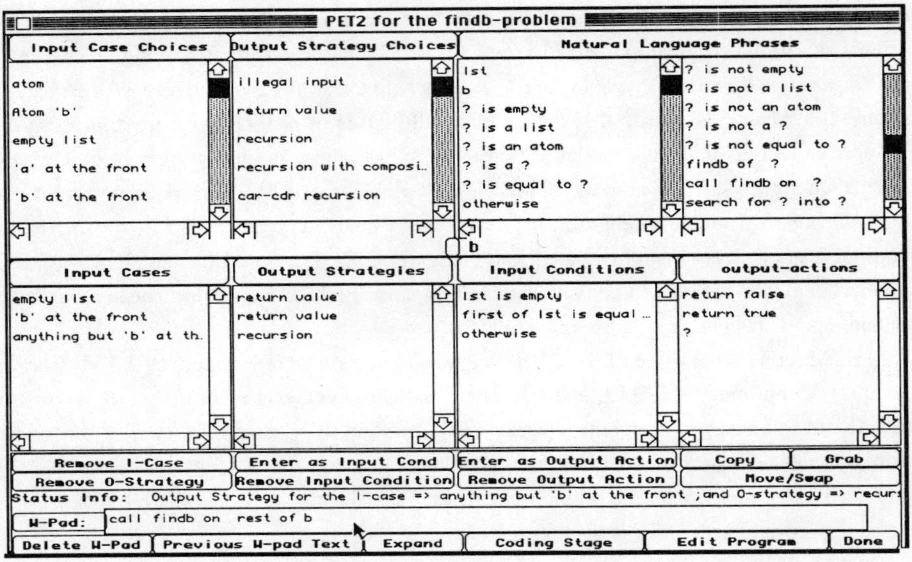

Figure 2 - Intention and Plan Screen from PET2

The other two PETs look fairly similar. Bhuiyan has tried to make a similar interface for each PET so that students won't be attracted or repelled by a PET for surface reasons. Their choice of a particular PET should be based on its deep support for the kind of problem solving they want to carry out. A complete discussion of these PETs can be found in [2].

Bhuiyan has recently carried out an empirical study of PETAL to see if it indeed does fulfill its goals of being both a learning tool for students and an experimental tool for empirical investigations. In this study a group of 9 students (near novices in programming and complete novices in the use of LISP) were given a 6 week introductory LISP course. During the first 2 weeks of the course both groups were introduced to the basics of LISP through lectures and individual problem solving using the standard LISP environment. Then, for the next three weeks they studied recursive problem solving, also through lectures and individual problem solving. For this phase, they were divided into two groups, a treatment group of 5 students who used PETAL and a control group of 4 who simply continued to use the standard LISP programming environment. For both groups, Bhuiyan sat with them, taking notes, dispensing occasional miminal advice and explaining solutions to problems when they ran into impasses. During this phase, he was able to collect a massive number of electronic protocols, along with videotapes of the students "in action" on PETAL. He also carried out post-session interviews with students as they went through the videotapes together. In these sessions he was able to elicit further information from the students about what they were thinking (or at least what they thought they were thinking) as they solved recursive programming problems. Finally, in the sixth week of the study he gave both control and treatment groups a pencil and paper post test of their recursive programming abilities. This study has resulted in a huge mass of data which

Bhuiyan is still analyzing. Nevertheless the preliminary analysis indicates that PETAL worked astonishingly well.

During the experiment, the 5 students using PETAL attempted an average of 8.8 problems, eventually got 82% of them correct, and took on average 30.64 minutes to solve a problem (or to reach an impasse). In contrast, the 4 non-PETAL students only attempted an average of 4.5 problems each, only got 15% of them correct (the rest were impasses), and took an average of 56.02 minutes on each problem. The difference in performance between the two groups on the pencil and paper post test was even more startling. On this test, Bhuiyan had the students solve 3 recursive programming problems and provide a trace of a recursive program. The PETAL students got 60% of the problems completely correct, 87% of them nearly correct (missing only one case), 93% of them syntactically correct, and got 100% of the traces right. The non-PETAL students solved none of the problems correctly, only one solution to one problem was nearly correct, none of their solutions were syntactically correct, and only one student got the trace right. Clearly, the support given by PETAL was crucial in the treatment group learning how to solve recursive problems. Why did PETAL work?

Looking in more detail at the particulars of each student's problem solving behaviour (through protocol and keystroke analysis), Bhuiyan has found that the PETAL students all eventually evolved an understanding of the syntactic method and then the analytic method (none of them developed or needed the analysis/synthesis method for these simple recursive problems). At some point they seemed to "catch on" (about the time they started to use the analytic model), and after this they became quite skilled problem solvers. In contrast, the non-PETAL students were still struggling with the basics of the syntactic method even at the end of the experiment, and never "caught on" to the analytic method. A more thorough analysis of the students' protocols is currently underway (see [2]), but it seems at this stage that the reasons for PETAL's success are two-fold. First, the various PETs directly support learning of the various methods by reifying for the students the conceptual primitives of each method. Second, the PETs help in the management of complexity, both by helping the students stage their thinking through phases and by supporting students in the creation of correct LISP syntax through the provision of a powerful editor. We are heartened by the success of PETAL and will be further analyzing the data and possibly running follow up studies to try to clarify "where the power is" in the scaffolding approach taken by PETAL.

The Potential of the SCENT and PETAL Approaches

In the SCENT advisor and the PETAL environment we have tried to tackle two very difficult problems in helping students as they learn to program: supporting their learning at the strategic or plan level, and helping them to use various deep mental methods as they construct solutions to recursive programming tasks. We believe both approaches have been successful, at least relative to our goals. In the SCENT advisor, we have generalized model-based recognition so as to minimize the usual problems of sporadic coverage of the domain, lack of context-dependent models, and inability to adapt and grow with experience. In the PETAL system we have reified aspects of three different mental methods for recursive problem solving, providing scaffolding for students as they use these methods, allowing the students to progress through increasingly sophisticated methods as their knowledge grows, and finally allowing us, as experimenters, to collect precise data about how students reason at the mental model level.

Although these systems are both domain-specific and task-dependent, their structure is general. It is easy to add a new task to the SCENT advisor: all that needs to be done is to come up with typical solutions (both good and ill-conceived) to the task, then use the granularity-based recognition scheme to generate the core of the case for the solution, and finally annotate the case with any task-specific information. Changing domains in the SCENT advisor is more difficult, since it requires a brand new static granularity hierarchy to be created to represent the basic concepts in the domain. Still, with experience, this is possible, and once the static hierarchy is created, it should remain relatively stable as more and more tasks are added to take care of variation within the domain. We anticipate that a SCENT-style approach will apply not only to other parts of the programming domain (e.g. iteration), but also to other problem solving domains. Adding a new task to the PETAL system is also fairly straightforward, since all that needs to be done is to choose a set of templates and descriptors relevant to the task. Often this simply requires slight changes to the templates and descriptors created for already existing tasks. Devising a new PET, however, is hard. Much of Bhuiyan's toughest work has been in coming up with the conceptual primitives for each mental method and then incorporating them into an appropriate screen design. His job has been complicated, of course, by his desire to have the various screens for each PET look similar to each other so as to minimize the students' difficulty in using the PETs and to not discourage students from trying increasingly sophisticated PETs. Still, Bhuiyan has shown the way, and we feel that this approach is amenable to creating support tools for deep mental methods in other problem solving areas.

Integrating the SCENT and PETAL Approaches

One of the intriguing possibilities we are considering is how to combine the PETAL and SCENT philosophies. It would seem that there are two basic ways of doing this. First would be to incorporate an advising capability into PETAL. There are doubtless various strategies as to how to put things together using Bhuiyan's mental methods, and presumably these could be modelled in terms of a granularity hierarchy. Cases could then be derived corresponding to typical student uses of each PET, and advice could be hung off the cases. If all of this could be done, then Bhuiyan's PETs could have available advice for students about their tentative mental model-level solutions to programming tasks. How hard this will be remains to be seen, but the many descriptors and templates used in PETAL seem to be a first step, at least, in beginning to form the appropriate abstractions and aggregations.

The other approach to merging the SCENT and PETAL philosophies is to deepen the SCENT system so that it can give advice about the student's deeper mental methods as well as the strategic levels of their solution to a programming task. A student using the new, souped up SCENT would find advice not only on missing base cases or fouled up composition steps, but might also get advice that he or she seems to have left out the base case because an intention was ignored, or has a weak composition step because recursion was being thought of in terms of a loop. This example points out immediately that in addition to the "correct" mental methods considered in PETAL, inappropriate mental methods (such as trying to analogize recursive programming in terms of loop structures) would have to be formalized. Even more difficult, however, is understanding just what the mental method level is relative to the strategic level. Maybe it constitutes a new and different granularity level at some deeper or finer grain size than the strategy level; or maybe it can be represented by other kinds of strategies intermingled with current strategies.

In choosing between these two approaches, it is important to watch how various types of novices actually create their code, and to be clear as to which type is the intended audience for the programming tool. For completely naive programmers, who need help not only with how to put together plans, but also lots of help in the deeper underpinnings of problem solving, the approach of adding advice to something like PETAL, i.e. the first approach, makes more sense. A hybrid system of the first type would be even more supportive than PETAL currently is for such students. On the other hand for sophisticated programmers who are only novices in the use of a new language, the second approach, adding deeper advice to SCENT, might make more sense. Such a programmer already has fairly well worked out mental methods, and would only need occasional advice about his or her mental methods (e.g. a FORTRAN programmer learning recursion in PASCAL might be thinking of recursion in terms of loops, despite his or her experience in other aspects of programming). A complete, mental method support tool, such as those devised by Bhuiyan, might just get in such a programmer's way.

Overall, in evaluating the direction to go in merging the PETAL and SCENT philosophies, it seems to us that perhaps the first direction is more tractable and more interesting from the point of view of producing a working application tool that would really help novices. The second approach may shed more light on theoretical issues like granularity, and might provide the foundations for a "help" tool for more expert programmers. It does seem harder, however, at this stage than the first approach. It will be interesting to see what happens as these investigations proceed.

But, Is Deep Knowledge Engineering Really Necessary?

Now we would like to discuss what many may see as a "half-baked" idea. The entire paper so far has been based on the assumption that, whatever else it may require, a system to support the learning of programming will entail considerable knowledge engineering. Is this really true? Perhaps, at least in certain cases, it will turn out to be possible to take advantage of aspects of the learning context in order to avoid the need for deep models of any sort. Such a "situated" system would need only insinuate itself appropriately into the interaction between the programmer and the world in order to enhance learning without the need to be concerned about the precise effects the system is having on the student's learning.

This kind of situation seems to arise in the programming domain. Every instructor of programming knows the phenomenom of the student who arrives with a gargantuan program listing inside of which lurks a subtle logic error. The instructor, actually having no idea of what the student is trying to accomplish with this mass of code, asks the student some fairly trivial questions about particular error messages, what the student is trying to accomplish at the points where these messages are generated, etc. The student, imbued with expectations that the instructor is a genius, assumes that the instructor's comments are based on deep and penetrating insights and looks carefully at the program. As often as not, this careful analysis helps the student to solve the problem. "Eureka!" The student leaves, still under the misapprehension that the instructor is a genius. What has happened here is that, much as in ELIZA [22], the instructor has taken advantage of his or her status as an authority in the eyes of the student to have the student solve their own problem. The social implications of the student-instructor interaction have conspired to provide relevant and useful advice without knowledge!

In our laboratory we have developed a system based on this scenario called G.E.N.I.U.S., an advisor for PL/C programming [17]. Students using G.E.N.I.U.S. are encouraged to enter the error message number of any error they think is significant. G.E.N.I.U.S. responds with some general advice about their error, and then prompts for more input from the student. The interactions produced seem quite natural, although as in ELIZA things can go seriously awry. G.E.N.I.US. achieves this with no real knowledge of the student or the domain; it is in a real sense "ignorance-based". Advice in the form of English "blurbs" is pre-stored in a large discrimination net, and is accessed through keywords in the student's input. The keywords themselves can trigger different advice depending on where in the network the system is currently focussed, making the system sensitive to context. Default answers are provided when the system can find no matching keywords in the student's input enhancing the robustness of the system. Moreover, it is a relatively simple task to engineer a large discrimination network and the relevant keywords for a domain.

G.E.N.I.U.S. has been used in a class of novice programming students with marginal success. Students tended to use the system 2 or 3 times before realizing that the air of authority essential for the student-tutor interaction to work properly was misplaced. Doubts arose when G.E.N.I.U.S. either became redundant or when students asked about errors not in G.E.N.I.US.'s storehouse of errors. This points out that it is crucial to maintain the social contract for a situated system to work properly. Anything violating that contract, for example obvious ignorance on the part of a supposed G.E.N.I.U.S., is likely to lead to the deterioration or collapse of the system's credibility, and hence its effectiveness.

Thus, it is an open question whether it is possible for an "ignorance-based" system like G.E.N.I.U.S. to indefinitely maintain its social contract with the student. It may turn out that building a system to take advantage of a social situation ultimately requires all the techniques so familiar to deep, knowledge-based systems like the SCENT advisor or the PETAL scaffolding environment. Nevertheless, we think that it may be worthwhile to consider the idea of building ignorance-based systems when the appropriate social context presents itself, thus achieving robustness and flexibility while vastly reducing the knowledge engineering task.

Acknowledgements: We thank Shawkat Bhuiyan, Randy Coulman, Kevin Murtagh and a host of other students over the years for developing and/or programming the PETAL, SCENT, and G.E.N.I.U.S. systems. We would also like to express our gratitude to the Natural Sciences and Engineering Research Council of Canada and the University of Saskatchewan for their financial support of various research projects in the ARIES Laboratory. Finally, the first author thanks NATO for supporting travel to the workshop in which this paper was presented, and Enrica Lemut, the director of the workshop, for organizing an outstanding event.

References

1. Anzai, Y. and Uesato, Y.: Learning recursive procedures by middle school children. Proceedings of the Fourth Annual Conference of the Cognitive Science Society, Ann Arbor, MI, pp. 100-102. 1982
2. Bhuiyan, S.H.: Supporting students in the use of mental methods of recursion (tentative title). Ph.D. Thesis, Dept. of Computational Science, U. of Saskatchewan, Saskatoon, SK, Canada. forthcoming
3. Bhuiyan, S.H., Greer, J.E., and McCalla, G.I.: Mental models of recursion and their use in the SCENT programming advisor. Proceedings of the Knowledge-Based Computer Systems Conference, Bombay, India, 135-144. 1989
4. Bhuiyan, S.H., Greer, J.E., and McCalla, G.I.: Characterizing, rationalizing, and reifying mental models of recursion. Proceedings of the 13th Meeting of the Cognitive Science Society, Chicago, 1991
5. Coulman R.A.: Combining case-based reasoning and granularity for educational diagnosis in an intelligent tutoring system. M.Sc thesis, Department of Computational Science, University of Saskatchewan, Saskatoon. 1991
6. Gentner, D. and Stevens, A. (eds.): Mental models. Hillside, NJ: Lawrence Erlbaum. 1983
7. Greer, J.E.: Empirical comparison of techniques for teaching recursion in introductory computer science, Ph.D. Thesis, U. of Texas, Austin, TX. 1987
8. Greer, J.E. and McCalla, G.I.: A computational framework for granularity and its application to educational diagnosis. Proceedings of the International Joint Conference on Artificial Intelligence (IJCAI), Detroit, pp. 477-482. 1989
9. Hobbs, J.: Granularity. Proceedings of the International Joint Conference on Artificial Intelligence, Los Angeles, pp. 432-435. 1985
10. Johnson, L. and Soloway, E.: Intention-based diagnosis of programming errors. Proceedings of AAAI 84, Austin, TX, 162-168. 1984
11. Kahney, H.: An in-depth study of the cognitive behaviour of novice programmers, TR 5, Open University, Milton-Keynes, UK. 1982
12. Kessler, C.M. and Anderson, J.R.: Learning flow of control: iterative and recursive procedures. Human-Computer Interaction 2, 135-166 (1986)
13. Kolodner, J.: Judging which is the best case for a case-based reasoner. Proceedings of the Second Case-Based Reasoning Workshop, Pensacola Beach, FL, pp. 77-81. 1989
14. Kurland, D.M. and Pea, R.D.: Children's mental models of recursive LOGO programming. Journal of Educational Computing Research 1, 235-243 (1985)
15. McCalla, G.I.: The central importance of student modelling to intelligent tutoring. In: New directions for intelligent tutoring systems (E. Costa, ed.). Berlin-Heidelberg-New York: Springer-Verlag forthcoming
16. McCalla, G.I., Greer, J.E., and the SCENT Research Team: Intelligent advising in problem solving domains: The SCENT-3 architecture. Proceedings of the First International Conference on Intelligent Tutoring Systems (ITS '88), Montreal, Canada, pp. 124-131. 1988
17. McCalla, G. I. and Murtagh, K.: G.E.N.I.U.S.: An experiment in ignorance-based automated program advising. AISB Newsletter 75, United Kingdom, pp. 13-20. Winter 1990/91
18. McCalla, G.I.,Greer, J.E., Barrie, B. and Pospisil, P.: Granularity hierarchies. International Journal of Computers and Mathematics with Applications (Special Issue on Semantic Networks), 23, 363-376 (1992)
19. Pirolli, P. A.: A cognitive model of a computer tutor for programming recursion. Human-Computer Interaction 2, 329-355 (1985)
20. Rich, C. and Shrobe, H.E. (1978) "Initial Report on a LISP Programmer's Apprentice", IEEE Transactions on Software Engineering, se-4, 6, November.
21. Weber, G.: Analogies in an intelligent programming environment for learning LISP, Proceedings of the Workshop on Cognitive Models and Intelligent Environments for Learning Programming, Genoa, Italy, pp. 85-94. 1992
22. Weizenbaum, J. (1966). "ELIZA - A Computer Program for the Study of Natural Language Communications Between Man and Machine", CACM, 9, 1, pp. 36-45.
23. Wills, L. M.: Automated program recognition: A feasibility demonstration. Artificial Intelligence 45, 113-171 (1990)

Knowledge Based Tools in Software Engineering Education

Paola Forcheri and Maria Teresa Molfino
Istituto per la Matematica Applicata - Consiglio Nazionale delle Ricerche
Via L.B. Alberti 4, 16132 Genova, Italy

Abstract: A computer based laboratory on abstract algebraic specifications was designed and implemented. The lab is intended as a tool to enable software engineering students to reason about programming problems abstractly. In particular, the lab provides students with a set of tools for building and modifying specifications, and allows them to effectively use specifications inside a program, written in a given programming language, by a process of automatic implementation.

Keywords: Programming learning, software engineering education, algebraic specifications

1. Introduction

The ability to specify programs on the basis of a formal description is one of the most useful requirements in designing and implementing reliable, re-usable, and easily maintained software, as specifications provide descriptions of software which are independent of the environment of implementation. Moreover, if these formal descriptions can be automatically executed, attention may be operatively focused on the main aspects of the programming activity, that is the data involved, the processes operating on them, their relationship and properties, the adherence of the program to the problem. Because of this, the teaching of algebraic specification methods is prominent in software engineering education.

However, the majority of students finds it difficult to appreciate the importance of these methods, as they are usually taught by using a theoretical approach and practical applications are not proposed. Consequently, in practical programming activities, students pay attention to the environment rather than the program design, thus making representation affect substantially software production.

These difficulties may be overcome by observing that it is much easier to understand abstractions when they derive from concrete experience which can only be had by using concrete tools and techniques.

On the basis of these considerations, a computer based laboratory on abstract algebraic specifications was realized. The lab, called MEMO, integrates the capacity to symbolically manipulate abstract objects and to describe computational processes operating on such objects, within a single computational context. MEMO places at the student's disposition a set of tools which allow him to develop all phases of software production by using the abstract specification directly, by-passing the phase of translation from a formal specification into its representation in a given programming language. Students can operatively define a program based on the concept of abstraction, they can analyse the properties of this abstraction, automatically obtain code in a given language and execute it.

The procedural interpretation of algebraic specifications of abstract data types, by means of the term rewriting system theory [5], underlies the system: the computational processes are described by rewrite rules that can be executed directly; the properties of the objects are examined by a process which adds the capacity of proving theorems by induction to that of performing equational reasoning.

MEMO provides for the building of equational specifications of programs; for the generation and verification of properties of a given specification; for the direct implementation, in Prolog language, of a given specification. The system is easy to operate, it produces solutions by using techniques similar to those employed by human experts; it explains the reasoning and the knowledge behind the solution of a problem. The capabilities of the system are interactively accessed by means of a series of commands. MEMO is written in Prolog and runs under operating system UNIX.

In the following, the main educational features of MEMO will be illustrated, through the analysis of an example of its use in the design and realisation of a program. This analysis aims at supplying an operative contribution to the discussion regarding how, and to what extent, automatic tools, endowed with the capability of reasoning about programs, can be employed to help students overcome the cognitive difficulties which underlie the learning of software production methods.

2. Features of the system

As noted by several authors [1,15], the cognitive difficulties which underlie the learning of programming regard mainly the phases of problem representation, testing, prototyping. As a consequence, it seems worthwhile to provide students with automatic tools which allow them to experiment with these activities. Powerful computing environments, based on different methods and techniques, have consequently been realised and experimented: automatic theorem provers [16], tools for visualizing sofware [8,9]; computer aided programming [2,14,17]; syntax-oriented editors [6]; specification systems [13], etc.. However, as different kinds of facilities are usually available from different tools, a considerable amount of time and effort is spent in learning to handle these tools, and students are led to concentrate on technical aspects rather than on the topic of interest. These problems can be overcome by placing at students' disposition a computational lab which adds the capability of reasoning about programs to facilities for rapid prototyping. MEMO has been designed on the lines of this pedagogical approach. The computational interpretation, via term rewriting, of algebraic specifications was the basis for the realisation of the system. In fact, under suitable conditions, a term rewriting system can be associated to a specification and, when this term rewriting system is proved to be canonical (i.e. noetherian and confluent) we can automatically obtain the code from the specification via a process of direct implementation and, at the same time, to prove properties of the specification via rewriting and induction.

To help students understand the different processes intervening into the building of programs, that is how a model is built and modified, how interesting conjectures are made and verified, how a representation can be derived, MEMO places a series of commands at the disposition of the user. Via the commands, the user autonomously decides on the specification to be explored, formulates properties which must be verified and the knowledge to be used in the proof, establishes which links with mathematical structures have to be analysed, decides which tests are to be carried out. The system helps the user in this activity by guiding him to describe the specification, by verifying its adequacy with respect to executability, by giving proof of the properties indicated by the student and by deriving programs from specifications.

The lab enables students to deal with problems pertaining to the following classes:

1. Representation of the problem. The student is given a language which allows him to model a problem by means of a collection of operators whose properties are defined by a set of equational laws.

2. Testing. The executability of a specification, that is, the possibility of using it for prototyping, is automatically verified.

3. Adherence of the representation to the programmers' idea. The system automatically checks whether properties that students think are owned by the specification.

4. Abstract modelling of the user's problem. The student can automatically analyse the mathematical structure of a specification.

5. Implementation of the problem. A specification can be effectively used within a program, written in Prolog, by automatically obtaining the corresponding code.

In the following, we will illustrate the capabilities of the lab by means of examples.

2.1 Building abstractions

To guide students in building abstractions, the lab sets at the user's disposition a language to describe a data type following the initial algebra approach to the specification used by Huet [12]. Moreover, the language makes it possible to specify a data type incrementally [4]. To correctly specify a program the user must express a "correct" idea of the objects of the type, by explicitly indicating the constructors. He has then to define the operations on the objects. Operations are specified by indicating their name and arity, and a set of "oriented" equations (that is, equations which are interpreted as rewrite rules), which give meaning to the names of the operations. For each operation, the definition must be given by taking into account that a computation unit will correspond to its axiomatic specification: thus, defining equations must be given in a way that allows carrying out a corresponding computation for all objects of the type; moreover, defining equations must guarantee that each corresponding computation terminates (normally or abnormally) and that it terminates in a unique way for each object of the type.

Specifications can be *generic* or *explicit*. A *generic* specification is a scheme that contains parameters (variables, operations and other types) that are instantiated when the specification is used in an actual program. An *explicit* specification is a refinement of a generic specification that substitutes actual arguments for the specification parameters.

For example, referring to the problem of reversing a list, the student can specify the program as shown in Figure 1.

2.2 Verifying executability of abstractions

The user is helped to build abstractions which verify the above properties (that is, that they are executable) by means of a tool, embedded in the lab, which automatically verifies the executability of the data type and guides the student in correcting errors [10]. The result of the process is a message informing the user as to executability of the specification at hand. When validation terminates with success we know that every instance of an abstract data type has a normal form which consists of constructors only, that every computation which entails only functions of the specification always terminates, and that the result is independent on the order in which "oriented equations" are applied. In case of error, the kind of error is pointed out and the editor is called in order to enable the student to modify the specification.

By means of the verification tool, relevant misconceptions are detected. For example, if the user gives the specification shown in Figure 2, where *lt* is the predicate "less than" on the data type listb, the system detects that the definition of *lt* is incomplete.

```
OBJECT list IS
SORT ls
CONSTRUCTOR
[]: --> ls;
cons: el x ls --> ls;

OBJECT listrev IS
ENRICHMENT OF list
OPERATION append:ls x ls --> ls IS AXIOM
append([],X) = X;
append(cons(X,Y),Z)) = cons(X,append(Y,Z)).
OPERATION reverse: ls --> ls IS AXIOM
reverse([]) =[];
reverse(cons(X,Y)) = append(reverse(Y),cons(X,[])).
```

Figure 1. Equational definition of the data type *listrev*. It is incrementally defined, starting from the definition of the data type *list*. The data type *listrev=(ls, [], cons, append, reverse)* we define consists of a base set *ls*, one operation with arity zero *[]: --> ls*, one unary operation *reverse: ls-->ls* and two binary operations *append: ls x ls-->ls, cons: el x ls-->ls*, where *el* indicates the base set of the elements of a list. In the equations, upper case identifiers indicate universally quantified variables.

In fact, the recursion on pairs of elements where the first is greater than the second does not terminate properly, since no true value can be derived from terms of the form

Specification given by the user

```
OBJECT listb IS
SORT ls
CONSTRUCTOR
[]: --> ls;
cons: el x ls --> ls;
SORT bool
CONSTRUCTOR
true: --> bool;
false: --> bool;

OPERATION lt: ls x ls --> bool IS AXIOM
lt([],[])= false;
lt([],cons(X,Y))=true;
lt(cons(X,Y),cons(Z,T))=lt(Y,T).
```

Message of the system

```
incompletely defined function
operation lt:ls x ls -->bool
```

Figure 2. Example of incomplete definition and corresponding output.

lt(cons(X,Y),[]).

Another example is shown in Figure 3. The definition of *le,* where *le* is the predicate "less or equal" on the data type listb, is inconsistent. In fact, the term le([],[]) can be reduced to false or true depending on the axiom chosen.

Specification given by the user

```
OPERATION le: ls x ls --> bool IS AXIOM
le([],X)= true;
le(X,[])=false;
le(cons(X,Y),cons(Z,T))=lt(Y,T).
```

Message of the system

```
axioms imply true=false
operation le: ls x ls --> bool
```

Figure 3. Example of inconsistent definition and corresponding output.

2.3 Analysing mathematical properties of a specification

To facilitate students in the process of analysing features of a program, the lab automatically performs proofs of properties of a formal specification, at the user's request [11].

The student indicates the property and the environment (the premisses) to be used to carry out the proof. The proof process is carried out by the system.

The properties, expressed in equational form, are analysed by using a many sorted version of the Boyer and Moore theorem prover, which performs proofs based on rewriting and induction [7]. The process is carried out in three steps; at first, the environment of the proof is determined; the inductive arguments for every defined operation of the specification are then automatically established; finally, an attempt is made to verify whether the given equation is a theorem.

For example, referring to the problem of proving that the *reverse* operation is idempotent, the student can give the command: *PROVE listrev reverse(reverse(X))=X*. The proof of the property and the print-out of the proof itself are the result of the execution of the command (see Figure 4).

The print_out explains the proof strategy and shows the individual steps of the solution with their justifications: at first the environment of the proof is visualized (the arrow is employed to clarify that equational deduction is replaced by computation); then, the property to be proved is displayed; finally, the complete proof process is shown. When the system decides to use induction as proof method, it informs the user

```
The axioms are:
 ax_1 append([],A0) -> A0
 ax_2 append(cons(A1,A2),A3) -> cons(A1,append(A2,A3))
 ax_3 reverse([]) -> []
 ax_4 reverse(cons(A4,A5)) -> append(reverse(A5),cons(A4,[]))

The theorem is:
 reverse(reverse(A6)) = A6
Begin induction on A6
Induction on A6 case []
 (L) reverse(reverse([]))     << subst A6 with [] <<
 (R) []     << subst A6 with [] <<
 (L) reverse([])     << reduct by ax_3 <<
 (L) []     << reduct by ax_3 <<
 *** equality obtained ***
Induction on A6 case cons(A7,A8)
 (L) reverse(reverse(cons(A7,A8)))     << subst A6 with cons(A7,A8) <<
 (R) cons(A7,A8)     << subst A6 with cons(A7,A8) <<
 (L) reverse(append(reverse(A8),cons(A7,[])))     << reduct by ax_4 <<
 (R) cons(A7,reverse(reverse(A8)))     << ind. hyp. on  A6 for A8 <<
 (L) reverse(append(A9,cons(A7,[])))     << gen of reverse(A8) <<
 (R) cons(A7,reverse(A9))     << gen of reverse(A8) <<
 *** equality depends on next lemma ***
The lemma is:
 reverse(append(A9,cons(A7,[]))) = cons(A7,reverse(A9))
Begin induction on A9
Induction on A9 case []
 (L) reverse(append([],cons(A7,[])))     << subst A9 with [] <<
 (R) cons(A7,reverse([]))     << subst A9 with [] <<
 (L) reverse(cons(A7,[]))     << reduct by ax_1 <<
 (L) append(reverse([]),cons(A7,[]))     << reduct by ax_4 <<
 (L) append([],cons(A7,[]))     << reduct by ax_3 <<
 (R) cons(A7,[])     << reduct by ax_3 <<
 (L) cons(A7,[])     << reduct by ax_1 <<
 *** equality obtained *** Induction on A9 case cons(B0,B1)
 (L) reverse(append(cons(B0,B1),cons(A7,[])))     << subst A9 with cons(B0,B1) <<
 (R) cons(A7,reverse(cons(B0,B1)))     << subst A9 with cons(B0,B1) <<
 (L) reverse(cons(B0,append(B1,cons(A7,[]))))     << reduct by ax_2 <<
 (R) cons(A7,append(reverse(B1),cons(B0,[])))     << reduct by ax_4 <<
 (L) append(reverse(append(B1,cons(A7,[]))),cons(B0,[]))     << reduct by ax_4 <<
 (L) append(cons(A7,reverse(B1)),cons(B0,[]))     << ind. hyp. on  A9 for B1 <<
 (L) cons(A7,append(reverse(B1),cons(B0,[])))     << reduct by ax_2 <<
 *** equality obtained ***
End induction on A9
End induction on A6
QED
```

Figure 4. Print-out of the proof of the property *reverse(reverse(X))=X*. The rewriting rules corresponding to the defining equations of the specification are displayed. At every proof step, the user is shown: the label (L for left and R for right) of the equation under examination; the expression obtained in one deductive step; a comment indicating the deduction.

by giving a message, by indicating the variable on which induction will be applied and the induction cases. The rewriting rules applied in an inductive proof are explicitly indicated.

2.4 Analysing the mathematical structure of a specification

Formal specifications seem to be an ideal bridge between user and programmer, as they allow to define the requisites which must be owned by a program by reasoning on the properties of its mathematical model, thus constituting a valuable help to interpret correctly the user's need. To help students understand, at least to some extent, the adherence of the program to the requirements, the lab enables them to analyse the mathematical structure of a specification.

The students indicates the specification of a data type, a mathematical structure and a functional association between them. MEMO verifies whether the data type constitutes a model for the abstract structure; the correctness of the functional association is tested, and an attempt is made to verify whether the axioms of the structure hold for the given data type. If so, knowledge of the specification (and, as a consequence, of the corresponding program), is automatically enriched, as all properties of the abstract structure obviously hold in the specification. Otherwise, an error message is displayed. By means of the automatic analysis of the mathematical properties of a data type, the student is given some indication about the substructure modeled by the data type, whenever the mathematical structure is specified hierarchically, or as composition of previously defined structures.

For example, referring to the problem of verifying that *list* forms a monoid with respect to the *append* operation, the student has to specify the *monoid* structure, by using a slight modification of the language described in paragraph 2.1 (see Figure 5); he then gives the command:

SPECIALIZE listrev to monoid BINDING ls TO mn [[],append] TO [e,comp].

The effect of the execution of the command is the proof of the validity of the association (see Figure 6).

2.5 Implementing a specification

To enable students to avoid representation problems, and to make them experiment with specifications as tools for rapid prototyping, the lab allows the execution of formal specifications. This capability is made possible by the procedural interpretation of algebraic specifications, which allows us to automatically derive code from specifications through a process of direct implementation. In MEMO, the target language is Prolog.

```
CLASS semigroup IS
 SORT mn;
 OPERATION comp: mn,mn -> mn IS AXIOM
 comp(comp(X,Y),Z) = comp(X,comp(Y,Z));
END

CLASS monoid IS
 USES CLASS semigroup;
OPERATION e: -> mn IS AXIOM
 comp(e,X) = X;
END
```

Figure 5. Equational definition of the structure *monoid.* In this example, the phrase *USES CLASS semigroup* enables the *monoid* specification to inherit the sort names, operation symbols and equations of the *semigroup* specification.
The *monoid* specification consists of a base set *mn,* a composition operation *comp:mnxmn->mn* which is associative, has an identity element *e.* In the equations of the specification, upper case letters indicate universally quantified variables.

The tool is aimed at being used for rapid prototyping of students' specifications. Given a specification, already verified w.r.t. executability, the student asks for its implementation. The corresponding Prolog code is generated automatically by the system, via a process hidden from the student. The code is then displayed and the student can execute it.

An example of the result of both encoding and execution processes, concerning the data type *listrev* is shown in Figure 7.

Roughly speaking, the direct implementation process is based on the fact that, when the set of definining equation can be interpreted as a canonical term rewriting system, every term has a *normal form,* that is, a representation that can not be further reduced by using the defining equations of the specification.

In a certain sense, the normal form of a term is its value. Following this viewpoint, we regard a term which is not in normal form as the invocation of a computation, whose result is the normal form of the term itself. Accordingly, terms which are in normal form are translated into identical Prolog terms; the translation of a defined operation of the specification into a Prolog predicate is based on a function which maps abstract terms into strings of Prolog terms. If f is a defined function with n arguments of the specification, its Prolog counter-part is a predicate with $n+1$ arguments. The additional argument is used to provide the result of f applied to the other arguments. A detailed description of the process can be found in [3].

```
The axioms are:
 ax_1 append([],A0) -> A0
 ax_2 append(cons(A1,A2),A3) -> cons(A1,append(A2,A3))
 ax_3 reverse([]) -> []
 ax_4 reverse(cons(A4,A5)) -> append(reverse(A5),cons(A4,[]))

The theorem is:
 append([],A6) = A6
 (L) A6      << reduct by ax_1 <<
 *** equality obtained ***
QED

The theorem is:
 append(append(A7,A8),A9) = append(A7,append(A8,A9))
Begin induction on A7
Induction on A7 case []
 (L) append(append([],A8),A9)      << subst A7 with [] <<
 (R) append([],append(A8,A9))      << subst A7 with [] <<
 (R) append(A8,A9)      << reduct by ax_1 <<
 (L) append(A8,A9)      << reduct by ax_1 <<
 *** equality obtained ***
Induction on A7 case cons(B0,B1)
 (L) append(append(cons(B0,B1),A8),A9)      << subst A7 with cons(B0,B1) <<
 (R) append(cons(B0,B1),append(A8,A9))      << subst A7 with cons(B0,B1) <<
 (R) cons(B0,append(B1,append(A8,A9)))      << reduct by ax_2 <<
 (L) append(cons(B0,append(B1,A8)),A9)      << reduct by ax_2 <<
 (L) cons(B0,append(append(B1,A8),A9))      << reduct by ax_2 <<
 (L) cons(B0,append(B1,append(A8,A9)))      << ind. hyp. on  A7 for B1 <<
 *** equality obtained ***
End induction on A7
QED
```

Figure 6. Proof of the fact that the data type *listrev* is a monoid w.r.t. the [] and append operations.

3. Conclusion

The lab herein described allows students to reason symbolically about programs and to compute with them in practice, working in a single computational environment.

The purpose of the lab is to provide an operative contribution to the analysis of two important pedagogical problems in software engineering education.

The first one concerns the cognitive difficulties underlying the learning of formal specification methods. To overcome these difficulties, our lab provides students with the possibility of experimenting concretely with data types presented precisely but independently of any concrete choice of the data objects and of any implementation of the operators of the types.

The second one regards the teacher's task of finding methods to operatively guide students in building software whose features satisfy the user's need. To handle this problem, our lab enables students to producepp code which is guaranteed to be correct and to satisfy the required mathematical properties.

A prototype version of the lab has been written in Prolog and runs on SUN 3/60.

```
TRANSLATE Prolog listrev

 The axioms are:
  ax_1 append([],A0) -> A0
  ax_2 append(cons(A1,A2),A3) -> cons(A1,append(A2,A3))
  ax_3 reverse([]) -> []
  ax_4 reverse(cons(A4,A5)) -> append(reverse(A5),cons(A4,[]))

 Prolog code:
 append([],A6,A6).
 append([A7|A8],A6,[A7|A9]) :-
   append(A8,A6,A9).

 reverse([],[]).
 reverse([B0|A7],A6) :-
   reverse(A7,A9),
   append(A9,[B0],A6).

 RUN Prolog listrev

 | ?- T isab reverse([1,2,3,4,5,6,7]).
 T = [7,6,5,4,3,2,1]
 yes

 | ?- T isab append([1,2,3],[4,5]).
 T = [1,2,3,4,5]
 yes

 | ?- T isab reverse(append([1],[2,3])).
 T = [3,2,1]
 yes

 | ?- T isab append(reverse([1,2]),reverse([3,4,5])).
 T = [2,1,5,4,3]
 yes

 | ?- halt.

[ Prolog execution halted ]
```

Figure 7. The operations *append* and *reverse,* their translation into PROLOG code and examples of execution.

References

1. Adams J.M., Kurtz B.L., "A State-of-the-Art CS Undergraduate Lab", in Lecture Notes in Computer Science 423, Springer-Verlag, Berlin, 1990, pp.85-94

2. Anderson J.R., Reiser B.J., "The LISP Tutor", Byte, 10-4, 1985, pp.159-175

3. Antoy, S., Forcheri, P., Molfino, M.T., "Specification-based code generation", Proceedings of the Twenty-third Annual Hawai Int. Conference on Systems Sciences, IEEE Computer Society Press, 1990, pp.165-173

4. Antoy, S., Forcheri, P., Molfino, M.T., C. Schenone, "A uniform approach to deduction and automatic implementation", to appear in Proceedings of DISCO92, Springer-Verlag, 1992

5. Avenhaus, J., Madlener K., "Term Rewriting and Equational Reasoning", in Formal Techniques in Artificial Intelligence, Banerji R.B. (Ed.), North Holland, 1990, pp.1-43

6. Barstow B.R., Shrobe H.E., Sandewall E., "Interactive programming environments", International Edition, 1986

7. Boyer, R.S., Moore J.S., "Proving Theorems about LISP Functions", JACM 22-1, 1975, pp.129-144

8. David J. et al., "An experimental learning environment for VLSI design", Proceedings PEG91, 1991, pp.110-119

9. Eisenstant M. et al., "Visual knowledge engineering", IEEE Transactions on Software Engineering, 16-10, 1990, pp.1164-1177

10. Forcheri P., Molfino M.T., "Educational software suitable for learning programming methodologies", Proceedings of CATS'90, 1990, pp.161-164

11. Forcheri P., Molfino M.T., "An intelligent tool for teaching programming techniques", Proceedings of ECOO/ICTE Joint Conference 1991, Toronto, Canada, 1991, pp.591-593

12. Huet G., Hullot J.M., "Proofs by induction in equational theories with constructors", JCSS 25, 1982, pp.239-266

13. Liskov B., Guttag J., "Abstraction and specification in program development", MIT Press, 1988

14. Rich C., Waters R.C., "The Programmer's Apprentice: a research overview, in Artificial Intelligence and Software Engineering", Partridge D. (ed.), Ablex Publ. Corp., 1991, pp.155-182

15. Rogalski J., Samurcay R., "Theoretical framework to analyse adequacy between cognitive models and environments for learning programming", in Proceedings of NATO Advanced Research Workshop: Cognitive Models and Intelligent Environments for Learning Programming, 1992, pp.1-12

16. Wang Y., "Automatic proof experiment report", Portland State University, Computer Science Dept., 1991

17. Wenger E., "Artificial Intelligence and Tutoring Systems", Morgan Kaufmann Publ., 1987

Analogies in an Intelligent Programming Environment for Learning LISP*

Gerhard Weber

Department of Psychology, University of Trier, D-5500 Trier, Germany

Abstract: When learning a new programming language, novices often use remindings of previous problems to solve new problems and to code programs. But, analogies and remindings are only helpful if they are based on elaborated explanations and higher-level structural similarities. ELM-PE, an intelligent programming environment supporting example-based learning, is designed to aid novices learning to program in LISP. For this system, an analogical component is developed to show up structurally similar problem solutions retrieved by an explanation-based retrieval method (EBR). Analogues are retrieved from a case-base where explanations of cases as analyzed by a cognitive diagnosis are stored. Two studies are reported indicating that the EBR-method retrieves analogues as well as the ARCS-model does or even better.

Keywords: Knowledge-based help system, intelligent programming environment, analogies, analogue retrieval, explanation-based learning, case-based learning.

Introduction

When learning a new programming language, novices often use examples and remindings of previous problem solutions to solve new problems and to code them correctly. Especially in the beginning of learning a first programming language, only a few analogies to other domains exist. During the first hours of learning most experiences are not generalized into abstract rules nor are they proceduralized into automatically applicable productions. So, learners heavily use remindings and previously studied examples to solve new problems [1, 14, 17]. Lewis and Olson [12] propose that the productivity of casual programmers can be increased by adopting a development style that emphasizes the use of example code. Example-based learning tools [16] are being developed to support learners in using examples during programming.

But, there is a debate about the question of whether learners are able to retrieve structurally and semantically similar analogues which are useful and helpful in the subsequent processes of analogical mapping and analogical transfer [6]. On the one side, Faries & Reiser [5] found that subjects who were learning LISP and were well-trained in this domain were able to retrieve structural remindings, despite the presence of competing surface similarities. On the other side, several studies find that subjects have a bias for retrieving surface-based

* This work is supported by the "Deutsche Forschungsgemeinschaft" under Grant We 498/12.

remindings and have difficulty retrieving helpful and useful structure-based analogies [7, 18, 19, 20]. Even instructing subjects to retrieve only structural matches that could be useful in solving an actual problem did not improve their performance [22]. Two factors might promote structure-based analogical access, the depth to which the original material is encoded and the degree of expertise. E.g., in a study of reminding using proverbs [22] increased relational reminding occured when subjects wrote out the meanings of the proverbs on the original study list. Gentner [6] argues that the main reason for the observed effects may be due to some type of encoding specificity. To the extent that the input is encoded in a way that is different from the way the later probe is encoded, there will be diminishing retrieval. This view is consistent with Schank's notation of a dynamic, case-based human memory [21].

From these findings one can conclude that it does not suffice to use any example or reminding that may come to mind. They must be based on structural similarity relations derived from an appropriate situation model [24] which in turn may stem from self-explanations [3]. In other words, a learner must know why an example or a previous episode led to a correct solution, which higher concepts and higher-level structures were relevant for solving the old problem and may have to be considered in the new problem, in what aspects the actual situation differs from previous solutions and where changes have to be made to fit the old solution to the problem at hand. In previous studies with students solving programming exercises, we often observed that novices used superficial similarities of the LISP-code when details of a programming algorithm (e.g., the principle of recursive programming) were not fully understood. This typically resulted in errors in which many parts of the solution were coded correctly by adequate analogical transfer, but some necessary, structurally related changes were omitted [27, 28].

Therefore, in order to support novices when learning to program it seems appropriate to empower a knowledge-based programming environment with necessary knowledge about the problem domain and, possibly, with information about the knowledge acquired by the particular user. If a help system comprises such knowledge, programming by examples can be supported in such a way that useful structural analogies as well as explanations of analogy errors can be offered to the learner.

In the following, ELM-PE, an intelligent programming environment supporting example-based learning will be presented. For this system, an analogical component is developed which is able to retrieve structurally and semantically similar problem solutions based on an explanation-based retrieval (EBR) method. This EBR method will be explained and discussed at the end of the paper.

ELM-PE - A Knowledge-based Programming Environment

The knowledge-based programming environment ELM-PE is designed to support novices learning the programming language LISP. It has several features which are especially useful in learning to solve problems in a new, complex domain. Some of these features will be sketched briefly in this section.

STRUEDI - a syntax-driven structure editor. In order to reduce syntax errors, coding function definitions is supported by a syntax-driven LISP-editor [11]. In the program window of the structure editor, LISP-code can be produced by filling in slots for LISP-expressions with syntactically correct LISP-code, or with schemata for function calls containing slots for their arguments. These schemata can be accessed from a menu of LISP-functions or from typing in the first part of a function call beginning with the function name. The structure editor accepts only syntactically correct LISP-expressions as input. Otherwise, the input is rejected and an explanation is given as to why the input would result in an incorrect expression.

Example-based programming. To support example-based learning [16], examples of LISP-code can be displayed in a separate example window. An example can be selected from examples discussed in the learning materials of the LISP-course as well as from the set of function definitions the student has coded already. The example window has the same functionality as the program window of the structure editor, so LISP-expressions can be altered and parts of the code can be copied into the program window.

Error and message explanation. All messages from the system displayed in the status line and all error messages displayed in the LISP listener can be explained. This is very helpful for novices because in the beginning most error messages may be more confusing than useful. That part of the code where the run-time error occured is highlighted in the program window and a short description is given why such a type of error can happen.

Visualization. One central principle in learning programming is to visualize the flow of data during evaluation of programs (e.g., Eisenstadt et al. [4]). This is supported by a stepper showing all evaluation steps indicating corresponding expressions of self-defined function definitions – including definitions of sub-functions – in the program window. The stepper is supposed to help students envision dynamic program properties and to encourage active and self-directed learning. Additionally, those parts of the program code which are responsible for errors or are explained by the knowledge-based diagnosis can be highlighted in the program window (Fig. 1).

Automatic cognitive diagnosis. The knowledge-based component of the programming environment consists of a cognitive diagnosis of the program code produced by a student. This diagnosis is based on the episodic learner model (ELM), a case-based learning model [25]. The diagnosis results in an explanation of how the program code could have been produced by the learner. This explanation is the basis for offering hints to the learner concerning what part of the code is incorrect, which plans must be followed to solve subgoals during problem solving and possibly partial solutions in the context of the learner's solution. As these explanations are the basis for retrieving structural and semantic analogies, the case-based learning model will be described in more detail in the following section.

ELM: A case-based learning model

ELM is a type of user or learner model storing knowledge about the user (learner) in terms of a collection of episodes. In the sense of *case-based learning*, such episodes can be viewed as cases. To construct the learner model, the code produced by a learner is analyzed in terms of the domain knowledge on the one side and to a task description on the other side (Fig. 2). This cognitive diagnosis results in a derivation tree of concepts and rules the learner might have used to solve the problem. These concepts and rules are instantiations of units from the knowledge base. The episodic learner model is made up of these instantiations and later generalization based thereupon. To understand this form of episodic learner model, a short description of the knowledge representation and the diagnostic process will be given.

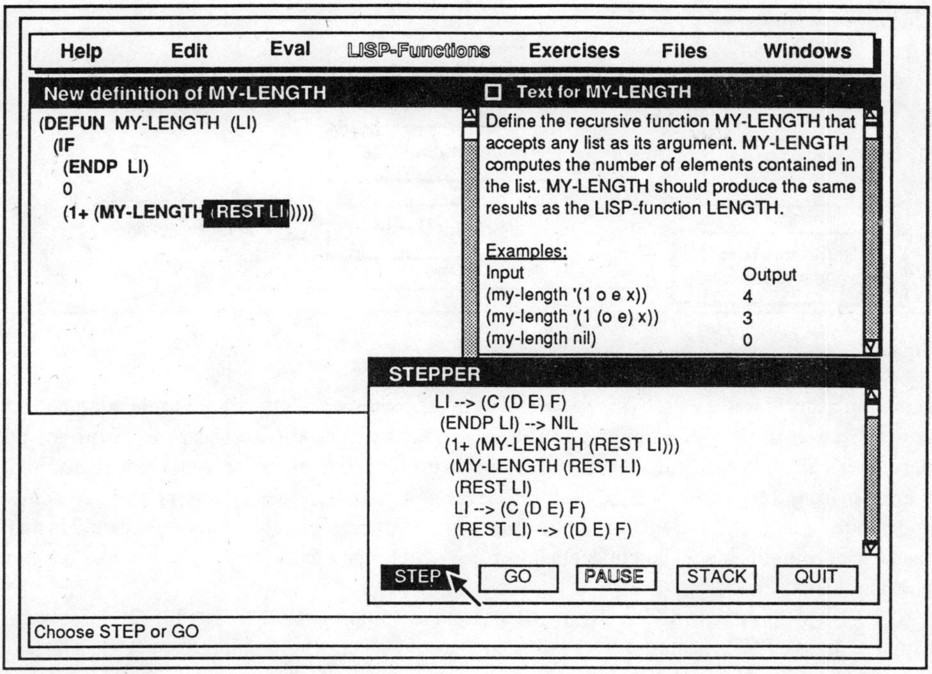

Figure 1: Visualization in the stepper.

Students using the environment code function definitions in a structured LISP-editor [11], so their function code is at least syntactically correct. The cognitive analysis of the program code employs an explanation-based generalization (EBG) method [15]. It starts with a task description related to higher concepts, plans, and schemata in the knowledge base. For every concept, a set of rules is stated describing different ways to solve the goal given by the plan of the concept. These rules are comparable to the notation of implementation methods for goals in PROUST [10]. There are "good", "suboptimal", and "buggy" rules explaining correct, correct but suboptimal, and incorrect solutions of the current goal or subgoal. The set of buggy rules is comparable to an error library in other ITSs (e.g., in Anderson's LISP-tutor [2]). Applying a rule results in comparing the plan description to the corresponding part of the student's code. In the plan description, further concepts may be addressed. The cognitive diagnosis is called recursively until a function name, a parameter, or a constant is matched.

The cognitive diagnosis results in a derivation tree [25] built from all concepts and rules identified to explain the student's solution. This derivation tree is an explanation structure in the sense of EBG and is the basis for building up the episodic learner model. Concepts and rules addressed in the derivation tree are the basis for creating episodic frames. These frames are integrated into the knowledge base as instances of their concepts and rules. Slots in these instances refer to the context where they were used (especially the current task), to the type of transformations of concepts, to the observed rules, and to the argument bindings.

In the next step, episodic frames are generalized. If an episodic frame is the first instance under a concept of the knowledge base, this single case is generalized from structural and

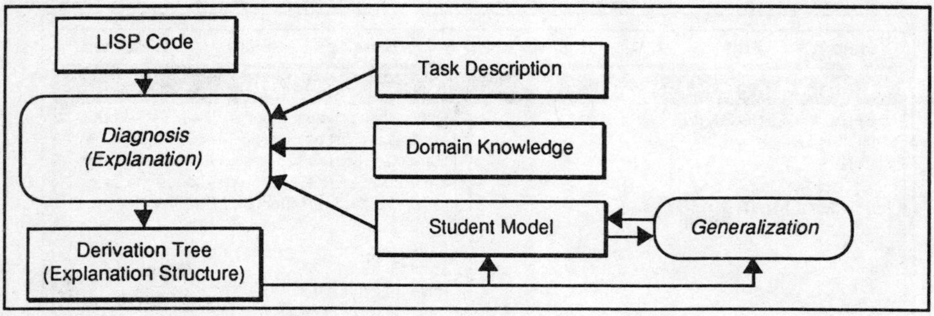

Figure 2: Components of ELM

semantic aspects in the data. This generalization mechanism is comparable to the single-case generalization in the EBG approach [15]. Additionally, similarity-based generalizations of data and plans can occur. Generalizations represent the class of types of plans and corresponding data which will be used in further cognitive analyses to interpret the student's code. With increasing knowledge about a particular learner, hierarchies of generalizations and instances are built under the concepts and rules of the knowledge base. They constitute the episodic learner model.

The ELM-approach differs from the case-based approach in SCENT [13] in several aspects. In SCENT, pre-analyzed cases are stored as a whole with respect to a static granularity hierarchy expressing aggregation and abstraction dimensions. These cases are used during analyzing the student's code to give detailed advice. In ELM, only examples from the course materials are pre-analyzed and the resulting explanation structures are stored in the individual case-based learner model. Elements from the explanation structures are stored with respect to their corresponding concepts from the domain knowledge base, so cases are distributed in terms of instances of concepts. Generalization hierarchies of instances are built up from explanations of the program code that a student produced to solve programming problems. Therefore, generalization hierarchies reflect the process of knowledge acquisition for a particular student. These individual cases – or parts of them – can be used for two different purposes. On the one side, episodic instances can be used during further analyses as shortcuts if the actual code and/or plan is matching corresponding patterns in episodic instances. On the other side, cases can be used by an analogical component to show up similar examples and problems for reminding purposes.

Analogies in ELM

When working with ELM-PE, two typical situations emerge where analogous cases have to be retrieved. First, analogues are needed by a tutorial component to offer the student remindings and analogies to examples in the materials when an error or a suboptimal solution is detected by the diagnostic component in the student's program code. Such remindings could be used to explain to the student how the error is similar to a previous error and how the problem can be solved, or how the incorrect part of the code resulted from superficial similarities to previous solutions which were incorrectly mapped to the current problem. Second, if the student asks for help while developing the code for the current problem the tutorial system should be able to offer the student analogies to similar previous problems or examples. Here, the analogical component has to look for analogies for the solution of the next subproblem to be solved in the context of subgoals solved up to that point. In both cases, existing program code is the basis for retrieving analogous cases from the case-base.

The EBR-Method

As an extension to ELM an explanation-based retrieval method (EBR) was developed [26, 27] that is suited to finding analogues in a case-memory of a case-based learning system. This method heavily depends on the distributed storing of cases in terms of instances of concepts identified during the explanation step of the EBG process. Concepts from the explanation structure for the current case are used as indexes to find corresponding instances from the student model. First, all concepts from the explanation structure are inserted as new instances into the existing hierarchy of instances of the learner model and are generalized if possible. For all new instances, all corresponding instances in the generalization hierarchy belonging to previous cases are collected. The more corresponding instances belonging to a previous case are found and the closer they are connected in the generalization hierarchy, the greater the evidence that the case is a good analogue. The case showing the most evidence computed by this algorithm is selected as best analogue and is therefore retrieved.

Evaluation of the EBR-Method

To validate the EBR-method we compared it with another retrieval method in a simulation study [26] and with preferences observed from humans in a second study.

Comparing the EBR-Method with the ARCS-Model: The ARCS-model [23] is a very general and psychologically validated program modeling human retrieval. In ARCS, potential analogous structures are noticed by sharing semantically similar concepts. ARCS sets up a constraint network considering the constraints of semantic similarity, structural consistency, and pragmatic centrality to compare their relevance to the target structure. A standard parallel connectionist relaxation algorithm is used to settle into a state that indicates the relative correspondence of the stored source structures to the probe structure. The algorithm of this retrieval method is fully described and easy to compute, so it can directly be compared to other retrieval methods. In ARCS, the target and the potential source candidates are represented in terms of the predicate calculus. As LISP-programs are composed of hierarchically nested function calls, they can easily be decomposed into predicates [9, 27]. Several studies show that semantic similarities are most important for retrieving analogues (e.g. [8, 18, 19]). So, the ARCS-model is designed to consider especially semantic similarities and not so much structural consistencies. Since analogues of LISP-programs are being retrieved, the case of within-domain analogies is given. Therefore, most semantic similarities stem from the identity of function names. Further degrees of semantic relatedness can be obtained from hierarchically clustering functions by their meaning. We call this version of the ARCS-model 'ARCS-P'.

One can argue that explanation structures used in the EBR-method comprise more information than a simple decomposition of LISP-code into propositions enabling the EBR-method to retrieve better analogues than the ARCS-method. So, explanation structures were decomposed into propositions, too (ARCS-E). Different semantic weights for concepts and rules were obtained from the hierarchy of concepts and rules in the knowledge base.

Data for the simulation study were gathered from interaction protocols of 13 students computing function definitions in the LISP structure editor STRUEDI [11]. For each student, the sequence of solutions for different tasks within each lesson of an introductory LISP-course was matched step by step against the examples from the materials for these lessons and against all previous solutions within the same lesson. 404 cases were observed where analogues could be retrieved. For each case, the best analogues retrieved by the EBR-method were compared to those retrieved by both versions of the ARCS-method (ARCS-P and ARCS-E) by two independent expert raters.

Results show that in most cases (94.6 %) the EBR method retrieves analogues as good as the ARCS-program does, or even better (Tab. 1). In 8.4 % and 16.1 % of all cases the EBR-method performed better than the ARCS-E and the ARCS-P-method, respectively. This indicates that the ARCS-model will be able to retrieve more useful and more helpful analogues if structures are stored with respect to a decomposition of an explanation structure (ARCS-E) instead of a simple decomposition of LISP-code into propositions (ARCS-P). Moreover, specific problems inherent to the constraint-satisfaction algorithm of the ARCS-method emerged with these structurally highly related and semantically very similar cases. These problems are discussed in more detail in Weber [27].

In less than 4 % of all cases the ARCS-method retrieved a better optimal analogue than the EBR-method. In some cases, this resulted from errors or combinations of errors which could not sufficiently be explained by the diagnostic component. In such cases, a retrieval process must be preferred which is based particularly on semantic similarities of predicates without knowledge about intentions and meaning of the program code and without interpretations of errors. Therefore, the ARCS-method performed slightly better when depending on a decomposition of the LISP-code (ARCS-P, 3.5 %) than on a decomposition of the explanation structure (ARCS-E, 3.2 %). In most other cases, the ELM-method failed because the current generalization mechanism in ELM is slightly too sensitive to structural differences in the student's LISP-code.

Comparing the EBR-Method with Human Analogical Retrieval and Mapping: It was shown in several experiments concerning analog retrieval that subjects have difficulty in retrieving useful structurally similar analogues, if there exist competing superficially similar cases [7, 18, 19, 20, 22]. As Gentner [6] points out, this bias for retrieving surface-based remindings may depend on the depth to which the original material is encoded and to the degree of expertise. That is, the less a learner knows about a new domain the more he or she must rely on superficial similarities to retrieve previous cases. This must hold for the process of analogical mapping, too, if learners are lacking knowledge to explain previous and new problems and their solutions to themselves. Therefore, a bias for superficial similarities in the mapping process will be observed when a subject is confronted with problems and with their solutions in a completely new domain and has not built up higher order concepts and relations. Such a situation occurs if a subject does not know anything about the programming language LISP and has to retrieve or to map analogues to programming problems or to their corresponding LISP-code.

To test this hypothesis a small experiment was done similar to the simulation study described above. Subjects were given three examples of function definitions and,

Table 1

Percentage of cases showing the same or different best retrieved analogues by the EBR- and the ARCS-method for a total of 404 cases. For different best retrieved analogues two independent expert raters whether the EBR-Method or one of the ARCS-methods retrieved the better analogue. In the "ARCS-P" column, the ARCS-method was run with a propositional decomposition of the LISP-code, in the "ARCS-E" column, the ARCS-method was run with a propositional decomposition of the corresponding explanation structure derived by the explanation-based diagnosis of the LISP-code.

		ARCS-E	ARCS-P
same		71.8	63.9
different	both methods equally effective	14.4	14.6
	EBR better	8.4	16.1
	ARCS better	3.2	3.5
	both methods failed	2.2	2.0

simultaneously, the LISP-code of another function definition serving as a probe. They had to rate how useful each example would be as an example to code the probe or to solve the probe problem. In the next trial, a new probe was given and was rated against all previous cases, that are the three examples and the previous probe. And in a third trial, a third probe was tested against all previous probes and examples. Ten students having no experiences in programming LISP served as novices whereas 10 students having at least completed an introductory LISP-course served as advanced programmers.

Subjects were given five series of trials with three series as described above, one series where examples were given as LISP-code and the probe consisted of the text of the programming task, and a fifth series where only texts were given. These series were selected from data observed from students in the first study. For each series, an optimal rank order for deep structural analogies between probes and examples was given by two LISP experts. For both groups of subjects, cumulated ratings from the three code-only series (all in all 100 cases) were compared to results from the retrieval methods considered in the first study (EBR, ARCS-E, ARCS-P) being applied to the same series of LISP-code. For each retrieval method and for each subject, it was tested whether subjects and the retrieval program selected the same best analogue. In the case of disagreement, it was tested whether preferences of the retrieval method or subjects' preferences were in concordance with experts' preferences.

Results shown in Figure 3 tend to support the hypothesis that the more deeply examples and probes are understood the more structure-based analogues are retrieved or chosen from a set of examples. Subjects having no knowledge about programming in LISP (Novices group) prefer examples which are in some aspects only superficially related and tend to neglect better, more structurally related examples. This is supported by the percentage of cases where the artificial retrieval methods retrieved better analogues than subjects did, 24 % – 28 %, whereas for the advanced LISP programmers (Advanced group), in only 8 % – 12 % of all cases the retrieval methods selected a better analogue compared to subjects' choices.

This study additionally shows that in many cases the EBR-method is able to retrieve better analogues than the ARCS-model, especially, if the ARCS-method is based on a decomposition of LISP-code only (ARCS-P). For the Advanced group, subjects retrieved in 24 % of all cases a better, more structurally related analogue compared to the ARCS-P-method, whereas for the EBR-method, in only 5 % of all cases subjects performed better than the simulation model.

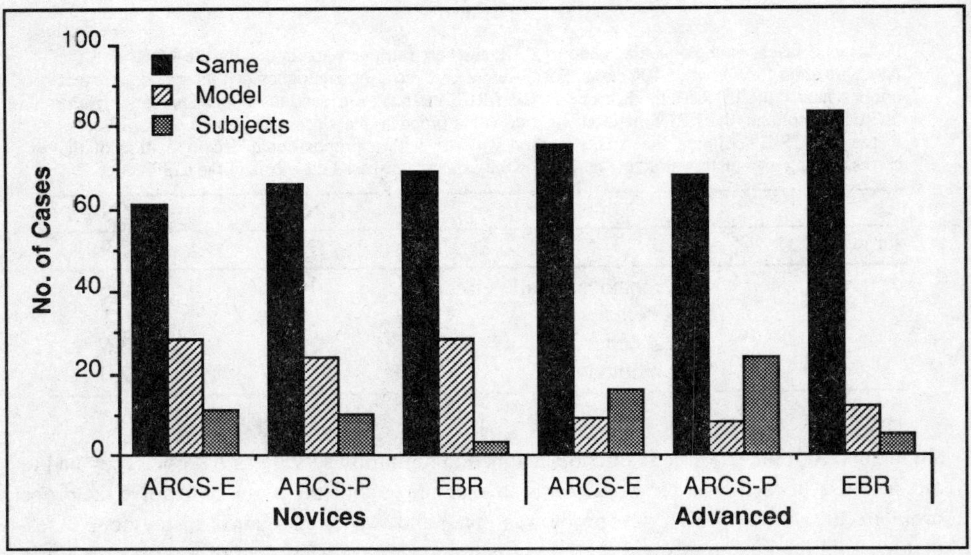

Figure 3: Results comparing subjects' similarity ratings with preferences computed by three retrieval methods (ARCS-E, ARCS-P, and EBR) for novices and advanced programmers. "Same" means cases where the retrieval method as well as subjects selected a structure-based, deep analogy, "Model" means that the case retrieved by the simulation model was a structure-based analogy whereas the case chosen by the subject was more superficially similar to the probe, and "Subjects" means that the subject selected a more structurally related example whereas the case chosen by the retrieval method was based on more superficial similarities.

Discussion

On the basis of the studies reported in this paper one can draw the following two conclusions.

(1) Results support the hypothesis that novices have difficulty in recognizing appropriate analogies [17], especially, if they are lacking necessary knowledge to understand examples and their solutions in full detail. According to Chi et al. [3], learners should have explained previous examples to themselves and should have stored these explanations in order to access them later. That is, people's ability to retrieve previous cases may be due to some type of encoding specificity [6]. Therefore, an intelligent programming environment supporting example-based learning should be able to show up explanation-based analogies allowing novices to understand problem solutions, to build an elaborated situation model [24], and to generalize appropriate abstractions and schemata.

(2) The EBR-method proved to be suited to retrieve analogues derived from explanations based on higher-order relations and schemata. Results are comparable to those produced by the ARCS-model or even better, especially when the ARCS-algorithm works on knowledge structures resulting from a decomposition of pure LISP-code into propositions.

However, the EBR-method is not able to simulate how and why novices prefer matches based on superficial similarities to retrieve examples. In the case of the ELM-model, the diagnostic component has to explain errors resulting from possibly misleading analogical transfer. If those errors are detected in the explanation step while diagnosing the program code, the EBR-method would be able to retrieve similar previous cases showing corresponding errors. These could be explained to the learner by a tutorial component.

References

1. Anderson, J.R., Boyle, C.F., Farrell, R., & Reiser, B. J.: Cognitive principles in the design of computer tutors. Proc. Sixth Annual Conference of the Cognitive Science Society, Boulder, CO. pp. 2-9. Hillsdale, NJ: Cognitive Science Society, Lawrence Erlbaum Associates 1984
2. Anderson, J.R., & Reiser, B.J.: The LISP tutor. Byte.10(4), 159-175 (1985)
3. Chi, M.T.H., Bassok, M., Lewis, M., Reimann, P., & Glaser, R.: Self-explanations: how students study and use examples in learning to solve problems. Cognitive Science. 13, 145-182 (1989)
4. Eisenstadt, M., Price, B.A., & Domingue, J.: Software visualization: Redressing ITS fallacies. (this volume)
5. Faries, J.M., & Reiser, B.J.: Access and use of previous solutions in a problem solving situation. Proc. Tenth Annual Conference of the Cognitive Science Society, Montreal. pp. 433-439. Hillsdale, NJ: Cognitive Science Society, Lawrence Erlbaum Associates 1988
6. Gentner, D.: Finding the needle: Accessing and reasoning from prior cases. In: Proc. Second Workshop on Case-Based Reasoning, Pensacola Beach, Florida. (K.J. Hammond ed.). pp. 137-143. San Mateo, CA: Morgan Kaufmann Publishers 1989
7. Gentner, D., & Landers, R.: Analogical reminding: a good match is hard to find. Proc. International Conference on Systems, Man and Cybernetics, Tucson, AR. pp. 607-613. 1985
8. Holyoak, K.J., & Koh, K.: Surface and structural similarity in analogical transfer. Memory & Cognition. 15, 332-340 (1987)
9. Holyoak, K.J., & Thagard, P.: Analogical mapping by constraint satisfaction. Cognitive Science. 13, 295-356 (1989)
10. Johnson, L.W.: Intention-based diagnosis of novice programming errors. London: Pitman 1986
11. Köhne, A., & Weber, G.: STRUEDI: a LISP-structure editor for novice programmers. In: Human-Computer Interaction INTERACT '87 (H.J. Bullinger, & B. Schackel, eds.). pp. 125-129. Amsterdam: North-Holland 1987
12. Lewis, C.H., & Olson, G.M.: Can the principles of cognition lower the barriers of programming? In: Empirical studies of programmers (G.M. Olson, S. Sheppard, & E. Soloway, eds.). Vol. 2, pp. 248-263. Norwood, NJ: Ablex Publishing Corporation 1987
13. McCalla, G., & Greer, J.: Helping novices laearn recursion: Giving granularity-based advice on strategies and providing support at the mental model level. (this volume)
14. McKendree, J., Reiser, B.J., & Anderson, J.R.: Tutorial goals and strategies in the instruction of programming skills. Proc. Sixth Annual Conference of the Cognitive Science Society, Boulder, CO. pp. 252-254. Hillsdale, NJ: Cognitive Science Society, Lawrence Erlbaum Associates 1984
15. Mitchell, T.M., Keller, R.M., & Kedar-Cabelli, S.T.: Explanation-based generalization: a unifying view. Machine Learning. 1, 47-80 (1986)
16. Neal, L.R.: A system for example-based learning. Proc. CHI'89: Human Factors in Computing Systems. pp. 63-68. 1989
17. Pirolli, P.L., & Anderson, J.R.: The role of learning from examples in the acquisition of recursive programming skills. Canadian Journal of Psychology. 39, 240-272 (1985)
18. Ratterman, M., & Gentner, D.: Analogy and similarity: determinants of accessibility and inferential soundness. Proc. Ninth Annual Conference of the Cognitive Science Society, Seattle, WA. pp. 23-35. Hillsdale, NJ: Lawrence Erlbaum Associates 1987
19. Ross, B.H.: This is like that: the use of earlier problems and the separation of similarity effects. Journal of Experimental Psychology: Learning, Memory, and Instruction. 13, 629-639 (1987)
20. Ross, B.H., Perkins, S.J., & Tenpenny, P.L.: Reminding-based category learning. Cognitive Psychology. 22, 460-492 (1990)
21. Schank, R.C.: Dynamic memory. Cambridge, MA: Cambridge University Press 1982
22. Schumacher, R.M.: Similarity-based reminding: The effects of distance and encoding on retrieval (Unpublished Master's thesis). University of Illinois, Champaign-Urbana, Illinois 1987
23. Thagard, P., Holyoak, K.J., Nelson, G., & Gochfeld, D.: Analog retrieval by constraint satisfaction. Artificial Intelligence. 46, 259-310 (1990)
24. van Dijk, T.A., & Kintsch, W.: Strategies of discourse comprehension. New York: Academic Press 1983
25. Weber, G.: Cognitive diagnosis and episodic modelling in an intelligent LISP-tutor. Proc. ITS-88, Montreal, pp. 207-214. Montreal: Université de Montréal 1988
26. Weber, G.: Explanation-based retrieval in a case-based learning model. Proc. Thirteenth Annual Conference of the Cognitive Science Society, Chicago, IL, pp. 522-527. Hillsdale, NJ: Cognitive Science Society, Lawrence Erlbaum Associates 1991
27. Weber, G.: Analogien in einem fallbasierten Lernmodell. In: Maschinelles Lernen - Modellierung von Lernen mit Maschinen (K. Reiss, M. Reiss, & H. Spandl, eds.). pp. 143-175. Berlin: Springer 1992
28. Weber, G., Waloszek, G., & Wender, K.F.: The role of episodic memory in an intelligent tutoring system. In: Artificial intelligence and human learning: Intelligent computer-aided instruction (J. Self, ed.). pp. 141-155. London: Chapman & Hall 1988

Redressing ITS Fallacies Via Software Visualization

Marc Eisenstadt, Blaine A. Price[1], and John Domingue

Human Cognition Research Laboratory, The Open University, Milton Keynes MK7 6AA, U.K.
Tel: +44 908 653149, Fax: +44 908 653169, E-mail: M.Eisenstadt@open.ac.uk
[1]also affiliated with: Dynamic Graphics Project, CSRI, The University of Toronto, M5S 1A1, Canada.

Abstract: The long-term future of Intelligent Tutoring Systems (ITSs) for the teaching of programming is severely hampered by a collection of fallacies which prevent ITSs from scaling up to cater for either a wide audience or a broad curriculum. The fallacies include the emphasis on toy examples and the belief that it is possible to create a comprehensive bug catalogue. We propose an alternative approach, based on examining the needs of expert programmers, and considering a pedagogical trajectory which caters for development from novice to expert by means of discovery-based learning. The common thread through this trajectory is "Software Visualization", a collection of techniques which allows beginners to see the innards of program execution clearly, and at the same time allows experts to view high level program abstractions which help them home in quickly on buggy code. We re-work a well known example from the ITS community, and then show how our approach scales up to handle a large programming problem.

Keywords: Intelligent Tutoring Systems, Programming, Program Visualization, Software Visualization, Programming Environments, Debugging, Discovery-Based Learning, Exploration-based learning

Introduction

How can we best facilitate the progress of students new to computer programming? This question has been of interest for many years to researchers in Cognitive Science, Artificial Intelligence, and Human-Computer Interaction. The scope of relevant emphases includes the use of clear execution models [13], cognitive models of learners' planning behaviour [2], and automatic program debuggers which provide tutorial advice [21]. Indeed, Intelligent Tutoring Systems (ITSs) in the domain of programming have combined many of these approaches to provide some important results. For example, the Lisp Tutor [3, 8] is a commercial product which is used regularly to teach a full semester of introductory Lisp programming at US universities, and the Advanced Placement Computer Science Practice and Feedback System (APCS) [37] is being developed by the US Educational Testing Service for large-scale tuition and testing of Pascal programmers.

Despite these apparent achievements, we are seriously concerned about the underlying premises of this work, and its prospects for future progress. In particular, we question the scale of the effort needed to provide coverage for a relatively small proportion of the programming population working on a very small class of problems. We are concerned with scale (of effort and of applicability) because systems that can not scale up to handle the large tasks faced by professional programmers may be an evolutionary dead-end, i.e. they are likely to lead users down a path which is not pertinent to their later experiences. Moreover, progression from novice to expert is a continuous learning experience, and therefore stepping back for a moment to think about the needs of experts can help us more clearly define a pedagogical "trajectory" which takes the life-long learner from metaphorical cradle to grave. These concerns suggest that our opening question emphasizes the needs of the few at the expense of the many. Thus, a better question would be "How can we best facilitate the progress of all computer programmers?" By addressing a larger population, we thereby ensure that coverage and scalability become primary concerns. But to succeed, we need to identify the shortcomings of existing approaches and to orient our research towards a tractable goal. Let's first consider the shortcomings of traditional ITS work.

As we see it, the conventional ITS paradigm, particularly for the teaching of programming, is plagued by four fallacies which will prevent any significant realization of its goals. Not all ITS research suffers from these fallacies, but the fallacies are nevertheless prevalent enough to warrant our concern:

- **The "Complete Bug Catalogue" Fallacy**: A successful ITS depends upon having a thorough bug catalogue, whether shallow or deep. Unfortunately, students can make bizarre errors which cannot be dealt with by an ITS because they deviate too far from the system's ability to cope, no matter how "complete" its bug catalogue may be. A common reason for such errors is that the students do not have a good model of the underlying machine [13], which is often due to the poor interface between the students and the programs that they write. Moreover, as Rosenberg [35] succinctly argues, "An exhaustive enumeration of error types is *not* a model [of the learner]."

- **The "Unix Helper" Fallacy**: For systems with dreadful user interfaces, one approach has been to provide sophisticated tutorial support and guidance to help the user deal with the difficulties. An alternative would be to re-design the interface from scratch, thereby eliminating the need for so much tutorial support and guidance. For many ITSs a thorough user interface overhaul is necessary since they provide a Unix-like textual interface which is inappropriate in the light of contemporary interface technology.

- **The "Toy Example" Fallacy**: An ITS must know its subject area thoroughly, and this invariably means it must be geared toward simpler problems. As the student learns more about programming and the problems being solved become more difficult, the effort that must be put into ITSs becomes dramatically larger and they cease to be cost effective when compared with human tutoring. This is a knock-on effect of the "Complete Bug Catalogue" fallacy: ITSs can only work for a limited range of programs and they are not sufficiently generalized to be of use after a programmer reaches a certain level of skill.

- **The "We Know Best" Fallacy**: An ITS depends on a limited number of paradigms for teaching which assume that no others will be more effective for a given student. Learning is a negotiation process between a teacher who knows the domain and the students who knows what they know. It is possible for students to embark on a correct solution path only to be told that they are wrong and have the ITS steam-roller them into the solution that it understands. Students need to be able to work through problems using their own methods and learn from their own mistakes in order to take advantage of discovery-based learning; remedial instruction should be used with particular students only when they are clearly unable to proceed on their own.

In many ways, the four fallacies are themselves knock-on effects of the limited focus implied by our opening question. In a nutshell, we feel that for the domain of teaching programming, the ITS paradigm offers only diminishing returns for the huge effort expended. In direct contrast, a thoughtful attack on the programming environments themselves (and particularly the way in which program execution is graphically portrayed) can pay much larger dividends, as we argue next. First, we suggest a shift of emphasis towards programming environments that scale up to the needs of experts and argue that one of their strengths, namely the clear visualizations that they provide, has such important pedagogical spin-offs that we can have our cake and eat it too (i.e. cater for the full range of programmers and possible programming tasks). We then describe our approach to "Software Visualization" in some detail, and show how it deals with an example taken from PROUST [21]. Finally, to emphasize the scalability of our approach, we present an example of Software Visualization applied to the debugging of an operating system comprising approximately 7,500 lines of code.

A proposed shift of emphasis

Over the past fifteen years, we have undergone a change of perspective in the way we teach programming. Having begun by worrying in detail about the needs of novices, and trying to understand their problems and misconceptions, we developed a range of environments, automated debugging assistants, and ITSs to help them (this work is described in detail in [16]). Our empirical studies [15] suggested that algorithm design and planning were not nearly as big an obstacle to our students as the lack of a clear execution model. For example, in tackling the averaging problem used by PROUST, our subjects had no trouble computing averages, but their algorithms were based on an intuitive approach of applying nested functions to aggregate data objects (i.e. first add up all the items, then tally them separately). The stumbling block was the mismatch between the subjects' intuitive approach and the rather artificial constraints imposed by the behaviour of a Pascal WHILE loop, and a critical issue for us was how to impart a clear model of this constrained behaviour. We therefore decided to place most of our emphasis on the "software maintenance" side of programming, as opposed to the "design" and "planning" sides. We realized eventually that the debugging/maintenance needs of experts were strongly related to the pedagogical needs of our novices: both needed to see in a perspicuous fashion what was happening during program execution, though at different levels of granularity. The difference between the viewpoints required by the two audiences was not simply one of physical scale size, such as might be provided for free on a graphics workstation, but rather one of *abstraction level* , which required careful attention. We decided that it would be possible to cater for quite a wide audience and a wide range of problems by focusing on the common thread which ran through the entire learning experience: visualization.

Software Visualization

There is an obvious pedagogic benefit in showing students how their programs are executing since it offers an opportunity to present a clear and consistent model of the language they are using [13]. However, providing this information in a suitable form without overwhelming the student is quite a challenge. The use of visualization in teaching is quite an old concept and the success of visualization in teaching programming is well documented. The motion picture (now videotape) *Sorting Out Sorting* [4] has been widely used in secondary and post-secondary schools for many years to explain how nine different sorting algorithms work. It uses colour animated graphics to show how the algorithms affect the data and how the algorithms compare with each other in terms of efficiency. The continuing work at Brown University on BALSA [7, 6] and TANGO [39] has extended this approach so that students can see graphical animations as they interactively run their programs. We use the term "Software Visualization" (SV) [31] to describe this and other such enterprises that use the crafts of typography, graphic design, animation, cinematography, and modern human-computer interaction technology to facilitate the human understanding and effective use of computer programs (Myers and others use the more ambiguous term "Program Visualization").

The literature of SV is full of anecdotes about ways in which animations of program execution have made the behaviour of a program "immediately clear" or helped in algorithm design [40]. Proper empirical study is needed to evaluate such claims and determine the value of various representations for SV applied to both novices and experts; we whole-heartedly encourage this work, although we have not yet seen a good methodology for evaluating SV systems [30]. Even so, Baek and Layne [5] conducted experiments to determine the effect of animated graphics, still graphics, and text in a computer-assisted learning tutorial and found that students using animated graphics had significantly higher test scores than the other groups, while those using still graphics had higher scores than the text-only group.

The SV and ITS communities (and approaches) are not inherently disparate, and there have been promising efforts which draw from both sides. Some researchers have tried to encourage students to use a graphical form to specify their programs (known as "Visual Programming" (VP) [28] in the literature) in order improve their model of the language. However, as Petre and Price [29] note, the VP paradigm is usually limited to either a data flow or control flow representation; some combination of both is required to properly convey the semantics of a language. The Graphical Instruction in LISP (GIL) ITS [33] draws its inspiration from both communities: it combines the traditional ITS model with a simple data flow VP window which allows students to construct small functions as a graph with nodes which are LISP atoms, lists, and functions. This system may have some value in showing the data flow relationships in small functions, but there is little evidence that students proficient with writing small programs in this environment will be any better off once they leave the environment to write larger programs, since they do not necessarily understand how control flow works or how the values of variables change during the code execution. One recent system which encourages discovery-based learning and provides the student with "a look inside" the virtual machine is DISCOVER [32] which is an ITS for a very simple algorithm-level pseudo-code language. DISCOVER augments the traditional ITS approach by providing a window with an example solution and a window showing the current values of all variables. This is a step towards the level of visualization required to allow students to debug their own programs without the overhead of learning a debugging language, but to understand which visualization systems are actually practical, we need to look at their characteristics.

Most of the SV systems that have been developed to date are what Price, Small, and Baecker [31] call *manual specification style* systems: each requires the author of the program to somehow annotate the programs to call animation routines. This practice might work in some situations for people near the middle of the novice-to-expert continuum, but those at the early novice end will certainly not have the skill to annotate their programs, and experienced programmers working on large software engineering projects will not have the time to annotate a huge program by hand. It is clear that fully *automatic* SV must be used at the novice end of the continuum and at least *semi-automatic* SV must be used for the rest.

Unfortunately, most of the automatic SV systems are not *intelligent*, i.e. the visualization relies on information that can be gathered from a simple parsing of the source code or from the operating system or interpreter/compiler. Since the SV system makes no attempt to understand this information, the resulting visualization does not display any of the abstractions in the code, but instead provides a dressed up version the information available in a textual debugger. The key to providing a useful tool for all programmers, from novice to expert, is *intelligent automatic* software visualization that provides a clear abstraction that is relevant to the task at hand. This in turn requires the use of AI program understanding techniques, to which we now turn.

Intelligent Automatic SV

A great deal of the program understanding work that has gone into ITS design is based on an approach whereby the system must have some kind of advance knowledge of the program to be understood. This work has ranged from systems which have detailed knowledge bases for only a few specific problems, (e.g. [18, 23, 26, 21]), to systems which require the user to submit some kind of specification (e.g. [36, 1, 27]), to recent work which attempts to debug arbitrary programs [42, 24]. One of the techniques common to several systems is the use of *plan recognition* where the system uses either a top-down or bottom-up approach to find the small programming plans or clichés that make up an algorithm. Often "buggy" plans (for bugs known to be commonly written by students) will also be recognized by the system so that it can offer advice as to reaching a solution.

One automatic SV system which uses some weak AI techniques is the University of Washington Program Illustrator (UWPI) [19]. It uses "shallow" idiom-recognition techniques applied to undergraduate programs written in a subset of Pascal to determine how data structures are being used. UWPI displays animated graphical abstract data type illustrations as the program runs and requires neither code alteration by the student nor a specification of the program from the instructor. The lesson of UWPI is that a collection of idioms or clichés is sufficient to recognize algorithm fragments even when the program as a whole can not be understood in a "deep" or principled way. This suggests that even in the worst case where no part of an algorithm can be recognized, it is still possible to provide a useful visualization of the data structure abstractions.

The AI portion of any ITS is by far the most time-consuming or costly portion, with the cost increasing exponentially with the amount of analysis desired. In some ITSs, much of the cost is due to the provision of a natural language-type output interface. In the program analysis or bug analysis portions of the system the ITS designer may choose to implement either a deep analysis for a narrow domain or a more shallow analysis for a broader range. It is clear that our goal of addressing the entire novice-expert continuum can not be done by attempting a deep analysis—we must avoid the Complete Bug Catalogue Fallacy and use an approach which will maximize the use of our AI investment across a wide spectrum of programs.

Fail-Safe Algorithm Fragment Recognition in "Fiz"

We are currently implementing a system called "Fiz," which builds upon our earlier SV work [30, 11]. Fiz aims to provide a wide range of views of program execution for traditional imperative languages such as C and Pascal. These views range from low level tracing of source code up to animations of programming abstractions such as "Sort These Array Elements." The motivation is to enable users to see at a glance what their programs are doing and why. Fiz recognizes standard algorithms encountered in the code using a library of "algorithm fragments." If variants are present, they are parsed as far as possible based upon Fiz's algorithm fragment library. Whenever Fiz is unable to recognize an algorithm within a particular code segment it falls back to a lower level, that of recognizing algorithm independent clichés, such as set membership tests, array initializations, or data structure abstractions. Only when it fails to recognize any structure or function within the code does Fiz fall back to tracing the program, but even here it has two options: coarse-grained visualizations and source-level stepping as in a conventional debugger. We have found [14, 10] that specially-designed coarse-grained visualizations afford better navigation capabilities for users than simple physical (scale-size) "zooming" facilities, and therefore we preserve that distinction in our current work. We call our approach "fail-safe" because there is always some level at which we can present a useful visualization to the user, even in the case of highly idiosyncratic variants. In contrast to the ITS approach, we do not have to anticipate these idiosyncrasies in advance, so the software environment will be of benefit to a wider audience. Thus we do not suffer from the Complete Bug Catalogue Fallacy or the problem of coming up with an incorrect analysis since we "fall back" to lower levels of abstraction. The SCENT system of McCalla and Greer [25] (also see chapter in this volume) uses a similar approach, but instead falls back on more coarse grained or abstract analysis, so the advice risks being at too high a level of abstraction to benefit the student.

Fiz analyzes programs using a language-independent "surface plan" (control-flow & data-flow) description, similar to the one developed by Rich and Waters [41, 34]. Such a notation is needed at the very least to abstract away from implementation-specific details, including choice of alternate constructs, open-coding vs. subroutine calls, etc. The class of objects we attempt to recognize are as follows:

- **Complete Algorithms:** these are the (fortunate) cases wherein a match can be made between part of the user's source code and a known algorithm.
- **Algorithm Fragments:** these are the more typical cases, in which parts of the source code, usually separated over disparate statements, correspond to a known fragment or cliché, such as "initializing and incrementing a counter" or "displaying formatted output."
- **Monitorable Constructs and Data Structures:** these are multi-line constructs such as while loops, recursive function calls, or data structures for which a specialized and meaningful coarse-grained view can be displayed.
- **Expressions:** these are the lowest level constructs which are amenable to visualization, and correspond to that which is normally observed using conventional tracing and single-stepping tools.

The first two of these embody the "intelligence," since they emphasize more abstract descriptions which can only be detected by analyzing and understanding what a piece of code is trying to achieve. The last two reflect less abstract (and therefore more conventional and easier to visualize) constructs.

The first step in the program recognition process is parsing what is known as the "surface plan graph" (internal representation of the control and data flow) of the program to find the base-level clichés—these are collections of a handful of lines in a program which perform a very simple function, such as "Initialize a sequence pointer" (the same lines of code may appear in more than one base-level cliché). Base level clichés may be combined to form higher-level, more abstract clichés (e.g. "Simple linear search"), which in turn may be part of a higher level cliché (e.g. "Search for element"), so the user may select the level of abstraction desired or if the system is unable to completely understand an algorithm fragment it can display the highest level of abstraction that it understands. By providing a broad library of base-level clichés from the start and relying on our strategy of "graceful degradation" for algorithm recognition, we avoid the Complete Bug Catalogue Fallacy since we provide *some* kind of analysis for every program.

Visualization in Fiz

Fiz builds upon the Viz software visualization framework [12]. In that framework, we consider program execution to be a series of *history events* happening to (or perpetrated by) *players*. A player can be any part of a program, such as a function, a data structure, or a line of code. Each player has a name and is in some *state*, which may change when a history event occurs for that player. History events are like "interesting events" in BALSA [6]—each event corresponds to some code being executed in the program or some data changing its value. These events are recorded in the history module, which allows them to be accessed by the user and "replayed". Events and states are *mapped* into a visual representation which is accessible to the end-user. But the mapping is not just a question of storing pixel patterns to correspond to different events and states—we also specify different views (e.g. trees vs. tables), and ways of navigating around them.

This framework is equally at home dealing with either program code or algorithms, since a player and its history events may represent anything from a low-level (program code) abstraction such as "invoke a function call" to a high level (algorithm) abstraction such as "insert a pointer into a hash table."

Examples

To make our approach more concrete, and to contrast our philosophy with that of the ITS community, we first rework an example taken from PROUST [22], and then describe how our approach scales up to handle the debugging of a 7,500 line operating system. Elsewhere [17], we describe our approach applied to an example taken from the Lisp Tutor.

PROUST

PROUST is an automatic program debugger that serves as the heart of an ITS for teaching Pascal to novices. PROUST helped to account in a principled way for the data of Soloway, Bonar and Ehrlich [38], which indicated that only 39% of their Pascal students could solve an elementary iterative programming problem after a full term of study. Their detailed analysis suggested that the source of difficulty was the mismatch between the way certain flow of control constructs work and the way novices think they ought to work. Figure 1 displays PROUST's analysis of a student's (buggy) Pascal program, which was intended to read in numbers repeatedly, stopping when the "sentinel" number 99 is encountered, and finally printing out the average of the numbers.

```
Student's  (buggy)  program

 1    PROGRAM average;
 2    VAR sum,count,x: integer;
 3        average     : real;
 4   BEGIN
 5       sum:=0;
 6       count:=0;
 7       read(x);
 8       WHILE x<>99 do
 9          BEGIN
10               count := count + 1;
11               sum := sum + x;
12              x := x + 1;
13          END;
14       average := sum/count;
15       write(average);
16   END

PROUST: It appears that you were trying to use line 12 to read the next input
value. Incrementing x will not cause the next value to be read in. You need to
use a READ statement here. The statement in question is:

        x := x + 1
```

Figure 1. Buggy averaging program, with increment at line 12 instead of read(x), and PROUST's analysis and advice. (Based on [22], and modified trivially for expository purposes).

PROUST's excellent analysis, and helpful description for the student, are dependent on being able to deal with stereotypical bugs (otherwise there is no way to *know* that x:=x+1 is intended to read the next value of x). Our analysis of the performance statistics given in [22] indicates that less than 70% of the students attempting this simple problem received useful advice. This is good from an AI point of view (because automatic bug correction is hard), but not from a pedagogical or software engineering point view (because all students deserve satisfactory treatment, as do all programs). Moreover, PROUST's output in Figure 1 exhibits the "We Know Best" fallacy. If the student had some clever way of using assignment (e.g. incrementing an array index, into which values were going to be stored on a second pass), then PROUST's advice could be misleading, demoralizing, or just plain wrong. Moreover, if the student could not work out what PROUST's remark meant, then there is a case for letting the student get on with his or her own debugging. It seems fair to say that "no one knows your plans and intentions better than you do," so trying to second-guess the student's intentions seems like a risky way to proceed. Our view is that it is far better to harness the student's own motivation and knowledge of the original intentions of the program, and couple that with good visualization techniques to let the student figure out what has gone wrong and why.

Fiz handles this same example by a combination of program visualization and algorithm fragment analysis. We note in passing that although many commercial programming environments (e.g. Borland C++ for PCs, CenterLine C++ for Unix workstations) provide nice source-level debugging by highlighting code statements and displaying views of variables in separate windows, they don't provide the sort of coarse-grained view that is useful for homing in on buggy code in large examples (or small examples with a large number of iterations). We handle this situation in Fiz by providing, among other alternatives, a "Table" view that portrays cycles of iteration over time (separate columns) and rows which depict the behaviour of different "players," in this case assignment statements and the "<>" test of line 8. Figure 2 shows a Fiz representation of what happens just within the main loop of the Pascal program of Figure 1 when the input data contains the following seven numbers: 54 8 15 32 10 7 99 (of which only the first, i.e. 54, is actually read). Note that this view is quite "cheap" from an AI perspective as no deep analysis was necessary to determine the players or how to display them.

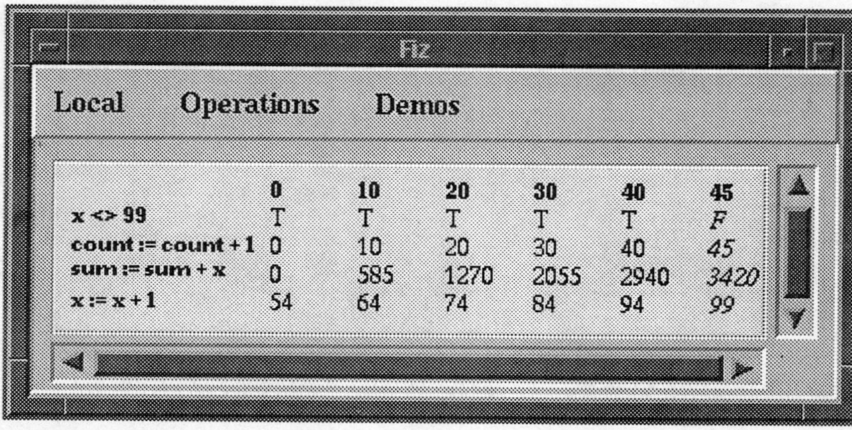

Figure 2. Fiz "compressed view" of 46 execution steps, given the buggy Pascal program shown in Figure 1 and the input data 54 8 15 32 10 7 99, of which only the first value is actually read in. The rightmost columns, by default, show the final step and the condition-failing (non-)step, respectively. The convention is that each column depicts an execution snapshot at the very *end* of that iteration. Fiz compresses the execution history by a factor of 10 (this factor is selectable by the user), and each bold-face step-number at the top of a column is mouse-sensitive let the user "expand-this-column" to have access to a more fine-grained presentation.

The notion of a *monitorable construct* introduced earlier is all we need to undertake the analysis presented in Figure 2. The construct in question is a WHILE loop, which has distinctive players, notably an exit condition and the individual statements (assignment statements in this case) within the body of the loop. Later we show how Fiz displays more abstract players such as "set flag." While not visually profound, Figure 2 ought to be highly meaningful to someone who has written the program presented in Figure 1. For one thing, the value of **sum** gets much higher than one would expect from a correctly-working solution. Secondly, the number of iterations is far higher than expected (after all, there were only 7 values to be read).

Fiz can automatically monitor the behaviour of an input buffer during program execution, treating it as just another player. The trick is to realize that it is interesting to observe the behaviour of this player during execution of the WHILE loop. As it turns out, a simple algorithm fragment matcher is sufficient to detect the potentially important relationship between the READ statement on line 7 and the WHILE loop which follows it, and to inform Fiz accordingly. Fiz's display of the state of the input buffer during execution is an animation, depicted statically for the purposes of this chapter in Figure 3. The left snapshot shows the input buffer before execution. The middle snapshot shows the buffer at the very moment the first element (54) is consumed. The right snapshot is how the buffer appears during the rest of the animation (i.e. throughout the WHILE loops).

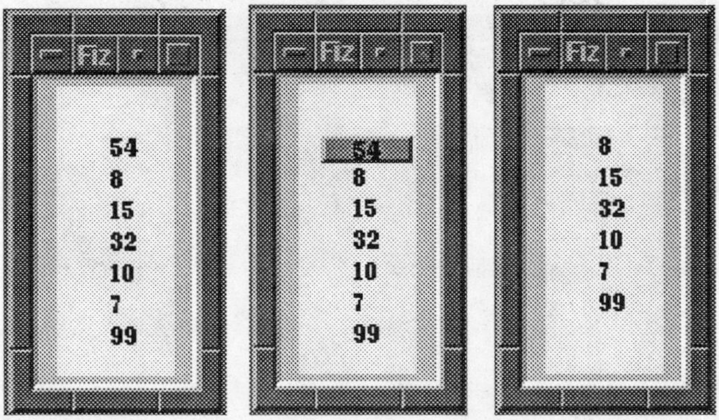

Figure 3. Snapshots of input buffer animation during execution of the buggy program presented in Figure 1. Left: before execution. Middle: the read statement is executed. Right: appearance throughout the WHILE loop. The contents of such buffers can be scaled automatically to suit the display size.

The burden is entirely on the user to detect that the input buffer is not being consumed beyond the first element. Our aim here is merely to bring this to the user's attention in as perspicuous (and problem-independent) a manner as possible.

The advantage of the approach advocated here becomes apparent as the examples increase in complexity. Understanding the user's true intentions automatically, or requiring a formal specification of those intentions, is simply not realistic. Providing the user with a way to observe the behaviour of a program is realistic. Moreover, the same algorithm and plan recognition technology can be harnessed to detect algorithm fragments or clichés, which can in turn be used to highlight players of *a priori* interest using Fiz's repertoire of software visualization techniques.

Scaling up

Only a handful of automatic SV systems clearly leave the realm of toy examples: TPM [14], TRI [9], and Paradocs [30] are all designed from the start to handle big problems. Here we look at one of these systems (Paradocs) in detail and show how its approach is incorporated and extended by Fiz. Paradocs shows a live animation of process behaviour in a small UNIX-compatible operating system simulator called Mini Tunis [20]. Mini Tunis consists of over 7500 lines of source code in 11 major modules and monitors (each with a number of sub-modules) and it is used to teach the senior operating systems course at the University of Toronto. As Mini Tunis runs, Paradocs shows a static hierarchical call-graph diagram of the top-level modules and monitors. The user is able to "open up" individual nodes so that the call graph changes to show a finer grained view with the enclosed sub-modules and procedures. While Mini Tunis is running, each active process is shown on the diagram as a coloured "marble" so that the marble moves from node to node on the diagram as the process executes in different modules and procedures (see Figure 4). In another window Paradocs displays larger versions of each process "marble" showing the state of the process. The user can pause and restart Mini Tunis (and thus the animation) and control the speed of execution. It is also possible to pause Mini Tunis and replay a recent animation either backwards or forwards at any desired speed.

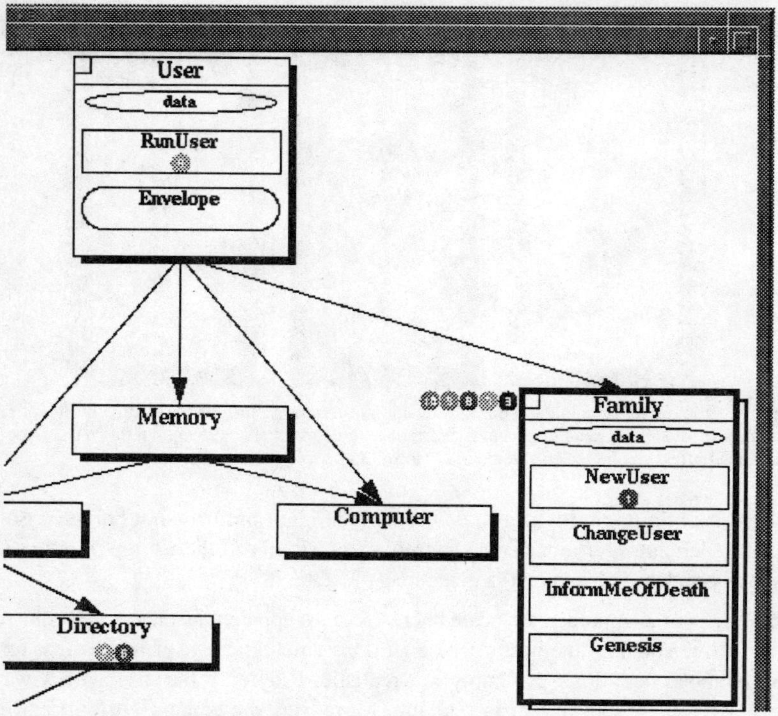

Figure 4. Paradocs snapshot of runaway process in Mini Tunis

The original version of Paradocs was completely automatic, but it was also *non-intelligent* since it only displayed control flow information and process status information (which can be gathered using a simple parsing of the source code). In the original empirical evaluation of Paradocs, subjects were trained then given a buggy version of Mini Tunis and told to find the bug using whatever methods they wished. We will now describe one of the original debugging scenarios showing how subjects used Paradocs, then we will show how Fiz is encompassing the Paradocs approach and adding fail-safe algorithm fragment recognition on demand to produce *intelligent automatic* visualizations for professional-level debugging and its concomitant pedagogical benefits.

One of the bugs which subjects were faced with involved a runaway process in the operating system's initialization sequence which results in too many processes being forked and the entire process table being filled. The symptom observed by the operating system users is a general and continuous degradation in performance as the system slows to a complete standstill when no more processes are left to be allocated. The subjects who used Paradocs to try to find this bug began by running Mini Tunis and looking at the high level view showing only the top level modules. This showed the initial process moving throughout the hierarchy as it initialized the devices, file system and memory, then it began a pattern of movement around the `User` and `Family` modules and new processes began to become active from the wait queue in the `Family` module. Most subjects then opened up the `User` and `Family` modules for a closer look and began replaying the animation to see where the initial process was executing in these modules.

After observing the animation closely and perhaps replaying sections a few times, most subjects concluded that the NewUser procedure in the `Family` monitor warranted closer inspection. At this point in the original Paradocs experiment the subjects had to resort to a paper printout of the procedure (which is a little over one page long). In Fiz, the users can invoke a view of the procedure using fail-safe algorithm recognition. Of course the system is not able to completely understand the procedure and come up with a high level description of what it does, nor is it necessarily able automatically to find the bug, since we are not trying to build a complete bug catalogue. Instead it can show a brief table view which summarizes the procedure and its execution history in only a few lines.

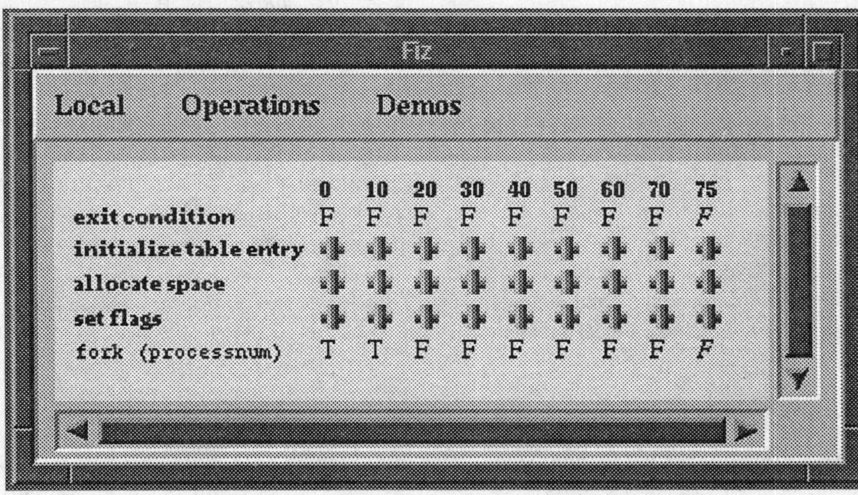

Figure 5. Fiz "table view" of critical (buggy) loop which spawns runaway process in Mini Tunis

The table view shown in Figure 5 summarizes the execution history for the main loop (which occupies most of one page) in the `NewUser` procedure. Our algorithm fragment recognizer has identified the loop's exit condition shown at the top of the first column. Following this, a number of lines have been identified as initializing entries in a table (likely the process table) and another group of lines have been identified as allocating space for the process. Following this we see that a number of flags are set before the unrecognized piece of code "`fork(processnum)`" is found (the experienced user will know that this is simply launching the next process). The execution history is automatically scaled by Fiz to fit the window and is compressed to show every tenth entry. This table reveals that the loop exit condition is always false up to the seventy-fifth iteration through the loop, so the loop has not yet exited. The next three parts of the algorithm have "pluses" to simply indicate that they have been executed while the `fork` entry shows that it was successful for at least the first 11 iterations but that a process was not successfully launched from iteration 20 onwards.

The main loop in the `NewUser` procedure is clearly launching too many processes and since there are only 11 processes available in this operating system, the system begins to grind to a halt as the initialization process is stuck in an endless loop. The obvious cause of the problem (given that the subject knows there are only 11 processes available) is the exit condition; a closer inspection reveals that the exit condition checks one of the process flags which is never set in the *set flags* section of the algorithm. Once this problem is corrected, the initialization runs correctly. The clear advantage of the Fiz approach is that the user can diagnose the problem by using the visualization and recognition software to lead the way.

Helping the student

Can such visualizations assist a really confused student? Frankly, we don't know, and this is a matter for future empirical work. Our focus is clearly on the debugging, maintenance, and diagnostic side of programming, for reasons we justified above. The point here is that by making the *symptoms* explicit, we can greatly facilitate diagnostic activity. The cause of the buggy behaviours is typically easy to see in the Fiz implementation, but more important is the fact that it can handle an unrestricted class of programs. The reason is that in the worst case there is always *something* that can be visualized, even if it is just a table that portrays cycles of iteration over time (separate columns) vs. the behaviour of different "players," such as loop variables and the exit tests (separate rows). The role of AI-based algorithm recognition techniques in Fiz is to provide annotations to such low-level visualizations, so that individual variables can be highlighted as part of, say, an "increment counter" plan when this is deemed appropriate. Even in the absence of such annotations, Fiz provides a compact coarse-grained view (unlike commercial source-level debuggers, single-steppers and tracers) which allows the user to home in quickly on problem areas.

Summary

We have argued that the ITS approach to teaching programming is limited in scope by the misguided goals which the traditional paradigm sets. By focusing the ITS approach on beginning novices, researchers are handicapping themselves from the start since the amount of effort they must expend to teach at higher levels grows exponentially with the difficulty of the problems. This approach has led to the development of four basic fallacies in the design of ITSs for computer programming which will prevent any significant realization of their goals.

In contrast, we suggest that the focus of ITS development should be on the continuum from novice through expert and that novices should be taught programming with professional-quality programming tools. The instruction-based learning process found in the traditional ITS approach prevents learning by experimentation and the poor or absent visualization of execution prevents the students from developing a good model of the abstract machine. By instead allowing a guided-discovery approach combined with a high-quality programming and debugging interface with good visualization, the students are able to teach themselves about how the machine works and solve problems on their own that otherwise would have required "spoon feeding."

We discussed *automatic* software visualization as a state-of-the-art programming interface and gave examples of its effective use in beginning and intermediate to senior level teaching as well as professional software engineering. One advantage is that good automatic SV systems (unlike ITSs) have a fall-back position which enables them to present *some* view of arbitrarily complex and novel programs which can still be of pedagogical benefit to the end-user. The real potential, as we see it, is to harness AI-based program-understanding and plan-recognition techniques to enhance these systems so that they can provide visualizations at a high level of abstraction so that we have *intelligent automatic* SV. This in turn provides a double-benefit: good low-level visualizations which work with any program, and good high-level visualizations which work at least on parts of programs which can be categorized sensibly. In all cases, the end-user, from novice to expert, wins.

Acknowledgment

This research was funded by the UK SERC/ESRC/MRC Joint Council Initiative on Cognitive Science and Human Computer Interaction Project 90/CS66 (Algorithm Visualization), and CEC ESPRIT-II Project 5365 (VITAL). We thank Ben du Boulay, Peter Pirolli and other attendees at the Genova workshop for their helpful comments on earlier drafts of this chapter and our related work.

References

1. Adam, A. and J. Laurent: LAURA: A System to Debug Student Programs. Art. Intell., 15, 75-122 (1980)
2. Anderson, J.R., R. Farrell, and R. Sauers: Learning to plan in LISP. Cognitive Science, 8, 87-129 (1984)
3. Anderson, J.R. and B.J. Reiser: The Lisp Tutor. BYTE, 10(4), 159-175 (1985)
4. Baecker, R.M. and D. Sherman: Sorting Out Sorting. narrated colour videotape, 30 minutes, presented at ACM SIGGRAPH '81 and excerpted in ACM SIGGRAPH Video Review #7, 1983. Los Altos, CA: Morgan Kaufmann 1981
5. Baek, Y.K. and B.H. Layne: Color, Graphics, and Animation in a Computer-Assisted Learning Tutorial Lesson. J. of Computer Based-Instruction, 15(4), 131-135 (1988)
6. Brown, M.H., Algorithm Animation. ACM Distinguished Dissertations, New York: MIT Press 1988
7. Brown, M.H. and R. Sedgewick. A System for Algorithm Animation. In: ACM SIGGRAPH '84. pp. 177-186. New York: ACM 1984
8. Corbett, A., J.R. Anderson, and E.G. Patterson, Student Modelling and Tutoring Flexibility in the Lisp Intelligent Tutoring System, in Intelligent Tutoring Systems: At the Crossroads of Artificial Intelligence and Education, C. Frasson and G. Gauthier, Editor. Ablex: Norwood, NJ. 1990
9. Domingue, J., TRI: The Transparent Rule Interpreter, in Research and Development in Expert Systems VII, N. Shadbolt, Editor. Cambridge University Press: 126-138. 1988
10. Domingue, J. and M. Eisenstadt. A New Metaphor for the Graphical Explanation of Forward Chaining Rule Execution. In: The Eleventh International Joint Conference on Artificial Intelligence. pp. 129-134. San Mateo, CA: Morgan Kaufman 1989
11. Domingue, J., B.A. Price, and M. Eisenstadt. A Framework for Describing and Implementing Software Visualization Systems. In: Graphics Interface'92. pp. 53-60. Palo Alto, CA: Morgan Kaufmann 1992
12. Domingue, J., B.A. Price, and M. Eisenstadt, Viz: A Framework for Describing and Implementing Software Visualization Systems, in User-Centred Requirements for Software Engineering Environments, D. Gilmore and R. Winder, Editor. (to appear) 1992
13. du Boulay, J.B.H., T. O'Shea, and J. Monk: The black box inside the glass box: presenting computing concepts to novices. Int. J. Man-Mach. Stud., 14(3), 237-249 (1981)
14. Eisenstadt, M. and M. Brayshaw: The Transparent Prolog Machine (TPM): an execution model and graphical debugger for logic programming. J. of Logic Prog., 5(4), 1-66 (1988)
15. Eisenstadt, M. and J. Breuker, An Account of the Conceptualizations Underlying Buggy Looping Programs, in Novice programming environments: explorations in human-computer interaction and artificial intelligence, M. Eisenstadt, M. Keane, and T. Rajan, Editors. Lawrence Erlbaum Associates: London. 1992

16. Eisenstadt, M., M. Keane, and T. Rajan, eds. Novice programming environments: explorations in human-computer interaction and artificial intelligence. London: Lawrence Erlbaum Associates 1992

17. Eisenstadt, M., B.A. Price, and J. Domingue: Software Visualization as a Pedagogical Tool: Redressing some ITS Fallacies. Human Cognition Research Laboratory, The Open University, Milton Keynes, UK Technical Report 91, April 1992

18. Goldstein, I.P.: Understanding Simple Picture Programs. MIT AI Lab Technical Report 294, 1974

19. Henry, R.R., K.M. Whaley, and B. Forstall. The University of Washington Illustrating Compiler. In: The ACM SIGPLAN '90 Conference on Programming Language Design and Implementation. pp. 223-233. New York: ACM 1990

20. Holt, R.C. and D.A. Penny: The Concurrent Programming of Operating Systems using the Turing Plus Language. Dept. of Computer Science, The University of Toronto Course Notes CSC 468/2204, 1988

21. Johnson, W.L., Intention-Based Diagnosis of Novice Programming Errors. Research Notes in Artificial Intelligence, London: Pitman 1986

22. Johnson, W.L. and E. Soloway: PROUST: Knowledge-Based Program Understanding. IEEE Trans. Software Eng., SE-11(3), 267-275 (1985)

23. Laubsch, J. and M. Eisenstadt. Domain Specific Debuggin Aids for Novice Programmers. In: IJCAI-81. pp. 964-969. 1981

24. Lutz, R., Plan Diagrams as a Basis for Understanding and Debugging Pascal Programs, in Novice programming environments: explorations in human-computer interaction and artificial intelligence, M. Eisenstadt, M. Keane, and T. Rajan, Editor. Lawrence Erlbaum Associates: London. 1992

25. McCalla, G.I. and J.E. Greer. Intelligent Advising in Problem Solving Domains: The SCENT-3 Arcitecture. In: International Conference on Intelligent Tutoring Systems (ITS'88) pp. 124-131. 1988

26. Miller, M.L., A Structured Planning and Debugging Environment for Elementary Programming, in Intelligent Tutoring Systems, D. Sleeman and J.S. Brown, Editor. Academic Press: Orlando. 1982

27. Murray, W.R. Heuristic and Formal Methods in Automatic Program Debugging. In: International Joint Conference on Artificial Intelligence. pp. 15-19. 1985

28. Myers, B.A.: Taxonomies of Visual Programming and Program Visualization. J. Vis. Lang. & Comp., 1(1), 97-123 (1990)

29. Petre, M. and B.A. Price. Why a Computer Interface is Not Like a Painting: the user as a deliberate reader. In: The St. Petersburg International Workshop on Human-Computer Interaction. pp. (to appear) 1992

30. Price, B.A. and R.M. Baecker. The Automatic Animation of Concurrent Programs. In: The First International Workshop on Computer-Human Interfaces. pp. 128-137. Moscow, USSR: ICSTI 1991

31. Price, B.A., I.S. Small, and R.M. Baecker. A Taxonomy of Software Visualization. In: The 25th Hawaii International Conference on System Sciences. pp. 597-606. New York: IEEE Computer Society Press 1992

32. Ramadhan, H. An Intelligent Discovery Programming System. In: ACM Symposium on Applied Computing: Special Track on Visuality in Computing. pp. 149-159. New York: ACM Press 1992

33. Reiser, B.J., *et al.*, Facilitating Students' Reasoning with Causal Explanations and Visual Representations, in Artificial Intelligence and Education: Proceedings of the Fourth International Conference. IOS: Amsterdam. 228-235. 1989

34. Rich, C. and R.C. Waters: Abstraction, Inspection, and Debugging in Programming. MIT AI Lab AI Memo 634, June 1981

35. Rosenberg, R.: A Critical Analysis of Reseach on Intelligent Tutoring Systems. Ed. Tech, 27(11), 7-13 (1987)

36. Ruth, F.G.: Intelligent Program Analysis. Art. Intell., 7, 65-85 (1976)

37. Sack, W., R. Bennett, and E. Soloway. The Advanced Placement Computer Science Practice and Feedback System. In: The NATO Advanced Research Workshop on Cognitive Models and Intelligent Environments for Learning Programming. pp. 291-297. 1992

38. Soloway, E., J. Bonar, and K. Ehrlich: Cognitive Strategies and Looping Constructs: An empirical Study. CACM, 26(11) (1983)

39. Stasko, J.T.: The Path-transition Paradigm: a practical methodology for adding animation to Program Interfaces. J. of Vis. Lang. and Comp., 1(3), 213-236 (1990)

40. Vitter, J.S. Design and Analysis of Dynamic Huffman Coding. In: The 26th Annual Symposium on Computer Science. pp. 293-302. New York: IEEE Computer Society Press 1985

41. Waters, R.C.: Automatic Analysis of the Logical Structure of Programs. Artificial Intelligence Laboratory, Massachusetts Institute of Technology AI Technical Report 492, December 1978

42. Wills, L.: Automated Program Recognition: A Feasibility Demonstration. Art. Intell., 45, 113-171 (1990)

Registermachine as a Mental Model for Understanding Computer Programming

Elmar Cohors-Fresenborg

Fachbereich Mathematik / Informatik, Universität Osnabrück, Postfach 44 69, D - 4500 Osnabrück, Germany

Abstract: From a cognitive science point of view and based on research concerning the resonance between external representations and cognitive structures of pupils we have developed a curriculum for introducing pupils of grade 7 into the world of computers. The mental model for computer programming with imperative languages is induced for the pupils by working with the demonstrative computer *registermachine*, which as a theoretical concept is known in the theory of computability. In this paper the fundamental ideas of the curriculum are presented as they are worked out in the textbook for pupils and evaluated in 50 experimental classes since 1987.

Keywords: Computer education / computer literacy / mental models of computer programming / (form of) representation / mathematics education / concept of function / algebra in school / curriculum development

1. Overview

In the following we report on curriculum development concerning the question, how can pupils at early secondary level get an insight into fundamental concepts of computer programming. It is based on research about the cognitive processes of the pupils, when they are inventing or analyzing algorithms ([4], [16], [19]). The work has been done by the research group "Foundations of Mathematics and Mathematics Education" at the University of Osnabrück since 1975 and the "Forschungsinstitut für Mathematikdidaktik" in Osnabrück since 1984.

The research we are reporting in this paper is part of the project "Integration of algorithmic and axiomatic reasoning into the mathematics lessons in grade 7 and 8 as a contribution to computer literacy", which is financed by the ministry of education in our state Niedersachsen. From 1987 until 1992 the curriculum and the textbooks ([6], [7], [8], [9]) have been evaluated in grade 7 and 8 in 52 classes respectively.

In our paper we will tackle our problem under different aspects, which depend each other: constructing curriculum elements has to start from mathematical ideas and to take into account psychological insights on learning and thinking processes of the pupils. As our research has shown, in this field the question of how to represent a mathematical concept plays an important role. Representation itself has two aspects: representing a mathematical idea means on the one hand, that there has to be constructed a conceptual framework, in which the new concepts are

implemented, on the other hand - if one deals with pupils - abstract concepts have to be represented by using materials or - more general - didactical situations.
If one has to teach fundamental concepts of algorithms and computer programs to pupils at early secondary level, there is the problem, that there does not exist a conceptual framework in which these new ideas could be implemented. For our approach we decided, to build up different microworlds as such a conceptual framework, which on one hand is complete in the sense, that it consists of all the fundamental concepts and allows to understand their relations but on the other hand is so small, that it can be taught within a very short time.

First (chapter 2) we explain our *theoretical background*. We start with an analysis of the idea of algorithm and computable function and compare the approach in the foundations of mathematics with findings in cognitive science: The two concepts are equivalent, but belong from a psychological point of view to different worlds. The first one is the world in which computational actions have to be organized, the second is where the structure of the functions has to be definded. This fits to the theory of Schwank ([19], [20]) concerning individual preferences for a functional or predicative cognitive structure.

Then (chapter 3) we introduce three different *forms of representation* for the ideal mathematical concept of algorithm: *RegisterBox, Computing Network, Registermachine*. Each of these contains the fundamental idea: an algorithm is constructed from elementary operations with a set of control structures. Our experimental research has shown, that pupils may have an individual preference for one of these microworlds ([16], [17]).

In the fourth chapter we are developing the *curriculum* "Introduction into the World of Computers with Registermachines" [6]. We have developed it from a cognitive science point of view ([20]) combining the process of making precise the idea of inventing programs for a computer and the idea of defining (recursive) functions. In the curriculum we are climbing up simultaneously on two ladders, using each step on one ladder as epistomological basis for understanding the next step on the other one.
In the following sections we briefly resume and analyse the content of the curriculum. We begin with *introducing the idea of algorithm* (section 4.1) to build up the idea in three forms of representation. In a next step we introduce the notation of functions (of several variables) from describing the handling of the registerbox. Using naively this notation it is easy to present functions, for which programs have to be developed. The idea of algorithmic complexity offers a frame in which both the analysis of algebraic terms and the training in programming is for the pupils an interesting and competitive first round in understanding the relation between the concepts of algorithms and functions. In this paper we resume it in section *(4.2) the concepts of function and complexity*. In a next spiral first the RM-language is extended for the use of *subprograms* (section 4.3). This section also containes the definition of the full RM-language. In the section (4.4) *computability and definability* we report, how pupils understand that there exist two different languages, in which one may describe a functional dependency: the programming language or the (traditional) representation as function terms in mathematics. The last turn in the didactical spiral is described in the section (4.5) *syntax and semantics*. To prepare the phenomenon, that a programming language has a grammar, we analyze the role which grammati-

cal mistakes play in understanding the meaning of a text written in a natural language. We discuss, that the grammar has been implemented into the computer, otherwise the RM could not "understand" the intended "meaning" of a program. It is quite astonishing for pupils that in mathematics lessons a grammar is an object of mathematical reasoning. This offers interesting aspects for a discussion with pupils about the nature of mathematics and mathematical thinking. It also enables a cooperation with the language teacher on the role, which grammar plays in formal and natural languages.

In the fifth chapter we report on the *evaluation* and give a *summary.*

2. Theoretical Background

2.1 Foundations of Mathematics

The establishing of a mental model for computer programming should be based on a deep analysis of the fundamental ideas which constitute the conceptual framework called algorithm. In the theory of computability the concept of registermachines (RM) was established by Rödding [18] 25 years ago. In the following years it turned out, that it was a fruitful concept to structure the theory and enable quite elegant proofs (see [1], [3]). The mathematical concept of RM describes an ideal computer. In each of its registers a natural number can be stored. The language of the RM is recursively defined from the elementary operations counting forwards and backwards (in each of the registers) by the control structures concatenation (linking) and iteration. The idea of RM was developed by us [3] to a theoretical model for an imperative programming language. (See section 4.3. In the RM-concept of Rödding [17] the "language" was more like a machine language. It consisted of the parts 1.1 a, 1.2 a and 1.2 b only, but for an arbitrary number n of registers).

The other fundament of the theory is the concept of recursive functions. Here complicated functions are defined from a small set of elementary functions by certain definition schemas. Both concepts are equivalent ([1], [3]).

From the philosophical point of view in the first approach the concept formation is based on the evidence of elementary operations and constructing principles. In a real computer the evidence has to be realized in the compiler or interpreter. In the second approach the concept formation is based on the evidence of elementary functions and the meaning of definitions.

2.2 Cognitive Science

We have developed our curriculum from a cognitive science point of view, as it has been introduced into mathematics education by Davis [10]. In consequence the concept of mental models as introduced by Johnson-Laird [14] plays an important role in our approach. During the last twenty years, starting with Bruner [2], the importance of different forms of external representations for the mathematical concept formation of pupils has been studied (f.e. [12], [13], [15]).

In our group different forms of representing algorithms have been developed (see [4] and chapter 3 in this paper). Kaune ([16], [17]) has shown, that these don't form an hierarchy (enactive, iconic, symbolic) in the sense of Bruner [2], because there exist individual preferences for one of these, if pupils are free to choose that form of representation, in which they would like to construct or analyse algorithms. Her research also pointed out, that there also exist individual differences concerning the performance in constructing versus analyzing algorithms.

The mentioned studies on algorithmic thinking have been the basis for a sophisticated analysis by Schwank, which led to a theory about individual differences in the preference for cognitive structures ([19], [20]). She distinguishes between a predicative and a functional cognitive structure. Predicative thinking emphasizes the preference for thinking in terms of relations and judgements; functional thinking emphasizes the preference for thinking in terms of processes and modes of action. There is a resonance between external representation and cognitive structure.
As she points out there is a correspondance between different ways in the foundation of the concept of functions (recursive versus computable) and the cognitive structures (predicative versus functional). This may be interpreted as a cognitive science explanation for the different points of view in the foundations of mathematics.

In our curriculum and textbook [6] we follow the results of Kaune [16] and Schwank [20] and combine it with the philosophy of constructivism, as von Glasersfeld [22] has introduced into mathematics education. It is important to mention, that the mental models is induced by a suitable form of external representation. Therefore these forms play the role of microworlds, in which the fundamental ideas are represented. By exploring that microworld pupils construct their mental model.

3. Forms of Representation

3.1 Register Box

In the form of representation "handling sticks in the register box" the stores are represented by various colored compartments in a so-called Register Box, the numbers in each corresponding to the number of sticks (of matching colour) in the compartments. The elementary operations of counting forwards and backwards corresponds to putting or removing single sticks. An algorithm consists of a suitable sequence of such elementary operations controlled by the test of zero. Curtains are fixed in front of the compartments so that the students, while organizing the course of action, cannot refer to the actual content of the compartments but have to invent these by using the concept of variable.

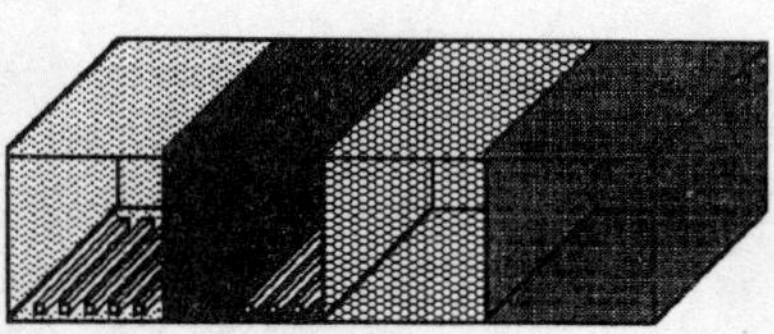

Register Box

An algorithm for addition could be described for this form of representation as follows:

> While the second (green) box is not empty, take one stick out of the green box and put one red stick into the first (red) box.

3.2 Computing Network

In the form of representation "computing network" the algorithm is represented by constructing it using the set of *Dynamic Mazes* ([4]). This contains bricks of the following type (see figures below): counters, straight lines, curves, crossings, and junctions.

Straight Line **Curve** **Crossing** **Junction**

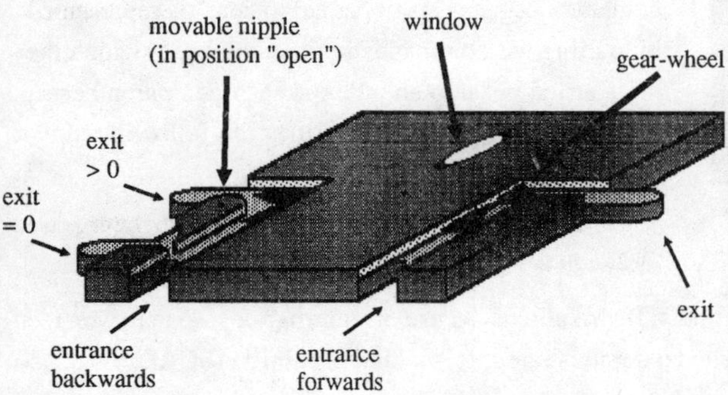

Counter

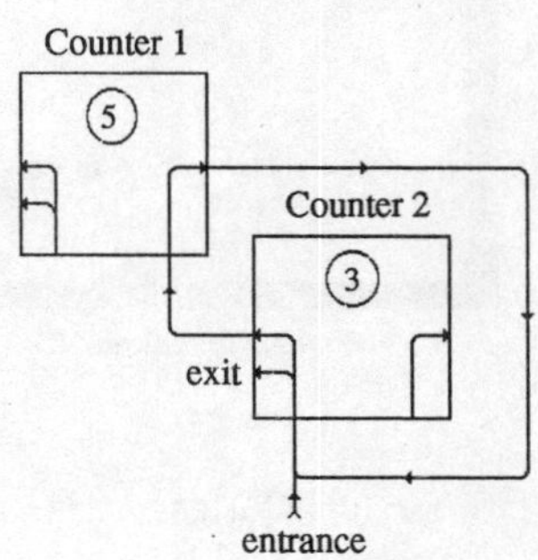

Computing Network

The counter building block contains a gear-wheel, and a round window where only one of the numbers from 0 to 10 is visible. When passing through the right entrance from the bottom to the top, the cog counts forwards. What happens passing through the left entrance depends on the position of the movable nipple. If the content of the counter is greater than zero, the movable nipple is in position "open" and passing through the left entrance will lead to counting backwards and the exit "> 0" will be reached. If the content is equal to zero, any further passage through this channel will be blocked up by the movable nipple, the exit "= 0" is reached without moving the cog. If it is in the zero position and the right entrance is used (for counting forwards), the content of the counter will change to 1, and the movable nipple will jump back into its position "open".

For constructing a computing network these bricks have to be fixed on a board in such a way that a kind of functioning flowchart is produced. The figure "Computing Network" above shows the abtract drawing of a constructed network, which computes the function "addition". By passing through the network starting at the entrance, the algorithm is executed, until the network is left at the exit.

In the computing networks, the idea that an algorithm does not depend on knowing the input values is illustrated by the fact that the algorithm works correctly even when the windows which show the numbers are covered.

3.3 Registermachine

In the form of representation "programs for the registermachine", the algorithm is represented by a program written in a simple program language for the registermachine (RM). In a microcomputer, the RM can be simulated using a special software system. In the following we denominate this demonstrative computer with registermachine also. The commands consist of the following. Counting forwards in register i is expressed by the symbol A_i, counting backwards in register i by S_i. The sequential execution of operations is represented by a serial notation of command chains, the iteration of command chains "while the content of register i is not equal to zero" is represented by putting the commands in parentheses, at which the register i is put into an index in the open parenthesis.. The program $(_2\ S_2\ A_1\ )$ describes the following algorithm for addition:

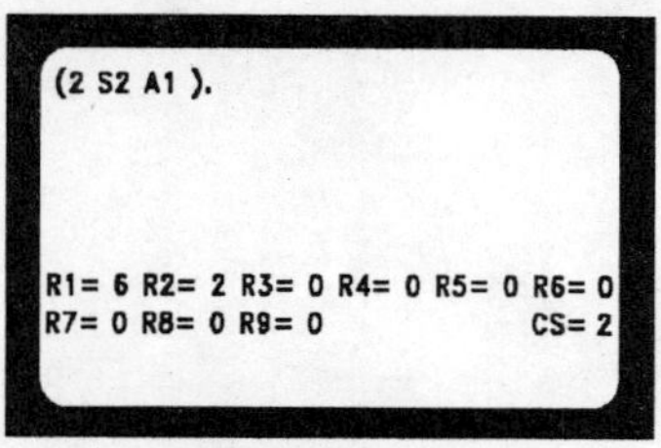

Registermachine

While the content of register 2 is not equal to zero, count backwards in register 2 and forwards in register 1.

The full RM-language (see section 4.3) also allows the use of subprograms, so that even the execution of recursive procedures can be demonstrated. It is a kind of mini-PASCAL.

On the monitor the pupils are able to follow the gradual process of the programs. At the same time, in all the bottom lines the gradual change of the register contents is shown. The RM has one line for the (main) program and 21 lines to define subprograms. If during the execution of a program an abbreviation is called, the complete definition is displaced on the screen. If during the execution of that subprogram another abbreviation is called (or in case of a recursive procedure the "same" abbreviation), the first 21 complete definitions occur in lines 2 to 22. If the depth of the calling hierarchy of subprograms is 22 or more (for example during the execution of a recursively defined subprogram), then in line 22 the complete definition of that subprogram is to be seen, which is just in execution.

Below these 22 lines for the program and complete definitions, there are two lines to show the actual value of the 9 registers (changing during the computation) and a counter for the number of steps (CS, see section 4.2), which the RM has executed. In the last line there occurs the error message.

4. Curriculum

4.1 Introducing the Idea of Algorithm

As we have pointed out earlier the fundamental concepts cannot be introduced by definition or explanation, they have to become evident by using them in different situations. We support the process of concept formation by offering different forms of representation as suitable micro-worlds and train the pupils to translate an idea from one world to the other. A benefit of such an approach is, that one form of representation now becomes an object of reflection, which is in a certain way "outside" the process of concept formation. The change of the forms of representation enables the pupils to become conscious about their own process of concept formation.

As a basis of evidence we use the microworld, that a robot has to execute a series of commands, using the register box (see section 3.2). The research of Schwank ([19], [20]) and our own investigations in the classroom have shown (even with deaf pupils [5]), that algorithms can be invented by pupils without first verbalizing the ideas. Our approach also supports the idea of Duchâteau [11], that the main difficulty in understanding programming is to switch from the task of solving a problem in the terms of "doing it" to "having it done by".

We use the pupil's naive understanding of addition and start with the problem to add two numbers, f. e. 5+3. The problem is concrete, but arbitrary. During the introductory lesson it has to be elaborated, what does it mean, that the algorithm is (exists) independent from the content of the compartments. A crucial situation for this is the question, whether it works, even if the heaps in the compartments are covered by the curtains, and next, uncounted heaps are thrown behind the curtains. In this microworld this is the test, whether the pupils have understood the concept of variable.

In a second approach the problem for the pupils is to construct a computing network with the bricks *Dynamic Mazes*. In this form of representation the algorithm is represented as an object, which can be seen: a foto is sufficient, but using the register box one needs a film. Therefore the pupils can be asked, which are the important parts of the network. Here the theory of Schwank ([20]) explains different types of answers. Generally the world of computing networks is not a suitable one for predicative structured pupils.
The representation of the concept of variable is in this form the arbitrary content of a counter. The representation of the concept of loop is really seen as the closed circle of bricks, in which the running is controlled by the zero test in a counter. An interesting problem is to discuss the difference between a WHILE-loop and a REPEAT-loop in the world of networks: the question is, where the entrance to the network is located.

The third form of representation is the simple version of the RM-language (see section 3.2). The framework for introducing is the idea, that a computer cannot "read" networks. Therefore it has to be described with "words" using "letters".

In the course of an ideal teaching all three forms of representing the algorithm for addition should be introduced in the first two lessons. During the following lessons simple algorithms for subtraction, doubling, copying should be invented in all three forms. Pupils should discuss the benefits of the different forms. It has been shown, that beside objective reasons for the choice there exist individual preferences: predicative structured pupils are not very successfull in handling (constructing or analyzing) networks. For them this form is only an image and not a structured microworld. On the other hand, functional structured pupils like networks and even later, when complex programs are to be invented, they use a mental model of organizing processes (like using networks) even if no real network is present. That means, later they will *not* first construct the algorithm as a network and then translate it to a program, but their way of talking about their ideas indicates their different mental model.

4.2 The Concepts of Function and Complexity

In our approach the concept of function is an undefined one. Therefore we have to introduce the talking (in the sense of Wittgenstein [23]) about functions and the functional notation. We construct the basis of evidence in the following way: We first remind pupils that we have invented algorithms for solving certain arithmetical problems. We had described them with words like addition, subtraction, doubling. But using the representation register box we can describe more problems, than we have common words for: we just say, what is in the compartments before the algorithm starts, and what is the result in the compartments. The notation of n-tupel is introduced by the story, that typewriters don't like to draw the register box so often. Therefore a register box-drawing is simplified by moving away top and bottom, replacing the sidewalls by parentheses and deminuting the walls between the compartments to commas. This procedure of simplifying is demonstrated with a sophisticated overhead folio. As a result of this folio artistic the idea of a n-tupel and in consequence the notation of functions of several variables has a very concrete mental representation and in future lessons causes no problem (even not for the more functional structured pupils, who don't tend to like written formal representations). The variables represent the idea of an uncounted heap behind the curtain, the index represents the number of the compartment. For the future the meaning of the following kind of sentences is established: Write a program for computing the following function:

$$f\colon (x_1, x_2, x_3) \to (x_1, x_2, x_3 \dot{-} 2(x_1+x_2))$$

After introducing the use of the description (which is more in favour for the predicative structured pupils), we start to implement the concept of functional dependency, based not on an input-output-relation but on an understanding of processes. For this approach we use the idea of algorithmic complexity: pupils have sometimes written more or less quick programs to compute the same function. Theyintroduce the concept of step counter functions as a measure for complexity: The number of executed elementary commands *depends* on the input. The step counter function describes the complexity of the process. Writing programs with simple complexity generates challenging series of problems for pupils. The mathematical techniques to find them are classical algebra combined with knowledge about the complexity of loops. This part of curriculum trains both, the formal aspect and the algorithmic one. We have observed, that for functional structured pupils the concept of functional dependency in processes is a fundamental one, which is deeper established than by verbal explanation. There is an interesting episode discussing the question, whether the step counter function for the addition program $({}_2S_2A_1)$ is a two digit or a single digit function:

$$CS_{Add}(x_1, x_2) = 2x_2 \qquad \text{or} \qquad CS_{Add}(x_2) = 2x_2$$

The explanation of a functional boy: "It is single digit, because all those (variables) are put in (the brackets), you can handle". The boy was obviously refering to the fact, that during executing that program with a register box only the sticks from compartment 2 are moved, therefore the process only depends on them. The idea of functional dependency is then turned back to the functions, which are computed. Pupils detect, that "real" dependency of functions is combined with the use of loops in RM-programs: the concept of loop represents the concept of functional dependency.

At the end of the first turn we give a feeling which problems occur while debugging algorithms (in the form of computing networks and RM-programs). Here again the two different cognitive structures induce different performance in handling the two microworlds.

4.3 Subprograms

Up to now the RM-programs are not too complex, because they only have single loops. The program for multiplication increases the complexity in a substantial way: the process cannot be understood by predicative structured pupils, because they cannot imagine two loops, one inside the other. They need support by reducing one *process* (here addition) to an *object*, which can be handled like an atomic operation and is accessable just by its name and the knowledge about its input-output behaviour. (Of course also functional structured people like the comfort of abstracting a process to a modul).
We introduce the idea of subprograms by using the idea to invent (and handle) abbreviations for parts in a RM-program. For such abbreviations the idea of interface has to be developed.
The introduction of the tool "subprogram" is done in a way, that it is a model for extending a programming language. First, on a naive basis, the syntax has to be extended by allowing, that correct abbreviations may be used like elementary operations. Second the RM must "know", how such an abbreviation is made explicit. This new tool immediately draws new demands: the RM should "learn" to understand abbreviations, which are described in an abstract way: instead of the names (numbers) of the registers it contains variables for the names. In all of our experimental classes this proposal was made by the pupils. This idea opens the next circle in extending the language. In the following we present the extended RM-language here, although the precise analysis is for the pupils done in a later part of the curriculum (see section Syntax and Semantics).

RM Language

1. Correct *RM-Programs*

1.1 a) A_i, S_i $(1 \le i \le 9)$ are correct programs.
 b) Correct abbreviations (for subprograms) are correct programs.

1.2 a) If P and Q are correct programs, then so is the *linking* PQ.
 b) If P is a correct program, then so is its *iteration* $({}_i\,P)$ for $(1 \le i \le 9)$.

2. Correct *abbreviations* consist successively of:

2.1 one character as a name

2.2 one footnote at the name, which may be a numeral from 1 to 9 or a character

2.3 a) the sign "<"

b) numerals or characters for registers, separated by a comma

c) the sign ">"

3. A *complete definition* (of a subprogram) consists successively of

3.1 one correct abbreviation

3.2 the sign "="

3.3 a correct program

4. A (syntactically) *complete RM-Program* consists successively of

- one correct program, in which only numerals (as names for registers) occur;
- a sequence of complete definitions under the condition, that all occuring correct abbreviations are completely defined in this RM-program.

The definition of the concept "complete RM-program", is recursive for the following reasons:

- The definition of "complete RM-program" contains the concepts "correct RM-program" and "complete definition".
- The definition of "complete definition" contains the concept "correct RM-program".
- The definition of "correct RM-program" contains the concept "correct abbreviation".

The reason for allowing only a single character as name for a subprogram is, that otherwise we would not have enough space to display totaly the execution of a complex RM-program on the screen (see section 3.3).

In section 4.4 you will find two examples for complete RM-programs. There you also see, how the idea of structured programming is linked with the mathematical idea of defining. We leave for a moment the developing of our lesson course and explain how the interpreter works on RM-programs.

Interpreter

As mentioned before we have developed a software-system, which enables us to use the RM-language on a microcomputer. The kernel is an interpreter for the language. The display on the screen shows how the RM-program (in the upper part) is working on the data (in the lower part). A cursor is moving from character to character (elementary operations or abbreviations). The speed can be varied. The running of the program can be interrupted at any time.

Let us now describe, how the interpreter handles the global and local variables. The register-numbers 1-9 are (the only) global variables. If a complete definition is called, which contents characters instead of register-numbers, then the interpreter first substitutes those characters which occur in the abbreviation of the subprogram as it is declared on the level above. If there occur characters (as variables for register-numbers) on the right side of a (complete) definition of a subprogram, which don't occur in the abbreviation on the left side, then the interpreter substitutes them by register-numbers following the rule: choose that register with smallest number which does not occur in this definition (line) and is empty in the moment of substitution. By this substitution the variable (in the mathematical sense) for a register-number has been replaced by a register-number and that plays the role of a global variable. One example is the definition of $F_r<i,j>$ in the example of section 4.4. Here the character/variable k has to be substituted by the interpreter appropriately after the definition is called during execution of the program. This handling of the variables makes it much easier to understand, what has to be done if a definition of a subprogram/procedure is used in a concrete situation, than it is the concept of variables in the language PASCAL.

4.4 Computability and Definability

Climbing up the two ladders RM and functions we now have reached a platform, from which we can reflect the two aspects which constitute the idea of a computable function. Let us do this from a cognitive point of view, using the theory of Schwank ([20]).

Let us take the two functions f: $(x_1,x_2) \rightarrow (0,0,2(x_1+x_2))$ and g: $(x_1,x_2) \rightarrow (0,0,2x_1+2x_2)$. The process orientated view, according to a *functional* cognitive structure, looks at the problem in terms of *organizing* the computational process. If one uses the technique of structured programming the complete programs F or G for computing f or g are given in the following way into the RM:

$F_3<1,2>.$

$F_r<i,j> = A_k<i,j>\ D_r<k>.$

$A_k<i,j> = ({}_iS_iA_k)\ ({}_jS_jA_k).$

$D_j<i> = ({}_iS_iA_jA_j).$

$G_3<1,2>.$

$G_r<i,j> = D_r<i>\ D_r<j>.$

$D_j<i> = ({}_iS_iA_jA_j).$

The stepfunctions for the programs are:

$CS_F(x_1,x_2) = 2x_1 + 2x_2 + 3(x_1 + x_2)$

$CS_G(x_1,x_2) = 3x_1 + 3x_2$

From a *predicative* point of view it could be more natural, first to analyze the way, how f and g are *defined*. The result is

$f(x_1,x_2) = d(a(x_1,x_2))$

$a(x_1,x_2) = x_1 + x_2$

$d(x_3) = 2x_3$

$g(x_1,x_2) = a(d(x_1),d(x_2))$

$a(x_1,x_2) = x_1 + x_2$

$d(x_3) = 2x_3$

Using this analysis the programming for the RM is indeed reduced to a *writing* of the program, following the insight "a composition of functions is computed by computing the suitable subprograms one after the other". Although the program for f is the same as before, the mental model is different: the intellectual work is done in a predicative structure: what is the structure of the given term, what is the meaning (definition) of the terms used in it? The "writing" of a program for g leads only to the following definition of G

$G_r<i,j> = D_k<i>\ D_l<j>\ A_r<k,l>.$

It is typical for a predicative approach, that the computational time measured by the stepfunction for that program is higher: $3x_1+3x_2+2(x_1+x_2)$. The efficient organizing is not a fundamental technique in a predicative cognitive structure as it is in a functional one.

Structured programming may be interpreted as making precise the intuitive knowledge about a given function for a functional structured pupil, while making explicit the definitions is the prefered technique for the predicative structered pupils. During the lessons we discuss the different cognitive points of view. It leads pupils to the insight, that giving a formal definition or writing a program are two sides of a medal and that turning the medal often may help for solving the problem.

4.5 Syntax and Semantics

During the lesson course the pupils have up to now learned the RM-language similar to a natural language. Especially functional structured pupils had the possibility first to organize the sequence of computing actions with structured material and then translate the result into a programming language. In a next step simultanously the mathematical language used for definitions and the programming language have been trained. The last part of our lesson course consists of a reflection about the role, which syntax and semantics play in understanding a text. For opening the pupils' view we start with several (german) sentences, in which grammatical mistakes and ambiguities hinder a context independent understanding of the meaning. With a series of examples we make the pupils aware, that in general the semantic of a language cannot be developed independent from the syntax and therefore grammatical mistakes are in general dangerous for detecting the meaning (and not only are reasons for bad marks by the teacher). In every experimental class pupils were astonished, that this interdisciplinary reflection about language is done during mathematics lessons.

After such a preparation it was natural to reflect on syntax and semantics of the RM-language, which was in the meantime successfully used by the pupils. We did it from a functional point of view: Which consequences have to be considered after the decision, that a RM should "understand" abbreviations (for subprograms)? What is the benefit of the decision, that (local) variables, which occur in a "right side" of an abbreviation must not occur on the "left side"? What are the consequences for the syntax, if the RM-interpreter should be available in a foreign language (for example in hungarian or indonesian, where A and S are not the first characters of the words for addition and subtraction)?

After that preparation we did the last step to show, that a formal language is not necessarily attached to a common sense understanding of language. We changed the syntax of the RM language using the following idea: a RM-program is a series of numbers, were the character A_i is replaced by the number 2i and S_i is replaced by 2i-1.
On the opposite we changed for the "old" RM-language the semantic in a way, that the elementary operations are interpreted as geometrical operations with geometrical figures on a sheet of paper.

The last step in this chapter was the link to the traditional mathematical language of terms, where all the dangerous brackets and computational signs are a cause for a distance to and failure in mathematics.

5. Evaluation and Summary

The lesson course "Introduction into the World of Computers with Registermachines" [6] is the introductory part in a new approach for combining algorithmic and axiomatic reasoning as two fundaments of mathematics in secondary schools.

In 1987 the first four lessons in constructing and analyzing algorithms were done as research project concerning the individual preferences for cognitive structures and strategies of the pupils. Instead of lessons in the classroom each pupil had four hours an individual interview situation. That research has been conducted by Inge Schwank. It is part of her research to evaluate her theory of predicative versus functional cognitive structures ([20], and her paper in this book).

The curriculum project started in 1987 with two classes grade 7 in a gymnasium. In the following year the project was continued for these pupils, while they were in grade 8, and for another two classes grade 7 the curriculum experiment was repeated.
The unforeseen success in increasing both the pupils competence in school algebra and their fun for mathematics lessons, lead to the decision of the ministry of education to extend the project: In 1989, 1990 and 1991 an each year revised version of the textbooks was taught each year in 16 classes grade 7 at 6 schools, continued in the following year in grade 8.

The competence of the pupils in handling the concept and notation of functions with several variables is used later in the curriculum project to teach linear functions and word problems ([7]). In grade 8 we start with constructing a mental model for understanding the axiomatic approach in mathematics ([8]). Using both, the algorithmic and axiomatic point of view, we introduce negative and then rational numbers and afterwards the solution of linear equations and inequations ([9]). It is important to mention, that the introductory part about RM, as it is reported here, is taught in addition to the normal curriculum. The time of about 3 months, which is needed for it, can be saved until the end of grade 8, because the competence of the pupils in handling and understanding the mathematical formalism, used in school algebra, has so much increased, that these classical parts of the curriculum become easy from the pupils' point of view. We see it in parallel with the results of Sutherland [21].

The important decision for our project was to lay preference on constructing mental models in the pupils' mind versus teaching mathematical facts and training skills. The research of Schwank on individual differences in the prefered cognitive structures enabled us to reach especially the functional structured pupils, which normally don't like the formal aspect of mathematics. We were able to demonstrate, how an introduction into the world of computers - understood as the mathematical aspect of computer literacy - can be combined with the introduction of the concept of function without changing the existing official curriculum, because we have fulfilled it. We have established the RM-language as a mental model for understanding an imperative programming language. The benefit of mental models, both about the programming ([6]) and the axiomatization ([8]), is now obvious in a small project continuing our ideas for grade 9, here we give an insight in programming with PROLOG.

6. References

1. Börger, E.: Berechenbarkeit, Komplexität, Logik. Braunschweig: Vieweg 1985
2. Bruner, J.: Beyond the Information Given. London: Allen & Unwin 1974
3. Cohors-Fresenborg, E.: Mathematik mit Kalkülen und Maschinen. Braunschweig: Vieweg 1977
4. Cohors-Fresenborg, E.: On the Representation of Algorithmic Concepts. In F. Lowenthal et al. (Eds.), Pragmatics and Education. New York: Plenum Press 1986
5. Cohors-Fresenborg, E.: Schulversuch "Algorithmisches Denken im Mathematikunterricht mit Hörgeschädigten". Beiträge zum Mathematikunterricht, pp. 102-105. Bad Salzdetfurth: Franzbecker 1988
6. Cohors-Fresenborg, E. & Kaune, C. & Griep, M.: Einführung in die Computerwelt mit Registermaschinen - Textbuch für Schüler, Handbuch für Lehrer. Osnabrück: Forschungsinstitut für Mathematikdidaktik [3]1991 (English translation available: Introduction into the World of Computers with Registermachines - Schoolbook for pupils, manual for teachers. Osnabrück: Forschungsinstitut für Mathematikdidaktik 1992)
7. Cohors-Fresenborg, E. & Kaune, C. & Griep, M.: Einführung in die mathematische Modellbildung mit Funktionen - Textbuch für Schüler, Handbuch für Lehrer. Osnabrück: Forschungsinstitut für Mathematikdidaktik [3]1992
8. Cohors-Fresenborg, E. & Griep, M. & Kaune, C.: Sätze aus dem Wüstensand und ihre Interpretationen - Textbuch für Schüler, Handbuch für Lehrer. Osnabrück: Forschungsinstitut für Mathematikdidaktik [4]1992
9. Cohors-Fresenborg, E. & Kaune, C. & Griep, M.: Vertragswerke für den Umgang mit Zahlen - Textbuch für Schüler, Handbuch für Lehrer. Osnabrück: Forschungsinstitut für Mathematikdidaktik 1990
10. Davis, R. B.: Learning Mathematics. Norwood, N.J.: Ablex Publishing 1984
11. Duchâteau, C.: From "DOING IT ..." to "HAVING IT DONE ...". In Preproceedings of NATO ARW "Cognitive Models and Intelligent Environments for Learning Programming", S. Margherita (Genova), Italy, (1992)
12. Goldin, G.: Cognitive representational systems for mathematical problem solving. In C. Janvier (Ed.), Problems of representation in the teaching and learning of mathematics, pp. 125-145. Hillsdale: Erlbaum 1987
13. Janvier, C.: Problems of representation in the teaching and learning of mathematics. Hillsdale: Erlbaum 1987
14. Johnson-Laird, P. N.: Mental Models. London: Cambridge University Press 1983
15. Kaput, J.: Representation of Systems and Mathematics. In J. C. Bergeron & N. Herscovics (Eds.), Proceedings of the Fifth Annual Meeting of PME-NA, Vol.2. Montreal: Concordia Uni. Dept. of Mathematics 1983
16. Kaune, C.: Schüler denken am Computer. Osnabrück: Forschungsinstitut für Mathematikdidaktik 1985
17. Kaune, C.: Fähigkeiten von Schülern beim Konstruieren und Analysieren von Algorithmen. *Journal für Mathematikdidaktik*, 8, 163-190 (1987)
18. Rödding, D.: Klassen rekursiver Funktionen. Lecture Notes in Mathematics, Vol. 70, pp. 159-222. Berlin: Springer 1968
19. Schwank, I.: Cognitive Structures of Algorithmic Thinking. In Proceedings of the 10th International Conference for the Psychology of Mathematics Education, pp. 195-200. London: University of London, Institute of Education 1986
20. Schwank, I.: On the Analysis of Cognitive Structures in Algorithmic Thinking. To appear *Journal of Mathematical Behaviour*
21. Sutherland, R.: Thinking Algebraically: Pupil Models Developed in Logo and a Spreadsheet Environment. In E. Lemut, B. du Boulay, G. Dettori (Eds.), Cognitive Models and Intelligent Learning Environments for Learning Programming. Berlin: Springer, NATO ASI Series F (this volume)
22. von Glasersfeld, E.: Representation and Deduction. In: Proceedings of the Ninth International Conference for the Psychology of Mathematics Education, pp. 484-489. Utrecht 1985
23. Wittgenstein, L.: Philosophical Investigations. Oxford: Blackwell 1953

Cognitive Structures and Cognitive Strategies in Algorithmic Thinking

Inge Schwank

Forschungsinstitut für Mathematikdidaktik e. V., Postfach 18 47, D-4500 Osnabrück, Germany

Abstract: Investigating the behaviour of (12-14 years old) students constructing and analyzing algorithms has shown that great individual differences in their methods of mental analysis of such mathematical problems do exist. We distinguish between predicative and functional cognitive structures. Predicative thinking emphasizes the preference for thinking in terms of relations and judgments; functional thinking emphasizes the preference for thinking in terms of courses and modes of action. There is a resonance effect between external representation and cognitive structure. The preference for predicative versus functional thinking seems to be gender related.

Keywords: Cognitive science / mental models / cognitive structures / cognitive strategies / representation / algorithmic thinking / individual differences / gender related differences.

1. Introduction

Concerning cognitive models for learning programming different approaches have been studied during the years. Most of them deal with the question, which is the best method to programm, e. g. top down versus bottom up. First this was discussed in a more normative way in the perspective to teach to program. Later it had been investigated, whether successful programmers do follow these guidelines. Recently the question has been asked, whether there are differences in the programming and planning behaviour between novices and experts. The question, whether differences in the planning and programming behaviour may be also explained by assuming differences in the individual preference for a cognitive style or a problem solving strategy is not addressed. We will make a contribution to it in our paper.

In cognitive science different theories concerning the construction of mental models and the representation of knowledge in memory have been established. The development of the theories has been driven by introducing different classes of problems or analyzing specific aspects. It is not widely discussed, whether there exist individual differences in the cognitive structure which may not be explained in terms of intellectual standard or the distinction experts versus novices, but could be explained by the existence of stable individual preferences for selecting a specific kind of mental model for representing knowledge about the external world.

In our paper we would like to present first such a theory concerning different cognitive structures and combine this with the assumption of individual differences for cognitive strategies. The research has been carried out during the last 10 years concerning first the question, how students in the early secondary level construct and analyse algorithms and which role different forms of external representations play in the process of concept formation. The concepts for which we do investigate the learning processes of pupils in terms of cognitive models build the basis for all programming languages (e. g. concatenation, iteration). Our findings have been the basis for a curriculum experiment ([5], in this book), in which pupils of grade 7 are introduced to the world of computers.

2. Predicative versus Functional Cognitive Structures

We distinguish between a predicative structure, which is more concentrated on networks of relations and structures, and a functional structure, which lays preference on thinking in terms of effects and organizing sequences of actions [21, 24]. For a predicative thinker logical judgments are important, for a functional one the dimension of cause is important. Figure 1 gives a survey about the polarization in predicative versus functional thinking concerning programming tasks.

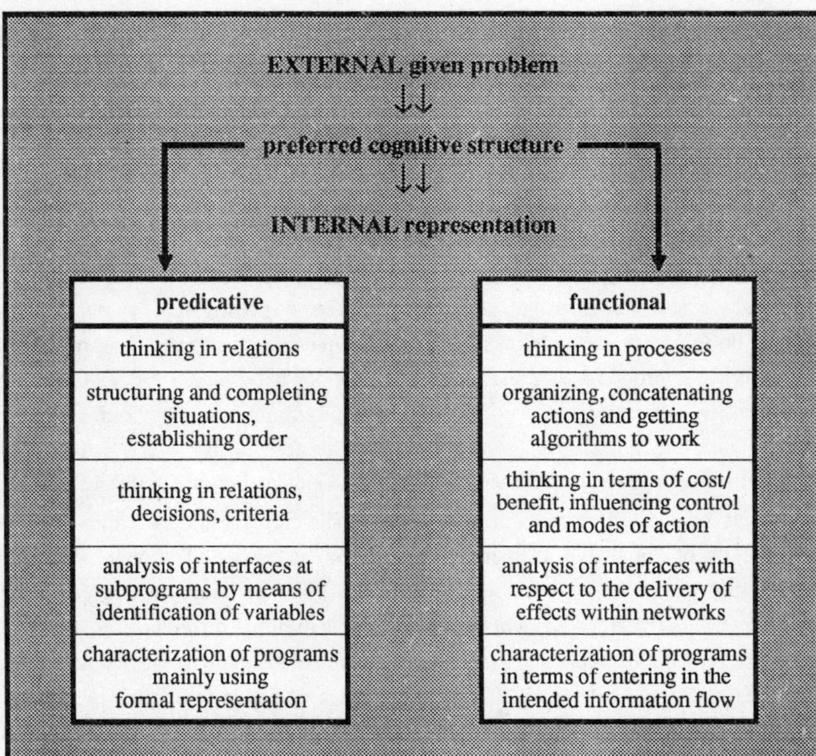

Figure 1: Survey of Predicative versus Functional Cognitive Structure

Our position is described best in analogy to the situation in the foundations of mathematics. There one has to choose while constructing a formal language, whether expressions for predicates and for actions (functions) are primitive elements, or whether one chooses one of these as undefined concepts and the other one as defined by nominal definitions. From a cognitive science point of view the differences in cognitive structures (predicative versus functional) are as follows: in a predicative cognitive structure the relations (predicates) are the fundamental primitive elements, from which the structure is built. If in such a structure something has to be expressed about actions, the idea of action is described by the relation between the states before and after executing the action. In a functional cognitive structure it is in the opposite way: the possibility to express something about processes is immediately given, statements about relations are constructed as derived statements about the process, which produces the relation. The predicative form of the formation knows intra/inner conceptual relations, deductions and general terms, abstraction as a tool for the formation of concepts, and logical operations. The functional-typical concept form examines the application of functions, the concatenations, (analogous) generalization of the application of tools, and the inversion of processes corresponding to a theoretical and experimental manner of thinking. The concepts predicative/functional can be related to single formations or single mental models. However, they also can be a basic characteristic feature of a person's way of constructing mental models. In such a case we speak of a predominant preference for a cognitive structure: predicative or functional.

It should be briefly noted that in stressing a mathematical perspective based on the concept of "function", one is not in general committed to a mathematical representation of what we have called "functional thinking". For example, this can be seen in a general definition of the concept of "function" resulting from special relations. In our terminology, this point of view could be described as a predicative simulation of the concept of "function". Another example is the use of production systems in cognitive science (e.g. [17, 19]). Mainly there is only formalized a relation between conditions and result and there is no formalisation of a process, in which the result is *produced.* Presenting our theory to a predicative thinking colleague we often have difficulties to introduce an independent functional point of view, because he may immediately see in the presented example concerning functions the predicative understood input/output relation.

Example

We want to illustrate with the help of the following example, that the differences in the cognitive structure are not mainly produced by the "matter" but by the differences of the individual conceptions which are produced by the "matter".

Within the scope of the lesson unit "Introduction into the World of Computers with Register Machines" [7, 5] in grade 7 students (12-13 years old) of a German Gymnasium had to work on the following problem:

> *What will be computed by the program (1 S1 A2 A2 A2) A2 ? In the beginning, only register 1 (R_1) is occupied.*

A: A boy wrote: "This program always counts one stick more than the triple of the content of counter R_1*."*

B: A girl wrote: "As long as something is in R_1*, take it off and multiply it by three. Then, at the end add one."*

Obviously, both students have different viewpoints of the role of an algorithm. For one student the algorithm leads to a *result* which is related to the input. For the other, the result is *derived* from the input. Based on our research work we believe that through an application of our research design the girl will be classified as being functional and the boy as being predicative. This example also shows that in the algorithmical world usually described as dynamic the differentiation between predicative and functional makes sense.

Relations to Other Cognitive Theories

In the following section, we would briefly like to try to connect our own theory with models of cognitive structure in psychology.

As a result of substantial research, Klix [15] puts forward his theory of the representation of knowledge in the human memory. From our point of view (details see [24]) this is a detailed analysis of a predicative thinking structure. It should be noted that a functional dimension is never mentioned. First of all, this statement refers to the fact that his experiments were planned in a way that relations which were predicatively understood were given by an external representation. Because of the resonance thesis which we introduced [24] it is not surprising that at first sight this external representation also corresponds to an internal predicative cognitive structure. In this respect the absence of functional structure, as we have noted, would be explained in the theory by exploring only this side of the experiments. On the contrary, we are convinced that only the availability of an effective external representation of the functional thinking - here presented in the form of the Dynamic Mazes [see 5 in this book] - allows *us* to make an experimental investigation of functional thinking.

It may be assumed that the difference between declarative and procedural knowledge as formed by Anderson ([1], see figure 2) corresponds to our distinction between predicative and functional thinking. But a precise analysis shows the following difference: predicative/functional is a property of the structure of the kind of knowledge representation and describes not different kinds of knowledge. Following Anderson's terminology we might have knowledge about effects (and not only about relations) in the declarative memory and knowledge about logical connections (and not only about calculating operations) in the production memory, as figure 3 shows. Here we have choosen as mathematical example a predicative versus a functional way of defining the function "division".

It should be noted that Johnson-Laird [12] also neglects to include an independent functional component in his theory of mental models.

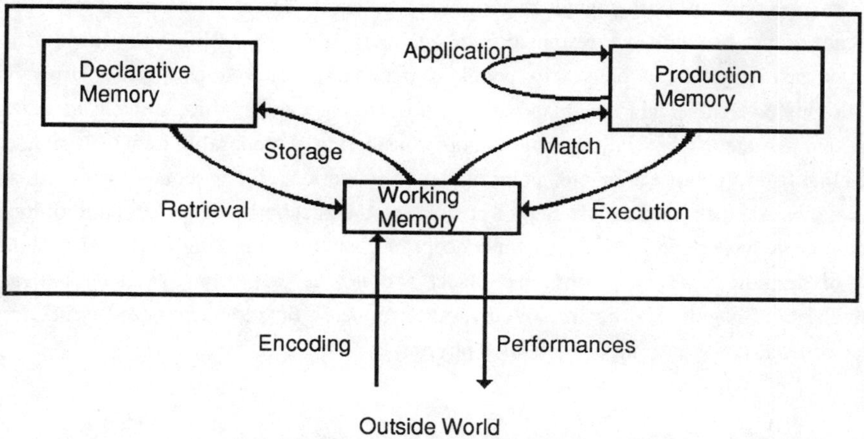

Figure 2: Anderson ([1], p. 19): Declarative Memory and Production Memory in ACT

	Predicative	**Functional**
Production Memory	**Connection of Predicates** Organisation of structures Construction of relations Logical argumentation	**Composition of Functions** Organisation of processes Control of processes
	$\frac{x}{y}$ is the number z such that $z \cdot y = x$	$d(x,y) = 0$ if $x = 0$ $d(x,y) = d(x-y,y) + 1$ else
	Procedures: Denotion	Procedures: Substitution, Control
Declarative Memory	**Predicates** Complex judgments Properties	**Functions** Processes Effects
	Predicate: Graph of the multiplication function	Function: Composition (f, g)
Encoding	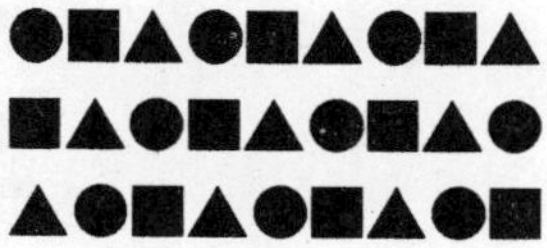	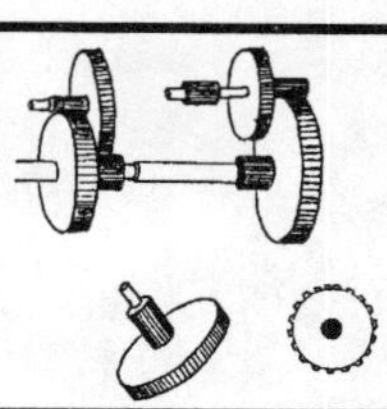
	(pattern)	(gear)
Outside World	⇑⇑⇑⇑⇑⇑⇑⇑⇑⇑⇑⇑⇑⇑⇑⇑	⇑⇑⇑⇑⇑⇑⇑⇑⇑⇑⇑⇑⇑⇑⇑⇑

Figure 3: Survey of Predicative and Functional Cognitive Strutures embedded in Andersons Model

The necessity of further analyzing thinking processes arises in a special way in the didactics of physics with the examination of qualitative thinking. Within the scope of their work on naive physics (i.e. physics for people who are not physicists), De Kleer & Brown [10] and Forbus & Gentner [11] have shown that a cognitive theory is not suitable to describe important aspects of physical thinking without considering procedural thinking. It should be noted that from a content orientated point of view they work out the particularity of qualitative thinking, but they do not take the step of postulating the peculiarity of the structure of mental models as we have done it with our own concept of "functional thinking". They describe this kind of thinking proceeding from the object and not as proceeding from an individual particularity of cognitive structures. We hypothesize, that a functional cognitive structure fits better with causual reasoning in qualitative physics.

3. Conceptual versus Sequential Cognitive Strategies

In the domain of cognitive stragies we distinguish between a conceptual and a sequential one:

<table>
<tr><th colspan="2">Analysis of the Students Behavior</th></tr>
<tr><td colspan="2">Problem
↓↓
Preferred Cognitive Strategy
↓↓
Solution</td></tr>
<tr><th>Conceptual</th><th>Sequential</th></tr>
<tr><td>Students begin with an analysis of the problem, structure it and try to construct a conceptual framework, which includes preknowledge.</td><td>Students begin with a first solution, before they have structured their ideas completely and in detail; they develop their ideas in a dialog with the material; they find the final solution by analyzing and modifying of partial solutions.</td></tr>
<tr><td>Problem
↓
Analysis
↓
Structuring
↓
Conceptual Frame
↓
Solution</td><td>Problem
↓
Partial Solution ←
↓
Analysis
↓
Modifying —
↓
Solution</td></tr>
</table>

Figure 4: Survey of Conceptual versus Sequential Cognitive Strategies

In the domain of cognitive stragies we distinguish between a conceptual and a sequential one. This terminology has been introduced by Cohors-Fresenborg & Kaune [6, 13] to describe individual differences of students, when they are constructing or analyzing algorithms. But a deeper analysis of the description had shown, that it consists of elements, which belong to the domain of cognitive structures, and those, which belong to the domain of cognitive strategies. In our paper [21] we postulated the independence of the two domains and proposed to reserve the terminology conceptual/sequential to that of cognitive strategies only. As figure 4 shows, the conceptual strategy includes a top-down problem solving behaviour. But the sequential strategy is neither bottom-up nor trial and error. It is goal orientated but interactive with the sequence of experience during the goal-directed activities. There is an analogy to the "visual moderated sequences" in the list of mental mechanisms introduced by Davis & McKnight [9], but the experience is not necessarily visual. Our hypothesis is, that for cognitive strategies there exist quite stable individual preferences, too.

4. Experimental Testing

Our research is part of a long tradition of studies concerned with examining mathematical thinking processes of students when they try to construct and analyze algorithms and while doing that, learn to program [3, 13-14, 16]. A common element in all these studies is the observation of students (ca. 12-14 years old) of grade 7 in the form of constructivist teaching experiments [2, 25] in which they try to solve programming problems. These studies have to be seen as a series or sequence of case studies involving more than a hundred students.

Problems

With respect to the problems concerning the mathematical structure [24], the mathematical content of our problems can be described as follows. We refer to the mathematical idea of a computer which at first has four boxes or stores for storing natural numbers. The computer can execute the elementary operations of counting forward and backward in each store. More complex instructions are built from simple ones by using the constructive processes of "concatenation" and "iteration". From the mathematical point of view, this is called a Register Machine [20]. The students have to construct or analyze algorithms for such a Register Machine. We have benefited from experiences which were obtained during the last thirteen years by the study group working around Elmar Cohors-Fresenborg at the University of Osnabrück. These helped us to select, arrange and present the set of problems.

The problems can be divided into three different forms of external representation ([3], see [5] in this book):

- manipulating sticks in the so-called Register Box,
- computing networks built with the didactical material Dynamic Mazes,
- programming for a Register Machine.

The fundamental translatability between predicative and functional worlds is related to the construction of experiments [24]. The students develop different mental models because of the forms of representation we used despite the fact that these representations are equivalent from the mathematical point of view. This can best be explained by the example of the computing networks built with Dynamic Mazes. While working with this material, a functional student makes frequent use of visualizing in detail the process of the functioning of the algorithm. By contrast, a predicative thinking student only uses the illustrative qualities of the computing networks and his knowledge that certain parts supply desired results under certain conditions. In other words, both types of thinking see and use different aspects of the same external situation. On the other hand there is a resonance effect between the external representation and the cognitive structure [24]: the "underlying philosophy" of an external representation asks for a specific kind of cognitive structure. If this structure is the individually preferred one, then it fits best. Following this hypothesis it seems not very useful to us to base an analysis for constructing tasks on constructing the problem space as an objective matter, as has been the tradition since Newell and Simon ([17], see also [19]).

Evaluation

As a first result of the applicability of our theory [21], we consider the fact that Marpaung [8, 16] was able to demonstrate that the two pairs of concepts predicative/functional and conceptual/sequential are of independent dimensions: The tested student Barus, a boy, shows a way of acting which can only be described with the combination "conceptual/functional", and the student Sriat, a girl, a behaviour which has to be described as a combination of "sequential/predicative" ([16], pp.81-99). For the first time it could be observed that individual preferences for a cognitive structure are more dominant than the structure given in the problem representation itself. We report here briefly the behaviour of these two students, because it may support our call for increasing the study of individual differences in constructing mental models of programming:

Here, it was a matter of two so-called debugging problems. One problem contained a mistake in an algorithm which was given as a constructed computing network. The mistake had to be found and corrected. In the second problem the algorithm was given in form of a program for the Register Machine. The (functional) student Barus was able to solve the debugging-problem given in the form of a computing network without any difficulties, but he had trouble in dealing with programs for the Register Machine. However, he could solve the problem after he had offered to first translate the program for the Register Machine into a computing network and then to search this for the mistake. The (predicative) student Listi was just the opposite: He found the mistake in the program at first sight but the computing networks were not his world. He solved the problem in the world of programs and then he was able to "translate" the correct program for the Register Machine into a correct computing network.

Our own studies [22, 23] dealt with grade 7 students (10 girls from the 12-13 years old age group of a Realschule). After making some revisions in our research design, we also studied students (boys and girls) from a Gymnasium. Each experiment consisted of three one hour sessions in which a test leader communicates with a single student while he is solving problems dealing with constructing, analyzing, and debugging algorithms in the three different forms of representation. All students received the same problems in the same sequence. For evaluation we proceeded from a list of categories in which the mathematical concepts represented in the given problems are enumerated. This one had to be used as a system of categories. So a model for each student is produced which can be regarded as a first formal representation of the process of his analysis with the algorithmical problems.The pilot study [22] pointed out that properly speaking only one of these 10 girls can be classified as being functional. We do not suppose that the different attitudes towards algorithms and computers can be explained only in terms of sociology. We believe that boys and girls do in fact differ in their preferred cognitive structures and the cognitive strategies they use. We set up the hypothesis that girls tend to more frequently have a predicative cognitive structure and use a conceptual strategy for solving problems than boys ([22], p. 80; [23]).

Curriculum Experiment as an Application

In addition to the discussed applications of our theory for explaining the different students' behaviour while constructing and analyzing algorithms, we would briefly like to explain how our ideas have influenced the curriculum experiment "Integration of Algorithmic and Axiomatic Ways of Thinking in Math-lessons of grades 7/8 as a Contribution to Computer Literacy and Communicative-Technological Education" of the Lower Saxon Ministry of Education [4, 5]. In the conception of his textbook [7] Cohors-Fresenborg tried to address the more predicative as well as the more functional students in consideration of our stated resonance thesis at the introduction of algorithmic thinking. But it turned out that the systematical consideration of functional thinking (except for the subject Dynamic Mazes) cannot easily be realized because of the experienced preference of the predicative view of math teachers during their studies at universities.

5. Summary and Prospects

In our paper, we have tried to present our theory about the existence of different cognitive structures, the resonance effect between external forms of representations and internal mental models of algorithmic ideas, and individual differences in cognitive strategies. Although our present research deals mainly with algorithmical concepts, it does have some general implications. Our general descriptions and our recourse to the situation in the foundations of mathematics should indicate our convinction that we have described (with the destinction between a predicative versus a functional cognitive structure) a relatively universal phenomenon, which is not only concerned with constructing and analyzing algorithms. We assume, that the cognitive structures are quite stable during the development of students and that they exist in different cultures.

For this hypothesis we have some support. The investigations of Marpaung [16, 8] have shown, that our theory is viable to explain the mathematical behaviour of Indonesian pupils, when they are dealing with the same algorithmic problems. For two years we have been conducting a pilot study with similar design in Shanghai, which has the same results. In this study we tried for the first time an experiment in naive physics. The results support our remarks about the usefulness of functional reasoning in physics. This branch of studies looks quite promising.

To support our ideas concerning the viability of our theory we would first mention our analysis [24] of the writing style of the poets Goethe and Fontane, in which we did find hints for the preference for a functional versus predicative cognitive structure. This idea, analyzing the reports of people concerning a room, we have tested for example in the above mentioned pilot study with chinese students with promising results: a predicative thinker describes a kitchen as it looks, a functional one more in a way, in which one understands the location of the furniture with respect to its usefulness.

Let us come back to the usefulness of the distinction between predicative versus functional cognitive structure for explaining different behaviours in programming. Let us consider the idea of recursion. The well known difficulties in learning recursive programming (see f.e. [19]) may be reconsidered from our point of view. We offer the hypothesis, that predicative and functional aspects have to be combined: on the surface the description is done in a predicative framework, but the execution is better understood in a functional one. It would be an interesting teaching experiment to construct in a functional thinking student a mental model of recursive organizing not by examples and abstraction [19], which is not a suitable cognitive tool for such a person, but by analogous generalisations of locally working processes.

The analysis of thinking processes which proceed while programming in different programming languages could also be an interesting application of our theories. This could not only help to explain the observed individual preferences (and corresponding aversions) for single programming languages (e. g. PASCAL versus LOGO). The example of the language PROLOG shows that concerning more complex programs a predicative form of representation leads to good results only if the programmer also has good functional conception of the process of the PROLOG program. The efficiency of PROLOG is based on a directed application of the functional effect of the predicative explicitely stated rules.

The general outcome of our studies is, that when analyzing cognitive models of learning programming, individual differences should play an important role. Before giving general outlines for teaching it should be more deeply analyzed, which effect in the individual student different strategies of planning have for constructing mental models of programming.

The results of the pilot study with girls constructing and analyzing algorithms with our design lead us to reconsider from a cognitive science point of view the explanations, which in literature are offered for the different behaviour of boys and girls ([22], pp. 81-98; [23]). We regard this as an interesting starting point for a cognitive anthropology, which investigates the central role which mental models play for understanding not only gender related differences but also cultural variances and invariances concerning thinking in mathematics, science and engineering.

6. References

1. Anderson, J.R.: The Architecture of Cognition. Cambridge: Harvard University Press 1983
2. Cobb, P. & Steffe, L.: The Constructivist Researcher as Teacher and Model Builder. *Journal for research in Mathematics Education*, 14, No. 2, 83-94 (1983)
3. Cohors-Fresenborg, E.: On the Representation of Algorithmic Concepts. In F. Lowenthal et al. (Eds.), Pragmatics and Education. New York: Plenum Press 1986
4. Cohors-Fresenborg, E.: Zur Integration algorithmischer und axiomatischer Denkweisen in den Mathematikunterricht der Klasse 7 des Gymnasiums. Beiträge zum Mathematikunterricht, pp. 130-133. Bad Salzdetfurth: Franzbecker 1987
5. Cohors-Fresenborg, E.: Registermachine as a Mental Model for Understanding Computer Programming. In E. Lemut, B. du Boulay, G. Dettori (Eds.), Cognitive Models and Intelligent Environments for Learning Programming. Berlin: Springer NATO ASI Series F (this volume)
6. Cohors-Fresenborg, E. & Kaune, C.: Sequential versus Conceptual - Two Modes in Algorithmic Thinking. In Proceedings of the 8th International Conference for the Psychology of Mathematics Education, pp. 261-267. Sydney 1984
7. Cohors-Fresenborg, E. & Kaune, C. & Griep, M.: Einführung in die Computerwelt mit Registermaschinen - Textbuch für Schüler. Osnabrück: Forschungsinstitut für Mathematikdidaktik 1988 (English translation available: Introduction into the World of Computers with Registermachines. Osnabrück 1993)
8. Cohors-Fresenborg, E. & Marpaung,Y.: Intercultural Studies between Indonesian and German Children on Algorithmic Thinking. In Proceedings of the 10th International Conference for the Psychology of Mathematics Education, pp. 404-409. London: University of London, Institute of Education 1986
9. Davis, R. B. & McKnight, C. C.: Modelling the Processes of Mathematical Thinking. *Journal of Children's Mathematical Behaviour*, 2, 91-113 (1979)
10. De Kleer, J. & Brown, J.S.: Assumptions and Ambiguities in Mechanistic Mental Models. In D. Gentner & A. L. Stevens (Eds.), Mental Models. Hillsdale: Lawrence Erlbaum 1983
11. Forbus, K. D. & Gentner, D.: Learning Physical Domains: Toward a Theoretical Framework. In R. S. Michalski et al. (Eds.), Machine Learning. Los Altos: Morgan Kaufmann 1986
12. Johnson-Laird, P. N.: Mental Models. London: Cambridge University Press 1983
13. Kaune, C.: Schüler denken am Computer. Osnabrück: Forschungsinstitut für Mathematikdidaktik 1985
14. Kaune, C.: Fähigkeiten von Schülern beim Konstruieren und Analysieren von Algorithmen. *Journal für Mathematikdidaktik*, 8, 163-190 (1987)
15. Klix, F.: Über Wissensrepräsentation im menschlichen Gedächtnis. In F. Klix (Ed.), Gedächtnis, Wissen, Wissensnutzung, pp. 9-73. Berlin: Deutscher Verlag der Wissenschaften 1984
16. Marpaung, Y.: Profile indonesischer Schüler beim Umgang mit Algorithmen und ihre Analyse. Osnabrück: Forschungsinstitut für Mathematikdidaktik 1986
17. Newell, A.: Production systems: Models of control structure. In E. G. Chase (Ed.), Visual information processing pp. 463-526. New York: Academic Press 1973
18. Newell, A. & Simon, H. A.: Human Problem Solving. Englewood Cliffs: Prentice Hall 1972
19. Pirolli, P. & Anderson, J. R.: The Role of Learning from Examples in the Acquisition of Recursive Programming Skills. *Canadian Journal of Psychology*, 39, 240-272 (1985)
20. Rödding, D.: Klassen rekursiver Funktionen. Lecture Notes in Mathematics, Vol. 70, pp. 159-222. Berlin: Springer 1968
21. Schwank, I.: Cognitive Structures of Algorithmic Thinking. In Proceedings of the 10th International Conference for the Psychology of Mathematics Education, pp. 195-200. London: University of London, Institute of Education 1986
22. Schwank, I.: Zur algorithmischen Begriffsbildung von Mädchen, Research Report Vol. I (theory), II (design). Osnabrück: Forschungsinstitut für Mathematikdidaktik 1990/1989
23. Schwank, I.: Untersuchungen algorithmischer Denkprozesse von Mädchen. In A. Grabosch & A. Zwölfer (Hrsg.), Frauen und Mathematik. Tübingen: Attempto 1992
24. Schwank, I.: On the Analysis of Cognitive Structures in Algorithmic Thinking, To appear *Journal of Mathematical Behaviour*
25. von Glasersfeld, E.: Learning as a constructive activity. In J. C. Bergeron & N. Herscovics (Eds.), Proceedings of the Fifth Annual Meeting of PME-NA, Vol. 1, pp. 41-69. Montreal: Concordia Univ. Dept. of Mathematics 1983

Young Novices Using an Intuitive Mental Schema to Construct Generalised Geometrical Tools

C. Kynigos

Department of Informatics, Faculty of Science, University of Athens,
Panepistimiopolis, TYPA Buildings, GR-15771, Athens, Greece

Abstract: Case study research is presented, focusing on the cognitive process by which 11–12 year-old children concurrently learned programming and geometry, developing understanding of structured programming and intrinsic, euclidean and cartesian geometrical ideas. They worked in geometrical Logo microworld environments. Programming and geometrical ideas embedded in generalised computational tools constructed by the children are analysed and discussed. This kind of activity is set against the importance of nurturing flexible learners who will feel at ease with programming as a means of communicating and exploring ideas, while learning content domain traditionally associated with their education.

Keywords: children's programming, flexible learners, computational tools, novice programmers, Logo microworlds, learning geometry through programming

Introduction

This paper discusses programming activity as a means of expressing domain-specific ideas and addresses young learners who concurrently develop their grasp of programming and of the concepts involved in exploring and solving problems within a domain other than programming, in this case geometry[1] (see also Sutherland, this volume). Case study research is presented, focusing on the cognitive process by which pairs of 11–12 year-old children developed understandings of structured programming and intrinsic, euclidean and cartesian geometrical ideas. They worked in geometrical Logo microworld environments designed to "bring out" the use of concepts belonging to the above domains. Programming and geometrical ideas embedded in generalised computational tools constructed by the children are analysed and discussed.

Programming as a Means of Expressing Ideas

What kind of programming activity encourages what has been described as a process of "learning how to learn" [19, 22]? The processes of discriminating, generalising and

[1] This distinction is only momentarily made in order to specify this particular kind of programming activity which, elsewhere, has been characterised as inherently mathematical [14].

synthesising concepts across contexts in which they are used and of thinking in the abstract [7], are considered not only as valuable qualitative components of scientific and intellectual activity, but also as important tools for the individual in everyday life. However, a large volume of research has been consistently showing us that this kind of thinking seems beyond children in primary and secondary education at least [3]. We also know that schooling seldom provides children with the opportunity to engage in such activity. This could be partly attributed to the large amount of information which has to be transferred from teacher to children as a requirement of curricula and (in the pre-computational era) to the lack of educational tools suitable for the generation of classroom environments providing this opportunity [17].

So, in response to the above question, one such activity is the process of programming as a means of expressing, structuring and abstracting ideas. The design of each worthwhile programming language has, of course an underlying philosophy, tightly related to the application in which it will be used. The philosophy underlying languages like LISP [2, 21] and LOGO [18, 6, 1] supports activity such as the above, by which programming, by an experienced or a child programmer, goes together with an evolutionary process of the programmer's grasp of the problem at hand. However, for children to be able to express their ideas, it is very important that the primitives of a programming environment make common sense to them, i.e. are designed to enable them to employ knowledge closely based on their intuitions, from which to construct more complex understandings [13].

Research in the 1980s has shown this experience to be educationally valuable (albeit under much debated circumstances [15]) and generalisable to more than one content domains (e.g., mathematics [15, 18], physics [4], creative writing [20]). This kind of programming activity has been seen as an essentially mathematical activity [14]. The process of thinking mathematically, however, has been studied not only in conjunction with specific mathematical content, but also as a thinking process in itself, relevant to many needs of everyday [16] and professional life.

So, if a programming environment may play the role of a catalyst in the practice of the above processes, partly by means of luring the user into a vivid interplay between expressing an idea and immediately observing its precise consequence, then we may well make a case for the learning of programming for everyone in school life [19]. If programming environments are used as a means of expressing, combining, generalising and abstracting ideas from the context in which they are actually used, the "quantitative" properties of programming may encourage qualitative development in the way we learn and in the way we use the knowledge that we acquire from school or from everyday experiences [12].

Set against the above arguments, this paper describes case-study research of the process by which children may use intuitive knowledge based on early experiences of movement and space in order to construct generalised computational tools constructing geometrical figures and subsequently to use these tools as primitives for more complicated constructions. The research involved a detailed observation and a subsequent qualitative analysis of the process and content of children's understandings of programming and geometrical ideas. The children worked in pairs in microworld environments specially designed to provide more focus on the use of geometrical ideas than in conventional Logo[2], but at the same time, to retain Logo's properties of allowing the children to construct their own knowledge, respecting their personal needs and styles. An elaboration of one of the case studies provides the ground for a discussion on the understandings formed by a pair of 12-year-old children who built a Circle microworld and then used its primitives to solve structured tasks requiring a combination of programming and intrinsic and euclidean geometrical ideas.

A Research Study

The empirical study presented here [9] was carried out to investigate children's use of specific intuitive conceptions [13, 11] while programming in Logo microworld environments designed to embed ideas belonging to intrinsic, euclidean and cartesian geometry. Four aspects of the problem were investigated.

a) the nature of the mental "schema" children form when they identify with the turtle in order to change its state on the screen in conventional Logo;
b) whether it is possible for them to use the schema to gain insights into certain basic geometrical principles of the cartesian geometrical system;
c) how they might use the schema to form understandings of euclidean geometry developed inductively from specific experiences;
d) the criteria they develop for choosing between intrinsic and euclidean ideas.

Method and Summary of the Results

Ten 11–12 year-old Greek children participated in the research, previously having had 40–50 hours of experience with conventional Turtle geometry. The research involved three case-studies of pairs of children engaging in cooperative activities, each case-study within a specially designed geometrical Logo microworld. The data included hard copies of everything that was said, typed and written.

A qualitative approach of progressive focusing was adopted for the analysis of the data [23, 5], the researcher adopting the role of a participant observer during the research sessions. Within the children's activities, episodes were identified which captured important insights into geometrical ideas, or which provided evidence of children adopting particular strategies or using specific ideas. These episodes are indicators within a continuous reality and not isolated instances with no relation between them.

---

[2] Research in children's learning with Logo has fallen short of Papert's vision of a spontaneous generation of self-created problem solvers. For a comprehensive debate on the circumstances in which Logo may be used as a base for children's learning of mathematics, arising from research during the 1980s, see [15].

Issues a) and b) were investigated by means of the first case-study which involved three pairs of children and a microworld embedding intrinsic and coordinate ideas [8]. A model of the children's intrinsic schema and a model of the coordinate schema which they formed during the study were devised. The analysis shows that the two schemas remained separate in the children's minds with the exception of a limited number of occasions of context specific links between the two.

Issue c) was investigated in the second case-study involving one pair of children and a microworld where the turtle was equipped with distance and turn measuring instruments and a facility to mark positions [10]. The analysis illustrates how a turtle geometric environment of a dynamic mathematical nature was generated by the children, who used their intrinsic schema and predominantly engaged in inductive thinking. The study elaborated how the children constructed a generalised computational tool for an isosceles triangle by *initially* using the microworld's measuring instruments to construct the figure, based on very little knowledge of its properties, and *then* exploring these in the process of generalising from their measurements.

Issue d) was investigated by means of the third case-study involving a pair of children constructing a Circle microworld comprised of four circle procedures embedding intrinsic and/or euclidean notions (Fig. 1a) and then choosing amongst those in order to construct figures of circle compositions (Fig. 1b). The analysis shows that the children employed their turtle schema in using both kinds of notions and did not seem to perceive qualitative differences between them. Their decisions on which type of notion to use were influenced by certain broader aspects of the mathematical situations generated in the study.

The findings from the three case-studies indicate that the children saw sense in identifying with the turtle and using experience based on bodily motion in order to change its state. Identifying the theorems the children seemed to have formed for controlling the conventional turtle was one of the research issues in focus during their activities with the microworld in the first case-study. The analysis of the data revealed episodes where the six children taking part in the case-study implicitly used one or more of the following notions:

a) an action-quantity notion, which involved a "turn degrees" notion for heading changes and a "move steps" notion for position changes, and
b) a sequentiality notion, which involved the notions of "one change after another" and "a change depends on the immediately previous state".

There is evidence of all six children readily using action-quantity and sequentiality notions during these activities. This, however, does not imply that they did not have difficulties with these ideas, such as problems with discriminating between the two states and between an action and its quantity, or with concentrating on one state change at a time.

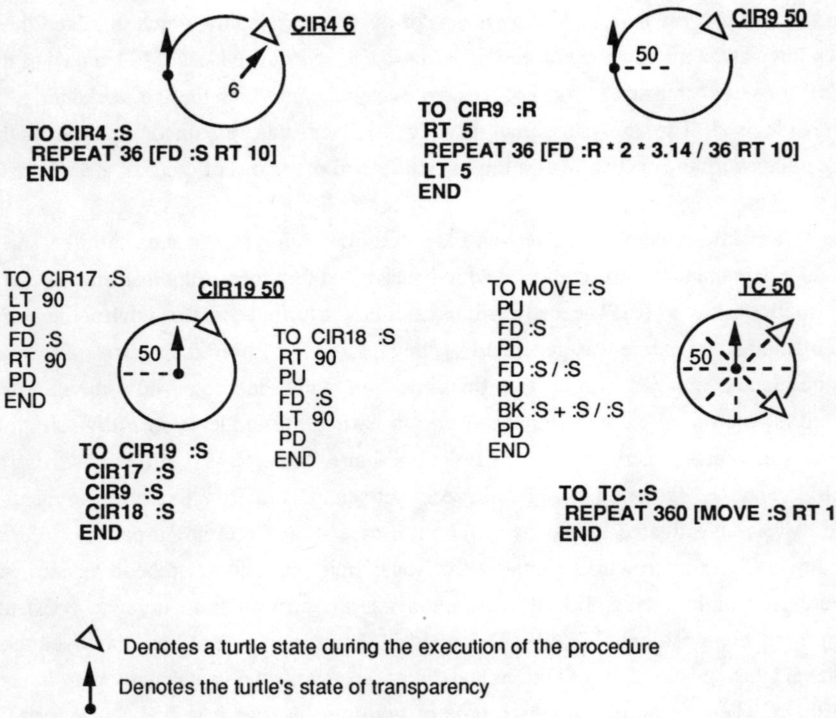

Figure 1a: The Circle microworld's primitives constructed by the children

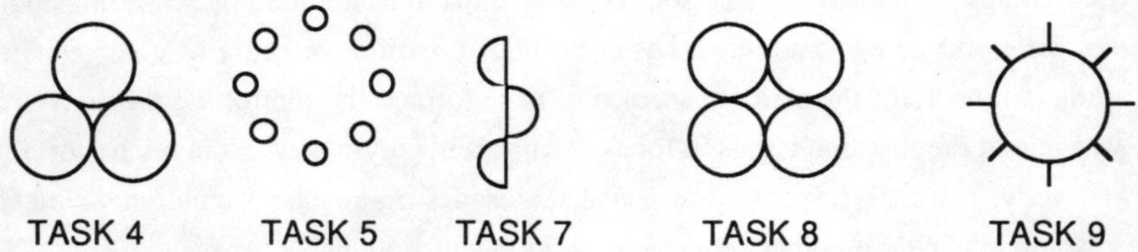

Figure 1b: Structured tasks involving Circle combinations

Using Ideas From Different Geometrical Systems

The analysis of the children's choices between using intrinsic and euclidean notions in constructing the task figures in the Circle Microworld study (Fig. 1b) provided evidence of a balance in their use of both kinds of notions, i.e., the children seemed to be quite prepared to use both intrinsic and euclidean ideas in planning and explaining turtle actions.

In order to illustrate the children's use of both types of geometrical ideas, an example is given of an episode which took place during their solution of task 4, Fig. 1b. The episode illustrates how the children saw the connection between the positions of the centre points of the three circles. After having tried out several strategies involving the construction of one circle after the other and stumbling on the working out of the interface between the second and third circle (Fig. 2), Alexandros seemed to spot the uniformity of the lengths between the circles' centres by revolving the piece of paper on which the figure was drawn, so that a bottom circle would go to the top and vice versa. Although the children seemed enthusiastic about their "discovery" concerning the distances between centres, they still did not consider the positions of the centres; although they had decided on the length of the second interface, they turned the turtle 45 degrees to the left apparently using their perceptual cues (Fig. 2).

```
CIR19 40
RT 90
PU
FD 80
LT 90
PD
CIR19 40
LT 45
```

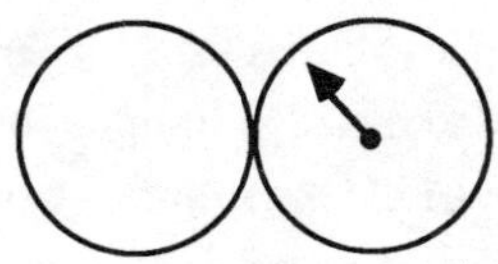

Figure 2: The children's perceptual strategy in task 4

The researcher decided to prompt them to focus their attention on the uniformity of the figure they had noticed from Alexandros' turning of the piece of paper. Their dialogue at this point illustrates how the relationship among the three centres was made explicit by the children:

V: *"You know what I'm thinking? Why should it be 45?* (the turn) *You know why? Since, if we join the three dots... a triangle is been done* (formed)... *an equilateral."*
A: *"Equilateral."*
V: *"Eh?"*
A: *"And the sum of the angles of a triangle... is 180?"*
V: *"Look. It goes forward. It goes left, you know how much? It goes left 360 divided by 3. So, how much is it? 3... 120. It goes left 120... it goes forward and does the circle...* (she observes that the turtle's current heading is zero)... *120... 30 because I was thinking that it's like that, so 90 plus 30...* (she types LT 30)."
(brackets are used for the researcher's comments).

This new strategy involved a rather complicated but coherent use of both intrinsic and euclidean notions. The reference to the two radii forming the sides of a triangle and the centres of the circles forming its vertices implies the use of euclidean ideas. On the other hand, deciding on the turtle's turning after constructing each circle was based on a partitioning of a total turtle turn. Furthermore, Valentini's argument for turning the turtle left from a zero heading to face the top vertice of the triangle, was based on partitioning the turtle's turn into a 90 plus 30 degree turn. The ability, inherrent in the programming environment, to use a computational tool (the procedure CIR19 + input, embedding geometrical ideas such as circle construction by use of a specific point, the procedure's state of transparency, and a variable radius), in conjunction with direct - driving commands, provided the children with a means to try out perceptual approaches to the problem before grasping its geometrical structure.

Discussing a Geometrical Theorem in a Circle Microworld

The analysis of the data suggested that using the above notions was not perceived by the children as using geometry, but as using experience which they had acquired irrespective of intended imposition of knowledge from the outside. This argument is further supported by specific findings in the Circle microworld study where, for example, the children themselves (Alexandros and Valentini) expressed the view that no knowledge is required in order to understand the total turtle turn theorem. In this study, however, the ideas used by the children were extended to those belonging to euclidean geometry as well as intrinsic [9]. The children expressed a preference for employing notions which they had previously used in personally meaningful contexts rather than those presented to them through the school system, as illustrated by the following episode.

REPEAT 4 [CIR19 20 PU FD 40 PD RT 90]

Figure 3: The children's solution of a structured task with circles

Within the context of discussing their solution of a task - figure involving circles placed in a square formation (Fig. 3), both children said that they preferred explaining the turtle's turn of 90 degrees by means of the partitioning of a total turn rather than adding up the internal angles of the formed square. What is interesting is not their preference as such (after all, they were using the turtle to construct the figure), but the reasons they gave for and against the two methods:

(The children's reasons on why they did not prefer the internal angles method)
V: "...they tell us, that definitely it's 360 (she means that the sum of the internal angles is 360 degrees) *and that's it, you can't say anything, it's definitely 360, I know and you can't ask, you can't do a thing."*

A: "It's like I told you the other time. Geometry forces us, we can't ask her... this, since it's been discovered that this is that much, that much we'll write it. We can't ask her why is it like that and why is it like this because they'll tell us because that's what it want's to be."

(Their reasons on why they preferred the total turn method)

V: "Because it's more natural... yes it's more natural, now I thought of that... anybody can understand it..."

A: "Even if he doesn't know turtle at all."

R: "Tell me something. What does someone have to know to understand this thing?"

V: "Nothing."

So, the children's perception of the "internal angles" rule as part of the geometry learned at school, portrayed geometry as a set of facts they were told of and not given the chance to question, let alone discover for themselves. Such ideas about school geometry are seldom made explicit by children in Greece, at least in the school where the research took place [12]. On the contrary their perception of the "turtle turn" rule seemed to be that they understood it even though they were not given any information about it. Thus, in contrast to school geometry, the children's view of the nature of a Turtle Geometric "rule", corroborates Papert and Lawler's contention that children base their understandings of Turtle Geometry on intuitive knowledge.

Conclusion

While programming in the above microworld environments, the children did seem to form certain theorems to control the turtle which based action-quantity and sequentiality processes on intuitions concerning movement *and* space. This would imply that prior contentions that only the former intuitions can be employed in conventional turtle graphics were dependent on the available programming tools rather than on children's choice or capability. However, the children in the study did not seem to relate these theorems to knowledge from a specific content domain, but rather perceived them as sense - making rules in themselves. The children's criteria for using the turtle metaphor tended to relate to its intuitive nature rather than to a particular type of geometrical notions. The children's critical remarks on generalised rules involving Intrinsic and Euclidean notions referred to whether the rules had been derived via an inductive method or not, rather than on which kind of such rules were easier to understand, as is evident from the episodes analysed in this paper. The programming and modularity involved in the children's strategies also influenced their choices on which notions to use. Specifically, their priorities in such decisions lay with the programming rather than with the type of geometrical ideas. What enabled the solution of task 4, for instance, was the children's initial coherent use of a "naive" trial and error sequence of primitive commands in conjunction with an analytical use of a generalised procedure. This allowed them to place the first two circles in position, conjecture about the interface between circles and subsequently write a structured program iterating circle procedure and interface, similar to the one they wrote to solve task 8. Thus the evidence from the study supports the argument that powerful computational tools in a Logo programming and geometric environment, such as the primitives of the Circle microworld, *may* be based on the turtle metaphor, enabling children to employ the intuitions which seem to accompany its use.

The analysis of the children's programming processes revealed how they learned programming through a process of forming "naive" or locally applicable theorems concerning key programming ideas such as the use of primitives, structuring a problem by means of writing procedures and constructing and working with generalised notional objects by means of defining procedures with variable inputs. For instance, the unsystematic bottom - up strategy in writing a structured program to solve task 4 was followed by a more or less top - down perception of task 8, *but not of task 5 or 9*, which to an adult programmer may seem like equivalent problems. Children have less ability to transfer techniques or strategies across problems and to perceive their generalisable nature. Learning environments encouraging local and inductively reached generalisations may therefore be important for subsequent higher - order abstractions, such as for instance, perceiving a circle procedure as a specific case of any regular polygon *and writing a procedure for the latter in order to construct the former*. It is suggested that such understandings of the above ideas are important both for the learning of content domains (in this case geometrical) and for the nurturing of flexible learners who will feel at ease with using the technology of tomorrow.

Primitives and tools with which children can *express meaning* ultimately derived from or constructed through their own experiences, are important ingredients of the kind of environment discussed in this paper, where programming and learning of some other content area such as geometry coexist in synergy. Programming in this case is seen as a means of *expressing, structuring and abstracting ideas* "belonging" to a specific domain and is intended for programmers who will potentially enhance their understanding of the problem at hand. Programmers' cognitive processes, teacher interventions and the educational culture in which these learning situations develop are research areas where interpretation of human behaviour is exponentially more complex than in the case of the use of tutoring systems (see duBoulay, Sumiga and the discussion concerning theme 3, in this volume). The design of such computer environments and the study of the cognitive models children form while working with these has thus been based on a growing volume of empirical research.

References

1. Abelson H., DiSessa A.: Turtle Geometry: the computer as a medium for exploring mathematics. Cambridge MA: MIT Press 1981
2. Abelson H., Sussman J.: Structure and interpretation of computer programs. Cambridge MA: MIT Press 1985

3. Collis K.: Cognitive development and mathematics learning. Shell Mathematics Unit Centre for Science Education, Chelsea College, University of London 1974
4. DiSessa A.: Phenomenology and the evolution of intuition. In Gentner D., Stevens A. (eds.) Mental models, pp. 15–33. Hillsdale NJ: Lawrence Erlbaum 1983
5. Goetz J.P., Lecompte M.D.: Ethnography and qualitative design in educational research. London: Academic Press 1984
6. Harvey B.: Computer Science Logo Style, Vols 1, 2 and 3. Cambridge MA: MIT Press 1985
7. Hoyles C.: Scaling a mountain – a study of the use, discrimination and generalisation of some mathematical concepts in a Logo environment. European Journal of Psychology of Education 1(2), 111–126 (1986)
8. Kynigos C.: Constructing bridges from intrinsic to cartesian geometry. In Borbas A. (ed.): Proc. Twelfth International Conference for the Psychology of Mathematics Education II, , pp. 449-456. Veszprem, Hungary 1988
9. Kynigos C.: From intrinsic to non-intrinsic geometry: a study of children's understandings in Logo-based Microworlds. PhD. Thesis, Institute of Education, University of London 1989
10. Kynigos C.: Can children use the turtle to develop understandings of euclidean ideas in an inductive way? In Leron U., Krumholtz N. (eds.): Proc. Fourth International Conference for Logo and Mathematics Education, pp. 115-124 The Israeli Logo Centre, Dept. of Education in Science and Technology, Technion – Israel Institute of Technology 1989b
11. Kynigos C.: The turtle metaphor as a tool for children doing geometry. In Hoyles C., Noss R. (eds): Learning Logo and mathematics, pp. 97–126. Cambridge MA: MIT Press 1992
12. Kynigos C.: Insights into pupils' and teachers' activities in pupil-controlled problem-solving situations: a longitudinally developing use for programming by all in a primary school. In Ponte J.P., Matos J.F., Matos J.M., Fernandes D. (eds.): Mathematics problem solving and new information technologies. NATO ASI Series F, Vol. 89. Springer-Verlag 1992
13. Lawler R. W.: Computer experience and cognitive development. a child's learning in a computer culture. Ellis Horwood 1985
14. Noss R.: Creating a mathematical environment through programming: a study of young children learning Logo. Ph.D. Thesis, University of London Institute of Education 1985
15. Noss R., Hoyles C.: Looking back and looking forward. In Hoyles C., Noss R. (eds): Learning Logo and mathematics. Cambridge MA: MIT Press 1992
16. Nunes Carraher, T.: Street mathematics and school mathematics. In Borbas E. (ed.): Proc. Twelfth Annual Conference of the International Group for the Psychology of Education 1, pp. 1–23. Vesprem, Hungary: OOK Printing House 1988
17. Paalz Scally S.: A clinical investigation of the impact of a Logo learning environment on students' van Hiele levels of geometric understanding. In Bergeron J, Herscovics N., Kieran C. (eds.): Proc. Eleventh International Conference for the Psychology of Mathematics Education, Montreal 1986, pp. 123–128
18. Papert S.: Mindstorms. Children, computers and powerful ideas. Harvester Press 1980
19. Papert S.: Computers and Computer Cultures. Creative Computing, 7, 82–92 (1981)
20. Sharples M.: Cognition, computers and creative writing. Ellis Horwood 1985
21. Sinclair K., Moon D.: The philosophy of LISP. Communications of the ACM 34(9), 41–47 (1991)
22. Solloway E.: Quick, where do the computers go?, Communications of the ACM 34(2), 29–33 (1990)
23. Vergnaud G.: Cognitive and developmental psychology and research in mathematics education: some theoretical and methodological issues. For the Learning of Mathematics 3(2), 31–41 (1982)

Thinking Algebraically: Pupil Models Developed in Logo and a Spreadsheet Environment

Rosamund Sutherland

Institute of Education, University of London, London, U.K.

Abstract: Project AnA is concerned with investigating the ways in which pupils' experiences with Logo and a spreadsheet environment influence their learning of algebraic ideas. The computer activities can loosely be described as programming although the emphasis is on the learning of mathematics. The study focuses on both the models developed within the computer environment and on how these models might influence pupils' work with "paper and pencil" algebra. The emphasis is on thinking and interacting with symbolic language as opposed to first developing a method and then translating this method into the appropriate symbolism. The results indicate that in both computer environments the models developed by pupils are as much linked to the problem situations as they are to aspects of the computer environment and individual pupils. Within this paper we describe the ways in which pupils can develop a more algebraic approach to problem solving in mathematics, discussing how this relates to their engagement in computer-based situations.

Keywords: Pupil models, programming, spreadsheets, algebraic processes

Introduction

Project AnA [8] is concerned with investigating the ways in which pupils' experiences with Logo and a spreadsheet environment influence their learning of algebraic ideas. In particular the research study is investigating the means by which pupils are able to negotiate and formalise a generalisation within a computer-based environment. The computer activities can loosely be described as programming although the emphasis is on the learning of mathematics. The study focuses on both the models developed within the computer environment and on how these models might influence pupils' work with "paper and pencil" algebra. Within this paper I firstly outline the theoretical and methodological influences on the study — the methodology involves collecting data from group teaching sessions and individual pupil interviews. The teaching sequences are then described as they have an influence on the models developed by the pupils. Finally I discuss the results concerned with two groups of pupils aged 10–11 (Group 1) and aged 11–12 (Group 2). The first group has worked on a range of spreadsheet tasks and the second on a range of Logo tasks.

Theoretical Background

In the early days our work with Logo was heavily influenced by previous research on children's understanding of algebra, which reported that pupils have considerable difficulties with the interpretation of letters and associated understanding of variable (for example [3]). This research suggests that pupils find it difficult to understand that a letter in algebra can represent a range of numbers and to accept "unclosed" expressions in algebra (for example x + 4). Most of this work on childrens' understanding of algebra was influenced by a Piagetian perspective. The implicit assumption often made in these studies is that if pupils cannot perform satisfactorily on certain algebraic tasks then they have not yet reached the stage of formal operations. Our Logo and spreadsheet studies have shown that many of the pupil misconceptions reported in the domain of paper and pencil algebra rarely occur in Logo or a spreadsheet environment[1] [7, 9]. This has caused us to re-question the earlier studies on pupils' misconceptions in algebra, in particular the attribution of pupil errors to cognitive obstacles situated within pupils. Our earlier work was also rather implicitly influenced by a Piagetian perspective and so for example during the first year of the Logo Maths Project [2] we tended to wait until pupils seemed to "need" the idea of variable within their own Logo programming projects. We also wanted to find out what pupils could do for themselves without instruction. One finding of the Logo Maths Project was that pupils very rarely chose to express a general relationship in their Logo work and consequently did not need to use variables. When presented with teacher-directed tasks pupils began to learn to use the idea, although there was often a gap between using the idea of variable in a teacher-directed task and choosing to use the idea in their own projects.

Work with Logo and spreadsheets has also shown that it may be mistaken to assume that pupils can first express a general relationship in natural language and then somehow translate this into computer language. When working on a new and challenging problem students tend to formulate general relationships by interacting with the computer language. The computer-based language becomes incorporated into their talk helping to structure the generalising process. In the spreadsheet environment the use of pointing (to different cells on the screen) is also an important mediator in the generalising process. By directly interacting with the language whilst working at the computer pupils develop a way of using the language to express their mathematical ideas. The emphasis on interaction and language, both in terms of communicating between themselves and communicating with the computer is now a feature of our work. This contrasts with the predominant approach amongst computer scientists in which the emphasis is on solving the problem before interacting with the computer (see for example [1] in this volume) although the notion of interacting with the computer is now receiving more attention [11].

---

1 These results have been obtained when pupils are solving tasks similar to those presented in Figs. 2 and 7.

In searching for an explanation for our empirical results we turned to the work of Vygotsky. Crucial to Vygotsky's theory is the idea that individual cognitive development results from social interaction in the world, and that speech, social interaction and cooperative activity are all important aspects of this social world. The active involvement of the child is a crucial part of the process and in this respect Vygotsky's theories are similar to those of Piaget. Vygotsky differs from Piaget in his views about the role of speech, and more generally symbol systems, in cognitive development.

> "The students of practical intelligence as well as those who study speech development often fail to recognize the interweaving of these two functions. Consequently the child's adaptive behaviour and sign-using activity are treated as parallel phenomena — a view that leads to Piaget's concept of "egocentric" speech. He did not attribute an important role to speech in the organization of the child's activities, nor did he stress its communicative functions, although he was obliged to admit its practical importance. Although practical intelligence and sign use can operate independently of each other in young children, the dialectical unity of these systems in the human adult is the very essence of complex human behaviour. Our analysis accords symbolic activity a specific organizing function that penetrates the process of tool use and produces fundamentally new forms of behaviour" ([10] p 24).

Vygotsky also stresses that developing an understanding of the relationship between sign and meaning does not result from discovery by the child — the teacher has an important role in this process. What is important for Vygotsky is what the child can do with instruction and he uses the term "the Zone of Proximal Development" to describe "the distance between the actual developmental level as determined by individual problem solving, and the level of potential development as determined through problem solving under adult guidance, or in collaboration with more capable peers" [10,86].

Methodology

Throughout Project AnA the aim is to describe and analyse the models used by pupils, linking these to the computer-based situations with which they have engaged — this involves analysing the problem situations and teacher and pupil language. As I have already discussed the emphasis throughout the teaching sequences is on thinking with the computer-based algebraic language, and not on developing a method (in for example natural language) and then translating this method into the computer language. The methodology used within Project AnA is essentially longitudinal case study, which involves detailed studies of small groups of pupils. Three groups[2] of pupils are being studied, with each group engaging in a sequence of

---

[2] Only part of the results of Project AnA are reported in this paper because the project is still ongoing. In the whole project Group 2 (the Logo group of this paper) will also engage in a spreadsheet sequence and a traditional algebra sequence. In addition there exists a Group 3 (aged 14-15) who have difficulties with school mathematics. Group 3 pupils are working on a spreadsheet sequence of activities. We are also carrying out a Mexican/British study [6] in which pupils in Mexico work on a range of spreadsheet problems.

individual interviews followed by teaching activities. This sequence is repeated at least three times for all groups.

The data collected includes: tape recordings of individual interviews; printouts of computer work; paper and pencil work; detailed notes of teaching sessions; occasional video recordings of computer work. Analysis of the data informs ongoing work. The analysis stage takes into account the fact that some teaching inevitably occurs during the individual interviews, and that information on pupil processes can also be obtained from the teaching sessions. Project AnA is carried out in schools and the details of the methodology are often constrained more by practical school considerations than by an ideal experimental design. This is mentioned because it is an issue which needs confronting within longitudinal school based studies.

We have developed an approach which views the teaching and learning of programming and domain specific ideas (in this case mathematical) as being linked. Problems presented to pupils are chosen because of their emphasis on both mathematical and programming ideas. The Logo activities are centred around the problem domain of geometry and the spreadsheet activities around the problem domain of arithmetic. In both environments pupils are initially asked to generalise from specific relationships using the appropriate symbolic language.

There are some differences between the use of variable in Logo and a spreadsheet. In Logo the variable is named (for example SIDE, X) in the editor (see for example Fig. 7) and pupils change the value of the variable when working in direct mode. In the spreadsheet Excel a variable is identified with a cell. The user interacts directly with a cell (by pointing with a mouse or typing the cell reference name). Values of the variable are varied by changing the number in the cell. This immediately produces visible effects in cells which contain functions depending on this variable.

An overall framework is being developed for analysing the models developed by pupils when working in a Logo, a spreadsheet and a more traditional algebra context. The following categories are being used to structure the analysis.

At a local level pupil focuses on :	When constructing a global mathematical relationship pupil focuses on:
• specific object	• process
• general object	• structure
• arithmetic code	• specific relationship
• algebraic code	• general relationship
• situation specific object	• constraints of situation

Discussion of Results from the Spreadsheet Group (Group 1)

A group of 8 pupils[3] (aged 10-11) worked in pairs on a sequence of spreadsheet (Excel) activities over a period of 5 months. The pupils had approximately 12 hours of hands-on spreadsheet time. The pupils were 4 girls and 4 boys who were chosen to represent a range of mathematical attainment. The spreadsheet activities were grouped around three sequences of problems:

Block 1: Function and inverse function (see for example Fig. 1) Within this sequence pupils were introduced to the following spreadsheet and mathematical ideas; entering a rule; replicating a rule; function and inverse function; symbolising a general rule; decimal and negative numbers.

Block 2: Equivalent algebraic expressions (see for example Fig 2) Within this sequence pupils were introduced to the ideas of: equivalent algebraic expressions; symbolising a general rule.

Block 3: Word problems (see for example Fig 5) Within this sequence pupils were introduced to solving a word problem in a spreadsheet by: representing the unknown with a spreadsheet cell; expressing the relationship within the problem in terms of this unknown; varying the unknown to find a solution.

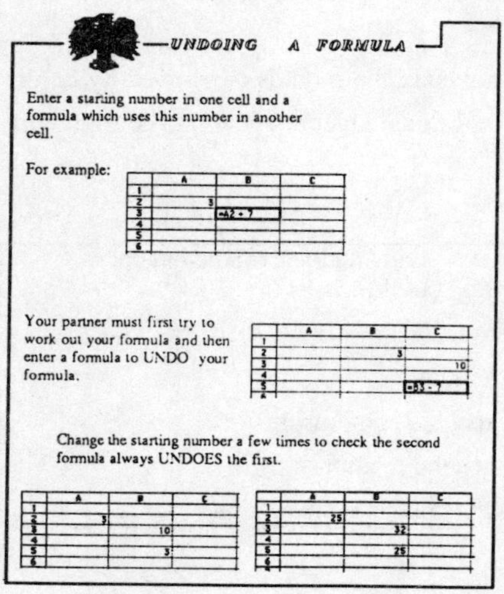

Figure 1: Undo the Formula

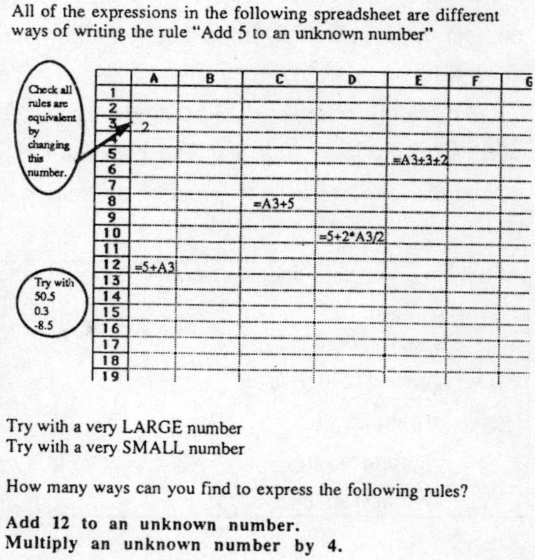

Figure 2: Equivalent Expressions

[3] These pupils had no previous experience of algebra.

All of the pupils in the spreadsheet group became competent at entering and replicating a rule in the context of solving the spreadsheet problems which were the focus of the study. At the beginning of the project this did not seem an inevitable outcome. In the first two sessions many of the pupils had difficulties with the idea of a entering a spreadsheet rule and were confused by the idea of an inverse rule. At this point the researcher felt that maybe the choice of working with 10 year old pupils was mistaken. These initial problems did not occur again when the pupils were faced with replicating a spreadsheet rule and it is likely that the initial difficulties were related to the pupils' inability to conceive of a spreadsheet cell as representing a general number (a central part of the introductory activity). Only one of the eight pupils was confident with this idea at the beginning of the study. However in the context of solving the function and inverse function problems four out of eight pupils developed an approach in which they were predominantly thinking with a general object[4]. It seems that for these four pupils we were working within their zone of proximal development with respect to the ideas of symbolising and generalising. Additionally the data suggests that those pupils (3 out of 8) who continued to think with a specific object at the end of the study did so because the idea of thinking with a general object was not yet accessible to them.

Although all of the activities in Blocks 1 and 2 were designed to provoke pupils to think in terms of a general mathematical object there was particular emphasis on this idea in the equivalent expressions problem. When first faced with this activity many pupils constructed equivalent expressions which only worked for specific cases as illustrated by the session in which Andrew and Graeme were finding expressions equivalent to "multiply an unknown number by 4" (Fig. 3). They entered the number 3 in cell A2 and then in another cell entered the rule A2*0.5*8 which produced a value of 12. In a new cell they then entered a new expression A2*3 + 3 which also produced a value of 12. The second expression suggested that they were thinking with the specific number 3 in order to construct the equivalent expressions. When they changed the number in A2 they realised for themselves that the second rule was not equivalent and changed it without any need for intervention from the teacher.

	A	B	C	D
1				
2	3	=A2*0.5*8		=A2*3+3
3				
4				
5				
6				

Figure 3: Andrew and Graeme's equivalent expressions for "Multiply an unknown number by 4"

---

4 The evidence for this comes from individual interviews and observations of pupils working on the spreadsheet tasks.

In the final interview pupils were asked (as they were working at the spreadsheet) to describe the way in which they thought of the spreadsheet cell. These results are presented in Table 1.

No of pupils who:	predominantly think with a **general object**	predominantly think with a **specific object**
think with[5] **arithmetic code** (i.e. a number)	1	2
think with **algebraic code** (e.g. C2)	4	1

Table 1: Overview of pupils' local models when working on Block 1 and 2 problems

Five of the pupils said that they thought in terms of the algebraic cell reference name (for example C6). However one of these five pupils, thought of this code as representing a specific object *"the place where you can put the unknown number"* suggesting that thinking with the algebraic code does not necessarily imply thinking with a general object. However the spreadsheet algebraic code does seem to play an important mediating role for the pupils who developed from predominantly thinking with a specific object to a general object. These pupils incorporated the algebraic code into their talk (for example *"unequal sides 5 cm.....right go up to B1....put the formula to calculate the equal sides to unequal sides....A2 is going to be times 2.....just put times 2...put 5 in there...equal 10.....right A2 times 2 in B2")*. They were also able to write down this code in response to a number of interview questions (Fig. 4a). This contrasts with the responses of the pupils who predominantly thought with an arithmetic object (Fig. 4b).

Question 3
a) Write down the rule which tells you the value of y if you know the value of x for the following table of values:

x	y
-2	-8
-1	-4
0	0
1	4
2	8
3	12

What is the rule? ....X x 4..................

What is the value of y if x is 50.....200...

Can you write it in spreadsheet language.= A1 x 4

What would be the undo rule? ~~=A1 ÷ 4~~ 1 ÷ 4

Can you write it in spreadsheet language:

..............................= A1 ÷ 4..................

Figure 4a: Use of spreadsheet algebraic code in response to interview item

b) Write down the rule which tells you the value of y if you know the value of x for the following table of values:

x	y
0	3
1	4
2	5
3	6

What is the rule? ....+3.......................

What is the value of y if x is 50.........46.....

Can you write it in spreadsheet language...............

What would be the undo rule? .....-3..............

Can you write it in spreadsheet language:

..............................= 46+3..................

Figure 4b: Use of arithmetic code in response to interview item

---

5 Category situation specific object is not included because in this type of problem this is the same as an arithmetic object.

When we turn to the analysis of Block 3 word problems the situation is more complex. These problems were difficult for the 10 year old pupils and for most of them the time constraints of the study were inadequate for them to develop competence in this approach to solving word problems. Nevertheless analysis of these sessions and the pupils' performance in individual interviews reveals some important aspects of the models used by pupils. The three pupils who continued to think predominantly with a specific object (within Block 1 and 2) had more difficulty with the word problems than those who thought with a general object. In order to solve these problems with a spreadsheet algebraic method pupils have to start from the unknown number (which in algebra would be represented by x for example) and then build up general relationship in terms of this unknown. Results from the pre-interview indicated that at least two pupils had efficient informal strategies for solving word problems. These strategies were not algebraic in that they involved working from the known to the unknown. So for example when solving the measurement of a field problem (Fig. 5) away from the computer Andrew used a non algebraic strategy. This involved dividing the given perimeter by 6 (102÷6) to give the width *"It says the length of the perimeter is twice as much as the width. So I just thought that there must be two of those in one length so there must be four of those for those in there and two of those"*.

Measurement of a Field

The perimeter of a field measures 102 metres. The length of the field is twice as much as the width of the field. How much does the length of the field measure? How much does the width of the field measure?

The Chocolates Problem

100 chocolates were distributed between three groups of children. The second group received 4 times the chocolates of the first group. The third group received 10 chocolates more than the second group. How many chocolates did the first, the second and the third group receive?

Figure 5: Algebra word problems

The "taught" spreadsheet solution involved representing the unknown by a spreadsheet cell and although the pupils' comments indicated that they initially found this a difficult idea they eventually accepted this idea. Pupils tended to enter a "good first estimate" of the unknown number into a cell as illustrated by Mike working on the Chocolates Problem (Fig. 5). Mike first carried out the calculation 100/3 in a cell and entered the result 33.3333333 in cell A5 (for the number of chocolates in the 1st group) (Fig. 6). It seems as if he started the solution by using a non-algebraic strategy (for further discussion of this strategy see [4]). He then entered the rule 33.3333333 * 4 (for the number of chocolates in the 2nd group) in cell A9 indicating that he was initially thinking with this specific value. He immediately changed this to the correct rule A5*4 indicating a shift from thinking with a specific object to thinking with a general object (a shift which was possibly provoked by the symbolic nature of the spreadsheet environment). This rule produced a number bigger than 100 which concerned him because *"there are only 100 chocolates altogether"* (indicating that he was also thinking with the constraints of the problem). However he continued and entered the correct rule A9 + 10 for the number of chocolates in the third group. He then changed the number in cell A5 (the number of chocolates in the first group) to 23.5. Until this point he had worked without support from the researcher. The researcher then suggested that he put in a rule to calculate the total number of chocolates and without any difficulty he entered a correct rule (Fig. 6) varying the number in the first group (cell A5) until he obtained a solution.

		A	B	C
No of chocs in 1st group	5	10		
	6			
	7			
No of chocs in 2nd group	8			
	9	=A5*4		
	10			
No of chocs in 3rd group	11	=A9+10		
	12			
	13			
Total No of chocs	14	=A5+A9+A11		

Figure 6: Mike's solution to the Chocolates Problem.

Mike's solution can be contrasted with Andrew's solution. Whereas Mike was a pupil who predominantly thought of a spreadsheet cell as representing a general number this was not the case for Andrew. When solving the Chocolates Problem Andrew firstly entered the number 100 in cell B4 and then in cell B5 carried out the calculation B4/3. This was similar to Mike's strategy for calculating a value (although incorrect) for the number of chocolates in the first group . Andrew then entered a correct rule (B5*4) for the number of chocolates in the second group. This produced a number greater than 100 for the number of chocolates in the first group which he knew could not be correct. Instead of changing the number in the first group Andrew then changed the correct general rule to B5*4/2 in order to try to reduce this unreasonably large number. This suggests that he was thinking with the objects and constraints of the situation at the expense of the general mathematical invariants of the problem. There was evidence from other occasions that Andrew predominantly thought with the objects of the situation, ignoring mathematical constraints as illustrated by the following comment *"How do we know how many teachers there are, is this a primary school or a secondary school?"*

Tom on the other hand, who was relatively unsuccessful with his school mathematics work, (possibly because of his great difficulty with arithmetic) developed a passion for the spreadsheet symbolism at the expense of considering the more practical aspects of the problem situation. So for example he would generate a negative number for the number of teachers in a school without noticing the unreasonableness of this solution. Perhaps his difficulties with number prevented him from calculating the value of a symbolic expression and this was maybe why he so readily accepted the spreadsheet symbols. However there was evidence that for Tom the symbol predominantly referred to a specific object *"the place where you can put the unknown number"* .

Discussion of Results from the Logo Group (Group 2)

A group of 16 pupils[6] (aged 11-12) worked in pairs on a sequence of Logo activities over a period of 6 months having approximately 11 hours of hands-on Logo time. The Logo sequence of activities were grouped around the following sets of problems:

Block 1: Operating on a Variable to write a procedure to draw a general geometric object (see for example Fig. 7) — the emphasis being on operating on a variable input and not on adding a string of unrelated variables to the procedure. The arithmetical relationships were kept simple in the initial problems (e.g. multiply by 2 or multiply by 5), becoming progressively more difficult.

Block 2: Changing the variable (see for example Fig. 8) In this sequence of activities pupils were introduced to the idea of changing the variable (parameter) in a general procedure. The focus in this activity was on analysing the structural relationships within a turtle geometry procedure.

From a programming point of view the majority (12 out of 16) of pupils in Group 2 were able at the end of the period of Logo activities to operate on a variable to construct a procedure to draw proportional representations of a pictorial image. In order to write this Logo procedure most of the pupils first constructed a procedure for a fixed shape and then modified this to make it general — which is how they had been introduced to the idea (Fig. 7).

In Logo pupils have to choose a name for their variable and at the end of the study all of the pupils were aware that they could use any name, with the majority predominantly choosing single letter names. The variable name becomes a symbolic object and all of the pupils who could successfully construct a procedure with variable said that they thought of this algebraic symbol (i.e. the variable name) as representing any number, which is consistent with the results from an earlier study with children who were two years older [7]. As Rachel says *"a variable is something which you can make in different sizes. You can start off with something small and variable it to get something bigger or smaller"*. This group of pupils are being asked both Logo

6 These pupils were from a mixed ability class and were chosen to represent a spread of mathematical attainment.

and traditional algebra[5] questions in their individual interviews. Their responses to the algebra questions also provide insight into the models being used.

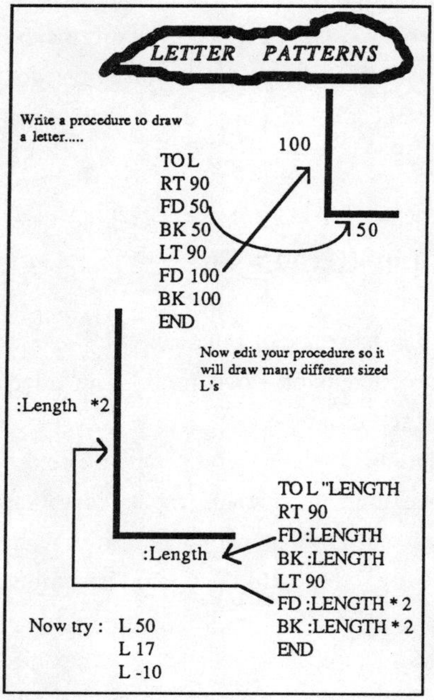

Figure 7: The "L" Task

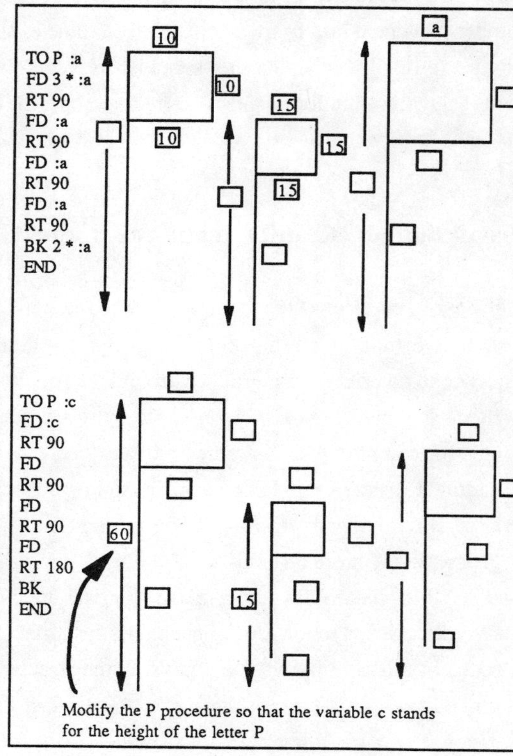

Figure 8: Changing the Variable

At the beginning of the study most of Group 2 pupils either said that they were not able to answer the algebra questions because they had never seen anything like them before or interpreted a letter as representing the position in the alphabet (a result which is consistent with previous algebra studies, [3]). In subsequent interviews some pupils began to refer spontaneously to their Logo work when presented with the algebra questions *"because we've done it on the computer.....because we've been using like ...ah ...variables and such and working out with the variables...... it just gave me a picture of how that might be done.* When

---

5 At the beginning of the study none of these pupils had carried out any traditional algebra as part of their normal school mathematics course. The pupils were working on an individualised mathematics curriculum and a few pupils began to encounter algebra as the study progressed. The algebra interview items were mostly taken from the CSMS study [3].

probed more about what this picture was this pupil said *"a formula with the letter and then it looked like that but with the little colons"* (referring to the Logo notation for signifying a variable). Another pupil Rachel wrote down the following solution to an algebra question :m x 3 + 1, again using the Logo notation for a variable. When Rachel was asked in the beginning interview the question *"If John had J marbles and Peter had P marbles what could you write down for the number of marbles they have altogether?"* she gave an answer of 25 (saying that the letters represented their position in the alphabet). In the final interview she responded *"Well J marbles could be anything and P marbles could be anything ....say J could be 10 and P could be 12....so the answer could be any number"*. More evidence that Rachel was using models developed in the Logo environment to answer these algebra questions came when she answered the question "Which is the larger 2n or n + 2?". She interpreted 2n as *"well 2n could just be say a name like BECKY"* indicating that for her 2n was a variable name (a permissible one in the Logo environment). Although Project AnA is not yet completed the evidence suggests that pupils without any previous experience of algebra do use the models developed in a programming context when solving traditional algebra questions. This result is similar to the finding of Samurçay [5] that older students (15-16 years) transfer their existing conceptions of algebra to the domain of programming. As the study progresses Group 2 pupils will be faced with more substantial algebra problems to probe this result in more depth.

In the context of their Logo work most of the pupils knew that some relationship had to be expressed within their "general" Logo procedure. They all started by learning an algorithmic method or process to generate a "general" procedure from a specific procedure (see Fig. 7) — a process which related very much to the specific numbers in the original fixed procedure. Pupils began to develop their own arithmetic strategies for dealing with any combination of numbers. The strategies often involved looking for a common factor and then thinking of the variable name as representing this specific number as they constructed their general procedure — most of them eventually realised that it was easier to think of the variable as the number 1 (a common factor for any number combination) when constructing their procedure *"it took us ages to just work out one thing so I thought that if I could get a number down to 1 it would be a lot easier"* — this strategy was never directly taught. In the final interview all of the pupils were asked whether they thought in terms of one or many images when they wrote a general procedure. The responses indicate that only 7 out of 16 think with many images *" different ones...all sizes big to small"*. So some pupils (in this study 5 out of 16) who can construct a "general" Logo procedure and who think with a general object at a local level still think in terms of a specific relationship at a global level. This result will be probed in more depth as the project continues.

Pupils also seem to have taken on board the idea that their general procedure should produce images which "look similar" and were aware that this constraint meant that they must only change the FD and BK commands in their procedure (and not the angle commands). They also learned that this constraint meant that *"take does not always work... times is better"* because they had seen the effect on the screen of not using a multiplicative strategy. In this sense they were aware of the global geometric constraints of the problem *"well the two sides there stay the same....it would still be the same distance between here and here"*, although none of them ever spontaneously expressed these constraints in terms of ratio or proportion.

Concluding Remarks

The results indicate that in both environments the models developed by pupils are as much linked to the problem situations as they are to aspects of the computer environment and individual pupils. Both the spreadsheet and the Logo problems centred around the idea of expressing a general mathematical relationship and in order to do this pupils must first think with a general object at a local level. Results from both groups of pupils suggest that the majority of pupils in the age range 10 to 12 do not do this spontaneously. It seems to be the interaction with the computer-based algebraic code which supports pupils development from thinking in terms of a specific to thinking in terms of a general object. In Logo it is the naming of the variable in the title line of the procedure which is important — pupils learn from experience that changing the value of this variable changes the size of the geometric image being generated. In the spreadsheet it is the cell itself which represents a general number — some pupils thinking with the cell reference code and others thinking with the number which appears in the cell. This suggests that pupils think with the object which they directly manipulate —which explains why for example in Logo pupils do not tend to think in terms of geometric lengths. There is also evidence (from Group 2 pupils) that pupils can transfer the model of a symbol representing a general number from Logo to a traditional algebra context[7].

When solving the more contextualised algebra word problems some pupils became inappropriately bogged down by situation specific objects and conversely other pupils thought inappropriately with symbolic objects. The Logo problems were essentially centred around geometric situations and there is some evidence that at a global level pupils think with the geometric objects of the situation, in that they distinguish between the angle and the distance commands in their procedures. This again could be explained by the fact that at a global level the geometric object becomes a focus of attention. However the "real world" situation of the word problems seems to have a stronger influence on pupils' global models than does the geometric situation of Logo.

Thinking in terms of a general object at a local level does not necessarily imply thinking in terms of a general relationship at a more global level. Some pupils seem to think of their apparently general looking Logo procedure in terms of the specific procedure from which it derived (*I see it as the size that I started off with*) although it is possible that this is a transitional stage. At a global level it seems that the spreadsheet environment more readily supports pupils

[7] This evidence comes from analysis of the interviews in which pupils were asked to solve a range of problems including items from the CSMS study (Küchemann, 1981).

to think in terms of a general relationship than does the Logo environment. This may be because the spreadsheet provides more immediate feedback from a general relationship, in that a pupil can interact with a spreadsheet cell (either by varying a number or by copying a rule) and watch the general relationship change, i.e., they can rapidly view a number of instantiations of their general relationship.

Within these studies we aim to analyse pupil models along the dimension process/structure although it is not easy to identify whether or not pupils are using a more structural or a more process model when solving a problem. However the results so far suggest that pupils can shift their models depending on the problem situation. So for example in the spreadsheet equivalent expressions problem (Fig. 2) the majority of pupils eventually thought with the structure of arithmetic when constructing equivalent expressions. Similarly when working on the Logo "Changing the Variable" activity (Fig. 8) many pupils began to think with the structural relationships embedded in the procedure. This could be because the computer frees pupils from the process activity of evaluating an expression, thus enabling them to focus more on the structural aspects of a situation.

These studies highlight the models pupils develop when working within both a Logo and a spreadsheet environment — a first stage in the development of a more coherent framework to explain and predict the potential of computer-based environments for learning mathematics.

Acknowledgement: The author would like to thank the Economic and Social Science Research Council for their support for this project (Grant number: R000232132).

References

1. Duchateau C. (1992) From "doing it....." to "having it done by ..." the heart of programming. Preproceedings of NATO ARW Cognitive Models and Intelligent Learning Environments for Learning Programming, S. Margherita, Genoa, Italy, 1992
2. Hoyles C., Sutherland R. (1989) Logo mathematics in the classroom. London: Routledge
3. Küchemann D. (1981) 'Algebra' in children's understanding of mathematics: 11-16, (K. Hart, ed). London: John Murray
4. Lins R. 1992, A framework for understanding what algebra thinking is. Unpublished Ph.D. Thesis, Shell Centre for Mathematics Education, Nottingham University
5. Samurçay R. (1985) Signification et fonctionnement du concept de variable informatique chez des élevès debutants. Educational Studies in Mathematics 16, 143 - 161
6. Rojano T., Sutherland R. (1992) Pupil strategies for solving algebra word Problems with a spreadsheet. Paper presented at 11th International Conference for the Psychology of Mathematics Education, USA
7. Sutherland R. (1989) Providing a computer-based framework for algebraic thinking. Educational Studies in Maths 20(3)
8. Sutherland R. 1990, Project AnA – the gap between arithmetical and algebraic thinking. Economic and Social Research Council, Project Proposal, Institute of Education, University of London
9. Sutherland R. (1992) Some unanswered research questions on the teaching and learning of algebra. For the Learning of Mathematics 11(3)
10. Vygotsky, L.S. (1978) Mind in society: the development of higher psychological processes. Cambridge MA: Harvard University Press
11. Young R., Howes A., Whittington J. (1990) A knowledge analysis of interactivity. In Diaper D et al. (eds.) Human-computer interaction. Elsevier Science Publishers

Learning Programming as a Cognitive Apprenticeship Through Conflicts

F. Arzarello[1], G.P. Chiappini[2], E. Lemut[2], N. Malara[3], M. Pellerey[4]

[1] Dipartimento Matematica Università, via Carlo Alberto 10, I-10123 Torino, Italy
[2] Istituto Matematica Applicata CNR, via L.B.Alberti, 4, I-16132 Genova, Italy
[3] Dipartimento Matematica Università, via Campi 213/b, I-41100 Modena, Italy
[4] Istituto Didattica Ateneo Salesiano, Piazza Ateneo Salesiano 1, Roma, Italy

Abstract: Learning to program is described as a cognitive apprenticeship, that is, as an apprenticeship where the interaction between expert and novice is aimed at enhancing the cognitive and metacognitive skills of the latter. Intellectual abilities involved in learning programming and emerging cognitive conflicts by the novices are illustrated. The development of intermediate supports able to help the transition from one problem solving environment to another is discussed. These intermediate supports are conceived as tools to stimulate a flexible and rich anticipatory thought, which seems to be necessary both for the mastery of the mentioned intellectual abilities and for recognizing and overcoming the cognitive conflicts.

Keywords: programming learning, cognitive apprenticeship, problem-solving, conflicts, anticipating thought, planning

Introduction

We shall present an overall picture of the research developed in the field of Learning Programming (LP) by various Italian research groups. All these groups have been supported by the Scientific Research Ministry and by CNR; most of them are in Maths Departments and work on research projects for improving the teaching of Mathematics. Their main interests in LP are as follows: (i) pupil and teacher awareness of what programming is; (ii) requirements, obstacles, difficulties in LP and related methodologies to overcome them; (iii) programming as a tool to learn mathematics in school.

In this paper we are mainly concerned with the performance of novices in programming; novices are both pupils of compulsory schools (6-13 years) and teachers engaged in refresher courses, while facing problem solving in BASIC, PASCAL, LOGO, Data Bases and Spreadsheet environments. We present and discuss LP as a *cognitive apprenticeship* aimed at learning programming as a tool for problem solving. This means to consider the LP process both as a process of *building* new (cognitive and metacognitive) knowledge and abilities, and as a process of *revision* of already acquired knowledge, and of *organization* of a new framework in which old and new knowledge must be compared and integrated. These processes are strictly connected, and require the capability to constructively handle conflicts that may arise when passing from the old knowledge system to the new one.

Based on our experience, the novice may have to face conflicts concerning abilities and habits which involve precise aspects of LP and can be strengthened by the actual style of teaching/ learning programming.

In the model of LP we are illustrating, cognitive apprenticeship is conceived as the natural scenario in which cognitive and epistemic conflicts should be monitored by experts, with the aim that novices acquire the main cognitive ingredients of LP; this implies that suitable teaching methodologies are adopted, so that methodological conflicts can be recognized by the expert and avoided.

In Sect. 1, we single out the intellectual abilities involved in LP, considering them as ingredients of LP from a conceptual point of view; cognitive conflicts in LP are presented in Sect. 2; in Sect. 3 we focus our attention on methodological aspects concerning recognition and management of conflicts.

1. Main Cognitive Ingredients of Learning Programming

The main cognitive ingredients in LP, at least those we are mainly interested in, are summarized below; the dynamics of their working in LP processes will be described.

1.1 PL as a Reading and Writing Activity

A first ingredient in programming is the competence in reading/writing programs. Reading also means understanding, analyzing and evaluating an existing program; writing means designing, implementing, testing, debugging and refining a program. Both abilities may have different levels and aims; they also have an important unifying aspect, in that in both cases it is necessary to *interpret* a problem by means of the syntax and semantics of the employed language.

Reading a program properly means understanding its algorithm and its coding in a specific language; this not only entails a syntactic knowledge of the language, but also its semantic mastery and a good acquaintance with the field of the problem. The process of understanding a program is developed through successive steps. Different parts of the algorithm can be focused through a complex sequence of cooperating moves which entails, on one side, the use of one's knowledge of the programming language, to associate each syntactic expression with its corresponding meaning in the program, and, on the other side, an inferential activity on schemes, or hierarchies of schemes, to match each expression with its operation. Hence, the interpretation is constantly mediated by the student's knowledge of the problem domain and by the quality and number of programming schemes he knows (see Sect. 1.2).

The reading activity requires a continuous and flexible interaction with the text of the program, by constructing anticipations which need to be actualized and verified. Interpretation strategies applied by the novice are usually different in relation both to the competence level that he attained in programming and to the situation where the comprehension is required (i.e., interpreting a program whose aim is known or nor known; interpreting a program which is certainly correct or possibly incorrect; interpreting a program with or without comments).

Analysing the different performances of experts and novices reading a program, Détienne [15] observes that experts know and use programming plans to understand and also to construct programs, whilst novices base their comprehension process on much more limited schemes. Moreover, she observes that experts are able to construct abstract representations of the program aims, while novices usually realize more concrete representations of its operation.

Also writing a program can be considered an interpretation activity. In this case, it is necessary to interpret the problem using the programming language as a tool for thought and action. A program can be viewed as an *interpreter* of a problem and its solution. As in reading activity, also in writing the competence of a subject is in relation to the quality and number of programming schemes that he has developed and is able to suitably apply as efficient programming moves (see Sect. 1.2). Writing a program requires, in general, a nontrivial ability to plan, which implies the use of anticipating thought aimed at determining a hierarchy of goals related to the problem representation that the subject constructs dynamically. The student can verify his anticipations when testing and debugging his program.

Reading and writing are complementary activities in learning programming; both aim at the interpretation of a problem by means of a programming language, each with its specific characteristics. When reading, the interpretation is based on information deduced from the text and on inferences on them according to the programming schemes of the subject; when writing, the interpretation is based on the construction of a suitable problem representation by means of the actualization of his programming schemes.

1.2 From "Statements" to "Plans"

In our analysis of LP processes, we distinguish four kinds of "working objects" for the novice: statements and control structures, programming schemes, programming moves, programming plans.

The simplest ones are single *statements* and *control structures* of the language, with their own syntax and semantics corresponding to their operative meaning.

For novices, these are the new elementary operations to build programs. In most cases, the spontaneous approach to the solution of a problem consists of a stepwise translation of the strategy developed in the more familiar environment. In these cases, novices are often not aware of having built a programming plan, as a result of repeated adjustments of such a strategy to the operative rules of the language.

Programming schemes are organized systems of operative rules. They have a certain degree of functionality, their own syntax and inner semantics. They maintain a static character and their semantics is embedded into the working of the device. The semantics of a scheme can be described in terms of actions performed by the computer, or of the sequence of internal execution states. Usually, there is a strict connection between the novice awareness of device working and the amount of programming schemes he masters.

To build a good programming plan for solving a problem (or understanding a program), it is necessary, but not sufficient, to have adequate programming schemes and to be able to use them in a relevant manner. To do this, programming schemes must be organized in (or interpreted as) *programming moves*, with respect to a goal, which is regarded (or anticipated by hypothetical reasoning) as a relevant point in the solution of the problem. Programming schemes are the main constituents of programming moves: the difference between them is mainly qualitative. A move can be made even by a single scheme, but it is conceived in a dynamic process; it is connected with other moves in a first nutshell of a plan, even if this is not yet organized at global level (terminology is from chess, where the playing move is how one plans to move to achieve some goal). We passe to moves when we use schemes as tools for anticipating, i.e., for building (or interpreting) partial solutions to a problem; in other words, while scheme semantics is in relation to device working (inner semantics), move semantics is in relation to the problem (outer semantics).

A *programming plan* is the global organization of moves, efficiently and effectively joined to solve the posed problem. A plan is built by carrying out programming moves; this may happen: (i) by analogy with an already known problem in its own domain; (ii) by analogy with an already known problem in the new programming environment; (iii) by elaborating some hypotheses with respect to an unknown situation.

In case (i), the used programming moves are deeply related to double contextualization and may stress cognitive and epistemic conflicts (Sect. 2). In case (ii), difficulties are typically concerned with interfacing variables [9]. In case (iii), more complex cognitive processes are involved, since different types of hypotheses must be formulated: a) heuristic hypotheses, while exploring the problem; b) interpretative hypotheses, while exploring the scheme-goal relevance; c) anticipating hypotheses, while searching for moves relevant to the goals. It is the mainly metacognitive mastery of all these abilities that characterizes the difference between novice and expert in planning.

1.3 Double Contextualization

Cognitive processes involved in solving programming problems are doubly bounded. From one side, they are linked to the logic-formal context, peculiar to the envisaged language. Also computing system constraints are looked at by novice as language constraints, through which he will obtain the desired performance from the computer. From the other side, he also will consider the special context, i.e., the problem domain where he habitually treats that particular problem.

Generally, each environment change (e.g., from paper and pencil to computer, or from one language to another) implies a double contextualization. A priori, double contextualization can have negative effects: the difficulty in shifting from one context to another may reduce intellectual efforts in solving the problem to a crude carrying over or translation of operations, instructions, structures, without any cognitive enrichment. The difficulty arises from the "einstellung effect" [19], which is the situation in which someone applies a less-than-optimal procedure to a new problem because that procedure is already known. In practice, it is the rigidity effect that emerges since the subject has effectively solved problems of a certain type through a specific procedure. This attitude is related to the cognitive conflict "performing versus designing" and "syntax versus semantics", which will be illustrated below (Sect. 2).

However, double contextualization may also have positive effects, since it helps in saving one's thought and is the conceptual basis for many positive processes, rooted in the parallel acquisition of syntactic and semantic knowledge: e.g., the so called "stepwise incremental learning approach" [3, 23], or the "spiral approach" [32]. Positive effects of double contextualization are related to the expert's ability in making the novice aware of it.

1.4 Learning to Program is Learning by Problem Solving

The problem solving is an intrinsic ingredient of programming activity, though some programmers, especially experts, can become unaware of it.

We distinguish a task from a problem in LP: following Hoc [17], a *task* is a goal together with a set of conditions to achieve it; a problem is a representation of a task a subject evokes or elaborates, that cannot yet trigger an acceptable procedure to reach the goal (i.e., a procedure which is in conformity with the prescribed conditions). For instance, to produce a program for a familiar task can be a problem for the novice.

Obviously programming can imply the resolution of an applicative problem and at the same time of a programming problem. This can cause a tension between processes and representations related to problem solving in the application field and those related to the use of a programming language.

Using the Representation and Processing System (RPS) architecture to describe learning mechanisms [17], it is easy to point out a major difference between the usual PS and the PS in LP: in the latter, the solver elaborates a procedure associated with the device he is becoming acquainted with. So he must adapt or abandon his previous procedural and declarative knowledge related to a certain field of problems for a new one, according to the characteristics of the new environment.

Here are the roots of all cognitive conflicts in LP (Sect. 2); however, it is worth pointing out that not all problem solving processes in LP entail real cognitive and epistemic conflicts.

The teacher must take charge of the problem of understanding where there is continuity or not in the problem solving process when passing from a familiar environment to a new one.

As we will see later (Sect. 3), a careful management by the teacher of the problem solving activity can foster the development of programming competencies and can help a novice to become aware of his misconceptions about device logic, and of the relationship between syntax and semantics in programming.

2. Cognitive Conflicts in Learning Programming

In this section we discuss some of the main cognitive conflicts in LP; most of them correspond to the cognitive ingredients discussed in Sect.1. Our interest here is in how they intervene in the dynamic of learning programming processes. Of course, we do not think that our list of conflicts is exhaustive, but it does suggest a way of modelling learning processes in LP.

Generally speaking, the reason for most conflicts in LP rests on the dramatic difference between programming environment as a knowledge domain and other scientific knowledge domains (i.e., mathematics, physics,...). Rogalski and Samurçay in [29] pointed out its main features: (i) there is no everyday intellectual activity that can form the basis for spontaneous constructions of mental models for programming concepts; (ii) the physical machine is not cognitively transparent.

2.1 Performing Versus Designing

The conflict, rooted in double-contextualization (Sect. 1.3), concerns the resolution approach that the novice activates to face and solve a problem. This conflict emerges when the novice must get away from natural language or another familiar one to express himself in a new artificial language, in which it is not possible to translate in a one-to-one fashion activities and operations performed differently. The problem of non-correspondence between the two processes consists both of the fact that questions must be asked in a different way (*procedural unbalance*), and in the necessity to recognize and overcome logical conflicts between computer environment and pen-and-paper or between different computer environments (*relational unbalance*). The latter is the most difficult .

This is a polarity widely faced in the literature; in our opinion, it makes sense to speak of a conflict in that this term allows us to catch a typical aspect of programming thinking, that is a sudden transition from simple computational attempts to the synthesis of the whole in a procedure or program. This is a delicate transition that poses complex didactical problems. In fact, on one side, suitable performing exercices seem necessary (but not sufficient) for the transition to designing, on the other side the performing activity can hinder the development of designing competencies. This fact poses delicate problems in the development of didactical plans in order to transform the *performing–designing* conflict into a fruitful relationship that can emphasize its complementarity.

In order to design the solution of a problem using the computer, the novice must overcome this conflict, on the one hand by conceptually and effectively separating its two aspects (designing and performing), on the other hand, by using both. In fact, he must express hypotheses and make choices to solve the problem, but he must also identify himself with the working modality of the device, to verify such hypotheses and choices.

Not always novices are able to make this transition. At opposite extremes, we find those who keep using a performing approach based on trial-and-error methods, and those who, at a higher cognitive level, make a global plan and/or revision, looking at the program as a whole from outside. The former ones are essentially executors: they simulate computer behaviour and only consider whether the whole program does the right things to solve the problem. The latter ones master the double contextualization and, in fact, they focus their attention not only on the program's correctness, but also on their own strategy validity, even if not yet translated into a program: they do not instantiate variables, but check strategy as external observers, looking at the verbal description of the process.

2.2 Syntax Versus Semantics

This conflict is mainly rooted in double-contextualization; it appears in the contrast between syntactic aspects of the programming language and the processes by which one solves a problem, using his inner and ordinary language. The translation of such processes into a programming language may be difficult insofar one must change deeply the processes' structure, because of the syntactic constraints of the formal language. Moreover, even if a novice knows how to make a precise translation of each single step of his solution process into a single sentence, this may not be the case when the whole stream of thought which has ruled the process of solution must be translated into a sequence of sentences, according to the syntactic constraints of the programming language.

We think appropriate to speak of syntax versus semantics as a conflict when learning a programming language, in that often the student is not able to operate recognizing that the two aspects are complementary as concerns reading/writing programs; he has the tendency to concentrate his attention on syntactic aspects and to transfer the semantics of a familiar environment (natural language, or a better known artificial one) to the new one, without being aware of semantic differences and analogies between the two environments.

The inability of the computer to interpret the student's intentions, sometimes expressed by means of meaningless (for the student) syntactic errors (such as a "," instead of a ";", a pair "begin...end" substituted by an indentation, etc), and the need to overcome this rigidity of the computer in order to realize executable programs, strongly moves the novice's attention from the semantic of the problem to the syntax of its implementation, and in particular to the syntax of a single program line. This attention completely concentrated on the syntax assumes for the student a value much bigger than it really has as a tool to make a program executable.

The fact that he is not familiar with the use of, and metalinguistic reflexion on, some complex structures of natural language (e.g., "*do* A and then *repeat* A *until* condition", "*repeat* A *until* condition", "*while* condition *do* B", "*if* condition *then* ...") and of the different meanings of a same linguistic connective (e.g. *until*, *while*, *if*) in different context, makes it very difficult to accept the attribution of a single conventional semantic to those structures which appear to the novice as a translation, according to purely syntactical rules, of structures of the natural language of a more familiar artificial one. In fact, the natural tendency of the novice is to associate to a structure of the programming language a meaning that is familiar to him from another environment. For instance, it is not easy for the novice dissociate the *while* (or, in some cases, the *until*) from their "natural" meaning of temporal continuity to discretize them; analogously, it is not easy for the novice to assign to the structure *repeat* ... *until* , the meaning of "do A and then repeat A until ..." in natural language.

2.3 Epistemic Conflicts

These are always cognitive conflicts, arising from epistemic issues, in particular between algebra and programming languages, and between real machine and internal states machine.

This is a crucial point for research, as it is the core of major conflicts (including of cognitive nature): for instance, one of the more dramatic conflicts to study is the one between algebraic variables in mathematics and variables in computer environments. Another conflict arises from the dichotomy discrete vs. continuous; a third one is between the usual mathematical logic and the logic incorporated in some control structures.

As many researchers have observed [13, 29, 30], the notion of the machine in computer environments is far from being transparent. It differs greatly from the notion of everyday life machines. In fact, A.Turing invented programming machines exploiting the new concept of *internal states:* the comparison between a sausage machine and a computer shows that both are devices with an input and an output, but the latter can only be described completely by using the very abstract notion of internal states. It is a very hard notion to assimilate, as many researches have proved. In fact, the knowledge used by an expert in programming extends beyond operating rules and involves the representation of the whole system (editor, operating system, I/O devices, etc.), namely what du Boulay has termed the notional machine [29].

A shifting of conceptions is required: from an approach based on "how to do it" to an approach based on "how to have it done" [14]; from the use of RPS constructed by mimicking man's or the sausage-machine's processes to the conceptualization of the notional machine. It is important to observe that mechanistic and anthropomorphic misconceptions may reinforce each other: for instance, the representation of what the computer knows (possible anthropomorphic misconceptions) is checked looking at the effect of single instructions and not considering how the inner structure of the information is elaborated (typical mechanistic conception).

Generally, novices who recognize the computer inner logic are not merely step by step translators of programs from one environment to another. They appear to be more flexible both in writing and in verifying–modifying their original program; moreover, their changes are made according to a new plan, not as a result of repeated trials.

3. Recognition and Management of Conflicts in a Cognitive Apprenticeship for Learning Programming

In learning programming, especially in school environments, it is methodologically relevant to distinguish between "cognitive apprenticeship" and "practical apprenticeship". It is also very important to single out the delicate interplay between teacher and student in order to make cognitive the apprenticeship process of the novice. Since it is not possible to separate them [12], we will discuss them together.

Practical apprenticeship is characterized by a specific learning method based on three phases, or developing moments: (i) observation, (ii) scaffolding, (iii) increasingly independent practice. Its main feature is imitative nature, aimed at reproducing, possibly with some changes, actions from a model usually given by an expert; a typical practical apprenticeship is learning in artisan workshops (such as barber, plumber, whitewasher, etc.).

Cognitive apprenticeship is not only aimed at practical abilities and processes, physically realized, but also (and mainly) at abilities and processes of a cognitive and metacognitive nature. Hence, the expert can model and scaffold the novice, and the novice can observe the expert, correct and refine his own practice looking carefully at the expert's *externalization* of his relevant internal cognitive processes and methods. The novice must observe, analyze and evaluate not only inner cognitive processes, which the expert externalizes, but he must also compare and contrast them with his own intellectual performance. A sort of continuous self-evaluation is required; the point is that the novice can activate it, only if his distance from expert performances is not too far; if not, this may cause stumbling blocks in cognitive apprenticeship.

The art of making *cognitive* the *apprenticeship* mainly consists in the creation of a balanced dialectic between scaffolding and challenging the knowledge of the novices, handling the conflicts which can emerge. The expert must clarify which are the points where there is contradiction between old and new knowledge and must propose problems to novices, which allow them to recognize conflicts, as a first step towards overcoming them. Apprenticeship becomes really cognitive in that the expert helps novices in modifying, re-organizing and developing their knowledge.

Hence, the interaction between expert and novices in cognitive apprenticeship is a very delicate point. There is always the risk that the novice misunderstands the expert's performance and/or viceversa; moreover, even when the expert externalizes his inner processes, it is not sure at all that novices interpret the expert's words in the right way, though both may be convinced of the contrary. The result is that the apprenticeship may be no longer cognitive and conflicts may not be overcome.

Our results [1, 2, 4, 5, 9, 10, 11, 20, 21, 22, 24, 25] confirm the importance of developing *intermediate supports,* able to help the transition from one problem solving environment to another. Intermediate supports must be identified in order to develop a flexible and rich *anticipating thought,* which seems to be necessary both for the mastery of the cognitive ingredients we mention in Sect. 1 and for recognizing and overcoming the cognitive conflicts we introduced in Sect. 2.

Sometimes, anticipating thought can operate on the basis of external representations, such as graphical outputs, diagrams, tables and so on, possibly, but not always, constructed by novices using the computer. Sometimes, anticipating thought can operate on the basis of internal dynamic representations, essentially generated and managed by hypothetical reasoning made in a mental space, which has spatial and temporal features [5, 6].

We consider these external and internal representations as intermediate supports. The real problem is how to make novices able to correctly develop and use these intermediate supports, both under the guidance of the expert and autonomously. This involves some important didactical implications as the expert has to solve two methodological problems which are closely connected to each other. On the one hand, the expert must analyze the nature and specific characteristic of various representations used in didactical practice, in order to understand if they are a useful means on which the subject's thinking can rely to overcome the cognitive conflicts; on the other hand, he must single out ways and forms of novice–expert interplay, able to favour the development of cognitive and metacognitive processes which characterize LP as a cognitive apprenticeship.

As regards the *external representation,* in our research we have observed that useful representations allow the novice to put into action a lot of mental experiments able of developing a closer link between action on data and variables of the problem, and device operation underlying the used language. For example, in many occasions, we have verified the usefulness of tables as a mediator for recognizing and overcoming many cognitive conflicts described in the previous section. In fact, tables can provoke anticipations: it becomes an ideal object and a real planning tool, in the sense that it is the starting point for experiments which soon become purely mental, induce hypothetical reasoning and validations, backward from the mental space to the table and forward again to new mental experiments; generally, each validation is made using the computer. Research work by Malara and her group [22], studied the role of tables in computer environments. For example, in a study in which pupils were asked to analyse, and "teach" to the computer, the method used by Russian farmers for calculating the product of two numbers, the table was used as a working tool to design the model of an algorithm working with the operating logic of the computer (or, rather, what they took to be its operating logic). As is well known, the product is found as follows: the first number is divided by two and its whole quotient is written beneath it; the second number is doubled and written beneath it; this procedure is repeated until the first number becomes 1; at this point the required product is given by the sum of the numbers in the second column that correspond to the odd numbers in the first column.

Analysis of the pupils' protocols, which illustrate each pupil's personalized approach to table use, highlights both the personal requirements of the pupils (as can be seen in the different ways the tables were organised) and their objective difficulties in transferring this algorithm to the computer. In order to demonstrate the mental processes followed by the pupils, Fig. 1 contains some of their protocols, showing prototype tables they produced. In protocols a) and b) the halving and doubling procedures are indicated to show how the initial values of the two numbers are progressively modified. This indication is achieved by leaving an appropriate space and with the use of a symbol, an arrow, as a general indicator of the operations. The arrow is an efficient way of emphasizing the progressive change in values of the variables, which somehow animates the intrinsic static nature of the tables, and in particular reveals the table to be a personal instrument of the pupil. Unlike the others, protocol c) contains a column of remainders. This pupil considered the need to tell the computer when a number is even or odd, but above all he attempted to find a mean to do it that was suitable for the computer. Normally, to distinguish between an odd and an even number, one checks the parity of the last digit; this is, however, a complicated procedure to transfer to the computer. This pupil realised it and overcame the difficulty by using the remainder function, thereby enabling them to insert the check in the table, or, more precisely, to insert the result of the check. Many others were not able to circumvent this obstacle and it is here that the differences between human modes of thought and those of the computer are evident. Protocol d) is representative of many pupils' reactions to another obstacle encountered in transferring this algorithm to the computer: how to tell the computer to perform the sum of the selected values to obtain the product. Once again we see the difference in procedure when using pencil and paper, where firstly the halving and doubling operation are carried out and secondly the sum of the selected values is carried out, and the procedure with the computer, where it is convenient to perform these operations simultaneously. Nearly all pupils, even though they included in their tables a column of values to be summed, did not realise that in this case not only it was necessary to control a number of different variables simultaneously, but also to introduce an accumulator variable. In fact, this is one of the difficulties inherent in this type of problem.

Tables are good tools for thinking and help novices in transferring algorithms to the computer. In fact, their use facilitates novices in overcoming the designing/performing conflict, namely tables spur a double outlook: from one side imagining machine actions stepwise (inner outlook), from the other grasping procedure globally, in order to forecast effects and fill in possible gaps (outer outlook). It is a typical representation and elaboration system [17], both for analyzing/planning procedures and for reflecting on self/others thinking processes. As Malara points out [22], table effectiveness depends strongly on the conditions in which it is used.

For example, its productiveness is spurred by allowing it to be used in an open and autonomous way; moreover, it is essential that verbal processing, possibly aloud, always supports its use: it is in this fashion that it can stimulate hypothetical thinking in novices.

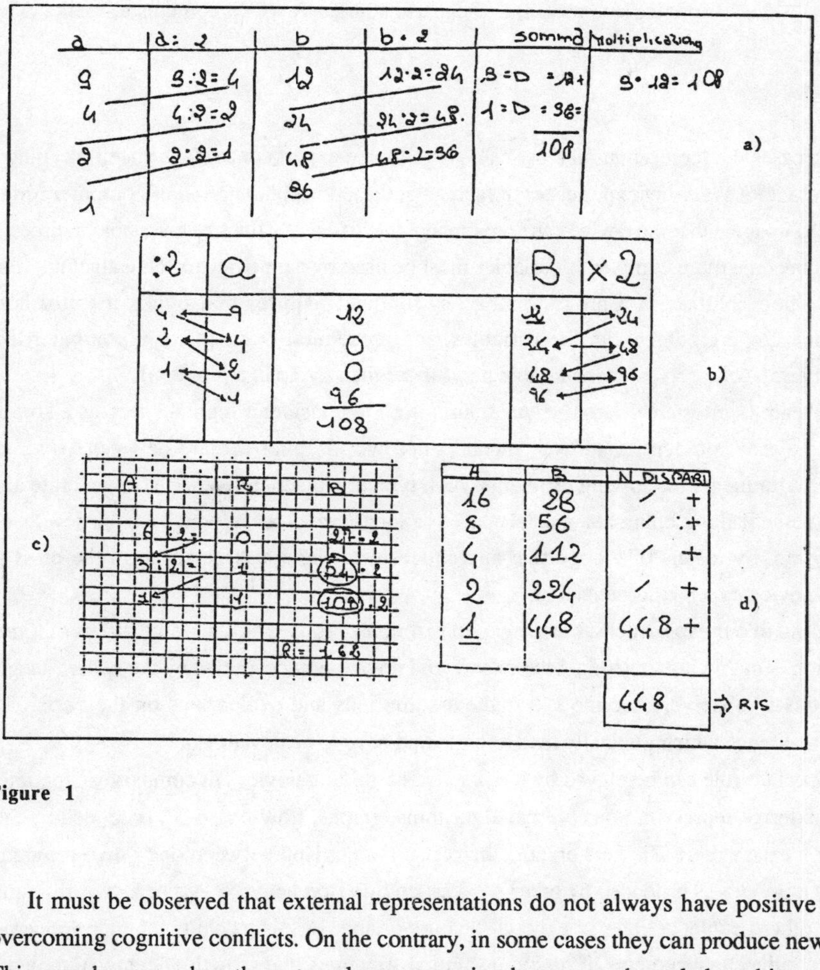

Figure 1

It must be observed that external representations do not always have positive effects on overcoming cognitive conflicts. On the contrary, in some cases they can produce new conflicts. This may happen when the external representation becomes a knowledge object, namely an external tool where knowledge is stored.

A typical example is given by "boxes" used by novices as models of variables in computer environments: such a picture may cause misconceptions and misunderstanding in the novice, while monitoring the programming schemes needed to build an accumulator-variable. Two typical situations of novice's ways of reasoning are illustrated in Figure 2:

(novice's comment) "There are 3 memories"

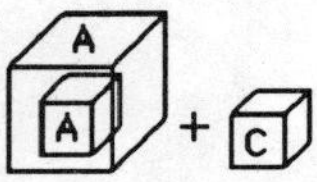

(novice's comment) "I can use a larger A which contains a smaller A"

Figure 2

In such cases the representation ("boxes") given by the expert contrasts the deep meaning it has in the novice's everyday experience: in fact, an anthropomorphic notion of computer forces the novice to imagine that the device can "remember" the different values of a variable in time.

Things become more complex if variables must be used by the novice to solve algebraic-like problems. Their solution in a programming environment requires that pupils monitor both systemic aspects, e.g., algebraic like variables, and procedural ones [1], e.g. computer-like variables [9,35], for errors when a variable plays more than a role in a problem).

As regards *internal dynamic representations,* we consider a mental space as a sort of imagined real environment, a sort of "mental microworld" intermediate between a pair of different environments for solving problems. As a typical metacognitive skill, to generate and manage hypothetical reasoning in a mental space is a long-term process, which can be developed in the long run by means of a cognitive apprenticeship, where a large space in the class is devoted to novice-expert externalizations.

According to our experiences, novice-expert externalizations should involve different forms of interaction, suitably integrated: novice-expert and novice-novice guided by the expert. In any case, abilities to observe, describe and make assumptions and evaluations on the basis of a common experience which gradually tend to be shared have to be developed.

An important role can be played by the practice of guiding novices in comparing programs and other external representations (verbal algorithms, graphs, flow-charts,...) produced by the novices or by the expert [7]. This practice involves: comparison between one's own program and one or more others produced by other novices; comparison between two or more programs written by other people, novices or experts. The importance of this teaching practice concerns its effects on: the enhancements of problem solution strategies; the growth of personal thought levels for understanding and constructing programs; the stimulation for many, even below-average, novices to produce hypotheses ("Should I do as he says..."). This teaching method allows novices to make the first steps towards overcoming cognitive conflicts, with particular respect to performing versus designing and syntax versus semantics. This teaching practice involves all the ingredients of LP already discussed. As a limitation of the positive effects of this teaching practice, we observe that, in our experience, it appears that only those novices who autonomously at least created a small solution strategy and translated it into a first approximate program are then able to examine the reasoning of other people. Also in these cases, at times, it appears that novices are only able to penetrate into reasonings which are similar to their own, while other times they are able to understand also different ones, though often losing the thread of thought and including their own way of thinking in some passages [7].

Another important role in learning programming is played by specific moments for the interaction between the expert and novices. This interaction concerns the formulation, the specification and subsequently the test of hypotheses inherent to interpreting the behavior of an analysed system (a program, a specialised software) and, above all, of anticipative hypotheses concerning the aptest procedure easily executed by the system, or its most appropriate use to perform the chosen solution procedure [7].

Classroom activities linked to requests for interpretative hypotheses about incorrect programs before, while and after their execution and to requests for anticipating hypotheses about the effectiveness of programs (written by other people) before their execution, are other examples of this form of social interaction in the production and handling of hypotheses.

References

1. Arzarello F. [1992] Algebraic problem solving. In: J.P. Ponte, J.F.Matos, J.M. Matos, D. Fernandes (eds.) Mathematical problem solving and new information technologies. NATO ASI Series F, Vol. 89. Berlin: Springer-Verlag
2. Arzarello F. [1991] Procedural and relational aspects of algebraic thinking. Proceedings of the 15th PME Conference, Vol.1, pp. 80–87
3. Ausubel D.P. [1968] Educational psychology: a cognitive approach. New York: Holt, Rinehart & Winston
4. Barbero R. [1991] Utilizzo dei linguaggi di programmazione nella scuola media: potenzialità didattiche e conflitti cognitivi. To appear in: L'insegnamento delle Matematiche e delle Scienze integrate
5. Boero P., Ferrari P.L., Lemut E., Martinelli A.M. [1989a] Lo spazio-tempo delle ipotesi nel Problem Solving. Publ. IMA-CNR n.19/89, Genova, Italy
6. Boero P., Chiappini G., Lemut E., Martinelli A.M. [1989b] Sul ragionamento ipotetico nell'approccio alla risoluzione di problemi con il calcolatore. Publ. IMA-CNR n.21/89, Genova, Italy.
7. Boero P., Carlucci A., Chiappini G., Ferrero E., Lemut E. [1991] Analysis of classroom experiences on automatic processes as cultural "objects" suitable to force pupils' cognitive development. Fourth International Conference on Children in an Information Age. Albena, Bulgaria (to appear)
8. Chi M.T.C., Glaser R., Rees E. [1982] Expertise in problem solving. In: R.J. Sternberg (ed.) Advances in the psychology of human intelligence, Vol. 1, pp. 7–76 London: Lawrence Erlbaum
9. Chiappini G.P. [1990] Acquisizione del concetto di variabile in campo matematico e informatico. Publ. IMA -CNR n.8/90, Genova, Italy
10. Chiappini G.P., Lemut E., Parenti L. [1991a] Analysis of the behaviour of mathematics teachers in problem solving situations with the computer. Proceedings of the 15th PME Conference, Assisi, Italy, pp. 207-214
11. Chiappini G.P., Lemut E. [1991b] Construction and interpretation of algebraic models, Proceedings of the 15th PME Conference, Assisi, Italy, pp. 199-206
12. Collins A., Brown J.S., Newman S.E. [1989] Cognitive apprenticeship: teaching the crafts of reading, writing and mathematics. In: L.B. Resnik (ed.) Knowing, learning and instruction, pp. 453–494. Hillsdale, NJ: Lawrence Erlbaum
13. Dagdilelis V. [1992] The "private" relation of the student with structured programming and verification. This volume

14. Duchateau C. [1992] From "doing it..." to "have it done by...": the heart of programming. some didactical thoughts. Preproceedings NATO ARW Cognitive Models and Intelligent Environments for Learning Programming, S.Margherita Ligure, Genova, Italy, 1992
15. Detienne F. [1989] Une revue des études psychologiques sur la comprénsion des programmes informatiques. Tecnique et Science Informatique 8(1), 5–20
16. Hillel J. [1990] Functions through the lens of computer algebra systems. Conference on the Learning and Teaching of the Concept Function, Purdue University, October 26-28
17. Hoc J.M., Nguyen-Xuan A. [1990] Language semantics, mental models and analogy. In: Hoc J.M., Green T.R.G., Samurçay R., Gilmore D.J. (eds.) Psychology of programming, pp. 139–156. London: Academic Press
18. Kieran C. [1989] A perspective on algebraic thinking. Actes de la 13e Conference Internationale PME, Paris, Vol.2, pp. 163–171
19. Luchins A.S. [1942] Mechanisation in problem solving. Psychological Monographies 54(248)
20. Lemut E., Ferrero E. [1988] Of the linguistic prerequisites of computing literacy. In: F. Lovis, E.D. Tagg (eds.) Computers in Education. IFIP 88, pp. 139-144. Amsterdam: Elsevier (North-Holland)
21. Lemut E., Chiappini G.P., Martinelli A.M. [1990] On the problem solving with the computer: analysis of difficulties and requirements. In: McDougall A., Dowling C. (eds.) Computers in education. IFIP 90, 409–414. Amsterdam: Elsevier (North-Holland)
22. Malara N.A., Garuti R. [1991] The table as a working tool for pupils and as a means for monitoring their thought processes in problems involving the transfer of algorithms to the computer. Proceedings of the 15th PME Conference, Vol.2, Assisi, Italy, pp. 373–380
23. Merrienboer J.J., Krammer H.P.M. [1987] Instructional strategies and tactics for the design of introductory computer programming courses in high school. Instructional Science 16, 251–285
24. Pellegrino C., Garuti R. [1989] Dall'avvio alla ricorsività ai cambiamenti di base nei sistemi di numerazione attraverso la simulazione in LOGO del contachilometri. La Matematica e la sua Didattica, IV, n.1, 1990, 19–30
25. Pellegrino C., Malara N. [1991] LOGO in the teaching of mathematics: problems, experiences and requests. In: E.Calabrese (ed.) Proc. third European Logo Conference
26. Pellerey M. [1986a] L'io della mente. Riflessioni si intelligenza artificiale, intelligenza naturale e dintorni. Orientamenti pedagogici, n.33, pp. 7–20
27. Pellerey M. [1986b] Informatica. Fondamenti culturali e tecnologici. Torino: SEI
28. Pellerey M. [1991] Processi cognitivi ed esperienze di programmazione. Proc. Didamatica '91, Cesena, Italy
29. Rogalski J., Samurçay R. [1990] Acquisition of Programming Knowledge and Skills. In: Hoc J.M., Green T.R.G., Samurçay R., Gilmore D.J. (eds.) Psychology of programming, pp. 157–174. London: Academic Press
30. Rogalski J., Samurçay R. [1992] Theoretical framework to analyse adequacy between cognitive models and environments for learning programming. This volume
31. Rouchier A. [1987] L'ecriture et l'interpretation des procedures récursives en LOGO. Psychologie Française, tome 32-4, 281–285
32. Schneiderman B. [1977] Teaching programming: a spiral approach to syntax and semantics. Computers and Education 1, 193–197
33. Schoenfeld [1985] Problem solving. London: Academic Press
34. Soloway E. [1982] Does computer programming enhance problem solving ability? Some positive evidence on algebra word problems. In: Computer Literacy, Academic Press, pp. 171-185
35. Spohrer, J.C., Soloway, E., Pope, E. [1985] A goal-plan analysis of buggy Pascal programs. Human-Computer Interaction 1, 163–207
36. Vergnaud G. [1990] La Théorie des Champs Conceptuels, Recherches en Didactique des Mathematiques 10(23), 133–170
37. Vygotsky L.S. [1978] Mind in society: the development of higher psychological processes. Cambridge MA: Harvard University Press

List of Contributors

List of Participants

NATO Advanced Research Workshop
Cognitive Models and Intelligent Environments for Learning Programming
S.Margherita, Genova, Italy, March 17-21, 1992

Ferdinando **Arzarello**
Dipartimento di Matematica, Università di Torino, Via Carlo Alberto 10, I-10123 Torino, Italy; tel. x-39-11-538855, fax: 534497, e-mail: arzarello@unimat.to.cnr.it.

Nicolas **Balacheff**
Laboiratoire IMAG - LSDD, BP53X, F-38041 Grenoble Cedex, France; e-mail: balacheff@imag.fr.

Rosa Maria **Bottino**
Istituto per la Matemetica Applicata del C.N.R, Via L.B. Alberti 4, I-16132 Genova GE, Italy; tel. x-39-10-515510/517639; fax: 517801; e-mail: bottino@image.ge.cnr.it

Benedict **du Boulay**
School of Cognitive and Computing Sciences, University of Sussex, Brighton BN1 9QH, U.K.; tel. x-44-273-678324, fax: 678188; e-mail: bend@uk.ac.susx.cogs.

Peter L. **Brusilovsky**
International Center for Scientific and Technical Information, Kuusinen str. 21b, Moscow 125252, Russia; fax: x-7-95-943-0089; e-mail: plb@plb.icsti.su.

Giampaolo **Chiappini**
Istituto per la Matemetica Applicata del C.N.R, Via L.B. Alberti 4, I-16132 Genova GE, Italy; tel. x-39-10-515510/517639; fax: 517801; e-mail: chiappini@image.ge.cnr.it

Elmar **Cohors-Fresenborg**
Fachbereich Mathematik/Informatik, Universität Osnabrück, Postfach 4469, W-4500 Osnabrück, Germany; tel x-49- 541- 9692514; fax: 9692770; e-mail: cohors@dosuni1.

Albert T. **Corbett**
Psychology Department, Carnegie-Mellon University, Pittsburgh, PA 15213, U.S.A.; tel x-1-412-268-2815; e-mail: corbett@psy.cmu.edu.

Martin B. **Curry**
University of York, Heslington, York YO1 5DD, U.K.; e-mail: mbci@uk.ac.york.

Walter **Daelemans**
Institute for Language Technology and AI, Tilburg University, P.O. Box 90153, NL-5000 Le Tilburg, The Netherlands; tel. x-31-13-663070; fax: 663110; e-mail: walter@kub.nl.

Vassilios **Dagdilelis**
Laboratoire des Structures Discrètes et Didactiques, IMAG, BP.52X, F-38000 Grenoble, France; fax: X-49-621-14375.

Simon P. **Davies**
Department of Psychology, University of Nottingham, Nottingham NG7 2RD, U.K.; e-mail: spd@uk.ac.nottingham.psyc.

Françoise **Détienne**
Project of Ergonomics Psychology, INRIA, Domaine di Voluceau, Rocquencourt, BP 105, F-78153, Le Chesnay Cedex, France; tel. x-33-1-39635522; fax: 39635330; e-mail: detienne@psycho.inria.fr.

Giuliana **Dettori**
Istituto per la Matemetica Applicata del C.N.R, Via L.B. Alberti 4, I-16132 Genova GE, Italy; tel. x-39-10-515510/517639; fax: 517801; e-mail: dettori@image.ge.cnr.it

Charles **Duchâteau**
CeFIS, Faculté N-D. de la Paix, Rue de Bruxelles 61, B-5000 Namur, Belgiulm; tel. x-32-81-725060; e-mail: cduchateau@bnandps1.

Margherita **Fasano**
Dipartimento di Matematica, Via N. Sauro 85, I-85100 Potenza PZ, Italy; tel. x-39-971-474155; fax: 470763.

David **Gilmore**
Department of Psychology, University of Nottingham, Nottingham NG7 2RD, U.K.; tel.x-44-602-484848; fax: 590339; e-mail: dg@psyc.nott.ac.uk.

Victor **Kaptelinin**
Institute of General and Educational Psychology, 20 "V", Marx Ave., 103009 Moscow, Russia; tel x-7-95-2028876; e-mail:vic@plb.icsti.su.

Chronis **Kynigos**
Deptartment of Informatics, Faculty of Science, University of Athens, Panepistimiopolis, TYPA Buildings, GR-15771 Athens, Greece; tel. 7221855; e-mail: sip60@grathun1.

Lyuba J. **Lazarova**
Institute of Education, 125 Trakia Boulevard, bl.V, 1113 Sofia, Bulgaria; tel, fax: x-359-2-652488.

Enrica **Lemut**
Istituto per la Matematica Applicata del C.N.R., Via L.B. Alberti 4, I-16132 Genova, Italy. tel. x-39-10-515510/517639; fax: 517801; e-mail: lemut@image.ge.cnr.it

Laura Marie **Leventhal**
Computer Science Department, Bowling Green State University, Bowling Green, OH 43403, U.S.A.; fax: x-1-419-372-8061; e-mail: leventha@andy.bgsu.edu.

Nicolina **Malara**
Dipartimento di Matematica, Università di Modena, Via Campi 213/b, 41100 Modena, Italy; tel. x-39-59-364416; fax: 35713.

Gordon **McCalla**
Department of Computational Science, University of Saskatchewan, Saskatoon, Saskatchewan S7N 0W0, Canada; tel. x-1-306-966-4902; fax: 966-4884; e-mail: mccalla@sask.usask.ca.

Maria Teresa **Molfino**
Istituto per la Matemetica Applicata del C.N.R, Via L.B. Alberti 4, 16132 Genova GE, Italy; tel. x-39-10-515510/517639; fax: 517801; e-mail: molfino@image.ge.cnr.it

Barbee T. **Mynatt**
Computer Science Department, Bowling Green State University, Bowling Green, OH 43403, U.S.A.; tel. x-1-419-372-8061; e-mail: mynatt@opie.bgsu.edu.

Maurice **Naftalin**
Department of Computer Science, University of Stirling, Stirling FK9 4LA, Scotland, U.K.; e-mail: mpn@cs.stir.ac.uk.

Peter **Pirolli**
School of Education, University of California at Berkeley, Berkeley, CA 94720, U.S.A., and Xerox Palo Alto Research Center, 3333 Coyote Hill Road, Palo Alto, CA 94304, U.S.A.; tel. x-1-415-812-4483; fax: 812-4777; e-mail: pirolli@park.xerox.com.

João Pedro **da Ponte**
DEFCUL, Av. 24 de Julho 134-4, P-1300 Lisboa, Portugal;
fax: 1-604546, e-mail: ejp@fcvax1.fcl.rccn.pt.

Blaine A. **Price**
Human Cognition Research Laboratory, The Open University, Milton Keynes MK7 6AA, U.K.; e-mail: doc@dgp.toronto.edu.

Maria **Reggiani**
Department of Mathematics, University of Pavia, Strada Nuova 65, I-27100 Pavia, Italy; tel. x-39-382-387333.

Janine **Rogalski**
CNRS - Université Paris 8 - URA 1297, Equipe de Psychologie Cognitive Ergonomique, 2, Rue de la Liberté, F-93526 Saint-Denis Cedex 2, France;
tel. x-33-1-49406488; fax: 49406754; e-mail: upsc001@frors31 (earn/bitnet).

Warren **Sack**
131 Peyton Street, Santa Cruz, CA 95060, U.S.A.; e-mail: wsack@mcimail.com.

Renan **Samurçay**
CNRS - Université Paris 8 - URA 1297, Equipe de Psychologie Cognitive Ergonomique, 2, Rue de la Liberté, F-93526 Saint-Denis Cedex 2, France;
tel. x-33-1-49406488; fax: 49406754; e-mail: upsc001@frors31 (earn/bitnet).

Zahava **Scherz**
Department of Science Teaching, The Weizman Institute of Science, Rehovot 76100, Israel; fax: 972-8-466964; e-mail: ntscherz@weizmann.weizmann.ac.il.

Jean **Scholtz**
Computer Science Department, Portland State University, Portland, OR 97207-0751, U.S.A.; tel: x-1-503-725-4103; fax: 725-3211; e-mail: jean@cs.pdx.edu.

Francisco C. **Simplicio-Filho**
Department of Computing, Imperial College, 180 Queen's Gate, London SW7 2BZ, U.K.; e-mail: fcs@doc.ic.ac.uk.

Mark K. **Singley**
User Interface Institute, IBM T.J.Watson Research Center, Yorktown Heights, NY 10598, U.S.A.; e-mail: singley@warson.ibm.com.

John **Sumiga**
School of Computing and Information Technology, Wolverhampton Polytechnic, Wolverhampton, U.K.; tel. x-44-902-322206 (h); 889-271070 (w); fax: 889-271070; e-mail: jsumiga@uk.ac.wolves.a.

Rosamund **Sutherland**
Institute of Education, University of London, London, U.K.

Gyulane **Radnai Szendrei**
Teacher's Training Institute of Budapest, Budapest, Racoczi u. 23.VI.20, h-1191 Hungary, tel. 361-1779-046.

Oleg K. **Tikhomirov**
Psychological Faculty, University of Moscow, Marx Avenue 18, Moscow, 103009, Russia; tel. x-7-95-938-14-11.

Haruki **Ueno**
Department of Systems Engineering, Tokyo Denki University, Hatoyama, Saitama 350-03, Japan; tel. x-81-492-96-2911; fax: 965060; e-mail: ueno@k.dendai.ac.jp

Gerrit C. **van der Veer**
Department of Computer Science, Free University, De Boelelaan 1081 A, NL-1081 HV Amsterdam, The Netherlands, and Department of Ergonomics, University of Twente, Enschede, The Netherlands; tel. and fax: x-31-20-5485591; e-mail: gerrit@vdveer.cs.vu.nl.

Boris **Velichkovsky**
Department for Psychology and Engineering of Knowledge, Moscow State University, Moscow 103009, Russia; e-mail: bmv@chair.cogsci.msu.su.

M. Felisa **Verdejo**
Escuela Técnica Superior de Ingenieros Industriales, U.N.E.D., Ciudad Universitaria s/n, 28040 Madrid, Spain; tel. 3413986483; fax: 3415446344.

Gerhard **Weber**
Department of Psychology, University of Trier, W-5500 Trier, Germany; e-mail: weber@cogpsy.uni-trier.de.

Observers

Fulvia **Furinghetti**
Dipartimento di Matematica, Universià di Genova, Via L.B. Alberti 4, I-16132 Genova GE, Italy, tel. x-39-10-353 8707, fax: 353 8769.

Bruria **Haberman**
Department of Science Teaching, The Weizman Institute of Science, Rehovot 76100, Israel; fax: x-972-8-466964; e-mail: nthaber@weizmann.weizmann.ac.il.

Subject Index

Printing: Druckhaus Beltz, Hemsbach
Binding: Buchbinderei Schäffer, Grünstadt

NATO ASI Series F

Including Special Programmes on Sensory Systems for Robotic Control (ROB) and on Advanced Educational Technology (AET)

Vol. 1: Issues in Acoustic Signal - Image Processing and Recognition. Edited by C. H. Chen. VIII, 333 pages. 1983.

Vol. 2: Image Sequence Processing and Dynamic Scene Analysis. Edited by T. S. Huang. IX, 749 pages. 1983.

Vol. 3: Electronic Systems Effectiveness and Life Cycle Costing. Edited by J. K. Skwirzynski. XVII, 732 pages. 1983.

Vol. 4: Pictorial Data Analysis. Edited by R. M. Haralick. VIII, 468 pages. 1983.

Vol. 5: International Calibration Study of Traffic Conflict Techniques. Edited by E. Asmussen. VII, 229 pages. 1984.

Vol. 6: Information Technology and the Computer Network. Edited by K. G. Beauchamp. VIII, 271 pages. 1984.

Vol. 7: High-Speed Computation. Edited by J. S. Kowalik. IX, 441 pages. 1984.

Vol. 8: Program Transformation and Programming Environments. Report on a Workshop directed by F. L. Bauer and H. Remus. Edited by P. Pepper. XIV, 378 pages. 1984.

Vol. 9: Computer Aided Analysis and Optimization of Mechanical System Dynamics. Edited by E. J. Haug. XXII, 700 pages. 1984.

Vol. 10: Simulation and Model-Based Methodologies: An Integrative View. Edited by T. I. Ören, B. P. Zeigler, M. S. Elzas. XIII, 651 pages. 1984.

Vol. 11: Robotics and Artificial Intelligence. Edited by M. Brady, L. A. Gerhardt, H. F. Davidson. XVII, 693 pages. 1984.

Vol. 12: Combinatorial Algorithms on Words. Edited by A. Apostolico, Z. Galil. VIII, 361 pages. 1985.

Vol. 13: Logics and Models of Concurrent Systems. Edited by K. R. Apt. VIII, 498 pages. 1985.

Vol. 14: Control Flow and Data Flow: Concepts of Distributed Programming. Edited by M. Broy. VIII, 525 pages. 1985.

Vol. 15: Computational Mathematical Programming. Edited by K. Schittkowski. VIII, 451 pages. 1985.

Vol. 16: New Systems and Architectures for Automatic Speech Recognition and Synthesis. Edited by R. De Mori, C.Y. Suen. XIII, 630 pages. 1985.

Vol. 17: Fundamental Algorithms for Computer Graphics. Edited by R. A. Earnshaw. XVI, 1042 pages. 1985.

Vol. 18: Computer Architectures for Spatially Distributed Data. Edited by H. Freeman and G. G. Pieroni. VIII, 391 pages. 1985.

Vol. 19: Pictorial Information Systems in Medicine. Edited by K. H. Höhne. XII, 525 pages. 1986.

Vol. 20: Disordered Systems and Biological Organization. Edited by E. Bienenstock, F. Fogelman Soulié, G. Weisbuch. XXI, 405 pages.1986

NATO ASI Series F

Including Special Programmes on Sensory Systems for Robotic Control (ROB) and on Advanced Educational Technology (AET)

Vol. 21: Intelligent Decision Support in Process Environments. Edited by E. Hollnagel, G. Mancini, D. D. Woods. XV, 524 pages. 1986.

Vol. 22: Software System Design Methods. The Challenge of Advanced Computing Technology. Edited by J. K. Skwirzynski. XIII, 747 pages. 1986.

Vol. 23: Designing Computer-Based Learning Materials. Edited by H. Weinstock and A. Bork. IX, 285 pages. 1986.

Vol. 24: Database Machines. Modern Trends and Applications. Edited by A. K. Sood and A. H. Qureshi. VIII, 570 pages. 1986.

Vol. 25: Pyramidal Systems for Computer Vision. Edited by V. Cantoni and S. Levialdi. VIII, 392 pages. 1986. *(ROB)*

Vol. 26: Modelling and Analysis in Arms Control. Edited by R. Avenhaus, R. K. Huber and J. D. Kettelle. VIII, 488 pages. 1986.

Vol. 27: Computer Aided Optimal Design: Structural and Mechanical Systems. Edited by C. A. Mota Soares. XIII, 1029 pages. 1987.

Vol. 28: Distributed Operating Systems. Theory und Practice. Edited by Y. Paker, J.-P. Banatre and M. Bozyiğit. X, 379 pages. 1987.

Vol. 29: Languages for Sensor-Based Control in Robotics. Edited by U. Rembold and K. Hörmann. IX, 625 pages. 1987. *(ROB)*

Vol. 30: Pattern Recognition Theory and Applications. Edited by P. A. Devijver and J. Kittler. XI, 543 pages. 1987.

Vol. 31: Decision Support Systems: Theory and Application. Edited by C. W. Holsapple and A. B. Whinston. X, 500 pages. 1987.

Vol. 32: Information Systems: Failure Analysis. Edited by J. A. Wise and A. Debons. XV, 338 pages. 1987.

Vol. 33: Machine Intelligence and Knowledge Engineering for Robotic Applications. Edited by A. K. C. Wong and A. Pugh. XIV, 486 pages. 1987. *(ROB)*

Vol. 34: Modelling, Robustness and Sensitivity Reduction in Control Systems. Edited by R.F. Curtain. IX, 492 pages. 1987.

Vol. 35: Expert Judgment and Expert Systems. Edited by J. L. Mumpower, L. D. Phillips, O. Renn and V. R. R. Uppuluri. VIII, 361 pages. 1987.

Vol. 36: Logic of Programming and Calculi of Discrete Design. Edited by M. Broy. VII, 415 pages. 1987.

Vol. 37: Dynamics of Infinite Dimensional Systems. Edited by S.-N. Chow and J. K. Hale. IX. 514 pages. 1987.

Vol. 38: Flow Control of Congested Networks. Edited by A. R. Odoni, L. Bianco and G. Szegö. XII, 355 pages. 1987.

Vol. 39: Mathematics and Computer Science in Medical Imaging. Edited by M. A. Viergever and A. Todd-Pokropek. VIII, 546 pages. 1988.

Vol. 40: Theoretical Foundations of Computer Graphics and CAD. Edited by R. A. Earnshaw. XX, 1246 pages. 1988.

NATO ASI Series F

Including Special Programmes on Sensory Systems for Robotic Control (ROB) and on Advanced Educational Technology (AET)

Vol. 41: Neural Computers. Edited by R. Eckmiller and Ch. v. d. Malsburg. XIII, 566 pages. 1988.

Vol. 42: Real-Time Object Measurement and Classification. Edited by A. K. Jain. VIII, 407 pages. 1988. *(ROB)*

Vol. 43: Sensors and Sensory Systems for Advanced Robots. Edited by P. Dario. XI, 597 pages. 1988. *(ROB)*

Vol. 44: Signal Processing and Pattern Recognition in Nondestructive Evaluation of Materials. Edited by C. H. Chen. VIII, 344 pages. 1988. *(ROB)*

Vol. 45: Syntactic and Structural Pattern Recognition. Edited by G. Ferraté, T. Pavlidis, A. Sanfeliu and H. Bunke. XVI, 467 pages. 1988. *(ROB)*

Vol. 46: Recent Advances in Speech Understanding and Dialog Systems. Edited by H. Niemann, M. Lang and G. Sagerer. X, 521 pages. 1988.

Vol. 47: Advanced Computing Concepts and Techniques in Control Engineering. Edited by M. J. Denham and A. J. Laub. XI, 518 pages. 1988.

Vol. 48: Mathematical Models for Decision Support. Edited by G. Mitra. IX, 762 pages. 1988.

Vol. 49: Computer Integrated Manufacturing. Edited by I. B. Turksen. VIII, 568 pages. 1988.

Vol. 50: CAD Based Programming for Sensory Robots. Edited by B. Ravani. IX, 565 pages. 1988. *(ROB)*

Vol. 51: Algorithms and Model Formulations in Mathematical Programming. Edited by S. W. Wallace. IX, 190 pages. 1989.

Vol. 52: Sensor Devices and Systems for Robotics. Edited by A. Casals. IX, 362 pages. 1989. *(ROB)*

Vol. 53: Advanced Information Technologies for Industrial Material Flow Systems. Edited by S. Y. Nof and C. L. Moodie. IX, 710 pages. 1989.

Vol. 54: A Reappraisal of the Efficiency of Financial Markets. Edited by R. M. C. Guimarães, B. G. Kingsman and S. J. Taylor. X, 804 pages. 1989.

Vol. 55: Constructive Methods in Computing Science. Edited by M. Broy. VII, 478 pages. 1989.

Vol. 56: Multiple Criteria Decision Making and Risk Analysis Using Microcomputers. Edited by B. Karpak and S. Zionts. VII, 399 pages. 1989.

Vol. 57: Kinematics and Dynamic Issues in Sensor Based Control. Edited by G. E. Taylor. XI, 456 pages. 1990. *(ROB)*

Vol. 58: Highly Redundant Sensing in Robotic Systems. Edited by J. T. Tou and J. G. Balchen. X, 322 pages. 1990. *(ROB)*

Vol. 59: Superconducting Electronics. Edited by H. Weinstock and M. Nisenoff. X, 441 pages. 1989.

Vol. 60: 3D Imaging in Medicine. Algorithms, Systems, Applications. Edited by K. H. Höhne, H. Fuchs and S. M. Pizer. IX, 460 pages. 1990.

NATO ASI Series F

Including Special Programmes on Sensory Systems for Robotic Control (ROB) and on Advanced Educational Technology (AET)

Vol. 61: Knowledge, Data and Computer-Assisted Decisions. Edited by M. Schader and W. Gaul. VIII, 421 pages. 1990.

Vol. 62: Supercomputing. Edited by J. S. Kowalik. X, 425 pages. 1990.

Vol. 63: Traditional and Non-Traditional Robotic Sensors. Edited by T. C. Henderson. VIII, 468 pages. 1990. *(ROB)*Vol. 64: Sensory Robotics for the Handling of Limp Materials. Edited by P. M. Taylor. IX, 343 pages. 1990. *(ROB)*

Vol. 65: Mapping and Spatial Modelling for Navigation. Edited by L. F. Pau. VIII, 357 pages. 1990. *(ROB)*

Vol. 66: Sensor-Based Robots: Algorithms and Architectures. Edited by C. S. G. Lee. X, 285 pages. 1991. *(ROB)*

Vol. 67: Designing Hypermedia for Learning. Edited by D. H. Jonassen and H. Mandl. XXV, 457 pages. 1990. *(AET)*

Vol. 68: Neurocomputing. Algorithms, Architectures and Applications. Edited by F. Fogelman Soulié and J. Hérault. XI, 455 pages. 1990.

Vol. 69: Real-Time Integration Methods for Mechanical System Simulation. Edited by E. J. Haug and R. C. Deyo. VIII, 352 pages. 1991.

Vol. 70: Numerical Linear Algebra, Digital Signal Processing and Parallel Algorithms. Edited by G. H. Golub and P. Van Dooren. XIII, 729 pages. 1991.

Vol. 71: Expert Systems and Robotics. Edited by T. Jordanides and B.Torby. XII, 744 pages. 1991.

Vol. 72: High-Capacity Local and Metropolitan Area Networks. Architecture and Performance Issues. Edited by G. Pujolle. X, 536 pages. 1991.

Vol. 73: Automation and Systems Issues in Air Traffic Control. Edited by J. A. Wise, V. D. Hopkin and M. L. Smith. XIX, 594 pages. 1991.

Vol. 74: Picture Archiving and Communication Systems (PACS) in Medicine. Edited by H. K. Huang, O. Ratib, A. R. Bakker and G. Witte. XI, 438 pages. 1991.

Vol. 75: Speech Recognition and Understanding. Recent Advances, Trends and Applications. Edited by P. Laface and Renato De Mori. XI, 559 pages. 1991.

Vol. 76: Multimedia Interface Design in Education. Edited by A. D. N. Edwards and S. Holland. XIV, 216 pages. 1992. *(AET)*

Vol. 77: Computer Algorithms for Solving Linear Algebraic Equations. The State of the Art. Edited by E. Spedicato. VIII, 352 pages. 1991.

Vol. 78: Integrating Advanced Technology into Technology Education. Edited by M. Hacker, A. Gordon and M. de Vries. VIII, 185 pages. 1991. *(AET)*

Vol. 79: Logic, Algebra, and Computation. Edited by F. L. Bauer. VII, 485 pages. 1991.

Vol. 80: Intelligent Tutoring Systems for Foreign Language Learning. Edited by M. L. Swartz and M. Yazdani. IX, 347 pages. 1992. *(AET)*

Vol. 81: Cognitive Tools for Learning. Edited by P. A. M. Kommers, D. H. Jonassen, and J. T. Mayes. X, 278 pages. 1992. *(AET)*

NATO ASI Series F

Including Special Programmes on Sensory Systems for Robotic Control (ROB) and on Advanced Educational Technology (AET)

Vol. 82: Combinatorial Optimization. New Frontiers in Theory and Practice. Edited by M. Akgül, H. W. Hamacher, and S. Tüfekçi. XI, 334 pages. 1992.

Vol. 83: Active Perception and Robot Vision. Edited by A. K. Sood and H. Wechsler. IX, 756 pages. 1992.

Vol. 84: Computer-Based Learning Environments and Problem Solving. Edited by E. De Corte, M. C. Linn, H. Mandl, and L. Verschaffel. XVI, 488 pages. 1992. *(AET)*

Vol. 85: Adaptive Learning Environments. Foundations and Frontiers. Edited by M. Jones and P. H. Winne. VIII, 408 pages. 1992. *(AET)*

Vol. 86: Intelligent Learning Environments and Knowledge Acquisition in Physics. Edited by A. Tiberghien and H. Mandl. VIII, 285 pages. 1992. *(AET)*

Vol. 87: Cognitive Modelling and Interactive Environments. With demo diskettes (Apple and IBM compatible). Edited by F. L. Engel, D. G. Bouwhuis, T. Bösser, and G. d'Ydewalle. IX, 311 pages. 1992. *(AET)*

Vol. 88: Programming and Mathematical Method. Edited by M. Broy. VIII, 428 pages. 1992.

Vol. 89: Mathematical Problem Solving and New Information Technologies. Edited by J. P. Ponte, J. F. Matos, J. M. Matos, and D. Fernandes. XV, 346 pages. 1992. *(AET)*

Vol. 90: Collaborative Learning Through Computer Conferencing. Edited by A. R. Kaye. X, 260 pages. 1992. *(AET)*

Vol. 91: New Directions for Intelligent Tutoring Systems. Edited by E. Costa. X, 296 pages. 1992. *(AET)*

Vol. 92: Hypermedia Courseware: Structures of Communication and Intelligent Help. Edited by A. Oliveira. X, 241 pages. 1992. *(AET)*

Vol. 93: Interactive Multimedia Learning Environments. Human Factors and Technical Considerations on Design Issues. Edited by M. Giardina. VIII, 254 pages. 1992. *(AET)*

Vol. 94: Logic and Algebra of Specification. Edited by F. L. Bauer, W. Brauer, and H. Schwichtenberg. VII, 442 pages. 1993.

Vol. 95: Comprehensive Systems Design: A New Educational Technology. Edited by C. M. Reigeluth, B. H. Banathy, and J. R. Olson. IX, 437 pages. 1993. *(AET)*

Vol. 96: New Directions in Educational Technology. Edited by E. Scanlon and T. O'Shea. VIII, 251 pages. 1992. *(AET)*

Vol. 97: Advanced Models of Cognition for Medical Training and Practice. Edited by D. A. Evans and V. L. Patel. XI, 372 pages. 1992. *(AET)*

Vol. 98: Medical Images: Formation, Handling and Evaluation. Edited by A. E. Todd-Pokropek and M. A. Viergever. IX, 700 pages. 1992.

Vol. 99: Multisensor Fusion for Computer Vision. Edited by J. K. Aggarwal. XI, 456 pages. 1993. *(ROB)*

Vol. 100: Communication from an Artificial Intelligence Perspective. Theoretical and Applied Issues. Edited by A. Ortony, J. Slack and O. Stock. XII, 260 pages. 1992.

NATO ASI Series F

Including Special Programmes on Sensory Systems for Robotic Control (ROB) and on Advanced Educational Technology (AET)

Vol. 101: Recent Developments in Decision Support Systems. Edited by C. W. Holsapple and A. B. Whinston. XI, 618 pages. 1993.

Vol. 102: Robots and Biological Systems: Towards a New Bionics? Edited by P. Dario, G. Sandini and P. Aebischer. XII, 786 pages. 1993.

Vol. 103: Parallel Computing on Distributed Memory Multiprocessors. Edited by F. Özgüner and F. Erçal. VIII, 332 pages. 1993.

Vol. 104: Instructional Models in Computer-Based Learning Environments. Edited by S. Dijkstra, H. P. M. Krammer and J. J. G. van Merriënboer. X, 510 pages. 1993. *(AET)*

Vol. 105: Designing Environments for Constructive Learning. Edited by T. M. Duffy, J. Lowyck and D. H. Jonassen. VIII, 374 pages. 1993. *(AET)*

Vol. 106: Software for Parallel Computation. Edited by J. S. Kowalik and L. Grandinetti. IX, 363 pages. 1993.

Vol. 107: Advanced Educational Technologies for Mathematics and Science. Edited by D. L. Ferguson. XII, 749 pages. 1993. *(AET)*

Vol. 108: Concurrent Engineering: Tools and Technologies for Mechanical System Design. Edited by E. J. Haug. XIII, 998 pages. 1993.

Vol. 109: Advanced Educational Technology in Technology Education. Edited by A. Gordon, M. Hacker and M. de Vries. VIII, 270 pages. 1993. *(AET)*

Vol. 110: Verification and Validation of Complex Systems: Human Factors Issues. Edited by J. A. Wise, V. D. Hopkin and P. Stager. XIII 704 pages. 1993.

Vol. 111: Cognitive Models and Intelligent Environments for Learning Programming. Edited by E. Lemut, B. du Boulay and G. Dettori. VIII, 305 pages. 1993. *(AET)*